D0218978

Taking Sides
Clashing Views
in Human Sexuality

**by Ryan W. McKee and
William J. Taverner**

http://create.mcgraw-hill.com

ISBN-10: 0078139589   ISBN-13: 9780078139581

Contents

Preface

In few areas of American society are clashing views more evident than in the subjects of human sexuality and sexual behavior. Almost daily, in the news and electronic media, in congressional hearings, and on the streets, we hear about Americans of all ages taking completely opposite positions on such issues as abortion, contraception, fertility, same-sex marriage, teenage sexuality, and the like. Given the highly personal, emotional, and sensitive nature of these issues, sorting out the meaning of these controversies and fashioning a coherent position on them can be a difficult proposition. The purpose of this book, therefore, is to encourage meaningful critical thinking about current issues related to human sexuality, and the debates are designed to assist you in the task of clarifying your own personal values in relation to some common, and often polar, perspectives on the issues presented.

Book Organization

This 13th edition of *Taking Sides: Clashing Views in Human Sexuality* presents many lively and thoughtful statements by articulate advocates on opposite sides of a variety of sexuality-related questions. Each issue includes:

1. A *question* (e.g., "Has sex become too casual?");
2. *Learning Outcomes* describing the knowledge or skills students should be able to achieve upon reading the YES and NO selections;
3. An *Issue Summary* that presents background information helpful for understanding the context of the debate and information on the authors who will be contributing to the debate;
4. Essays by two authors—one who responds *Yes*, and one who responds *No* to the question; and
5. *Exploring the Issue* that presents questions for critical thinking and reflection; a summary of the arguments, including discussion about whether common ground exists and additional questions to help you further examine the issues raised (or not raised) by the authors; and print and Internet sources for further reading.

It is important to remember that for the questions debated in this volume, the essays often represent but two perspectives on the issue. Remember that the debates do not end there—most issues have many shades of gray, and you may find your own values congruent with neither author. Since this book is a tool to encourage critical thinking, you should not feel confined to the views expressed in the articles. You may see important points on both sides of an issue and may construct for yourself a new and creative approach, which may incorporate the best of both sides or provide an entirely new vantage point for understanding.

As you read this collection of issues, try to respect other people's philosophical worldviews and beliefs and attempt to articulate your own. At the same time, be aware of the authors' potential biases, and how they may affect the positions each author articulates. Be aware, too, of your own biases. We all have experiences that may shape the way we look at a controversial issue. Try to come to each issue with an open mind. You may find your values challenged or strengthened after reading both views. Although you may disagree with one or even both of the arguments offered for each issue, it is important that you read each statement carefully and critically.

A word to the instructor An *Instructor's Manual* with issue synopses, suggestions for classroom discussions, and test questions (multiple-choice and essay) is available from McGraw-Hill/CLS. This resource, authored by Karen Rayne, makes a very useful accompaniment for this text. A general guidebook, *Using Taking Sides in the Classroom,* which discusses methods and techniques for integrating the pro/con approach into any classroom setting, is also available. An online version of *Using Taking Sides in the Classroom* and a correspondence service for Taking Sides adopters can be found at www.mhhe.com/createcentral

Taking Sides: Clashing Views in Human Sexuality is one of the many titles in the Taking Sides series. If you are interested in seeing the table of contents for any of the other titles, please visit the Taking Sides website at www.mhhe.com/cls or www.mhhe.com, or by contacting the authors at ryan@ryanmckee.com or sexedjournal@hotmail.com. Ideas for new issues are *always welcome!*

Ryan W. McKee

Widener University

and

William J. Taverner

Center for Family Life Education

Editors of This Volume

RYAN W. MCKEE, MS, MEd, is a doctoral candidate in the Center for Human Sexuality Studies at Widener University. His research interests include the intersections of masculinity and sexual health, the health behaviors of fraternity men, online health and sexuality education, and sexual health and technology. Along with William J. Taverner, Mckee coedited the 11th and 12th editions of *Taking Sides: Clashing Views in Human Sexuality*. As an adjunct instructor, he teaches a variety of health- and sexuality-related courses for Montclair State University, Kean University, and Widener University. In addition to teaching, he works as a sexuality education consultant and program evaluator. Recent projects include the development and implementation of an online sexuality education course for seminary students. He is a member of the American Association of Sexuality Educators, Counselors, and Therapists (AASECT) as well as the Society for the Scientific Study of Sexuality (SSSS). He is the winner of the 2011 AASECT Schiller Prize, awarded for best conference workshop using interactive strategies, and the 2011 SSSS Eastern Region Student Paper Award. He can be reached at ryan@ryanmckee.com.

WILLIAM J. TAVERNER, MA, CSE, is the editor-in-chief of the *American Journal of Sexuality Education* and is the executive director of the Center for Family Life Education, the nationally acclaimed education division of Planned Parenthood of Central and Greater Northern New Jersey. He has coauthored many sexuality education resources, including *Making Sense of Abstinence; Older, Wiser, Sexually Smarter; Positive Images: Teaching about Contraception and Sexual Health; Sex Ed 101;* and eight editions of *Taking Sides: Clashing Views in Human Sexuality.* He served as editor-in-chief for the two-volume third edition of *Teaching Safer Sex,* which received the 2013 Book Award from the American Association of Sexuality Educators, Counselors, and Therapists (AASECT). A trainer of thousands throughout the United States, who has twice advocated for sexuality education at U.S. congressional briefings, Taverner has received other national awards recognizing his leadership in sexuality education: AASECT's first "Schiller Prize" for best workshop using interactive strategies; Planned Parenthood's "Golden Apple Award" for leadership in education; a *Sexual Intelligence* award naming him as "one of the country's preeminent sex educators, trainers, and sex education theorists"; and the "Golden Brick Award" for "encouraging the growth of sex education professionals." He can be reached at sexedjournal@hotmail.com.

Acknowledgments

Thanks from Ryan W. McKee

First and foremost I would like to thank William J. Taverner for bringing me on board to work on this amazing series over 7 years ago. I never imagined it would be so challenging and rewarding. I owe so much of my professional success to the lessons Bill has taught me about hard work and dedication over the years. I'm proud to call him my colleague, but I'm happy to also call him a friend.

I'd also like to thank Dr. Robert Francoeur, founding editor of this Taking Sides series. Bob passed away last fall. He was a brilliant and kind man, dedicated to challenging those around him to think differently about sex and sexu-

ality. I had the privilege of working with him, albeit briefly, at Fairleigh Dickinson University several years ago. I learned so much from him in such a short time.

Thanks to Jill Meloy at McGraw-Hill for her help, support, and patience throughout the process of developing this edition. As always, she has been a pleasure to work with. Thanks to Karen Rayne for developing the Instructor's Resources for this edition, as well as helping review our progress and suggesting resources. Thanks also to Olivia Von Kohorn and Jeffrey Anthony for their help and feedback.

I'd also like to thank my colleagues, professors, and students at Widener University. I'm especially thankful for the support of Dr. Dyson, Dr. Sitron, Dr. Crane, Dr. Satterly, and Dr. Browne. I've learned so much from these kind and caring people. I hope to have the same impact on my students that they have had on me. Thanks to my other Widener colleagues, classmates, and friends, including Kelly Wise, Julissa Coriano, Jayleen "Dr. Jay" Galarza, Tracie Gilbert, Becky Anthony, and Elliot Ruggles. Extra thanks are due to my frequent collaborator and writing partners Eli Green and Amelia Hamarman.

Thanks to my colleagues and students at Montclair State University and Kean University. Dr. Elisha Nixon at Kean has been incredibly supportive of me over the years. And without Dr. Eva Goldfarb in my corner at Montclair State, I don't know where I would be. Thanks also to my friends and mentors Dr. Daphne Rankin and Judith Steinhart.

I consider myself fortunate to have a large and supportive family. To my parents, Paul and Erma McKee, I owe everything. My brothers, sisters, niece and nephews are a constant source of support and motivation. I can't possibly thank them enough.

Finally, I want to thank my partner Alison Bellavance. She is dedicated to making the world a better, healthier and kinder place. Her example motivates me to achieve my goals. She is always there for me with patience and grace when I need it. Her love and support keeps me focused on our future together.

Thanks from William J. Taverner

It is always exciting to put out a new edition, and Ryan W. McKee is an absolute joy to work with! A strong writer and editor with a knack for finding articles that are relevant and capture the pulse of sexual debates in America, Ryan provides a depth of context to the many issues we present in this book. I think what I appreciate most about Ryan is his integrity and ethics. It would be a mistake to assume that we, as editors, are completely neutral and opinionless. To the contrary, like everyone, we have many strongly-held values and beliefs, and I love how we keep each other in check, asking each other if we have enough websites and references for a viewpoint contrary to our own, or requesting a careful review from the other editor when one of us writes on a subject that hits pretty close to home.

Thanks to Jill Meloy at McGraw-Hill, who gave us great feedback on articles, and prodded us along when we needed prodding. Thanks to Karen Rayne, who helped us find websites and references, and also authored the Instructor's Manual of this edition. Thanks, too, to Eli R. Green and Allyson Sandak, authors of the two prior Instructor's Manuals. Thanks to Jeffrey Anthony for his feedback and suggestions. Thanks to my friend and occasional coeditor Susan Milstein, who did not coedit this book, but I feel like we work together so often I should thank her anyway.

Thanks to my family who keep me on my toes thinking about various sides of issues. My wife, Denise, sometimes leaves me with articles about sex in the news, and these are sometimes discussed in Taking Sides. My children, Christopher and Robert, share their opinions—on all matters, not just sexual—that continue to broaden my perspective.

The publication of the 13th edition of *Taking Sides: Clashing Views in Human Sexuality* is a bittersweet time for me. My friend and mentor, Dr. Robert T. Francoeur, died this past October. Bob was the original editor of this series, as well as the author of 21 other books in human sexuality, and author or contributor to more than 100 encyclopedias, handbooks, journal articles, and textbooks. Bob's masterpiece was the *Continuum Complete International Encyclopedia of Sexuality,* for which he served as lead editor. He and coeditor Raymond J. Noonan arranged for its donation to the Kinsey Institute, so you can look up any chapter you like at www.kinseyinstitute.org/ccies.

I met Bob 22 years ago when he was a member of the faculty for an international studies program titled "Sex in Two Cultures," which met for three weeks in New York City and three more weeks in Copenhagen, Denmark. We used the 4th edition of Taking Sides in that class. I don't think I made the connection immediately that my professor was also my textbook author. The realization of Bob's prolific fame as one of the world's leading sexologists came later, when a classmate and I were walking down Copenhagen's famed Stroget, or main street. As we stopped to examine magazines at a newsstand, we were dumbstruck when we saw Bob's name on the cover of the Danish version of *Penthouse*. Not able to decipher the Danish text, we rushed back to the hotel, and asked Bob why on earth his name was on the cover of an erotic magazine. This modest, unassuming man simply said, "Oh. I wrote an article about pheromones. I guess they printed it."

Bob and I would eventually edit two editions of Taking Sides together, and we would also teach different sections of human sexuality at Fairleigh Dickinson University, Madison, NJ, for many years. I miss Bob.

"The future is what we decide to make it.

We are all co-creators of the world to be."

—Robert T. Francoeur

Academic Advisory Board Members

Members of the Academic Advisory Board are instrumental in the final selection of articles for Takings Sides books

and ExpressBooks. Their review of the articles for content, level, and appropriateness provides critical direction to the editor(s) and staff. We think that you will find their careful consideration reflected in this book.

Dr. Donald Dyson
Widener University

Janna Edrington
Luther College

Marina Epstein
University of Washington

Andrea Ericksen
San Juan College

Allan Fenigstein
Kenyon College

Christopher Ferguson
Texas A&M International University

Edward Fernandes
Barton College

James Ferraro
Southern Illinois University, Carbondale

Edward Fliss
St. Louis Community College, Florissant Valley

Franklin Foote
University of Miami-Coral Gables

Pamela J. Forman
University of Wisconsin-Eau Claire

Richelle Frabotta
Miami University Br-Middletown

James S. Francis
San Jacinto College—South Campus

Bernard Frye
University of Texas, Arlington

Ana Maria Garcia
Arcadia University

Bertram Garskof
Quinnipiac University

Joanna Gentsch
University of Texas, Dallas

Elham Gheytanchi
Santa Monica College

Timothy Gobek
Calumet College of St. Joseph

Debra Golden
Grossmont College

Jerry Green
Tarrant County College—Northwest Campus

Janet Griffin
Howard University

Timothy Grogan
Valencia Community College, Osceola

Nicholas Grosskopf
York College

Mercedes Guilliaum
California State University, Long Beach

Kevin Gustafson
University of Texas—Arlington

C. Lee Harrison
Miami University, Oxford

Marissa A. Harrison
Penn State Harrisburg

Susan Heidenreich
University of San Francisco

Lisa Justine Hernandez
Saint Edwards University

Norene Herrington
College of DuPage

Margot Hodes
Teachers College

Steven Hoekstra
Kansas Wesleyan University

Alice Holland
Penn State-Berks

Sabra Jacobs
Big Sandy Community and Technical College

Ethel Jones
South Carolina State University

Jennifer Jossendal
Kishwaukee College

Janice Kelly
Purdue University

Bree Kessler
Hunter College

Caitlin Killian
Drew University

Keith King
University of Cincinnati

Kim Kirkpatrick
Fayetteville State University

Kenyon Knapp
Mercer University

Harold Koch
Penn Valley Community College

Jess Kohlert
King's College

Mindy Korol
Mount Saint Mary's College

Charles Krinsky
Northeastern University

Shanti Kulkarni
University of North Carolina, Charlotte

Leslie Lamb
Dowling College

Justin Lehmiller
Harvard University

Joseph Lopiccolo
University Of Missouri-Columbia

Fredanna M'Cormack
Coastal Carolina University

Priscilla MacDuff
Suffolk County Community College

J. Davis Mannino
Santa Rosa Junior College

Amy Marin
Phoenix College

Lis Maurer
Ithaca College

Konstance McCaffree
Widener University

Kathy McCleaf
Mary Baldwin College

Mary McGinnis
Columbia College Chicago

Susan Milstein
Montgomery College

Deborah Mitchell Robinson
Valdosta State University

Adina Nack
California Luthern University

Jenny Oliphant
University of Saint Thomas

Natasha Otto
Morgan State University

Carol Oyster
University of Wisconsin, La Crosse

Jane Petrillo
Kennesaw State University

Terry Pettijohn II
Coastal Carolina University

Mindy Puopolo
California Luthern University

Karen Rayne
AUSTIN Community College

Sandra Reineke
University of Idaho

Steven Reschly
Truman State University

Doug Rice
California State University—Sacramento

Christine Robinson
James Madison University

Christopher Robinson
University of Alabama-Birmingham

Dennis Roderick
University of Massachusetts-Dartmouth

Louise Rosenberg
University of Hartford

Martha Rosenthal
Florida Gulf Coast University

Daniel Rubin
Valencia Community College-West Campus

Catherine Salmon
University of Redlands

Aimee Sapp
William Woods University

Jillene Seiver
Bellevue College

Phyllis Shea
Worcester State College

John G. Shiber
Big Sandy Community & Technical College

Lawrence A. Siegel
Palm Beach State College

Sue Simon Westendorf
Ohio University-Athens

B. Jill Smith
University Of Wisconsin—Eau Claire

Stanley Snegroff
Adelphi University

David Stewart
Sanford-Brown College

Linda Synovitz
Southeastern Louisiana University

Tony Talbert
Baylor University

Adrian Teo
Whitworth University

Sandra M. Todaro
Bossier Parish Community College

Alisa Velonis
University of Colorado-Denver

Lenore Walker
Nova Southeastern University

Sara Walsh
Indiana University-Bloomington

Estelle Weinstein
Hofstra University

Casey Welch
Flagler College

Maria Theresa Wessel
James Madison University

Laura Widman
University of Tennessee-Knoxville

Lou Ann Wieand
Humboldt State University

Roberta Wiediger
Lincoln Land Community College

Chris Wienke
Southern Illinois University, Carbondale

Jessica Willis
Eastern Washington University

Midge Wilson
DePaul University

Kelley Wolfe
University of North Carolina-Asheville

David Yarbrough
University of Louisiana, Lafayette

Correlation Guide

The *Taking Sides* series presents current issues in a debate-style format designed to stimulate student interest and develop critical thinking skills. Each issue is thoughtfully framed with an issue summary, learning outcomes, an issue introduction, and an exploring the issue section. The pro and con essays—selected for their liveliness and substance—represent the arguments of leading scholars and commentators in their fields.

Taking Sides: Clashing Views in Human Sexuality, 13/e is an easy-to-use reader that presents issues on important topics such as *sexual expression, sex and society,* and *sex and reproduction.* For more information on *Taking Sides* and other *McGraw-Hill Contemporary Learning Series* titles, visit www.mcgrawhillcreate.com.

This convenient guide matches the issues in **Taking Sides: Human Sexuality, 13/e** with the corresponding chapters in two of our best-selling McGraw-Hill psychology textbooks by Hyde/DeLamater and Yarber/Sayad.

TAKING SIDES: Human Sexuality, 13/e	Understanding Human Sexuality, 11/e by Hyde/DeLamater	Human Sexuality: Diversity in Contemporary America, 8/e by Yarber/Sayad
Issue: Is Pornography Harmful?	**Chapter 1:** Sexuality in Perspective **Chapter 3:** Sex Research **Chapter 14:** Variations in Sexual Behavior **Chapter 16:** Sex for Sale **Chapter 19:** Ethics, Religion, and Sexuality **Chapter 20:** Sex and the Law	**Chapter 1:** Perspectives on Human Sexuality **Chapter 2:** Studying Human Sexuality **Chapter 18:** Sexual Explicit Materials, Prostitution, and Sex Laws
Issue: Should Condoms Be Required in Pornographic Films?	**Chapter 16:** Sex for Sale **Chapter 18:** Sexually Transmitted Infections **Chapter 20:** Sex and the Law	**Chapter 15:** Sexually Transmitted Infections **Chapter 16:** HIV and AIDS **Chapter 18:** Sexual Explicit Materials, Prostitution, and Sex Laws
Issue: Do Reality TV Shows Portray Responsible Messages about Teen Pregnancy?	**Chapter 1:** Sexuality in Perspective **Chapter 7:** Contraception and Abortion Hormonal Methods **Chapter 9:** Sexuality and the Life Cycle: Childhood and Adolescence	**Chapter 1:** Perspectives on Human Sexuality **Chapter 6:** Sexuality in Childhood and Adolescence **Chapter 11:** Contraception, Birth Control, and Abortion **Chapter 12:** Conception, Pregnancy, and Childbirth
Issue: Should Sexual Problems Be Treated Pharmaceutically?	**Chapter 8:** Sexual Arousal **Chapter 17:** Sexual Disorders and Sex Therapy	**Chapter 3:** Female Sexual Anatomy, Physiology, and Response **Chapter 4:** Male Sexual Anatomy, Physiology, and Response **Chapter 13:** The Sexual Body in Health and Illness **Chapter 14:** Sexual Function Difficulties, Dissatisfaction, Enhancement, and Therapy
Issue: Should Prostitution be Legalized?	**Chapter 10:** Sexuality and the Life Cycle: Adulthood **Chapter 16:** Sex for Sale **Chapter 19:** Ethics, Religion, and Sexuality **Chapter 20:** Sex and the Law	**Chapter 1:** Perspectives on Human Sexuality **Chapter 7:** Sexuality in Adulthood **Chapter 18:** Sexual Explicit Materials, Prostitution, and Sex Laws
Issue: Is Monogamy a More Sustainable Relationship Style than Polyamory?	**Chapter 1:** Sexuality in Perspective **Chapter 2:** Theoretical Perspectives on Sexuality **Chapter 10:** Sexuality and the Life Cycle: Adulthood	**Chapter 1:** Perspectives on Human Sexuality **Chapter 7:** Sexuality in Adulthood **Chapter 8:** Love and Communication in Intimate Relationships
Issue: Is There a Valid Reason for Routine Infant Male Circumcision?	**Chapter 1:** Sexuality in Perspective **Chapter 4:** Sexual Anatomy **Chapter 9:** Sexuality and the Lifecycle: Childhood and Adolescence	**Chapter 1:** Perspectives on Human Sexuality **Chapter 4:** Male Sexual Anatomy, Physiology, and Response
Issue: Are Puberty-Blocking Drugs the Best Treatment Option for Transgender Children?	**Chapter 5:** Sex Hormones, Sexual Differentiation, and the Menstrual Cycle **Chapter 9:** Sexuality and the Life Cycle: Childhood and Adolescence **Chapter 12:** Gender and Sexuality **Chapter 13:** Sexual Orientation: Gay, Straight, or Bi? **Chapter 14:** Variations in Sexual Behavior	**Chapter 5:** Gender and Gender Roles **Chapter 6:** Sexuality in Childhood and Adolescence **Chapter 9:** Sexual Expression **Chapter 10:** Variations in Sexual Behavior

TAKING SIDES: Human Sexuality, 13/e	Understanding Human Sexuality, 11/e by Hyde/DeLamater	Human Sexuality: Diversity in Contemporary America, 8/e by Yarber/Sayad
Issue: Is Sexual Orientation Biologically Based?	**Chapter 2:** Theoretical Perspectives on Sexuality **Chapter 13:** Sexual Orientation: Gay, Straight, or Bi?	**Chapter 1:** Perspectives on Human Sexuality **Chapter 6:** Sexuality in Childhood and Adolescence
Issue: Should Same-Sex Marriage Be Legal?	**Chapter 1:** Sexuality in Perspective **Chapter 2:** Theoretical Perspectives on Sexuality **Chapter 12:** Gender and Sexuality **Chapter 13:** Sexual Orientation: Gay, Straight, or Bi? **Chapter 19:** Ethics, Religion, and Sexuality **Chapter 20:** Sex and the Law	**Chapter 1:** Perspectives on Human Sexuality **Chapter 5:** Gender and Gender Roles **Chapter 7:** Sexuality in Adulthood **Chapter 9:** Sexual Expression **Chapter 18:** Sexually Explicit Materials, Prostitution, and Sex Laws
Issue: Is Abortion Moral?	**Chapter 7:** Contraception and Abortion Hormonal Methods **Chapter 19:** Ethics, Religion, and Sexuality	**Chapter 1:** Perspectives on Human Sexuality **Chapter 11:** Contraception, Birth Control, and Abortion **Chapter 18:** Sexually Explicit Materials, Prostitution, and Sex Laws
Issue: Should Pharmacists Have the Right to Refuse Contraceptive Prescriptions?	**Chapter 6:** Conception, Pregnancy, and Childbirth Conception **Chapter 7:** Contraception and Abortion Hormonal Methods **Chapter 19:** Ethics, Religion, and Sexuality	**Chapter 11:** Contraception, Birth Control, and Abortion **Chapter 12:** Conception, Pregnancy, and Childbirth **Chapter 18:** Sexually Explicit Materials, Prostitution, and Sex Laws
Issue: Should Parents Be Allowed to Select the Sex of Their Baby?	**Chapter 6:** Conception, Pregnancy, and Childbirth Conception **Chapter 19:** Ethics, Religion, and Sexuality	**Chapter 12:** Conception, Pregnancy, and Childbirth **Chapter 18:** Sexually Explicit Materials, Prostitution, and Sex Laws
Issue: Has Sex Become Too Casual?	**Chapter 1:** Sexuality in Perspective **Chapter 10:** Sexuality and the Life Cycle: Adulthood **Chapter 11:** Attraction, Love, and Communication **Chapter 18:** Sexually Transmitted Infections	**Chapter 1:** Perspectives on Human Sexuality **Chapter 6:** Sexuality in Childhood and Adolescence **Chapter 8:** Love and Communication in Intimate Relationships **Chapter 9:** Sexual Expression
Issue: Is Oral Sex Really Sex?	**Chapter 8:** Sexual Arousal **Chapter 14:** Variations in Sexual Behavior **Chapter 19:** Ethics, Religion, and Sexuality	**Chapter 1:** Perspectives on Human Sexuality **Chapter 6:** Sexuality in Childhood and Adolescence **Chapter 9:** Sexual Expression
Issue: Is Sexting a Form of Safer Sex?	**Chapter 14:** Variations in Sexual Behavior **Chapter 19:** Ethics, Religion, and Sexuality	**Chapter 1:** Perspectives on Human Sexuality **Chapter 6:** Sexuality in Childhood and Adolescence **Chapter 10:** Variations in Sexual Behavior
Issue: Is BDSM a Healthy Form of Sexual Expression?	**Chapter 8:** Sexual Arousal **Chapter 14:** Variations in Sexual Behavior	**Chapter 8:** Love and Communication in Intimate Relationships **Chapter 9:** Sexual Expression **Chapter 10:** Variations in Sexual Behavior
Issue: Can Sex Be Addictive?	**Chapter 4:** Sexual Anatomy **Chapter 8:** Sexual Arousal **Chapter 14:** Variations in Sexual Behavior **Chapter 15:** Sexual Coercion **Chapter 17:** Sexual Disorders and Sex Therapy	**Chapter 9:** Sexual Expression **Chapter 10:** Variations in Sexual Behavior **Chapter 14:** Sexual Function Difficulties, Dissatisfaction, Enhancement, and Therapy

Topic Guide

This topic guide suggests how the selections in this book relate to the subjects covered in your course. You may want to use the topics listed on these pages to search the web more easily.
All issues and their articles that relate to each topic are listed below the bold-faced term.

Abortion

Do Reality TV Shows Portray Responsible Messages about Teen
    Pregnancy?
Is Abortion Moral?
Should Pharmacists Have the Right to Refuse Contraceptive Prescriptions?

Adolescence

Are Puberty-Blocking Drugs the Best Treatment Option for Transgender
    Children?
Do Reality TV Shows Portray Responsible Messages about Teen
    Pregnancy?
Has Sex Become Too Casual?
Is Oral Sex Really Sex?
Is Sexting a Form of Safer Sex?

Aging

Are Puberty-Blocking Drugs the Best Treatment Option for Transgender
    Children?
Should Sexual Problems Be Treated Pharmaceutically?

Addiction

Can Sex Be Addictive?

Biotechnology

Are Puberty-Blocking Drugs the Best Treatment Option for Transgender
    Children?
Should Parents Be Allowed to Select the Sex of Their Baby?
Should Sexual Problems Be Treated Pharmaceutically?

Civil Rights

Is Abortion Moral?
Is Pornography Harmful?
Is Sexual Orientation Biologically Based?
Should Condoms Be Required in Pornographic Films?
Should Pharmacists Have the Right to Refuse Contraceptive Prescriptions?
Should Prostitution Be Legalized?
Should Same-Sex Marriage Be Legal?

Children

Do Reality TV Shows Portray Responsible Messages about Teen
    Pregnancy?
Is There a Valid Reason for Routine Infant Male Circumcision?

Evolution

Is Monogamy a More Sustainable Relationship Style than Polyamory?
Is Sexual Orientation Biologically Based?

Human Development

Do Reality TV Shows Portray Responsible Messages about Teen
    Pregnancy?

Is Sexual Orientation Biologically Based?
Should Parents Be Allowed to Select the Sex of Their Baby?

Gender

Are Puberty-Blocking Drugs the Best Treatment Option for Transgender
    Children?
Is Monogamy a More Sustainable Relationship Style than
    Polyamory?
Is There a Valid Reason for Routine Infant Male Circumcision?
Should Parents Be Allowed to Select the Sex of Their Baby?

Government Regulation

Is Abortion Moral?
Should Parents Be Allowed to Select the Sex of Their Baby?
Should Pharmacists Have the Right to Refuse Contraceptive
    Prescriptions?
Should Prostitution Be Legalized?
Should Same-Sex Marriage Be Legal?

Health Care

Are Puberty-Blocking Drugs the Best Treatment Option for Transgender
    Children?
Is Abortion Moral?
Is Pornography Harmful?
Is Sexting a Form of Safer Sex?
Is There a Valid Reason for Routine Infant Male Circumcision?
Should Pharmacists Have the Right to Refuse Contraceptive
    Prescriptions?
Should Sexual Problems Be Treated Pharmaceutically?

Homosexuality

Is Sexual Orientation Biologically Based?
Should Same-Sex Marriage Be Legal?

Marriage

Is Monogamy a More Sustainable Relationship Style than Polyamory?
Should Same-Sex Marriage Be Legal?

Medicine

Are Puberty-Blocking Drugs the Best Treatment Option for Transgender
    Children?
Should Pharmacists Have the Right to Refuse Contraceptive
    Prescriptions?
Should Sexual Problems Be Treated Pharmaceutically?

Parenting

Are Puberty-Blocking Drugs the Best Treatment Option for Transgender
    Children?
Do Reality TV Shows Portray Responsible Messages about Teen
    Pregnancy?
Is Oral Sex Really Sex?
Is Sexting a Form of Safer Sex?

Is There a Valid Reason for Routine Infant Male Circumcision?
Should Parents Be Allowed to Select the Sex of Their Baby?

Pornography

Can Sex Be Addictive?
Has Sex Become Too Casual?
Is Pornography Harmful?
Is Sexting a Form of Safer Sex?
Should Condoms Be Required in Pornographic Films?

Pregnancy

Do Reality TV Shows Portray Responsible Messages about Teen
    Pregnancy?
Is Abortion Moral?
Is There a Valid Reason for Routine Infant Male Circumcision?
Should Parents Be Allowed to Select the Sex of Their Baby?

Public Health

Are Puberty-Blocking Drugs the Best Treatment Option for Transgender
    Children?
Do Reality TV Shows Portray Responsible Messages about Teen
    Pregnancy?
Is Abortion Moral?
Is Oral Sex Really Sex?
Is Pornography Harmful?
Is Sexting a Form of Safer Sex?
Is There a Valid Reason for Routine Infant Male Circumcision?
Should Condoms Be Required in Pornographic Films?
Should Parents Be Allowed to Select the Sex of Their Baby?
Should Pharmacists Have the Right to Refuse Contraceptive
    Prescriptions?
Should Prostitution Be Legalized?
Should Sexual Problems Be Treated Pharmaceutically?

Relationships

Can Sex Be Addictive?
Has Sex Become Too Casual?
Is BDSM a Healthy Form of Sexual Expression?
Is Monogamy a More Sustainable Relationship Style than Polyamory?
Is Oral Sex Really Sex?
Should Same-Sex Marriage Be Legal?

Sex Crimes

Is BDSM a Healthy Form of Sexual Expression?
Is Sexting a Form of Safer Sex?
Should Prostitution Be Legalized?
Is Pornography Harmful?

Sex Discrimination

Are Puberty-Blocking Drugs the Best Treatment Option for Transgender
    Children?
Is Sexual Orientation Biologically Based?
Should Parents Be Allowed to Select the Sex of Their Baby?
Should Pharmacists Have the Right to Refuse Contraceptive
    Prescriptions?
Should Same-Sex Marriage Be Legal?

Sex Roles

Are Puberty-Blocking Drugs the Best Treatment Option for Transgender
    Children?
Do Reality TV Shows Portray Responsible Messages about Teen
    Pregnancy?
Has Sex Become Too Casual?
Is Abortion Moral?
Is Monogamy a More Sustainable Relationship Style than Polyamory?
Should Parents Be Allowed to Select the Sex of Their Baby?

Introduction

Sexual Attitudes in Perspective

To many, America can seem like one seriously divided country, with a blue northern and coastal perimeter, and a bright red center! On television and in print media, this is the overly simplified caricature of American politics and social attitudes. Are you from a *red state,* perhaps Utah or maybe Texas? Then surely you supported the G.O.P. in the most recent elections. You also oppose abortion and same-sex marriage, and you probably love hunting and NASCAR. Are you from a *blue state,* perhaps California or maybe Massachusetts? Then surely you are a Democrat who votes for the party line every chance you get. You support a woman's right to choose, are a staunch supporter of civil rights, and maybe have plans to attend a friend's same-sex wedding. Oh, and you are also a vegan who bikes to work in order to reduce greenhouse gas emissions!

If you are scratching your head thinking that neither profile describes you, you are not alone. Texas and Utah may be "red states," but how do we reconcile with the fact that millions of Americans in these two states vote for Democrats in general elections? Or that millions of other people who voted in favor of conservative candidates are from the "blue state" of California? Moreover, what about voters in the so-called "swing states," who have the power to sway elections in favor of one party or the other from term to term. And what do we know about those who choose not to vote? It's an important question as these nonvoters make up over 90 million Americans! The reality is that our opinions, attitudes, and values on social and sexual issues are as diverse as we are. They are formed by numerous factors that we will explore in this introduction.

As you examine the eighteen controversial issues in human sexuality in this volume, you will find yourself unavoidably encountering the values you have absorbed from your society, your ethnic background, your religious heritage and traditions, and your personal experiences. Because these values will influence your decisions, often without being consciously recognized, it is important to actively think about the role these undercurrent themes play in the positions you take on these issues.

How Social and Ethnic Factors Influence Our Values

American society is not homogeneous, nor is it even red or blue! People who grow up in rural, suburban, and large urban environments sometimes have subtle differences in their values and attitudes when it comes to gender roles, marriage, sexual diversity, and sexual behaviors. Growing up in different areas of the United States can influence one's views of sex, marriage, and family. This is also true for men and women who were born and raised in another country and culture.

Many researchers have found that values can be affected by one's family income level and socioeconomic status. Researchers have also indicated that one's occupation, educational level, and income are closely related to one's values, attitudes, sex role conceptions, child-rearing practices, and sexual identity. Our values and attitudes about sex are also influenced by whether we are brought up in a rural, suburban, or large urban environment. Our ethnic background can also be an important influence on our values and attitudes.

There are many classic examples of the role of ethnicity on sexual values and behaviors. Traditionally, a boy growing up among certain Melanesian cultures in the Southwestern Pacific was taught to avoid any social contact with girls from the age of three or four. While adolescent Melanesian boys and girls were not allowed to have sex with each other, boys were expected to have sex both with an older male and with a boy of his own age. Their first heterosexual experiences came with marriage. In the Cook Islands, Mangaian boys were expected to have sex with many girls after an older woman taught them about the art of sexual play. Mangaians also accepted and expected both premarital and extramarital sex. While these norms may seem peculiar to many Americans, it is important to consider that American norms may seem just as strange to those other societies.

But one does not have to look to anthropological studies to find evidence of the importance of cultural values. Even within the United States, one can find subtle but important differences in sexual attitudes and values among its diverse population. Though the authors included in this volume have differing opinions on the controversial issues they debate, they often find some common ground in their arguments. Within each issue, there are many shades of gray to consider.

Religious Factors in Attitudes Toward Sex

In the Middle Ages, Christian theologians divided sexual behaviors into two categories: behaviors that were "natural" and those that were "unnatural." Since they believed that the natural function and goal of all sexual behavior and relations was reproduction, masturbation was unnatural because it frustrated the natural goal of conception and continuance of the species. Rape certainly was considered illicit because it was not within the marital bond, but since it was procreative, rape was also considered a "natural" use of sex. Homosexual relations were considered both illicit and unnatural. These religious values were based on the view that God created man and woman at the beginning of time and laid down certain rules and guidelines for sexual behavior and relations. This view is still very influential in our culture, even for those who are not active in any religious tradition, as recent political controversies surrounding same-sex marriage, access to contraception and abortion, and comments over sexual assault have shown.

These perspectives have been synthesized into a model proposed by the late Dr. Robert T. Francoeur, a Catholic priest, former editor of this Taking Sides volume, and coeditor of the *International Encyclopedia of Sexuality.* Understanding these two perspectives or "worldviews" is important in any attempt to debate controversial issues in human sexuality.

Two Major Sexual Value Systems

Fixed or Absolutist Worldview

- Sexuality is basically an animal passion and must be controlled.
- The main goal of sex is marriage and reproduction. Sex is only acceptable in heterosexual marriages.
- Masturbation, oral sex, anal sex, and other nongenital sex—all impede God's purpose for sex. They are forbidden.
- Same-sex relationships are forbidden.
- Gender roles are strictly defined, and the male is superior in relationships.
- The emphasis of sex should be on genital acts.

Process or Relativist Worldview

- Sexuality is a natural and positive life force with both sensual and spiritual aspects.
- Pleasure, love, and celebration of life are goals in themselves. Sex does not have to be confined to marriage.
- The purpose of sex is to celebrate life; masturbation, oral sex, anal sex, and other nongenital sex can express the celebratory and communal nature of sex.
- Same-sex relationships are accepted.
- Gender roles are equal and flexible.
- The emphasis should be on people and their relationships, rather than on what they do sexually.

Adapted from a summary of the work of sexologist and biologist Robert T. Francoeur (1991) by Linda L. Hendrixson.

Judeo-Christian tradition allows us to examine two distinct worldviews, the *fixed worldview* and the *process worldview.* The fixed worldview says that morality is unchanging. Right and wrong are always right and wrong,

regardless of the situation or circumstances. The fixed worldview relies on a literal interpretation of its religious or ethical teachings, without regard for context. The process worldview examines issues of morality in an ever-changing world. What is right or wrong may require a contextual examination, and rules and ethics must constantly be reexamined in light of new information and the world's evolving context.

Take for example the question of masturbation. Where does the Christian prohibition of masturbation come from? If you search the pages of the Bible, you will discover that the words "masturbate" and "masturbation" are never mentioned. Yet much of what has been taught in Christianity regarding masturbation comes from the story of Onan:

> Then Judah said to Onan, "Go in to your brother's wife and perform the duty of a brother-in-law to her, and raise up offspring for your brother." But Onan knew that the offspring would not be his. So whenever he went in to his brother's wife he would waste the semen on the ground, so as not to give offspring to his brother. And what he did was wicked in the sight of the Lord, and he put him to death also.
>
> —Genesis 38:8–10, English Standard Version

Many theologians point to this passage as evidence for a masturbation prohibition. The passage describes how Judah asked his brother Onan to help him to bear a child, and how Onan had sexual intercourse with his sister-in-law, but "waste[ed] his semen on the ground." This phrase has been interpreted literally by fundamentalist Christians to say that semen must never be wasted, that is, no masturbation. Indeed, Catholic theologians in the Middle Ages even examined whether or not sperm cells had souls! This interpretation led to prohibitions on masturbation and other sexual behaviors that do not produce pregnancy. The fixed worldview is that God did not want any semen wasted—what Onan did was "wicked," and so masturbation will always be wicked.

Process worldview Christians may read the same passage differently. They might ask "What was the thing Onan did that was 'wicked in the sight of the Lord'?" Was God condemning the wasting of semen? Or was God angry at Onan's selfishness—or disobedience—with his intentional failure to produce a child for his brother, as was his traditional obligation at the time? A process worldview Christian might also point out that even if the passage is to be interpreted as a masturbation prohibition because of the spilling of one's seed, the passage says nothing about female masturbation, which involves no release of any seed. Is female masturbation therefore permissible?

This example only serves to illustrate only two possible values related to the sometimes controversial issue of masturbation. It may be tempting to stop there and look only at two perspectives, but consider that there are many other reasons people may support or oppose masturbation. The ancient Chinese Tao of love and sex advises that semen should be ejaculated very rarely, for reasons related to mental and physical (not moral) health. Masturbation aside, the Tao advises that males should only ejaculate one time per every 100 acts of intercourse, so that female—not male—pleasure is maximized! Another position on masturbation may be its functionality, as viewed by sex therapists, for treating sexual dysfunction. Another perspective is to evaluate the morality of masturbation on whether or not it causes physical harm. Since masturbation—a very common behavior, from birth to death—causes no physical harm, it might be regarded as a healthy sexual alternative to other behaviors that may be dishonest or exploitative. There are many perspectives on this one topic, and there are similarly many perspectives beyond the two articles presented for every issue in this book.

Consider a non-Western, non-Christian example from recent history: the Islamic cultures of the Middle East and the politics of Islamic fundamentalists. On the fixed worldview side are fundamentalist Muslims who believe that the Muslim world needs to return to the unchanging, literal words of Mohammed and the Koran (the sacred book of the teachings of Allah, or God). Again, there is no gray area in a fixed worldview—what Allah revealed through Mohammed is forever the truth, and the words of the Koran must be taken as literally as the day they were first recorded. There is no room for mitigating factors or new or unique circumstances that may arise.

On the other side of fixed worldview of fundamentalist Muslims are Muslims who view the world through a process worldview—an ever-changing scene in which they must struggle to reinterpret and apply the basic principles of the Koran to new situations. They consider as progress the new rights that some Muslim women have earned in recent years, such as the right to education, the right to vote, the right to election of political office, the right to divorce their husbands, the right to contraception, and many other rights.

The fixed and process worldviews are evident throughout the history of American culture. Religious fundamentalists believe that Americans need to return to traditional values. This worldview often shares a conviction that the sexual revolution, changing attitudes toward masturbation and homosexuality, a tolerance of premarital and extramarital sex, sexuality education in the schools, and the legality of abortion are contributing to a cultural decline and must be rejected.

At the same time, other Americans argue for legalized abortion, civil rights for gays, lesbians and transgender individuals, and the decriminalization of prostitution. For a time, the process worldview gained dominance in Western cultures, but renewed influences of such fixed worldview groups as the Moral Majority and Tea Party have manifested in the recent elections of conservative and other fundamentalist politicians.

Sexological Worldview

In recent years, continued emphasis has been placed on the importance of understanding worldviews when considering one's sexual attitudes and behaviors. Sitron and Dyson (2009) advocated for students and professionals in the field of sexology (the academic study of sexuality) to cultivate a sexological worldview in order to gain and transform their perspective on, and better understand, sensitive topics in sexuality. Through interviews with sexologists they defined the construct of sexological worldview as follows:

> Sexological worldview is the often unexamined but changeable perspective held by each person about the world around them with regards to sexuality. Sexological worldview emerges throughout life experiences and the socialization proves and is influenced by the presence or absence of infinite combinations of the following components and their variations: culture, knowledge, values, beliefs, religion or spirituality, opinions, attitudes and concepts specific to sexuality, relationship style and type, sexual behavior, sexual orientation, and gender identity. Sexological worldview develops across a continuum with worldviews at one end being expressed as "dualistic (right or wrong)" and at the opposing end as "relativist (possible perspectives are endless and no one perspective is right or wrong)" and varied expressions in between (p. 12).

Closing Thoughts

The worldviews described here characteristically permeate and color the way we look at and see everything in our lives. One or the other view will influence the way we approach a particular political, economic, or moral issue, and the way we reach decisions about sexual issues and relationships. However, one must keep in mind that no one is ever fully and always on one or the other end of the spectrum. The spectrum of beliefs, attitudes, and values proposed here is an intellectual abstraction. Real life is not that simple. You may find yourself holding fixed worldviews on some issues, and process worldviews on others. Your views may represent neither worldview. Just like there are no pure blue and red states, there are no absolutes when it comes to sexual values. There is a continuum of values, with the fixed worldview on one end, and the process worldview on the other. Your sexual values for each issue presented in this text will likely depend on the issue, your personal experiences with the subject matter, and the values and beliefs that you have accumulated by important sources within your own life.

Personal connection with an issue may be a strong indicator of one's sexual values. If you are among the millions of Americans who has had a sexually transmitted infection, that firsthand experience will likely affect what you believe about mandatory condom usage in pornography. If you identify as gay, lesbian, or bisexual and live in a state that prohibits same-sex marriage, your views on marriage equality may be strong and well-formed. If a family member that you love and respect taught you that pornography is wrong, it may be difficult for you to accept the proposition that it is not harmful. There may be other issues presented that you have no strong opinion on, or are simply unfamiliar with. As we are all sexual beings, so many of the issues presented here provide an opportunity for a personal connection to an issue, beyond a simple academic exercise.

As you plunge into the eighteen controversial issues selected for this volume, try to be aware of your own predispositions toward certain topics, and try to be sensitive to the kinds of ethnic, religious, social, economic, and other factors that may be influencing the position a particular author takes on an issue. Understanding the roots that support a person's overt position on an issue will help you to decide whether or not you agree with that position. Take time to read a little bit about the authors' biographies too, as their affiliations may reveal something about their potential biases. Understanding these same factors in your own thinking will help you to articulate more clearly and convincingly your own values and decisions.

References

Francoeur, R. (1991). *Becoming a sexual person* (2nd ed.). New York, NY: Macmillan.

Sitron, J. and Dyson, D. (2012). Validation of a sexological worldview: A construct for use in the training of sexologists in sexual diversity. *SAGE Open, 2,* DOI: 10.1177/2158244012439072

Unit 1

UNIT

Sex & Society

*C*ompeting philosophical forces drive concerns about human sexuality on a societal level. Some are primarily focused on the well-being of individuals (or groups of individuals) and their right to individual expression versus their protection from harm; others are mainly concerned with either maintaining or questioning established social norms; still others are engaged by the extent to which the law should impose on a citizen's privacy. This unit examines six such questions that affect our social understanding of sexuality.

Selected, Edited, and with Issue Framing Material by:
Ryan W. McKee, *Widener University*
and
William J. Taverner, *Center for Family Life Education*

ISSUE

Is Pornography Harmful?

YES: **Pamela Paul**, from "The Cost of Growing Up on Porn" (March 7, 2010), www.washingtonpost.com/wp-dyn/content/article/2010/03/05/AR2010030501552.html?sid=ST2010030502871

NO: **Megan Andelloux**, from "Porn: Ensuring Domestic Tranquility of the American People," an original essay written for this volume (2011)

Learning Outcomes

After reading this issue, you should be able to:

- Explain the limitations and difficulties in defining "pornography."
- Describe some of the recent research that has been done on pornography.
- Critique research methods on the effects of pornography.
- Discuss specific reasons why pornography might be considered harmful, or beneficial.

ISSUE SUMMARY

YES: Pamela Paul, author of *Pornified: How Pornography Is Transforming our Lives, Our Relationships, and Our Families*, argues that studies declaring the harmlessness of pornography on men are faulty, and that consequences of porn consumption can be seen in the relationships men have with women and sex.

NO: Megan Andelloux, sexuality educator and founder of the Center for Sexual Pleasure and Health, argues that the benefits of porn on American society outweigh the questionable consequences. Andelloux outlines several arguments for how porn may be beneficial.

"The Internet is for porn!" Or, so sings a muppet from the hit Broadway show *Avenue Q*. As in-home access to the Internet has risen, so has access to a seemingly unlimited supply of pornography. But is pornography harmful? And whom, if anyone, does it harm? While the debate over erotic and explicit material is nothing new, the widespread availability of online pornography has raised new concerns about an old issue.

Debates over pornography in the United States have largely focused on the perceived negative impact of porn versus free-speech arguments that oppose censorship of any kind. While many see this conflict as a feminist issue, even feminists can find themselves on opposing sides of the argument. In the 1970s and 1980s, an often intense academic debate (referred to as the feminist sex wars) raged between "radical feminists" and a new school of feminist thinkers who labeled themselves "sex-positive." Radical feminists, such as Andrea Dworkin and Catharine MacKinnon, opposed pornography. Sex-positive feminists were weary of calls for censorship and alarmed by anti-porn feminists who were now allied with the conservative movement they saw as in opposition to women's liberation.

A key part of the debate hinges on the effects of the consumption of pornography. Opponents point to researchers who have found connections between porn and a decrease in compassion toward rape victims and the support of violence against women. Recently several popular authors (including Pamela Paul, whose essay is featured in this issue) have warned against the negative impact easily accessible porn can have on relationships, masculinity, and femininity.

On the other hand, supporters of porn point to other studies that show no significant correlation between sexually explicit material and attitudes that are supportive of violence against women. Anti-censorship advocates like Nadine Strossen and sex-positive feminists like Susie Bright and Violet Blue have written about the ways pornography can empower both performers and viewers. The growing market for feminist and queer erotica, featuring films produced and directed by women such as Candida Royalle, Tristan Taormino, and Jayme Waxman, suggests women are supporting porn in increasing numbers.

While the feminist sex wars cooled over time, the debate was never settled—thanks in large part to the ambiguous definition of porn. What, exactly, is pornography?

Is there a line between art and pornography? Between pornography and obscenity? In 1964 Supreme Court Justice Potter Stewart, in an opinion stating the scope of obscenity laws should be limited, famously said of hard-core porn, "I know it when I see it." Nearly 50 years later, controversial porn producer Max Hardcore was sentenced to 46 months in prison (though the sentence was later reduced) for violating federal obscenity laws by distributing his films and promotional material via mail and over the Internet.

The issue of pornography and its potential harms, particularly in reinforcing the subjugation and humiliation of females, is a perplexing one. Efforts to censor speech, writing, and pictorial material (including classical art) have been continuous throughout American history. The success of censorship efforts depends mainly on the dominating views in the particular era in which the efforts are being made, and on whether conservative or liberal views dominate during that period. In the conservative Victorian era, morals crusader Anthony Comstock persuaded Congress to adopt a broadly worded law banning "any book, painting, photograph, or other material design, adapted, or intended to explain human sexual functions, prevent conception, or produce abortion." That 1873 law was in effect for almost a hundred years, until the U.S. Supreme Court declared its last remnants unconstitutional by allowing the sale of contraceptives to married women in 1963 and to single women in 1972.

In 1986, a pornography commission headed by then-Attorney General Edwin Meese maintained that the "totality of evidence" clearly documented the social dangers of pornography and justified severe penalties and efforts to restrict and eliminate it. At the same time, then-Surgeon General C. Everett Koop arrived at conclusions that opposed those of the Meese commission. Koop stated that "Much research is still needed in order to demonstrate that the present knowledge [of laboratory studies] has significant real world implications for predicting [sexual] behavior.

It is doubtful that Justice Stewart, the feminists of the 1970s, or the Meese commission could have foreseen the impact of the Internet and "smart phones" (such as iPhones, Androids, and Blackberries) on the availability or distribution of porn. The seemingly unlimited availability of free hard-core porn at our fingertips has been cited by many as a need for further restrictions. The implications of porn consumption, however, are still hotly debated. While accurate statistics are difficult to come by, there is no debating porn's popularity or billion dollar revenues.

As you read the selections, think about how *you* define pornography. Does it need to be explicit to be considered pornographic? How should feminist, gay, lesbian, or queer-produced porn that portrays people of various genders and body types enjoying sex be viewed in the conversation? What about erotic novels, like *Fifty Shades of Gray*, or paintings, illustrations, and sculptures depicting nudity or sex? Should soft-core porn be treated the same way as hard-core? What about animated scenes of nudity or sexual intercourse that are often depicted in video games? Consider your own porn-viewing habits, or the habits of people you know. Do you think it has had an impact on your (or your friends') attitudes toward women, men, or sex in general? If you believe pornography to be harmful, do you feel it is more damaging to women or men? Do you believe society would benefit from restricting or banning some types of sexually explicit material? Where would you draw the line (or lines) in deciding something was illegal?

In the following selections, Pamela Paul, author of *Pornified: How Pornography Is Transforming Our Lives, Our Relationships, and Our Families*, calls into question the findings of a Canadian researcher who found that viewing pornography had no negative effects on men in his sample. Megan Andelloux, sexuality educator and founder of the Center for Sexual Pleasure and Health, argues that pornography is not only healthy, but it is a valuable part of the fabric of American society.

YES ↵

Pamela Paul

The Cost of Growing Up on Porn

Guess what, guys? Turns out pornography—the much-maligned bugaboo of feminists, prigs and holy rollers—is nothing more than good, not-so-dirty fun.

The proof comes from the University of Montreal, where recent research showed that connoisseurs easily parse fantasy from reality, shudder at the idea of dating a porn star (what would Maman think?) and wholeheartedly support gender equality. "Research contradicts anti-pornography zealots," gloated a column's headline in the *Calgary Sun.*

So, I've been contradicted. Presumably, I'm one of the zealots in question. My anti-porn fanaticism took the form of a 2005 book, "Pornified," in which I dared to offer evidence that all is not well in the era of Internet porn. Today, 20-somethings, teenagers and even—sorry to break it to you, parents—tweens are exposed to the full monty of hard-core pornography.

Wasn't it time someone asked some obvious questions? What will happen now that the first generation of men raised on Internet porn is making its way onto the marriage market? What influence does the constant background blare of insta-porn have on their ideas about women and monogamous relationships?

The answers I found to those questions were less than cheering. In dozens of interviews with casual and habitual porn users, I heard things such as: "Real sex has lost some of its magic." "If I'm looking like eight or 10 times a day, I realize I need to do something to build my confidence back up." "My wife would probably think I was perverted and oversexed if she knew how much I looked at it every day."

In the years since I wrote the book, I have heard from dozens of readers who described the negative effects of porn. One was a student at Berkeley, who observed that "ever more deplorable acts needed to be satiated" and noted: "As a child, we are exposed to things that we may not realize have formative effects. As adults, many times we simply continue without questioning." (Women, it seems, also turn to iVillage.com, where a board devoted to "relationships damaged by pornography" contains more than 32,280 messages to date.)

Yet there's still so much we don't know. Perhaps we can learn from the scintillating news out of Montreal. Let's have a closer look at that—oops!—turns out there is no study. Simon Louis Lajeunesse, a postdoctoral student and associate professor at the university's School of Social Work, has yet to publish a report. His findings, such as they exist, were based on interviews with 20 undergraduate males who detailed their views on sex, gender and pornography in one to two lickety-split hours.

Granted, it's qualitative, not quantitative, research, but the brevity of the interviews is concerning. While reporting "Pornified," I felt the need for more than four hours with many of my 100 interviewees. Of course, my guys could talk anonymously to a disembodied voice on the phone; the poor fellows in Montreal had to sit down and look a male social worker in the eye before confessing a penchant for three-ways. Lajeunesse asked 2,000 men before he found 20 willing subjects. Most of them, he said, were referred by women in their lives. Hmm.

And just how did Lajeunesse learn that pornography hadn't affected their views of said women? Why, he asked and they said so! "My guys want to have equal relationships, equal income, equal responsibility domestically," Lajeunesse told me. Color me dubious, but I hardly think most men would own up to discriminating against women, spurred on by porn or not.

To be fair, researching the relationship between men and pornography isn't easy. My methods had flaws, too. The most methodologically sound study would involve gathering a sample of men, scheduling regular sessions to view online porn, and comparing their subsequent sexual attitudes and behaviors with those of a control group that did not use pornography. Through a series of measures—interviews, questionnaires, observations—the data would be collected and analyzed by a team of objective academics.

That's not going to happen now, though it once did. Back in 1979, Jennings Bryant, a professor of communications at the University of Alabama, conducted one of the most powerful peer-reviewed lab studies of the effects of porn viewing on men. Summary of results: not good. Men who consumed large amounts of pornography were less likely to want daughters, less likely to support women's equality and more forgiving of criminal rape. They also grossly overestimated Americans' likelihood to engage in group sex and bestiality.

Yet Bryant's research (conducted with colleague Dolf Zillmann) was carried out long before the Internet brought on-demand porn to a computer screen near you. So why no update? Other than a spate of research in the '80s and '90s that attempted to link pornography with violence (results: inconclusive), nobody has looked at the everyday impact of hard-core porn. "That's a catch-22 with most studies about media effects," Bryant told me. "If you can't demonstrate that what you're doing to research participants is ultimately beneficial and not detrimental, and you can't eradicate any harm, you're required not to do that thing again."

Every university has a review board for the protection of human subjects that determines whether a study is ethically up to snuff. "It is commonly the case that when you get studies as clear as ours, human subjects committees make it difficult to continue to do research in that area," Bryant explained. "Several graduate students at the time wanted to follow up, but couldn't get permission." In other words, the deleterious effects were so convincing, ethics boards wouldn't let researchers dip human subjects back into the muck.

No matter—people will take care of that on their own. As one young man explained, after mentioning that "porn may have destroyed my relationship with my girlfriend" in an e-mail: "I always feel that I'm over porn, but I find myself keep coming back to it. There seems to be an infinite number of porn sites with limitless variations, one never becomes bored with it. . . . It's a very difficult habit to break."

Or as one 27-year-old female lawyer noted recently: "All of my girlfriends and I expect to find histories of pornographic Web sites on our computers after our boyfriends use it. They don't bother erasing the history if you don't give them a lot of hell." The implications troubled her. "I fear we are losing something very important—a healthy sexual worldview. I think, however, that we are using old ideas of pornography to understand its function in a much more complex modern world."

Of the many stories I've heard revealing the ways in which young men struggle with porn, I offer here just one, distilled, from a self-described "25 year old recovering porn-addict" who wrote to me in October. "Marc" began looking at his father's magazines at age 11, but soon, he wrote, he "turned to the Internet to see what else I could find." This "started off as simply looking at pictures of naked women. From there, it turned into pictures of couples having sex and lesbian couples. When I got into

watching videos on the Internet, my use of porn skyrocketed." At 23, he began dating a woman he called "Ashley." "However, since Ashley's last boyfriend had been a sex/porn addict, I was quick to lie about my use of porn. I told her that I never looked at it. But after 5–6 months, Ashley discovered a hidden folder on my computer containing almost a hundred porn clips. She was devastated."

Marc and Ashley broke up, got back together and spent several months traveling in India. He continued to look at porn behind her back, and on a trip to Las Vegas, he got lap dances despite promising not to. Ashley broke up with him again. "I had never thought about the adverse effects of my use of porn. . . . I want to change. I want to be a respectful human being towards all human beings, male and female. I want to be a committed and loving boyfriend to Ashley."

This is hardly solid lab research. But it is one of many signs of pornography's hidden impact. And flimsy "if only it were true!" research isn't an acceptable substitute for thorough study. An entire generation is being kept in the dark about pornography's effects because previous generations can't grapple with the new reality. Whether by approaching me (at the risk of peer scorn) after I've spoken at a university or via anonymous e-mails, young people continue to pass along an unpopular message: Growing up on porn is terrible. One 17-year-old who had given up his habit told me that reading about porn addicts "was like reading a horrifying old diary, symptoms, downward spirals, guilt, hypocrisy, lack of control, and the constant question of to what degree fantasy is really so different from reality. I felt like a criminal, or at the very least, a person who would objectively disgust me."

Let's not ignore people like him, even if it's tempting to say, as one headline did, "All men watch porn, and it is not bad for them: study."

That's just one more fantasy warping how we live our real lives.

PAMELA PAUL is a journalist and author. Her books include *Parents, Inc.,* and *Pornified: How Pornography Is Damaging Our Lives, Our Relationships, and Our Families.*

Megan Andelloux

 NO

Porn: Ensuring Domestic Tranquility of the American People

Pornography. Images of happy people rolling over one another, flashes of arched backs, moans that cannot be ignored, and giggles pouring from the mouths of stars. Out of the corner of the eye a flash of skin on the monitor catches our attention and draws us in. Porn has become ubiquitous on the Internet in the modern day, but its existence has graced the surface of the Earth since humans first began tracing stick figures on cave walls. One of its earliest forms comes to us from the town of Santillana del Mar, in the Cantabria region of northern Spain during the Upper Paleolithic Period.[1] Coital scenes were drawn out on cave walls 40,000 years ago depicting oral sex, voyeurism, and sex for the sake of fun! Records of these "graphic" images coming from France, Portugal, and Egypt beg the question: did rulers like the great Pharaoh Ramses have to hide his papyrus porn from the royal court? Were our ancestors riddled with angst and shame about the potential damage of gazing at naked bodies drawn on scrolls? Probably not. The danger of depicting human nudity wasn't a social concern until the middle of the 18th century, when the written word made erotica available to the common man.[2] Suddenly, politicians, clergy members, and authority figures of all types decried the erotic word and spread fear of its supposed dangerous and corrupting influence. Today, alas, we still face the same argument: Is pornography harmful?

Not all porn is created equal, but it is a form of speech that has been and must continue to be protected in our society. What may be found offensive by one citizen or group of citizens should not dictate whether or not the rest of society is to be allowed free access to it, lest tyranny of minority opinion rule the day. It's clear the American court systems agree.[3] If the US Supreme found that the Westboro Baptist Church's hate speech is to be afforded protection, how could one ever think to outlaw pornography's message of pleasure? Porn virtually embodies everything the founders envisioned when they penned "the right to life, liberty, and the pursuit of happiness!"

It's been reported that over 372 million websites are devoted to displaying images of people having sex of one sort or another.[4] There are untold thousands of magazines, flash drives, comic strips, and pornographic images that circulate around us every day. Porn is a major part of our American culture, and it could be argued that watching porn is America's real pastime. Now before I start getting hate mail for an inflammatory statement like that, let me point out that regardless of a person's religious preference or political affiliation, about 36% of the American population uses porn at least once a month.[5] One would never know it because very few people publicly claim to enjoy pornography. It's understandable why. Acknowledging that you watch pornography is tantamount to identifying yourself as a "pervert" in our society.

It is astonishing that 40 years after a conservative administration spent years and millions of dollars trying to find a correlation between violence and porn (which they were unable to do), and show that porn has damaging effects on individuals and their personal relationships (which they have not), Americans are still shamed when they enjoy such a basic, ancient part of our humanity.

So, when we have hard, reputable data that tens of millions of Americans have watched porn in the past month, that our crime rates are lower when we have access to it,[6] that the most prevalent images *by far* are of adults having sex,[7] and that the performers in the field like the work they do,[8] why then is porn still vilified? It's because a group of highly motivated, yet select few people yell hard, long, and loud. They shame both people who watch and the actors who perform in porn. They portray those who stand up for porn as being misguided, or as duped by the industry itself, and browbeat people with their opinion that looking at images of people having sex is somehow immoral. We rarely hear that using porn is beneficial, empowering and a healthy choice in sexual development, exploration and expression.

Let's look at why pornography is indeed, good for society and individuals.

Pornography Shows Human Beings as Being Sexual Creatures

Pornography exposes sexual desire, and it is unashamed of what it produces. It shows the lust, the yearning, and the appreciation of other human bodies and their sexual energy. Pornography rejoices in the very things society works so hard to suppress.

Whether stumbled upon or sought out intentionally, porn is a part of society because we enjoy it. People derive pleasure seeing other people be sexual. Porn helps individuals explore behaviors they may feel alone in experiencing, such as fetishes, non-heterosexuality, or even simple masturbation. The anti-porn folks are right in at least one thing: We do learn from the images. Although, the moral crusaders will then go on to argue that we in the audience are without free will and are forced to mimic the most degrading images we see in pornographic films. But just as I will continue to come to a full stop at the next red light I see despite having enjoyed *The French Connection* last night, free will gives us the option to imitate movie scenes or not at will. Nearly everyone is sexual. Porn helps us to share in our sexuality without overriding or sublimating it.

> "Old, young, black, white, male, female, trans, pretty, ugly, tall, short, big, little, all types are represented on screen. A wider variety of body types are welcome on the porn screen as opposed to mainstream media representations of love, sex and romance. We may not look like Angelina Jolie, but we can find someone on a porn screen who looks a lot like we do, having a fun time and living to tell the tale. That's no small thing."
>
> —*Nina Hartley*
> *Porn Performer, Sex Educator*

Pornography Shows the Wide Variety of Human Sexual Desires and Actions

Porn gives hope to those who feel alone and/or sexually isolated. Queers, women, the elderly, or any marginalized group can see, with full representation, that there may be others out there, sexual like they are.

> "I started performing in pornography so that I could participate in what I felt is much needed visibility of queer sexuality, gender expressions, and sex-positive behaviors and culture. My work reflects the minority/marginalized communities that I am a part of, while allowing me to connect with a universal audience who can all appreciate great sex."
>
> —*Jiz Lee, Feminist Porn Award's Boundary Breaker*
> *and AVN Nominated Best New Web Star*

And now with amateur porn being the highest accessed sexually explicit material,[9] we have more evidence of the sex-lives of average Americans! We have proof that it's not just the "evil" porn industry that wants ejaculation scenes or spankings. We see normal bodies on film, flaws and all, having the best most creative sex.

And rather than a for-profit corporation behind the production, amateur porn has become the sexual art of folk. It's Bob and Jane playing here, or Jane and Jane, or Bob and Bob—beer belly, thick legs, short hair and . . . all frolicking around in sexual bliss.

> "Porn has afforded me the ability to feel out my sexuality without the fear of rejection or humiliation."
>
> —*Mark Farlow*

Ethically made pornography is a sub-genre of porn comprised of actors who are paid living wages for depiction of realistic sex. Ethically made pornography allows a performer to participate as more than just an actor in the sexual act being depicted. Ethical porn is an emerging powerful field within the adult market. The individuals and companies behind this movement seek out participants who DON'T look like the typical porn-stars. The ultimate goal seems to be to bring real sex to the masses. Some notable companies in this field include:

- Comstock Films
- Pink and White Productions
- Good Releasing
- Fatale Media
- Reel Queer Productions
- Sir Video
- Tristan Taormino's Expert Guide Series
- Nina Hartley's Guide Series

> "Independent and feminist porn especially can be an incredible validation for those who don't see their own desires reflected in mainstream media."
>
> —*Alison Lee, Good For Her Feminist Porn Awards*

Pornography Is a Risk Reduction Method It Is the Safest of Safe Sex

Watching porn is one of the safest ways to explore sexuality. There is no risk of STI transmissions, no risk of an unwanted pregnancy, no risk of feeling disappointed by the way our body performed, no risk of cheating, and no risk of violence. Human beings fantasize about forbidden fruit. We often wonder what it would be like to be with someone of the same gender, experience a threesome, engage in anal play, explore power dynamics, or talk dirty to our lover. Porn lets us find out, risk-free.

> "Pornography can be a great way for people to explore their sexuality and fantasies without affecting others in society. Through pornography, they are able to jump their pizza delivery person or proposition their car dealer without actually disturbing others."
>
> —*Shanna Katz, Sexologist*

Pornography Gives Access to Sex Information to All

While pornography isn't the best way to educate individuals on how to have sex, it does grant access to sexual information. It allows a great number of people to see what it means to have oral sex, pull-my-hair-play, or cis-gendered experiences. They say a picture is worth a thousand words. There is a clear difference between reading about it in a book and seeing it live in front of you, where you can watch the emotions, see the actual behaviors that take place, and process that information in a different way.

A person may feel titillated or disgusted, intrigued or off put, but all of these feelings are important parts of the learning process. What better starting point could one have when making decisions about the type of sexual behavior one wants to engage in?

I'm not arguing that pornography pretends to be educational. But it does purport to be experiential. Not everyone goes to college, nor do they have access to a sex educator, nor sex education programs, nor even a well stocked sex-ed self-help bookshelf. Accessing pornography can often be the first guidepost pointing the way to what one may want to do (or not do) in bed. The experience that porn brings, surrogate to real life as it may be, helps create a more informed decision making process.

> "We know that many people turn to porn for sex information because there is a dearth of sex ed media. So even if we're making a movie that is in no way intended to be primarily educational, (that is, porn) we want to show sex as people actually have it."
>
> —Carol Queen, Good Releasing Films

Pornography Encourages Conversations to Take Place about Sex

Hate it or love it, pornography is part of America.

Whether you call the risqué PETA commercial banned from prime-time porn, or find Charlie Sheen's latest sexual adventures pornographic, porn can start a conversation. We can turn to our neighbor or friend and ask, with all good intentions and proper decorum, "What do you think about Sasha Grey going into mainstream movies? Do you think she's going to make it? Why?" These probing questions serve a vital public service of allowing us to learn the sexual attitudes of our neighbors and friends.

American culture doesn't speak openly about sexuality yet harbors a judgmental attitude. Knowing the sexual mores of our peers can be vital for our social well-being. With the pornography industry putting "sexy time" out there for everyone to see and critique, seize the opportunity and talk about it!

> "Viewing porn was helpful to convey what turned me on (and off) to my partner, ultimately making the sex and relationship stronger."
>
> —Kim Chanza

Myth-Busting

In cultures that have access to pornography, violent crimes rates decreased. Yes, decreased. The US Government shows there is no correlation between violence and having access to and watching pornography.

The media routinely blares headlines bearing shocking titles such as "Porn made him sodomize his child!" Therefore, one would think that porn contributes to all manner of bad outcomes. The facts show, however, that pornography has been established not to increase rates of sexual violence. In 1970, the President's Commission on Obscenity and Pornography (also known as The Lockhart Report) found no link between pornography and delinquent or criminal behavior among youth and adults.[10] William B. Lockhart, Dean of the University of Minnesota Law School and chairman of the commission, famously said that before his work with the commission he had favored control of obscenity for both children and adults, but had changed his mind as a result of scientific studies done by commission researchers.

Similarly, in 1984 the Metro Toronto Task Force on Public Violence against Women and Children failed to demonstrate a link between pornography and sex crimes,[11] as did the 1994 US National Research Council Panel on Understanding and Preventing Violence.[12] Even the Meese Report, a famously biased hand-picked group of anti-pornography advocates hired by Ronald Reagan to prove the damaging effects of pornography failed to show any hard evidence. In fact, they got more than they bargained for when they hired Canadian sociologist Edna F. Einsiedel to summarize the current scientific studies linking pornography and violence. Her conclusion was that "No evidence currently exists that actually links fantasies with specific sexual offenses; the relationship at this point remains an inference.[13]"

Those talking heads who cling to the canard that porn leads to violence, rape, sexual assault, or child molestation are preaching from emotion, not facts. They fear what horrors "might" come to pass, and their fear is contagious. Terrifying tales without background or prelude are woven in the media to provoke a base response in their audience. Unfortunately, American history is littered with examples of just such emotional arguments being more powerful than well-reasoned counterparts. Witness the Salem witch trials, Japanese internment camps during WWII, or the sordid history of the House Un-American Activities Committee.

The anti-porn community (be it conservative religious or liberal feminist) stuffs the news media with anecdotal evidence of the danger posed by porn. Anecdotal evidence is of course the least reliable type of scientific data; one person, with a pretty face and a sob-story, can be more convincing than stacks of peer-reviewed journal articles. Though it can be moving to hear stories such as "Porn made me masturbate all day," or, "Porn made me see people as if they were naked," porn has not been actually shown to cause any such behavior.

Porn is an easy target for attack, but here is the thing: Humans have free will. We can choose to act one way or another, but pornography does not force us to do evil.

In all seriousness, rape and sexual assault are caused by violent antisocial tendencies, complete disregard for another's rights, and pure self-interest. To pin it on porn relieves the rapist of the guilt and blame.

One may not like certain aspects of pornography, but that discomfort should not restrict other's access to it. A society that produces legal pornography, a people that have access to pornography, is a sexually healthy nation. Pornography, a blessing of liberty, creates for us a more perfect union.

Resources

- Feminists for Free Expression
- ACLU
- Woodhull Freedom Foundation
- National Coalition for Sexual Freedom
- Free Speech Network
- Society for the Scientific Study of Sexuality
- America's War on Sex, Marty Klein
- Planned Parenthood of Western Washington, Pornography: Discussing Sexually Explicit Images, Irene Peters, Ph.D.

References

1. Cave paintings show aspects of sex beyond the reproductive. (2006, May 2). *Dominican Today,* Retrieved from http://www.dominicantoday.com/dr/people/2006/5/2/12982/Cave-paintings-show-aspects-of-sex-beyond-the-reproductive.
2. Carroll, J.L. (2007). *Sexuality now.* Belmont, CA: Wadsworth.
3. Corry v. Stanford University, Case No. 740309 (Cal. Super. Ct. 1995); Dambrot v. Central Michigan University, 839 F. Supp. 477 (E.D. Mich. 1993); Doe v. University of Michigan, 721 F. Supp. 852 (E.D. Mich. 1989).
4. Joseph, M. (Producer). (2007). *Internet porn* [Web]. Available from http://www.good.is/post/internet-Porn.
5. Media Metrix Demographic Profile—Adult. (2008, June). comScore
6. Kendall, T.D. (2006). Pornography, rape, and the internet. *Proceedings of the law and economics seminar* Stanford, CA: http://www.law.stanford.edu/display/images/dynamic/events_media/Kendall%20cover%20+%20paper.pdf.
7. Diamond, M. (2009). Pornography, public acceptance, and sex related crime: a review. *International Journal of Law and Psychiatry* 32 (2009) 304–314; corrected with Corrigendum IJLP 33 (2010) 197–199.
8. Paulie & Pauline. (2010). *Off the set: porn stars and their partners.* Glen Rock, NJ: Aural Pink Press.
9. Klein, M. (2006). *America's war on sex: the attack on law, lust, and liberty.* Santa Barbara, CA: Praeger.
10. The Commission on Obscenity and Pornography, (1970). *President's commission on obscenity and pornography.* Washington, DC: U.S. Government Printing Office.
11. Task Force on Public Violence against Women and Children, Final Report (1984). *Metro Toronto.* Toronto, Canada.
12. Reiss, A.J., & Roth, A.J. National Research Council, (1993). *Understanding and preventing violence.* Washington, DC: National Academy Press.
13. United States Attorney General, Commission on Pornography. (1986). *Attorney general's commission on pornography.* Washington, DC.

MEGAN ANDELLOUX, a certified sexologist and sexuality educator, is the director of the Center for Sexual Pleasure and Health, a sexuality resource center for adults in Pawtucket, Rhode Island. Ms. Andelloux lectures at major universities, medical schools, and conferences on issues surrounding sexual freedom and the politics of pleasure.

EXPLORING THE ISSUE

Is Pornography Harmful?

Critical Thinking and Reflection

1. What types of harm or benefits could result from consuming pornography?
2. Do you think that the ways men and women consume pornography are different? Explain.
3. How has technology changed the way porn is consumed?

Is There Common Ground?

Is there the potential for middle ground between vehemently anti-porn and resoundingly pro-porn camps? Is all porn bad and inherently harmful? How does the age of the viewer impact the potential for harm? There does appear to be general consensus that child pornography is harmful. However, defining child pornography may prove just as challenging as defining all porn. And should the viewer's age be taken into account? At what age should the line be drawn? 12? 16? 18? 21? Is there a difference between a 14-year-old watching online porn versus a 24-year-old? Should two high school students "sexting" each other be viewed the same way as a much older adult looking at nude images or video of a high school student?

In his book, *America's War on Sex*, Marty Klein reports that 50 million Americans use legal adult pornography. A 2013 *Huffiington Post* article reported that 30 percent of all data transmitted on the Internet is porn, and that porn websites are visited more frequently than Amazon, Netflix, and Twitter combined. Most people do not publicly acknowledge their use of pornography, and many even adopt shameful attitudes about it. So, in this way, the arguments presented by Paul and Andelloux may reflect American attitudes and experiences, in general. The common ground may be that people will continue to consume pornography, while many—even the same consumers of pornography—will be silent about it, or condemn it.

Create Central

www.mhhe.com/createcentral

Additional Resources

Blue, V. (2006). *The Smart Girl's Guide to Porn*. San Fransisco, CA: Cleis Press.

Klein, M. (2012). *America's War on Sex*. Santa Barbara, CA: Praeger.

Levy, A. (2006). *Female Chauvinist Pigs: Women and the Rise of Raunch Culture*. New York, NY: Free Press.

Nathan, D. (2007). *Pornography*. Toronto, ON: Groundwood Press.

Paul, P. (2006). *Pornified: How Pornography Is Transforming Our Lives, Our Relationships, and Our Families*. New York, NY: Holt.

Sarracino, C. & Scott, K.M. (2009). *The Porning of America: The Rise of Porn Culture, What It Means, and Where We Go from Here*. Boston, MA: Beacon Press.

Internet References . . .

Academia Does Porn

This article describes a brand new peer-reviewed academic journal devoted to pornography.

www.salon.com/2013/05/03/academia_does_porn/

Cindy Gallop Wants to Change the Future of Porn

Cindy Gallop, creator of www.makelovenotporn.com, shares some of her thoughts on intimacy, pornography, social media, and how these things will come together in the future.

www.businessinsider.com/make-love-not-porn-cindy-gallop-2013-4

Porn Study: Does Viewing Explain Doing—Or Not?

This is a discussion of a new study investigating the relationship between porn use, risky behavior, and erectile dysfunction.

www.psychologytoday.com/blog/cupids-poisoned-arrow/201304/porn-study-does-viewing-explain-doing-or-not

The History of Pornography No More Prudish than the Present

A history of pornography from the ancient to the current.

www.livescience.com/8748-history-pornography-prudish-present.html

Selected, Edited, and with Issue Framing Material by:
Ryan W. McKee, *Widener University*
and
William J. Taverner, *Center for Family Life Education*

ISSUE

Should Condoms Be Required in Pornographic Films?

YES: **Aurora Snow**, from "Condoms in Porn: One Adult Star Says Yes to Measure B," *The Daily Beast* (October 18, 2012), www.thedailybeast.com/articles/2012/10/18/condoms-in-porn-one-adult-star-says-yes-to-measure-b.html

NO: **Hugo Schwyzer**, from "Why Porn Sex Is the Safest Sex," *Jezebel* (October 5, 2012), www.jezebel.com/5948719/why-porn-sex-is-the-safest-sex

---

Learning Outcomes

After reading this issue, you should be able to:

- Explain the existing policy on testing for sexually transmitted infections (STIs) in the adult film industry.
- Discuss the public health arguments for mandatory condom usage in adult films.
- Discuss both the business and free-speech arguments against mandatory condom usage in adult films.

ISSUE SUMMARY

YES: Aurora Snow, adult film performer, believes that gaps in STI testing and filming, as well as a culture of intimidation, put performers at risk for infection despite the mandatory nature of testing. She argues that mandating and enforcing both testing *and* condom use is the best way to ensure performer safety.

NO: Hugo Schwyzer, an author and professor at Pasadena City College, believes that adult film industry is a unique work environment that is quite different from one's personal bedroom. Through interviews with several adult performers, he argues that mandating condom usage in porn, while well intentioned, is unnecessary thanks to a culture of testing and care for oneself and other performers.

For years, the production and economic center of the adult film industry, which generates billions of dollars annually, has been Los Angeles, California. In a typical year, there are about 500 applications for adult film permits. But between January 1 and April 14, 2013, only two were requested.[1] Why the sudden drop? Los Angeles County voters had just passed a controversial law, the County of Los Angeles Safer Sex in the Adult Film Industry Act, also known as "Measure B." The new law requires adult film performers to wear condoms during all scenes filmed in Los Angeles involving anal and vaginal intercourse.

Like all industries that operate within the United States, the adult film industry is subject to health and safety regulations developed and enforced by government agencies. The California Occupational Safety and Health Act (Cal/OSHA), passed in 1973, mandated "safe and healthful working conditions for all California working men and women by authorizing the enforcement of effective standards, assisting and encouraging employers

to maintain safe and healthful working conditions, and by providing for research, information, education, training, and enforcement in the field of occupational safety and health." Further, "Employers must protect employees from blood-borne pathogens and not discriminate against employees that complain about safety and health conditions. Companies are required to prevent workers from coming into contact with blood or other potentially infectious material, including semen and vaginal fluid, and to provide post-exposure prophylaxis."[2] While this law was not written specifically for adult performers, the occupational risks are similar to health care workers or researchers who may come into contact with such "infectious material." In 2006, Cal/OSHA recommended, but did not require, several policies to increase safety on porn sets, including the use of condoms and latex dams during filmed sexual activity.

Though Cal/OSHA regulations were on the books, enforcement of the law was minimal. Porn producers required mandatory monthly testing of each performer to stay in compliance, but did not require that condoms be used. The adult industry occasionally experienced outbreaks of various STIs, including HIV, during which production would stop and all performers who had been put at risk were immediately retested. Industry insiders, as well as many performers, felt that this policy was the best way to protect the safety of performers.

But in 2012, a male performer who altered his paperwork, hiding a positive syphilis test result, infected several of his fellow performers. This was the impetus for the HIV advocacy group AIDS Healthcare Foundation to successfully push for the passage of Measure B in Los Angeles County. Measure B, which passed with nearly 57 percent of the vote, requires the use of condoms for all on-camera acts of vaginal and anal sex. Those in favor of the law, including some performers, said that it would help to ensure the safety on the set and help promote condom usage among viewers. They likened the law to those requiring the use of hard-hats and safety goggles on construction sites. Opponents, including other performers, argued that,

thanks to rigorous testing, the mandatory use of condoms was not needed. They also noted that the new regulations might make the adult film industry consider taking their highly profitable business outside of Los Angeles to areas with less regulation.

In the following selections, both written during the lead-up to the vote on Measure B, adult film performer Aurora Snow speaks to the need for condoms in porn. She believes that the gaps between STI testing and the filming of scenes, as well as a culture of intimidation for those who speak up, put performers at risk for infection. She argues that mandating and enforcing both testing *and* condom use is the best way to ensure performer safety. Author and professor Hugo Schwyzer argues against the need for mandatory condoms. Through interviews with other adult performers, he reasons that requiring condoms is unnecessary because of rigorous testing and the performers' desire for a work environment that allows them to make their own decisions about health and safety.

YES ↵

Aurora Snow

Condoms in Porn: One Adult Star Says Yes to Measure B

I would prefer to have both condoms and testing in porn. It doesn't have to be one or the other; it makes sense to have both. This is not what a girl in the industry is supposed to say, but it is what a lot of us think when quietly eyeing Los Angeles County's ballot initiative—known as Measure B—mandating condoms in adult films.

Safety isn't sexy. Wearing a helmet while riding a motorcycle makes me feel like a dork, but I do it because I know what's at risk if I don't. No one feels or looks sexy wearing a safety hat or knee pads. That's what the condom is for the porn industry, it's our safety hat.

No one wants to wear the safety hat, it's uncomfortable, it doesn't look pretty and it may make the day longer. Condoms are known to rip. Who knows how many condoms one scene will take. If it's a three guys-on-one-girl scene and the condoms keep ripping it could go from a two-hour scene to a four-hour scene. Only one porn company that I know of is and always has been all condoms: Wicked. They have been doing what other companies fear: selling safe sex.

I have done the majority of my six-hundred scenes without condoms, but I predominately use condoms in my personal life. In real life, I ask that my partners both wear condoms and get tested. Yet when I go to work I follow the standard procedure of working without a condom and taking my fellow actor's most recent test at face value.

Every month when I get tested, I wonder if I'll have to come home to my guy and say, "Please don't be mad at me, but we have to go see a doctor because you might have been exposed." Because even though I primarily use condoms in my personal life, like most people I know, I don't use them with oral sex. While it's not as easy to catch something through oral, the possibility remains, and due to the nature of my work the risk is high. Luckily, most STDs that float around the world of porn—most often referred to as the "industry flu"—can be cured with a single shot of antibiotics. Because these STDs are so easy to get rid of, most performers have a certain level of comfort with them. It's almost common. There are other not-so-easily cured STDs that aren't tested for in the adult business. We test monthly for gonorrhea, chlamydia, and the big one, HIV. There are zero requirements to be tested for anything else, but there are other risk factors, such as herpes, HPV, and syphilis. Thanks in part to the recent syphilis outbreak, there may now be a standard monthly syphilis test.

When I heard about the syphilis outbreak, my first feeling was one of relief. For the first time ever, I was so removed from the Los Angeles porn scene that I didn't have to check my calendar and start calling every partner I'd had in the last two weeks to see whether I was at risk. There have been several HIV scares when I had to make those phone calls and figure out for myself how close I was to patient zero. There are no groups within porn protecting performers; it's always been up to performers to keep track of their scene partners, to check tests for themselves, and to make those phone calls no one wants to make.

It isn't safe to rely on someone else to keep me safe on set. I showed up one day with a fresh test, still a newbie to porn and very trusting. What happened? The other girl in our scene couldn't seem to "find" her test. She was a big star at that time, and she was an exclusive performer for this company. The director did his best to persuade me and the male performer to work with this prized performer despite her lack of a test. When we both refused, he yelled at us, but didn't fire us. That could have happened. Instead, we shot the scene without the untested girl. That was the first time I understood porn directors aren't looking out for me, so I have to.

While that situation doesn't happen often, it does happen. Here is another example. I arrived on time for work. I sat through an hour and a half of hair and makeup, went through wardrobe options with the director, and then shot glamour photos for the box cover. Before any bodily fluids are exchanged, performers share their test results. I showed the male performer my test results and waited patiently for his. Somehow he never produced them and got ready for the scene anyway. I persisted in asking for his test. His answer, "Baby girl, you know me. We work together all the time, you know I get tested baby." That answer didn't go over well with me. I sought out the director and asked for the test results. No one could produce a test and the scene was canceled. I didn't get a kill fee, neither did the male performer, the director lost out shooting a scene that day, not to mention the location fees he paid. Will they hire me again? I don't know. That's a risk I take when I speak up for my own safety concerns. Unfortunately, the idea of losing money is sometimes enough to make a performer overlook little things like double-checking a scene partner's test. And, of course, the money at stake sometimes has made other performers fake, doctor, or bluff their tests.

Knowing that a person I am working with is tested doesn't always mean they are STD free. Not everyone that works in porn has sex within the industry, nor do they always use condoms in their private lives, which increases the STD transmission risk from performer to performer between tests. Some of the industry men I know often date three or four girls at a time: there is the main squeeze, the distant girlfriend, the mistress, and the random one-night stand. I have been one of those girls, and not known I was one of a crowd. With the high sexual activity of performers both in and outside of the business, when an STD scare happens it can be lengthy due to reinfection rates from partners that have been treated still having sex with those that haven't. Even though telling someone you gave them an STD is the right thing to do so they can be treated for it, it is a talk most people would rather avoid. This is a part of being in the adult business; it's the less glamorous side.

Bringing something like condoms into porn may contribute to ruining the fantasy, because in fantasy land no one has to think about safety. But if I were your girlfriend, your sister, your mother, or your daughter, what would you want the law to be?

Aurora Snow is an adult film performer and director. She is also a contributor to *The Daily Beast,* where she writes about sex and the adult industry.

Hugo Schwyzer

 **NO**

Why Porn Sex Is the Safest Sex

"The safest sex you can have is in the adult film business." So porn star James Deen tells me during an interview about Measure B, a Los Angeles County initiative on the November ballot that would mandate the use of condoms on set. With just weeks to go until the election, one of Southern California's iconic industries faces a crisis that threatens to force porn production out of Tinseltown—and, unintentionally, make porn sets much less safe for performers. With November 6 fast approaching, Deen and other high-profile stars are banding together in what industry insiders call "an uphill battle" to defeat the initiative.

Placed on the ballot by the Aids Healthcare Foundation, Measure B seems commonsensical enough: make male performers wear condoms during scenes that involve vaginal or anal penetration. After all, aren't porn stars at especially high risk of contracting HIV and other sexually transmitted infections? The initiative's proponents claim it's a no-brainer issue of workplace safety, as basic as requiring that construction workers wear hard hats or machinists wear safety goggles.

As it turns out, it's not that simple. For starters, as Deen and sexual health experts familiar with the industry agree, what makes for safer sex in private doesn't translate well to an adult film set. In an email interview, porn legend Nina Hartley explained that in her business, "condom burn is a real issue. The friction from the latex, even with lubrication, is painful and breaches the integrity of my mucosal membranes, putting me at greater risk for disease transmission." Pointing out that the average length of sexual intercourse in "civilian life" is only a few minutes, Hartley noted, while the shortest porn scenes require an absolute minimum of "half an hour of hard thrusting by a well-endowed young man. It's hard enough to deal with w/o condoms. Add latex to the mix and I'm down to being able to work with a man once a week at best, to say nothing of the damage it would do to my private life and intimacy with my husband." Veteran sex educator Charlie Glickman agrees, pointing out that "what you do in your home kitchen never has the same protocols as you have in a catering business." Adding to Hartley's concerns about the damage rubbers can do to women's mucosal membranes, Glickman notes that condoms themselves degrade rapidly over the course of scenes that can last upwards of two hours to film, making them less effective as barriers to infection.

What does work, according to Hartley, Deen, and other performers, is testing. Porn actors are tested for HIV and other STIs at least once every 28 days (Deen notes he's tested twice as often) at a variety of private testing sites overseen by Adult Production Health and Safety Services, a service administered by the industry's trade group, the Free Speech Coalition. The track record of these testing protocols has been extraordinary, with even critics of the industry willing to admit that porn performers test positive for STIs at a rate well below that of the sexually active "civilians" who are their fellow Angelenos. Vivid Video CEO Steven Hirsch told me that the porn industry has produced "more than 300,000" hardcore sex scenes since 2004, with only two cases of HIV infection—both in performers who contracted the virus from untested civilian partners. That remarkable safety record is attributable to testing and what Deen describes as a "close-knit family atmosphere . . . where mutual trust is sacred" in the business.

As any sexual health advocate will tell you, condoms—even when they work properly—don't protect against every STI. Condoms make sex safer, but they never make sex entirely risk-free. They provide what porn scholar Chauntelle Tibbals calls "at best, visible 'evidence' of mitigated STI risk"; the danger (for both porn performers and the general public) is that condoms will come to be seen as the only protection necessary against transmission. Hirsch told me that mandatory condom use will mean a likely end to the industry's assiduous reliance on testing; Glickman agrees, suggesting that cases of STI infection may even rise as a consequence of the false security provided by Measure B.

Yet despite the powerful case against the initiative on grounds of performer health, the industry argument against Measure B focuses on two other concerns: government waste and free speech. James Deen told me he suspects voters will have an easier time understanding the huge costs associated with enforcing the measure than they will [have understanding] the public health problems with the initiative. Nina Hartley wrote that "the money issue alone should sink it" in a state and county where firefighters are being furloughed and classroom sizes skyrocketing. Vivid Video's Hirsch, meanwhile, thinks the No on B campaign should build its case at least in part on issues of artistic freedom. "We shouldn't be compelled to make films the public doesn't want to see," he argues, adding that that argument should carry weight in a region heavily dependent on mainstream films that appeal to popular tastes. Hartley sums up the problem: "Are we really prepared to force an expressive, made-for-entertainment form of speech (porn) to act as a back-door sexual education medium? That fails the sniff test."

What will happen if the initiative passes? Here, porn insiders disagree. "I doubt we'll leave town," Nina Hartley says; "we live here, our kids go to school here. We'll go underground, with no filming permits pulled." Steven Hirsch, on the other hand, assured me that Vivid and its nearly 100 non-performing full-time employees will pack up and leave L.A. "We can't be in a position where it's an unlevel playing field," he explains; "the performers will leave first, and the rest of the business will follow." If Hirsch is right, that's the potential loss of what the *Los Angeles Times,* in an article highly critical of Measure B, calls a $1-billion business in the county alone.

In our phone conversation, Deen spoke animatedly about the huge missed opportunity that Measure B represents. "There is so much good we could do with the AIDS Health Care Foundation," he insists, "I wish we could be partners." Sex educator Lanae St John suggests a more effective public health strategy would be to have AHF and the porn industry jointly create short public-service announcements to run at the start of porn videos, an idea that Deen heartily endorses. "There ought to be condom ads on every porn site," he says, "condoms are a great idea. They just aren't the best way to keep performers safe on camera."

"No one really understands how the porn industry works," Deen says at the end of our conversation. "They think we're reckless and easily exploited; what people don't understand is just how much we care about our health and the health of the all the performers in our community." The most-celebrated male porn star of his generation sighs, and offers his own take on why the condom law may pass: "I think people feel guilty about watching porn. They want to clear their conscience about it by trying to make us safer. But that's more about their shame than it is about our health." Before hanging up (and telling me to "say hi to everyone at Jezebel for me!") Deen reiterates his central point: that the most unsafe sex porn performers have is in their off-set private lives.

Is it misplaced guilt about masturbating to the images of performers Deen, Stoya, and Hartley that drives the Measure B campaign? Perhaps. A more likely explanation lies in the misperception of fucking on camera bears much resemblance to sex without a film crew present. We shouldn't be getting all our tips on how to make love from watching porn. And we shouldn't assume that responsible risk-reduction in the bedroom has much to do with keeping performers safe on set.

HUGO SCHWYZER, PhD, teaches history and gender studies at Pasadena City College. He is an author and speaker focusing on gender and sexuality. His writing has been featured in a variety of outlets, including *The Atlantic,* the *Guardian,* and the *Los Angeles Times.*

EXPLORING THE ISSUE

Should Condoms Be Required in Pornographic Films?

Critical Thinking and Reflection

1. What safety precautions were taken to protect performers before the passage of Measure B? What new practices did Measure B mandate?
2. What were the arguments in favor of Measure B? What were the arguments against?
3. How might mandatory use of condoms in porn impact the performers? The viewers?
4. Do you think adult films become more or less erotic with on-screen condom use? Or does it make no difference to the viewer?

Is There Common Ground?

The debate over Measure B was often framed as a public health and workplace safety issue. Public health advocates, adult performers, and producers agree that safe work environments for those involved in the porn industry are important. What they disagree on is the role of government in regulating safety practices. Opponents argued that increased regulation could actually decrease safety and impact the industry in other ways as well. The lack of condoms in porn is said to have been in response to viewer demand. Consumers, producers say, don't want to watch porn with condoms. Additionally, some filmmakers argue, requiring performers to use condoms would infringe on their artistic freedom. Supporters of the law note that condom use is the norm in the majority of gay male-oriented porn films, and that consumers have no problem with this. Additionally, they argue that condom requirements for porn produced in other parts of the world have not hindered sales of their films.

Rather than find out the impact of condoms on sales of their films, the porn industry quickly sought other locations for filming in the wake of Measure B. In response, many other communities are exploring the possibility of enacting similar laws in order to keep adult film productions out.

What is your take on the controversy? Do you feel, like Aurora Snow, that condoms would increase safety on the set, and reduce the spread of STIs? Or, do you believe, like Schwyzer and the performers he interviews, that mandatory condom use is unnecessary in adult films? Are analogies between condoms and hard-hats appropriate? Are adult film sets just another work environment? Why might condoms only be required for vaginal and anal sex and not oral sex? Should condoms and dams be required for oral sex as well? Would the use of condoms make you more or less likely to watch adult films? Why? Does the

porn industry have a responsibility to lead by example and promote safer sex practices? Or are adult films simply a form of artistic expression, like any other film? Do other types of media, like action or comedy films, television, or music, have a responsibility to promote healthy behaviors?

Create Central

www.mhhe.com/createcentral

References

1. Abram S., "Porn Film Permits Have Dropped Dramatically in L.A. County," *Los Angeles Daily News*, April 14, 2013. www.dailynews.com/ci_23024668/porn-film-permits-have-dropped-dramatically-l-county?source=rss_emailed
2. Grudzen C. & Kerndt P. (2007). "The Adult Film Industry: Time to Regulate?" *PLOS Medicine*, 4(6). doi:10.1371/journal.pmed.0040126

Additional Resources

Businesswire. "Study Shows STD Rates Much Higher in Adult Film Performers," July 28, 2011. www.businesswire.com/news/home/20110728006637/en/Study-Shows-STD-Rates-Higher-Adult-Film.

Hess, A. "Porn Stars May Soon Have to Wear Condoms. Will You Still Watch?" *Slate*, October 25, 2012. www.slate.com/blogs/xx_factor/2012/10/25/california_s_measure_b_what_s_so_bad_about_condoms_in_porn.html

Los Angeles Times, "No on Measure B," October 18, 2012.

Internet References . . .

Adult Production Health and Safety Services (APHSS)

APHSS provides guidelines and services, including resources, testing sites, and electronic access to test information to ensure the safety of the adult film industry.

www.aphss.org

AIDS Healthcare Foundation

The AIDS Healthcare Foundation is an advocacy organization for those infected with HIV/AIDS. They are the largest provider of HIV/AIDS medical care in the United States. In 2012, they successfully advocated for the passage of Measure B in Los Angeles County.

www.aidshealth.org

Free Speech Coalition

This organization is the trade association for the adult film industry. The website addresses many issues, legal and otherwise.

www.freespeechcoalition.com

Selected, Edited, and with Issue Framing Material by:
Ryan W. McKee, *Widener University*
and
William J. Taverner, *Center for Family Life Education*

ISSUE

Do Reality TV Shows Portray Responsible Messages about Teen Pregnancy?

YES: Amy Kramer, from "The REAL Real World: How MTV's '16 and Pregnant' and 'Teen Mom' Motivate Young People to Prevent Teen Pregnancy," Original essay for this edition (2011)

NO: Mary Jo Podgurski, from "Till Human Voices Wake Us: The High Personal Cost of Reality Teen Pregnancy Shows," Original essay for this edition (2011)

Learning Outcomes
After reading this issue, you should be able to:
• Describe the current rates of teen pregnancy in the United States.
• Compare the rates of teen pregnancy in the United States to other developed nations.
• Describe how shows like "16 and Pregnant" might affect and impact American attitudes and behaviors.
• Explain some of the possible negative effects of reality TV shows about teen pregnancy.

ISSUE SUMMARY

YES: Amy Kramer, director of Entertainment Media & Audience Strategy at the National Campaign to Prevent Teen and Unplanned Pregnancy, argues that reality television shows engage teens in considering the consequences of pregnancy before they're ready for it, and motivate them to want to prevent it.

NO: Mary Jo Podgurski, EdD, founder of the Academy for Adolescent Health, Inc., argues that though such television shows have potential benefits, they inadequately address the issue, and may even have a negative impact on those who participate in them.

Television has evolved during the past five decades. Just 50 years ago, families could gather around one immovable set with a limited number of channels, and observe Desi Arnaz and Lucille Ball occupy different beds in the wildly popular sitcom "I Love Lucy." Considered prudent for television standards at the time, it would strike many today as an odd family life arrangement for the famous couple—who were married both off-the-air and in-character! Fast forward two decades, and we see Mike and Carol Brady sharing the same bed on "The Brady Bunch," with not a hint of sexual interest or attraction between them.

Today's television has a much more substantial representation of sexual relationships and themes. Leaps and bounds from then-landmark events such as William Shatner and Nichelle Nichol's "first interracial kiss" on television's "Star Trek," Ellen DeGeneres coming out on-the-air in the mid-1990s, and Kerr Smith's and Adam Kaufman's "first gay male kiss" on primetime television in 2000, many of today's television programs include overtly sexual messages, and a greater range of sexual identities and orientations. Indeed, many shows rely and bank on sexual innuendo, humor, and steamy scenes. While the representation is greater, the *accuracy* of the portrayals is questionable. Is the infrequent gay character actually a *caricature* manifesting common stereotypes? Is sex so closely and frequently tied to crime as portrayed in various crime dramas? Does the constant use of sexual humor mirror and reinforce society's discomfort with sex? Do sexual scenes in prime-time dramas make sex appear seamless—and only for the young and beautiful? (Note the hilarious response to 90-year-old Betty White discussing her "Dusty Muffin" on "Saturday Night Live.")

Another way in which television has changed is with the emergence of the so-called "reality TV show" genre. Popularized with the success of MTV's "The Real World" and CBS's "Survivor," many reality TV shows and formats have followed. Perhaps it was inevitable that the worlds of reality TV and sexuality would collide, and new shows addressing specific sexual themes emerged in the last few years. Some shows address issues of pregnancy and family life. In 2007, we were introduced to the family life of parents of octuplets on Discovery Health's "Jon and Kate Plus 8." Later, MTV introduced the real-life teen-focused pregnancy dramas "16 and Pregnant" and "Teen Mom," which follow the lives of real young people dealing with teen pregnancy, parenting, and in some episodes, abortion. VH-1 also airs "Dad Camp," a show in which young men go through "boot camp-style group therapy" in preparing them to take responsibility for fatherhood.

Some sexuality educators, looking for ways to connect with students in authentic, meaningful ways, have embraced the popularity of these shows for their potential as teachable moments. Educators can show a clip to build discussion questions themed around the premise, "What would you do if . . .?"

Other sexuality educators express concern over the reality and impact of the shows. Do the networks do an adequate job of portraying all the hardships of teen pregnancy, or will students perceive the characters as TV stars to be admired and emulated?

In the following selections, Amy Kramer, the director of Entertainment Media & Audience Strategy at The National Campaign to Prevent Teen and Unplanned Pregnancy, describes the positive potential these shows can have as allies in sexuality education. Kramer explains how the shows help motivate young people to want to prevent pregnancy before they are ready to be parents. Mary Jo Podgurski, founder of the Academy for Adolescent Health, Inc., who routinely works with pregnant and parenting teens, explains her reasons for declining the opportunity to work with "16 and Pregnant" when producers approached her. While noting the potential benefits of such shows, Dr. Podgurski expresses reservations about the impact the shows might have on the teens who appear on a national stage.

YES ↵

Amy Kramer

The REAL Real World: How MTV's "16 and Pregnant" and "Teen Mom" Motivate Young People to Prevent Teen Pregnancy

Like it or not, media is a huge influence in the lives of young people. Teens spend more hours each week in front of a screen than they do in a classroom.[1] Many teens know a lot more about their favorite shows than they do about any academic subject, and characters on television are often more familiar than neighbors. What young people learn in sex ed, if they have sex ed at all, is a fraction of what pop culture serves up on a daily basis. Which is why parents and educators alike should be thankful that MTV has emerged as a sort of accidental hero in the campaign against teen pregnancy.

Thanks to the reality shows "16 and Pregnant" and "Teen Mom," millions of young people are now thinking and talking about teen pregnancy. These shows were developed as nothing more than good entertainment but they have succeeded in ways public health initiatives have not—that is getting young people to stop, pay attention, consider, and discuss what happens when someone becomes a parent before they're ready.

Although we know how to avoid teen pregnancy—get teens to avoid having sex at all or to use contraception carefully and consistently when they do have sex—prevention isn't always as easy as it looks. Getting young people to commit to waiting or protecting themselves is tough. After all, they're kids. The consequences of their actions might not seem as likely as the benefit of the risks. Nearly half of teens admit they've never thought about how a pregnancy would change their lives[2] and most girls who get pregnant say they never thought it would happen to them. It's no wonder young people don't always take precautions to prevent pregnancy—if you never consider that something might happen to you, or what life would be like if it did, why would you consider taking steps to prevent it?

But "16 and Pregnant" and "Teen Mom" seem to be changing that. These shows are bringing the reality of too-early pregnancy and parenthood smack into the middle of the lives and minds of young people in powerful and important ways. Teens come to these shows on their own and they say they come away with a new appreciation for some of the consequences of unprotected sex. In fact, in a nationally representative poll conducted by The National Campaign to Prevent Teen and Unplanned Pregnancy in

2010, 82% of teens who had seen "16 and Pregnant" said that watching the show "helps teens better understand the challenges of pregnancy and parenthood." Only 17% said the show makes teen pregnancy look glamorous.[3] Already, the fact that young people are tuning in week after week makes what MTV is doing more successful than many PSA campaigns could ever hope to be.

* * *

Rates of teen pregnancy and birth are higher in the United States than in any other industrialized nation. The teen birth rate in the U.S. is more than three times higher than the rate in Canada, and nearly twice that of the United Kingdom (which has the highest rate in Europe). One out of every ten babies born in the U.S. is born to a teen mother. Three out of every ten girls in the U.S. get pregnant before their 20th birthdays—750,000 girls each year. That's 2,000 girls getting pregnant *every day*. These numbers—as shocking as they are—actually represent dramatic improvements. In the past two decades, rates of teen pregnancy and childbearing in the U.S. have dropped by more than one-third.[4]

According to the National Center for Health Statistics, in early-1990s America, 117 out of every 1,000 girls ages 15–19 got pregnant, and 62 out of every 1,000 girls ages 15–19 gave birth. Not even twenty years later those rates are down to 72 per 1,000 teens getting pregnant and 39 per 1,000 teens giving birth. Put another way, teen pregnancy has declined by 38% and teen births are down by one-third. Still too high, but a remarkable improvement on an issue once thought to be intractable.

To what do we owe this astonishing decline in teen pregnancy and teen births? Quite simply and perhaps not surprisingly, it's a combination of less sex and more contraception. According to the National Survey of Family Growth (NSFG), a household-based nationally representative survey conducted periodically by the Centers for Disease Control and Prevention to study families, fertility, and health in the U.S., in 1988, 51% of girls and 60% of boys ages 15–19 had ever had sex. In 2006–2008 those numbers had declined to 42% of girls and 43% of boys. Condom use increased during that time as well: In 1988, 31% of girls and 55% of boys who had sex in the past 90 days said they used a condom the last time they had sex. In 2006–2008,

Do Reality TV Shows Portray Responsible Messages about Teen Pregnancy? by McKee and Taverner

37

those numbers had grown to 53% for girls and 79% for boys. So, for a complicated array of reasons, teens have been doing the only two things you can do to prevent pregnancy: delaying sex and being better about contraception when they do have sex.

It's also important to note that abortions to teens declined as well over that same time period. In 1988, 39% of pregnancies to teens ended in abortion, in 2006, it was 27%, meaning that the decline in teen births was not due to an increase in terminations.[5]

* * *

Consider the following: While rates of sexual activity, pregnancy, birth, and abortion among teens were declining enormously, the media was growing exponentially and becoming coarser and more sexualized. There are hundreds of channels now and an infinite number of websites. Finding sexually suggestive content on television and explicit content online—or it finding you—is a fact of life for many young people. If media influence on teens' decisions about sex is so direct and so negative, why might it be that teen sexual behavior has gotten more responsible at exactly the same time the media and popular culture has become more sexualized? Simply put, the media can't be solely to blame for teens having sex, or having babies. However, the media can help write the social script and contribute to viewers' sense of what's normal and acceptable—and can make sex seem casual, inconsequential, or serious. In fact, polling for The National Campaign to Prevent Teen and Unplanned Pregnancy shows that year after year 8 in 10 teens say they wish the media showed more consequences of sex (not less sex).[6]

So television alone doesn't cause teen pregnancy, but could it actually help prevent it? Teens themselves suggest that it can. Most teens (79% of girls, 67% of boys) say that "when a TV show or character I like deals with teen pregnancy, it makes me think more about my own risk of becoming pregnant/causing a pregnancy, and how to avoid it," according to the National Campaign to Prevent Teen and Unplanned Pregnancy.[7] "Thinking about my own risk" is an important piece of the prevention puzzle.

In that same study from The National Campaign, three-quarters of teens (76%) and adults (75%) say that what they see in the media about sex, love, and relationships can be a good way to start conversations about these topics. Communication between parents and teens about their own views and values regarding these issues is critical. Children whose parents are clear about the value of delaying sex are less likely to have intercourse at an early age. Parents who discuss contraception are also more likely to have children who use contraception when they become sexually active.[8] These conversations can be awkward and intimidating (on both sides), but they are important. So anything that encourages such talk, or makes it easier to start the conversation, is valuable.

MTV's "16 and Pregnant" is a conversation starter. Certainly among teens, but also within families. In a 2010 study of more than 150 teenagers involved with Boys & Girls Clubs after-school programs in a southern state, 40% of teens who watched "16 and Pregnant" with their group at the Club, and then talked about it in a facilitator-led discussion, also talked about it again afterward with a parent. One-third discussed it with a boyfriend/girlfriend. More than half discussed it with a friend.[9] That 40% went home and talked about with mom or dad is particularly exciting—because the more opportunities parents have to discuss their own ideas and expectations about pregnancy and parenting, the better. Teens talking about these shows—articulating their own thoughts about a teen parent on MTV or a situation depicted in an episode—brings them one step closer to personalizing it, which is an important step along the behavior change continuum, and the path to prevention.

Educators and leaders in youth-serving organizations are using the MTV shows as teaching tools. A social worker in the Midwest who frequently speaks at schools in both urban and rural areas, has used episodes of "16 and Pregnant" in her work: "With the boys, we had great discussion about what makes a man a 'father'." Boys were a little defensive about the portrayal of the teen dads, but after talking it through, began to empathize more with the young women." A teacher in the South incorporated the series into high school lesson plans: "I use it as part of a unit on teen parenting and parenting readiness to discourage teen pregnancies and to encourage students to wait until they are older and 'ready' before having children. . . . Students enjoy watching the 'real-life' stories of teens and are able to really identify with them." A private special education teacher who works with a teen population especially vulnerable to abusive relationships and pregnancy has also watched the series with students: "The kids were very much engaged because it was something they would watch at home. Some of them had seen the episodes already but looked at them differently once viewed in a group, clinical setting. The conversations were often very serious and enlightening for the students. They were able to put themselves into the girls' shoes and talk about how they would feel, react, respond in each of the situations that came up." Staff at a county juvenile detention center in the Southwest includes the show in teen pregnancy prevention programs and calls it "heavy-hitting and impactful": "They cater to the very media-driven nature of teens today—they aren't dry book material, but rather a great combination of reality and entertainment in a condensed format. . . . A whole year in the life of these teen parents in just an hour of viewing."[10]

* * *

Television shows like MTV's "16 and Pregnant" and "Teen Mom" are created for entertainment purposes with the hope of attracting viewers and keeping them engaged. By that measure, these shows are indisputably successful. Millions of people tune in to each new episode—and the ratings are among the highest on the cable network. Recent episodes have drawn more viewers than even the major broadcast network competition. Public attention to the storylines extends beyond the episodes themselves and into Internet discussion forums, where theories and speculation about the lives depicted on the shows are rampant.

Thanks to these very real reality programs, teen pregnancy is no longer a mysterious topic to millions of young people. Viewers have seen in the most vivid way possible what happens when contraception fails, when babies arrive, when boyfriends leave, when money is tight, when parents are disappointed, and when graduating from high school is impossible. Conversations are happening around dinner tables and in carpools, allowing parents and teens to explore their own opinions and behavior. Parents now have an opportunity to discuss their own values and expectations as they pertain to family formation and romantic responsibility. Friends, siblings, and partners are talking to each other about what happens when young people become parents before they're ready. Maybe they're even talking about how to prevent it from happening in the first place.

Every episode of "16 and Pregnant" includes a scene in which the expectant teenager talks about how she got pregnant. Many weren't using any protection at all, others had problems remembering to take their pills every day, some found out that prescribed antibiotics can interfere with the effectiveness of birth control pills, a few missed their Depo shot appointments, others stopped using a method after a break-up and then never returned to its use after reconciliation, etc. This information is presented honestly and in peer-to-peer terms, inviting viewers to listen and learn, and perhaps explore a type of contraception they hadn't previously known about. On "Teen Mom" viewers see the young parents taking steps to prevent subsequent pregnancies: cameras have captured the girls' discussions with their doctors about the vaginal ring, IUDs, and other long-acting methods of contraception. Even the "reunion" episodes devote time to discussion about birth control between updates on the babies and the relationship drama.

Watching what happens to girls who "never thought it would happen to them" encourages viewers to assess their own risk. When teenage fans of the shows see time and again that having a baby as an adolescent often means educational goals are abandoned, family relationships erode, financial challenges become insurmountable, and romantic fantasies are dashed, the prospect of early parenthood in their own lives becomes far less attractive. Rosier depictions of teen pregnancy and its consequences from movies, scripted television shows, and daydreams start to look silly in comparison. Seeing that teen pregnancy happens in the lives of girls from every sort of background (even a familiar one) reminds viewers that it could happen to them and it pushes them to figure out how to avoid a similar fate.

Separate from the shows themselves is the tabloid coverage they receive, though it is so pervasive right now it deserves mention here. That the tabloid media have decided to treat these struggling young mothers like celebrities is certainly unfortunate. That the real-life people around the teen mothers have obviously decided to cooperate with the tabloids (in the form of photos, tips, and other information) is sadder still. However, the bulk of even that coverage focuses on the turmoil in their lives. These are young mothers agonizing over money, men, family drama, health issues, the law, and the unending responsibility of parenthood. Followers of this often repugnant news stream may know even more about the chaos that swirls around young parents than do mere viewers of the show. Coverage does not necessarily equal glamorization. Bottom line: if you sit through a full episode, any episode, of "16 and Pregnant" or "Teen Mom," glamour is totally absent.

* * *

MTV's "16 and Pregnant" and "Teen Mom" are not evidence-based teen pregnancy prevention programs. They aren't a substitute for talented teachers or comprehensive sex ed curricula. These shows aren't more meaningful than traditions of faith. They aren't more important than access to quality healthcare or relevant health information. They aren't more powerful than engaged parents willing to talk openly about tough topics. But teen pregnancy prevention needs to happen everywhere, including in the popular media teenagers love to consume. Everyone who cares about teens, babies, and the next generation of Americans needs to do their part to keep rates of teen pregnancy on a downward trajectory. Families, schools, health care professionals, businesses big and small, religious communities, and yes, the media, all have a role to play. Teen pregnancy prevention requires sustained effort over time by all sectors. This isn't an issue where a vaccine or a cure will lead to a drop in incidence. Even new and better methods of contraception won't do the trick if young people aren't motivated to use them. Making headway on this complex topic requires young people to make better choices over and over again. Any way they can get the message that the teen years are not the appropriate time for parenthood matters.

MTV is doing more than most—even if inadvertently—with "16 and Pregnant" and "Teen Mom." Millions of young people tune in each week and four out of five viewers say that doing so "helps teens better understand the challenges of pregnancy and parenthood." Anyone who cares about reducing rates of teen pregnancy and teen birth should listen to what teens themselves are saying and tune out the rest.

Footnotes/Sources

1. Kaiser Family Foundation, (2010). *Generation M2: Media in the Lives of 8- to 18-Year-Olds*. http://www.kff.org/entmedia/upload/8010.pdf

2. National Campaign to Prevent Teen and Unplanned Pregnancy, (2007). *With One Voice 2007: America's Adults and Teens Sound Off about Teen Pregnancy*. http://www.thenationalcampaign.org/resources/pdf/pubs/WOV2007_fulltext.pdf

3. National Campaign to Prevent Teen and Unplanned Pregnancy, (2010). *With One Voice 2010: America's Adults and Teens Sound Off about Teen Pregnancy*. http://www.thenationalcampaign.org/resources/pdf/pubs/WOV_2010.pdf

4. National Campaign to Prevent Teen and Unplanned Pregnancy, various fact sheets. http://www.thenationalcampaign.org/resources/fact-sheets.aspx

5. Guttmacher Institute, (2010) *U.S. Teenage Pregnancies, Births and Abortions: National and State Trends and Trends by Race and Ethnicity*. http://www.guttmacher.org/pubs/USTPtrends.pdf

6. National Campaign to Prevent Teen and Unplanned Pregnancy, (2007, 2004, 2002). *With One Voice 2007/2004/2002: America's Adults and Teens Sound Off about Teen Pregnancy*. http://www.thenationalcampaign.org/resources/pdf/pubs/WOV2007_fulltext.pdf http://www.thenationalcampaign.org/resources/pdf/pubs/WOV_2004.pdf http://www.thenationalcampaign.org/resources/pdf/pubs/WOV_2002.pdf

7. National Campaign to Prevent Teen and Unplanned Pregnancy, (2010). *With One Voice 2010: America's Adults and Teens Sound Off about Teen Pregnancy*. http://www.thenationalcampaign.org/resources/pdf/pubs/WOV_2010.pdf

8. Blum, R.W. & Rinehard, P.M. (1998). *Reducing the Risk: Connections that Make a Difference in the Lives of Youth*. Center for Adolescent Health and Development, University of Minnesota. Minneapolis, MN.

9. Suellentrop, K., Brown, J., Ortiz, R. (2010) *Evaluating the Impact of MTV's '16 and Pregnant' on Teen Viewers' Attitudes about Teen Pregnancy*, The National Campaign to Prevent Teen and Unplanned Pregnancy, Washington DC. http://www.thenationalcampaign.org/resources/pdf/SS/SS45_16andPregnant.pdf

10. Telephone interviews and email inquiries by the author.

AMY KRAMER is the director of Entertainment Media & Audience Strategy at The National Campaign to Prevent Teen and Unplanned Pregnancy.

Mary Jo Podgurski  **NO**

Till Human Voices Wake Us: The High Personal Cost of Reality Teen Pregnancy Shows

Having a baby young took away my childhood and there's no way I'll ever get it back.

—16–year-old mother

I wouldn't be alive today if I hadn't had her. She's the reason I'm still alive.

—15–year-old mother

The "voices" above are direct quotes from the video I produced in 1998 entitled *Voices: The Reality of Early Childbearing—Transcending the Myths*. The video was marketed nationally by Injoy Productions until 2009 and is still used in the Lamaze teen program Creativity, Connection and Commitment: Supporting Teens During the Childbearing Year (Lamaze International, 2010). Over the course of a year my team interviewed and videotaped young parents with the intent of using their voices and wisdom as a catalyst for teen pregnancy prevention. I share these voices to underscore an acute need to protect teens. When editing the film I discovered that the teen mothers consistently wanted to reveal very intimate aspects of their lives. Data including early drinking, number of sexual partners, an incestuous relationship, nonconsensual sex, and sexual experimentation were all freely revealed. I cautioned them to think of the future. Would their children relish such revelations a decade later? Were these details pertinent to their messages? I persisted, and only information that was truly educational and not sensationalized remained in the film. I believed then that 16-year-old parents could provide a priceless service to other teens as peer educators; I continue to believe such teaching is effective and significant. I simply refused to expose the truly personal details of their lives to scrutiny. I was interested in education, not drama.

My staff and I remain in contact with many of the teen parents in *Voices*. More than ten years after its production they are in 100% agreement: our careful screening spared their children (now young teens) embarrassment. The young parents I've served have taught me to put a face on the statistics surrounding teen pregnancy; while I will always strive to educate all young people about the

risks associated with bearing children young, I am deeply cognizant of the price a teen parent pays when offering his or her life as a lesson plan.

The last 30 years of my life have been dedicated to providing comprehensive sexuality education to young people; our programs reach over 18,000 youth a year in all 14 Washington County school districts. Concurrently I've mentored young parents. I served as a doula (providing labor support) for my first adolescent in the '70s; that young mother became one of many. My staff and I provide educational services and support for nearly 100 pregnant and parenting teens annually. When the MTV program "16 and Pregnant" was in its planning stages I was approached by the producers and asked to provide teens for the show. I declined after much soul searching. This article explores my rationale for that decision.

Why Rethink Reality TV Using Teen Parents?

As an educator I seek teachable moments in everyday life. I am thrilled to have the opportunity to teach; I consider the field of sexuality education a vocation and am blessed to be in a role where life-affirming information is at my disposal and I am free to convey it to teens. I don't deny the impact reality shows like "16 and Pregnant" and "Teen Mom" (now "Teen Mom 2") can have on teens. The April 10, 2011, edition of *The New York Times* reports anecdotes of teachers using the shows as a part of curriculum in life skills and parenting classes (Hoffman, 2011, April 10). The National Campaign to Prevent Teen and Unplanned Pregnancy has distributed DVDs and teacher guides on "16 and Pregnant" and these materials seem to be well received by educators. I also am not deterred by fears that these reality shows glamorize teen pregnancy. The Campaign conducted a national telephone poll of young people ages 12 to 19; 82% said that the shows aided their understanding of the reality of teen pregnancy. Only 17% stated that the shows gave pregnancy a glamorous spin (Albert, 2010). In the hands of a skilled educator the shows' influence can be directed away from glamour to empathic awareness. There is no doubt that there are lessons to be learned from these shows, but at what price?

My primary concern with reality TV shows like "16 and Pregnant" and "Teen Mom" deals with the human cost of these lessons. Young parents, like most young people, are not immune to the appeal of fame. I question a teen's ability to give full permission to a life-changing activity that will reframe his or her identity on a national stage. I am concerned that these young people cannot developmentally grasp the far-reaching implications of their decision to participate. Exploitation is a strong word and I use it with a caveat; I do not believe the shows aim to exploit. I believe that their intentions are good; it is society that removes all boundaries and exposes tender lives to the scrutiny of tabloids and the manipulation of the media. When I filmed *Voices* I stressed the need for discretion; in ten or twenty years, I said, would your baby want to be known for the things you now reveal? In a decade and more, how will the babies in "16 and Pregnant" view their lives? How will they react to their parents, their families, and their infancy and toddler years exposed for posterity?

I am also troubled by a nagging sense that these shows hope to provide a simple solution to the problems associated with adolescent sexuality in America. There are no Band-aids that can be applied to the multi-faceted, complicated situations that arise when teens are sexually involved, yet our culture consistently seeks an easy fix. I was afforded the privilege of attending an Advocates for Youth European Study Tour in 2001. As part of that experience I was exposed to European approaches to sexuality education. In contrast to American culture, European culture does not deny the fact that teens need education that helps them achieve sexual health; comprehensive sexuality education is the norm. Are reality TV shows that focus on the lives of young parents yet another simplistic answer that distracts from the need to mandate comprehensive sexuality education to all of our children?

No Band-Aids

Research points to antecedents to early pregnancy and risky behavior; I question whether the teen parents in reality TV shows reflect those antecedents or are selected for their "camera" quality and the appeal of their families' dramas. I also ponder the use of dollars to develop these TV shows instead of creating programs that would target youth that evidence-based data show are at risk.

Dr. Doug Kirby's work (2002, 2007) alone and with colleagues (Kirby, Lepore, & Ryan, 2006) is considered seminal in the areas of comprehensive sexuality education and teen pregnancy antecedents. Research into the role of siblings in early childbearing from East and associates (1996 through 2007) is pivotal to understanding generational teen pregnancy (East, Reyes, & Horn, 2007; Raneri & Constance, 2007). Kristen Luker (1999, 2006) is considered a founding theorist of the sociological and political theories surrounding early childbearing and linked poverty to teen pregnancy as an antecedent, not a consequence of the pregnancy. Young people who are survivors

of sexual and physical abuse (Boyer & Fine, 1992) are at risk for early childbearing, as are children in placement or foster care (Kirby, Lepore, & Ryan, 2006) and children living with domestic violence, drug/alcohol abuse, or incarcerated parents (Coyle, 2005; Goode & Smith, 2005; East & Khoo, 2005; Jekielek, Moore, Hair, & Scarupa, 2002). Do the teens in reality TV reflect these antecedents?

Research at the University of Arkansas showed that girls are more likely to experience teen pregnancy if they live with internal poverty (measured as a low locus of control and future expectations) as well as external poverty (Young, Turner, Denny, Young, 2004). Internal poverty "describes a person's lack of internal resources, such as attitudes and beliefs that attribute outcomes to individual effort, high future expectations, and few perceived limitations for life options" (Coles, 2005, 10). Certainly internal and external poverty are antecedents in the pregnancies of some reality TV participants; at any time are those teens given guidance that will help them develop the skills and self-efficacy they need to succeed?

Antecedents to teen pregnancy in the United States lead dedicated sexuality educators to explore the need for education that affects behavioral change. Dr. Michael A. Carrera's Children's Aid Society is a well-respected and researched youth development approach that targets the whole child through early intervention (Children's Aid Society, 2010). On a much smaller scale, my team and I have tried to emulate his efforts. Although we remain committed to comprehensive sexuality education, we first approached teen pregnancy prevention through proactive education in 1999 with the initiation of an early intervention educational mentoring program entitled Educate Children for Healthy Outcomes (ECHO). ECHO provides one-on-one mentoring to young people who have been identified as at risk for engaging in high-risk behavior. Specifically, we target girls in grades 2–12 who have experienced sexual abuse, abandonment issues, placement problems, truancy, early sexual acting out, and/or familial teen pregnancy and provide them with a supportive, consistent, empowering educator and role model. Our advisors educate participants on youth development topics that guide them in making healthy life choices. Our program topics include: decision making, refusal, communication, and problem solving skills, assertiveness training, anger management, conflict resolution, puberty education, socialization skills, life skills, and prevention education. We strive to empower families to communicate well with each other, help children avoid risky behavior during their adolescent years, and strengthen the family unit as a whole. Only three of the 511 high-risk girls we've mentored since 1999 experienced a pregnancy, and all three of those young women were older than 18 when they gave birth.

Reality shows target all teens without the capacity to address the real and complicated issues that may lead to actual teen pregnancy. Focusing on sexual health for all young people is vital; providing personalized instruction to teens at highest risk, while costly, could maximize positive outcomes.

Voices to Break the Cycle: A Phenomenological Inquiry into Generational Teen Pregnancy

I completed my doctoral work late in life; my dissertation was not only informative but also humbling. I looked at the lived experiences of women who gave birth as adolescents to investigate how these adults might help their pubertal aged children avoid teenage pregnancy. Research participants gave birth as teens (defined as under 19 years of age) and were parenting their biologic children ages 10–15. A key criteria for selection in the study was generational teen pregnancy; participants in the study came from families with a history of teen pregnancy through at least one generation prior to the former teen mother's birth. The study reinforced the antecedents of poverty, foster placement, sexual abuse, and familial patterns of early childbearing (Podgurski, 2009).

Stigmatizing women who conceive and bear children during adolescence is common in American culture and can lead to social inequalities (McDermott & Graham, 2005). Data reinforces young mothers' continuing need for support while teens (Pai-Espinosa, 2010) and as their lives move forward beyond adolescence (Jutte et al., 2010). The voices of former teen mothers in my study also revealed lives deeply affected by their adolescent pregnancies. Many women expressed a desire to move away from the community in which they gave birth; 30% of the former teen mothers in the study did relocate. One participant in the study stated: "When I got married I left the area. I found it easier to reinvent myself than deal with people who had labeled me as that pregnant girl. My life here is better than it would have been if I'd stayed where I was." Where can a teen parent whose life has been exposed on a national reality TV show relocate?

Adult empathic understanding and compassion for the lives of teen parents was not common among the participants in my study; over 80% described self-reported disrespectful treatment during their births, upon their return to school, or while seeking employment. If, as the National Campaign for Teen and Unplanned Pregnancy reports, 41% of adults report the show "16 and Pregnant" glorifies teen pregnancy (Albert, 2010), will that compassion diminish?

Till Human Voices Wake Us

What is the effect of fame on the young parents made into instant celebrities by reality TV? What do they and their children sacrifice to the altar of TV ratings?

To examine the possible long-term effects of fame and celebrity status on young parents, it is illustrative to look at fame as it is perceived in youth culture. Halpern

(2007) surveyed 5th to 8th grade students in Rochester, New York, and found 29% of males and 37% of females selected fame over intelligence as a desired trait. The study participants viewed at least five hours of TV daily; that figure is consistent with other studies of youth screen time (defined as TV and computer time). For example, Burnett and her research team (2008) found that 60% of teens spent an average of 20 hours in screen time, a full third spent closer to 40 hours per week and 7 percent were exposed to greater than 50 hours of viewing time weekly. Perhaps most significantly, Halbern's work showed that 17% of the students felt that celebrities owed their fame to luck, and believed that TV shows had the power to make people famous. If fame is valued over intelligence and luck is perceived as a better indicator of future well-being than industry among average children, would pregnant and parenting teens buy into that delusion as well?

An intense desire for fame can lead reality TV participants to believe that "every reality show is an audition tape for future work" (Wolk, 2010, p. 32). If adults are affected by fame hunger that directs their actions and choices, how can adolescents avoid influence from reality TV fame? The sad drama of Amber, violence, and child custody revealed on the show "Teen Mom" was popular among tabloids, magazines, and advertisers. As an educator I am troubled. Did Amber receive guidance or were her actions considered fodder for higher ratings? One need go no further than the cover story of a current *OK! Magazine* to read that "More Teen Mom Babies!" are planned, including one baby that is being conceived to save a relationship (2011, April 18). The same issue proclaims that Amber and Gary will reunite. What type, if any, relationship skill education do these young "reality celebrities" receive as their lives are broadcast nationally?

Putting a Face on the Numbers

The names of the young parents in the following anecdotes are fiction but their stories are not. Any of these young people would produce high ratings on a reality TV show. Protecting their anonymity is a fundamental educational task. Ethical treatment of pregnant and parenting youth demands that respect is rendered at all times.

Picture Tracy: This lively young woman was a National Honor Society student when she found she was pregnant at the age of 16. Articulate, empathetic, and soft-spoken, she is now a caring social worker completing her master's degree in counseling. Tracy did not disclose her history of sexual assault until the baby she birthed as a teen was four years old; she now uses her life experiences to help her connect with young women at risk for early childbearing.

Nina is a bright, intelligent 27 year old. Her hair color and body piercings change often but her striking hazel eyes and determined expressions remain constant. She is perceptive, a hard worker, and one of the most resilient young people I've ever known. Nina is also the parent of a 12 year old. She lived in a series of foster homes while pregnant and parenting; her mother gave birth to her as a 15 year old and her grandmother had her first pregnancy as a 16 year old. Nina was born into poverty and continues to struggle to make ends meet. She left school at 17 and hasn't completed the GED (General Equivalency Diploma) she frequently talks about. She often bemoans the fact that her daughter "does without" things she too was denied as a teen. She is proud that she has been her child's only parent and that her daughter has never been in foster care. Like her own parents, Nina fights addiction to alcohol and drugs and has been in and out of rehab several times.

Meet Samantha: Sammy planned her baby to prove that she was heterosexual. Her first kiss at 11 was with a girl; she reacted violently to the fear that she was lesbian in a homophobic family and made a conscious decision to conceive a baby to a man ten years her senior. She was only 12 when her pregnancy was discovered; she didn't tell anyone until she was in her third trimester. She came out when her son was two years old and is currently in a five-year relationship with her female partner.

Jodi gave birth as a tenth grader but only disclosed her stepfather as her baby's daddy when he starting hitting on her younger sister. Her baby was two years old at the time. Disclosure led to her stepfather's arrest and incarceration for over four years of sexual abuse. Her five siblings were divided and sent to three different foster homes. While Jodi is intermittently proud of her disclosure, she blames herself for the dissolution of her family. She is in a new school district where few know her family's history and is starting to shine academically.

Trevor's father reacted to his girlfriend **Amy's** pregnancy by denying his parentage; within an hour he was homeless at 18. Too old for children and youth services, he wandered from one friend's sofa to another until the single mother of his girlfriend allowed him to move in with her family. The baby is due this spring. Trevor is determined to remain with his partner and states firmly that he will not "be a statistic." His girlfriend's mother, while kind and supportive, is skeptical. She sees Amy's father in Trevor. Although she hopes for the best, she expects him to leave before the baby is two.

It's Not about the United States

Those in the United States who have committed our lives to supporting, empowering, and educating young people approach this charge in unique ways. I humbly acknowledge that there are many paths to reaching youth. I have learned more from listening to the young people I serve than from any other resource. When I train new staff I reinforce a common theme: our work is not about us, it's about the young people. I am reminded of the old admonition: First, Do No Harm. As adults we are responsible for the needs of all youth, regardless of sexual orientation, gender and gender identity, race, ethnicity, socio-economic status, religion, or level of sexual involvement. I challenge

all who serve pregnant and parenting teens to examine the effects adult interventions have upon the lives of these young people and their children, bearing in mind that we do not yet have full knowledge of the long-term implications of national exposure at a time of great vulnerability. When in doubt, protect.

References

Albert, B. (2010). *With one voice 2010: Teens and adults sound off about teen pregnancy.* National Campaign to Prevent Teen and Unplanned Pregnancy. *Retrieved from* http://www.thenationalcampaign.org/resources/pdf/pubs/WOV_2010.pdf

Barnett, T., O'Loughlin, J., Sabiston, C., Karp, I., Belanger, M., Van Hulst, A., & Lambert., M. (2008). Teens and screens: The influence of screen time on adiposity in adolescents. *American Journal of Epidemiology, 172*(3), 255–262.

Boyer, D. & Fine, D. (1992). Sexual abuse as a factor in adolescent pregnancy and child maltreatment. *Family Planning Perspectives, 24*(1), 4–11.

Children's Aid Society. (2010). Dr. Michael A. Carrera, Retrieved from http://www.childrensaidsociety.org/carrera-pregnancy-prevention/dr-michael-carrera

Coles, C. (2005). Teen pregnancy and "internal poverty." *Futurist, 38*(7), 10.

Coyle, J. (2005, September). Preventing and reducing violence by at-risk adolescents common elements of empirically researched programs. *Journal of Evidence-Based Social Work, 2*(3/4), 125.

Goode, W. W. & Smith, T. J. (2005). *Building from the ground up: Creating effective programs to mentor children of prisoners.* Philadelphia, PA: Public/Private Ventures.

East, P. L., & Khoo, S. (2005, December). Longitudinal pathways linking family factors and sibling relationship qualities to adolescent substance use and sexual risk behaviors. *Journal of Family Psychology, 19*(4), 571–580.

East, P. L., Reyes, B. T. & Horn, E. J. (2007, June). Association between adolescent pregnancy and a family history of teenage births. *Perspectives on sexual and reproductive health, 39*(2), 108–115.

Halpern, J. (2007*). Fame junkies: The hidden truth behind America's favorite addiction.* New York: Houghton Mifflin Company.

Hoffman, J. (2011, April 10). Fighting teen pregnancy with MTV stars as Exhibit A. *The New York Times,* p. ST 1, 11.

Jekielek, S. M., Moore, K.A., Hair, E. C., & Scarupa, H.J. (2002, February). Mentoring: A promising strategy for youth development. *Child Trends Research Brief.* Retrieved from www.mentoring.ca.gov/pdf/MentoringBrief2002.pdf

Jutte, D., Roos, N., Brownell, M., Briggs, G., MacWilliam, L., & Roos, L. (2010). The ripples of adolescent motherhood: social, educational, and medical outcomes for children of teen and prior teen mothers. *Academic Pediatrics, 10*(5), 293–301.

Karcher, M. (2005). The effects of developmental mentoring and high school mentors' attendance on their younger mentees' self-esteem, social skills and connectedness. *Psychology in the Schools, 42*(1), 65–77. Retrieved from www.adolescentconnectedness.com/media/KarcherPITS_mentoring&conn.pdf

Kirby, D. (2002). Antecedents of adolescent initiation of sex, contraceptive use, and pregnancy. *American Journal of Health Behavior, 26*(6), 473.

Kirby, D. (2007). *Emerging answers: Research findings on programs to reduce teen pregnancy and sexually transmitted diseases.* Washington, DC: National Campaign to Prevent Teen Pregnancy.

Kirby, D., Lepore, G., & Ryan, J. (2006). *Sexual risk and protective factors—Factors affecting teen sexual behavior, pregnancy, childbearing and sexually transmitted disease: Which are important? Which can you change?* Scotts Valley, CA: ETR Associates.

Lamaze International. (2010). *Creativity, connection and commitment: Supporting teens during the childbearing year.* Retrieved from http://www.lamaze.org/ChildbirthEducators/WorkshopsConference/SpecialtyWorkshops/SupportingTeensDuringtheChildbearingYear/tabid/494/Default.aspx

Luker, K. (1997). *Dubious conceptions: The politics of teen pregnancy.* Boston: Harvard University Press.

Luker, K. (2006). When sex goes to school: Warring views on sex—and sex education since the sixties. New York: W. W. Norton & Company.

McDermott, E. & Graham, H. (2005). Resilient young mothering: social inequalities, late modernity and the 'problem' of 'teenage' motherhood. *Journal of Youth Studies, 8,* 59–79.

(2011, April 18) More teen mom babies. *OK! Magazine, 16,* 32–35.

Pai-Espinosa, J. (2010). Young mothers at the margin: why pregnant teens need support. *Children's Voice, 19*(3), 14–16.

Podgurski, MJ. (2009). *Voices to break the cycle: A phenomenological inquiry into generational teen pregnancy.* (Doctoral dissertation). University of Phoenix, Phoenix, AZ.

Raneri, L., & Constance, M. (2007, March). Social ecological predictors of repeat adolescent pregnancy. *Perspectives on Sexual & Reproductive Health, 39*(1), 39–47.

Young, T., Turner, J., Denny, G., Young, M. (2004, July). Examining external and internal poverty as antecedents of teen pregnancy. *American Journal of Health Behavior, 28*(4), 361–373.

Wolk, J. (2002). Fame factor. *Entertainment Weekly,* (665), 32.

MARY JO PODGURSKI is the founder of the Academy for Adolescent Health, Inc., in Washington, Pennsylvania. She is an adjunct professor in the Department of Education at Washington and Jefferson College.

EXPLORING THE ISSUE

Do Reality TV Shows Portray Responsible Messages about Teen Pregnancy?

Critical Thinking and Reflection

1. In what ways could reality TV programs educate the public and impact the prevention of teen pregnancy?
2. How might reality TV programs about teen pregnancy have a negative impact on the teens involved?
3. What strategies, other than television, might be effective in addressing high rates of teen pregnancy?
4. European nations have much lower teen pregnancy rates than the United States. Why might this be?

Is There Common Ground?

Amy Kramer notes that the shows depict realistic consequences of sexual activity and teen pregnancy without glamorizing these outcomes. She says, "Families, schools, health care professionals, businesses big and small, religious communities, and yes, the media, all have a role to play." Do you agree with her assessment of the role of various institutions, including the media in addressing teen pregnancy prevention?

Mary Jo Podgurski does not dispute the potential benefit that reality TV shows about teen pregnancy can have. She notes their merits and their good intentions. However, she is concerned about the potential for teens who appear on the show to be exploited. She says that, developmentally, teens can't fully "grasp the far-reaching implications of their decision to participate." What might be some examples of far-reaching implications? Think back to when you were 15 or 16. How prepared do you think you would be to share your life story on national television, if you experienced early pregnancy or became a teen parent?

Noting that young people may be blinded by fame, Podgurski also commented on how participants on the show may be selected for their "camera quality." What do you think she meant, and how do you think this might be problematic? Podgurski also expressed concern about society applying a "Band-aid" solution to a complex, multifaceted issue, and that perhaps money would be better invested in programs that actually address the variety of

antecedents to early pregnancy and risky behavior. Kramer likewise acknowledges that these TV programs do not make a singular solution. Is there room for *both* evidence-based teen pregnancy prevention programs *and* media-driven shows that open the door for discussion between parents and children? Is one approach better than the other? If you were in a position to award a million dollar teen pregnancy prevention project, would you invest in both approaches, or would you support one more than the other?

Create Central

www.mhhe.com/createcentral

Additional Resources

Alford, S. & Hauser, D. (March, 2011). *Adolescent Sexual Health in Europe and the United States: The Case for a Rights, Respect, Responsibility Approach*. Washington, DC: Advocates for Youth.

Chang, J. & Hopper, J. "Pregnancy Pressure: Is MTV's 'Teen Mom' Encouraging Pregnancy for Fame?" *ABC News*, February 11, 2011.

Sharp, S. "16 and Pregnant and Almost True," *Mother Jones*, April 21, 2010.

Stanley, A. "Motherhood's Rough Edges Fray in Reality TV . . . And Baby Makes Reality TV," *New York Times*, January 21, 2011.

Internet References . . .

16 and Pregnant: Important Things to Know about Teen Pregnancy

Developed by the National Campaign to Prevent Teen and Unplanned Pregnancy, this page presents a summary of key facts about teen pregnancy.

www.thenationalcampaign.org/resources/pdf/16-and-preg-fact-sheet.pdf

Evaluating the Impact of MTV's *16 and Pregnant* on Teen Viewers' Attitudes about Teen Pregnancy

This page, also by the National Campaign to Prevent Teen and Unplanned Pregnancy, has links to fact sheets about the media and teen pregnancy.

www.cnn.com/2011/SHOWBIZ/TV/05/04/teen.mom.dolgen/index.html

Sexuality and Reality TV

This article critically examines the portrayal of gender identity, sexual orientation, and other aspects of sexuality on reality television.

http://mkopas.net/courses/soc287/2012/08/06/sexuality-and-reality-tv/

Why I Created MTV's "16 and Pregnant"

Laura Dolgen, senior vice president for MTV series development, explains her rationale for creating "16 and Pregnant" and "Teen Mom."

www.cnn.com/2011/SHOWBIZ/TV/05/04/teen.mom.dolgen/index.html

Selected, Edited, and with Issue Framing Material by:
Ryan W. McKee, *Widener University*
and
William J. Taverner, *Center for Family Life Education*

ISSUE

Should Sexual Problems Be Treated Pharmaceutically?

YES: Connie B. Newman, from "Pharmacological Treatment for Sexual Problems: The Benefits Outweigh the Risks," Original essay for this edition (2011)

NO: Anita P. Hoffer, from "The Hidden Costs of the Medicalization of Female Sexuality—How Did We Get Here? An Overview," Original essay for this edition (2013)

Learning Outcomes

After reading this issue, you should be able to:

- Describe some of the sexual problems experienced by women and men.
- Explain some of the factors that may contribute to sexual problems.
- Describe some of the treatments available for sexual problems.
- Differentiate between treatments available to men and those available to women.

ISSUE SUMMARY

YES: Connie B. Newman, MD, an endocrinologist and adjunct associate professor of medicine at New York University School of Medicine, explores the definitions and causes of sexual dysfunction and explains how sexual medicines can improve sexual response.

NO: Anita P. Hoffer, PhD, EdD, former associate professor at Harvard Medical School and former director of research in urology at the Brigham and Women's Hospital, argues that the rise of sexual medicine has created a market that benefits the pharmaceutical industry at the expense of the individual.

If you watch much television, chances are you have seen ads for Viagra, a drug that treats erectile dysfunction in men. In fact, 2013 marked the 15-year anniversary of the "little blue pill." Since its release, several additional erectile dysfunction drugs, including Levitra and Cialis, have made the process of getting erections much easier for millions of men around the world. The products have been so successful that pharmaceutical companies have, for years, been attempting to replicate their success with medications for a variety of sexual dysfunctions in women (including hypoactive sexual disorder, otherwise known as low libido). Authors of a controversial study from 1999 found that 43 percent of women between the ages of 18 and 59 had some type of sexual dysfunction (1). Pharmaceutical companies invested billions of dollars into research for elusive remedies. It was thought that the profits from women's treatments would rival, if not surpass, those of male treatments.

Clinical trials of a women's version of Viagra, as well as several other potential medications, ended with mixed results. Intrinsa, a testosterone patch designed to increase women's libido, showed promise, but did not get approval from the Food and Drug Administration (FDA) (the patch was approved in several European countries, however). The desire for the product was there; the desired results, on the other hand, were not.

Why has the search for a women's prescription treatment proven so challenging? If men can have some of their sexual issues taken care of with a prescription medication, critics argue, why have women's sexual problems proven so difficult to treat? Some women's health advocates take issue over the disparity between FDA-approved drugs available for men and women. Some saw sexism and a fear of women's sexuality at play in the FDA's decisions. Others theorized there were subtle differences between the ways men and women experienced arousal. A pill may have a difficult time differentiating between such body–mind nuances.

Another camp holds that pharmaceutical treatments for such complex issues (for both men and women) may be off-base to begin with. Many therapists and sexologists warn against what they see as the "medicalization" of sexual problems. An over-reliance on prescription drugs is seen as a one-size-fits-all approach that ignores larger issues. Some point to the far more common psychogenic causes of sexual dysfunction that cannot be treated by medication. They contend that nonmedical treatments (improving partner communication, for example) would be far more effective. They charge that pharmaceutical companies are making a hefty profit through the "medicalization" of sexuality. Still others argue that the estimated number of sexual dysfunction cases is inflated, and that the vast majority of real cases of both female and male sexual dysfunction are caused by psychological or interpersonal factors that are better treated with nonmedicinal interventions like counseling or therapy.

In the following selections, Dr. Connie B. Newman describes the common problem of sexual dysfunction in both men and women, and explores the ways that sexual medicines may alleviate these problems. Dr. Anita P. Hoffer argues that pharmaceutical companies, not their patients, are the primary beneficiaries of sexual medicine.

YES ↵

Connie B. Newman

Pharmacological Treatment for Sexual Problems: The Benefits Outweigh the Risks

Introduction

In the past decade considerable controversy has emerged over whether medicines that improve sexual function are truly needed. In fact, some experts have accused the pharmaceutical industry of creating sexual diseases in order to profit from new medicines specifically designed for these "invented" diseases (1, 2). In November 2010, while at a sex education conference sponsored by The Center for Family Life Education (The CFLE), I had the opportunity to preview the movie *Orgasm Inc.*, a documentary about the development of therapies to improve women's sex lives. The movie questioned whether female sexual dysfunction was a real disorder or a pseudo-disease created by the pharmaceutical industry in order to develop and market sex-enhancing medicines for women. In doing this, the movie made light of the real sexual problems that some women have. It did not explain the nature of the highly regulated drug development process, which requires pharmaceutical companies to adhere to strict standards in developing safe and effective medicines. It also put forth a distorted image of practicing doctors, showing them to be too eager to fix their patients' problems by prescribing medications.

To my surprise many people in the audience seemed to believe every word in the film and did not understand that there might be another side to this story. I am writing this article to explain the other point of view, or at least a more balanced point of view. Sexual dysfunction is a real disorder that occurs in women, especially as they age, as well as in men. Women's sex problems can have a physiological as well as a psychological basis, and are not solely due to lack of sex education, poor relationships, or working long hours. Sexual medicines that enhance sexual performance can benefit individuals and society. Pharmaceutical companies are interested in making a profit (after all they would not be in business if they did not), but in addition many scientists who work in pharmaceutical companies want to help people have healthier and more satisfied lives. Doctors prescribe medicines for patients only after a diagnosis is reached by evaluation of the patient's history, symptoms, physical findings, and laboratory tests, and after consideration of the benefits and risks of available therapies.

This article assesses the benefits and risks of using pharmacological treatments (sexual medicines) for individuals with sexual dysfunction. The following topics will be considered: the definitions and causes of sexual dysfunction in men and women, the prevalence of sexual dysfunction, therapeutic options for individuals with sexual problems, and an analysis of currently available medicines for sexual dysfunction.

Changing Definitions of Sexual Dysfunction: A Shift from Psychological Factors to Combined Organic and Psychological Causes

Sexual dysfunction is a broad general term that includes abnormalities in libido (sex drive), erections, orgasms, and ejaculation in men, and in sexual desire, arousal, orgasm in women, as well as painful intercourse and vaginal spasm. The sexual response cycle differs in men and women (3). In men, sexual desire often occurs before sexual stimuli and subsequent arousal. In contrast, women, especially those in established relationships, often engage in sex with their partners for reasons other than desire (3). Data suggest that sexual desire, as expressed by fantasizing, anticipating sexual experiences, and spontaneously thinking about sex in a positive way, varies in frequency among women and may be infrequent in many women who have normal sexual function (3, 4). In women, desire can be triggered during the sexual encounter (5), and desire then follows sexual arousal.

In both men and women many hormones, peptides, and neurotransmitters have a role in sexual desire and arousal. One of these hormones, testosterone, and its potential therapeutic uses, will be discussed later. Various medical conditions can adversely affect sexual responsiveness, as can depression, other psychiatric diseases, and psychological and social factors. In addition, medications including antidepressant agents can cause sexual problems as a side effect.

Defining sexual dysfunction has been difficult because of incomplete understanding of sexual disorders, especially in women. Classification of sexual disorders has been based on the *Diagnostic and Statistical Manual of Mental Disorders, 4th Ed. (DSM-IV)*, a manual published by the American Psychiatric Association, reflecting the long-held belief that most sexual problems are psychologically based (6). This in itself might explain some of the resistance to pharmacological therapies that is still present today. *DSM-IV* recognized five disorders in female sexual function: hypoactive sexual desire disorder (reduced desire for sexual activity), female sexual arousal disorder, female orgasmic disorder, dyspareunia (genital pain associated with sexual intercourse), and vaginismus (spasm of the muscles of the outer third of the vagina that interferes with sexual intercourse). *DSM-IV* classified sexual disorders in men into the following main categories: erectile disorder, orgasmic disorder, premature ejaculation, hypoactive sexual desire disorder, and dyspareunia due to general medical condition. A new, revised manual of sexual disorders, with more precise definitions, is targeted for publication in 2012 [DSM-5 published May 27, 2013].

Prevalence of Sexual Disorders: What Do We Really Know?

It is difficult to know the true prevalence of sexual disorders in different age groups because most of the information comes from large surveys, rather than from detailed assessment by interviews. Although both the Food and Drug Administration (FDA) and the American Psychiatric Association require personal distress as part of the definition of sexual dysfunction, some of the older studies did not specifically evaluate this parameter. In the following section, data from the following surveys are presented: Massachusetts Male Aging Study (MMAS) in 1,709 men ages 40–70 years (7) and in 847 men ages 40–69 years (8); National Health and Social Life Survey (NHSLS) in 1,749 women and 1,410 men ages 18–59 years (9); National Social Life, Health and Aging Project (NSHAP) in 1,550 women and 1,455 men ages 57–85 years (10); Prevalence of Female Sexual Problems Associated with Distress and Determinants of Treatment (PRESIDE) in 31,581 women ages 18–102 years (11).

Estimates of Prevalence of Sexual Disorders in Men

Premature ejaculation is the most prevalent sexual disorder in young adult men and is defined by *DSM-IV* as "persistent or recurrent ejaculation with minimal sexual stimulation, before, upon, or shortly after penetration and before the person wishes it." In addition, the disturbance must cause marked distress or interpersonal difficulty. This definition of premature ejaculation has been criticized because it is not precise and is dependent upon the judgment of the clinician as well as the patient (12). The exact prevalence is unknown because of the lack of a universally accepted definition and the fact that, like most data on sexual function, the available data are self-reported. In NHSLS, early climax was reported by 30% of men between the ages of 18 [and] 29 years, and by 28–32% of men in the older age groups: 30–39, 40–49, 50–59 (9). Performance anxiety was less common than premature ejaculation, and was reported by 19%

of men in the youngest age group, and 14% of men in the oldest age group.

Erectile dysfunction also occurs in younger men, although less frequently than in older men. How much of this is related to performance anxiety in younger men is not known. In NHSLS (9), difficulty in maintaining an erection was reported in less than 10% of the youngest men (18–29 years), and in 18% of men between the ages of 50 [and] 59 years. As men are more likely to overstate than understate their sexual capacity, these percentages are probably underestimates. Among older men the most prevalent sexual problem is erectile dysfunction (7, 8, 10), which increases with age and disease. In MMAS (7, 8), 52% of men between the ages of 40 [and] 70 years reported some degree of erectile dysfunction. With more advanced age, the prevalence of erectile dysfunction increases, affecting as many as 75% of men over the age of 80.

Lack of interest in sex is a less frequent complaint for men than either premature ejaculation or erectile dysfunction. In NHSLS, about 15% of men reported lack of interest in sex (9). In NSHAP, in older men between the ages of 57 and 85 years, lack of interest in sex was reported by 28% of respondents (10).

Estimates of Prevalence of Sexual Disorders in Women

There is uncertainty about the overall prevalence of sexual problems in women. NHSLS concluded that in women aged 18–59 years the prevalence of sexual dysfunction was 43%. More recently, PRESIDE, a survey of about 31,000 women (age 18–102 years, mean age 49), found that while 43% had at least one sexual problem, only 22% reported sexually related personal distress (11). The most common sexual problems reported by women are low desire, low sexual arousal, and inability to achieve an orgasm (9–11). In PRESIDE, 27% of women in the youngest age group reported any of these sexual problems, compared with about 45% of middle-aged women, and 80% of women 65 years of age or older (11). In NHSLS, in the youngest women studied (ages 18–29), 32% reported lack of interest in sex, 26% reported inability to achieve orgasm, 21% reported pain during sex, and 16% reported performance anxiety (9). In PRESIDE low desire was the most common sexual problem reported by 39% of the entire group; less common were low arousal (26%) and orgasm difficulties (21%) (11). Distressing sexual problems were more common in middle-aged than in younger or older women. Women with depression had more than twice the chance of having distressing sexual problems. This may be due in part to the adverse sexual side effects of antidepressant drugs, which can interfere with the ability to have an orgasm.

Taking all these data into consideration, it appears that at least one-third of men and women of all ages report sexual problems. In younger men, premature ejaculation is the most commonly reported problem, and in younger women, the most commonly reported problems are low desire, low arousal, and difficulty achieving an orgasm. Problems due to low libido and orgasm difficulties in women and to erectile dysfunction in men increase with age.

Therapeutic Options for Sexual Dysfunction

The "VIAGRA Revolution"

As noted by Segraves (6), after the publication of *Human Sexual Inadequacy* by William Masters and Virginia E. Johnson (13) the majority of sexual problems were considered to be treatable by psychologically based methods. Psychosexual counseling to reduce performance anxiety, develop sexual skills, change sexual attitudes, and improve relationships became first-line therapy for sexual dysfunction, regardless of cause (3). The introduction of sildenafil (VIAGRA) in 1998, dramatically changed the therapeutic approach to men with erectile problems. VIAGRA quickly became accepted as first-line therapy for male patients with erectile dysfunction. Now doctors had available an oral medication that was effective in about 70% of men with this problem, effective both in those with organic (vascular and neurologic disease) and psychological causes. The use of VIAGRA and similar medications changed the emphasis of treatment for erectile dysfunction from psychological and behavioral therapies to medicinal interventions. Improved sexual performance increases self-confidence and improves interpersonal relationships. Thus, in individuals with a psychological basis for erectile dysfunction, pharmacological treatment may be used together with psychological therapies.

Medicines for Men

Table 1 lists approved medicines that are used to treat disorders of sexual function in men along with the approved indications. Information about potential side effects may be found in the Patient Information and Important Safety Information brochures (available on the medication's website). Although all of these medicines are approved by the FDA, not all are approved for use in sexual dysfunction. Premature ejaculation is the most prevalent sexual dysfunction in men aged 18–59 years, but there is no FDA-approved medication for premature ejaculation. Ejaculation is regulated by serotonin, and similar chemicals produced by the brain that are responsible for good feelings (14, 15). This has led to the off-label use of some medications that block serotonin, known as "selective serotonin reuptake inhibitors" (SSRIs), including fluoxetine (PROZAC), sertraline (ZOLOFT), and escitalopram (LEXAPRO) for the treatment of premature ejaculation.

Conversely, the use of SSRIs for depression and other psychiatric diseases has led to sexual side effects such as difficulty in reaching orgasm and difficulty maintaining an erection. SSRI-induced sexual dysfunction is often

Table 1

Medical Therapies for Sexual Dysfunction in Men

Drug (Brand Name)	Therapeutic Use	Approved Indications in United States
Sildenafil (VIAGRA) Vardenafil (LEVITRA) Tadalafil (CIALIS)	Erectile dysfunction, Selective Serotonin Uptake Inhibitor (SSRI)—induced sexual dysfunction*	Erectile dysfunction
Alprostadil [intraurethral (MUSE), intracavernosal]	Erectile dysfunction	Erectile dysfunction due to neurogenic, vasculogenic, psychogenic, or mixed etiology
Fluoxetine (PROZAC, SARAFEM) Sertraline (ZOLOFT) Paroxetine (PAXIL) Escitalopram (LEXAPRO) Citalopram (CELEXA)	Premature ejaculation*	Depression, obsessive compulsive disorder, panic attacks, post traumatic stress disorder, social anxiety disorder, premenstrual dysphoric disorder, generalized anxiety disorder
Bupropion (WELLBUTRIN, ZYBAN)	SSRI-induced sexual dysfunction*	Depression, seasonal affective disorder, smoking cessation
Testosterone†	Hypoactive sexual desire disorder when low testosterone is present	Replacement therapy in men with deficiency or absence of endogenous testosterone

Information is from the United States Product Circulars for the medications listed. Approved indications may not apply to all drugs in that class. Information about possible side effects can be found in the "Patient Information" for each drug, and the "Important Safety Information" which are available on each product's website.

*Off-label use in the United States SSRIs include fluoxetine, sertraline, paroxetine, escitalopram, citalopram.

†Preparations include injectable testosterone, transdermal gels, transdermal patches, buccal tablets, implantable pellets.

treated with VIAGRA and similar medications, although VIAGRA is approved for use in erectile dysfunction but not for orgasmic difficulties.

Although libido is not completely understood in either men or women, the hormone testosterone is necessary for sexual desire in men and is also believed to contribute to sexual desire and function in women. The average testosterone level in premenopausal women is about 10% of the average male level. Hypoactive sexual desire disorder in men, commonly known as decreased libido or lack of sexual interest, can have many causes including depression, medications, and chronic illness, but may also be due to deficiency of testosterone (16, 17), especially in older men. A variety of testosterone preparations are available for treating men with low levels of testosterone, and this treatment usually restores libido. Testosterone is not recommended for use in men with normal levels of testosterone or in men who simply want to increase their sexual desire, as levels above normal increase the risk of prostate cancer.

Medicines for Women Are Lacking

Unfortunately, there are few medications available for the sexual disorders that affect women (Table 2). This is particularly true for younger women who most commonly suffer from low desire, low arousal, or difficulty with orgasm. More research is needed. Presently, the only FDA-approved medications for treating sexual dysfunction in women are estrogen preparations for dyspareunia related to vulvovaginal atrophy (a post-menopausal condition that is associated with vaginal dryness, irritation, soreness, urinary frequency and urgency, and pain during intercourse).

The clinical success of VIAGRA in men increased interest in finding pharmacological treatments for women with sexual dysfunction. However, trials of VIAGRA in women failed to show significant benefit and the drug development program for this indication has been discontinued. Unfortunately, the quest for medications to help women with sexual problems has led to criticisms of both the pharmaceutical industry and physician-experts who consult for the industry. Despite the epidemiological data, which shows that a significant proportion of women have sexual dysfunction, these critics insist that female sexual dysfunction is an illness created by doctors under the influence of their pharmaceutical industry allies.

Many factors—biological, psychological, and social—contribute to sexual response in women, and it is challenging to find an abnormality that can be corrected with medication. Thus, behavioral, cognitive, and sexual therapies continue to be the main therapies for sexual dysfunction in women (3). While some studies have found varying degrees of improvement with non-pharmacological therapies [with response rates varying from 37% to 82% in 9 studies reviewed by Basson (3)], outcome data evaluating these non-pharmacological approaches are severely limited by the different durations of treatment and follow-up, different methods for assessing the benefits of treatment, and the fact that not all studies are controlled (3, 18).

Clearly there is still a need for safe and effective sexual medicines that can be used in younger as well as older women. Fortunately research efforts continue. Investigational drugs which act upon neurotransmitters, increasing dopaminergic and decreasing serotoninergic activity, are postulated to have a favorable effect on sexual responsiveness (19), and several compounds are under evaluation in younger women (20).

Should Testosterone Be Used to Treat Low Sexual Desire or Low Arousal in Women?

It should be pointed out that testosterone is a promising treatment for older, postmenopausal women with decreased libido and low levels of testosterone. Testosterone, long considered the "male hormone" because of its role in the development of secondary sex characteristics in men (deeper voice, facial hair, etc.), is also produced in women and is thought to have an important role in female sexual function. Some but not all studies

Table 2

Medical Therapies for Women with Sexual Dysfunction

Drug (Brand Name)	Therapeutic Use	Approved Indications in United States
Estradiol vaginal tablets (VAGIFEM); Conjugated estrogens vaginal cream (PREMARIN vaginal cream); Estradiol vaginal ring (ESTRING)	Vaginal atrophy in menopausal women (vaginal dryness, pain during sexual intercourse, vaginal itching)	Vagifem: atrophic vaginitis in menopausal women. Estring: moderate to severe symptoms due to postmenopausal vaginal atrophy (dryness, burning, itching, and pain during intercourse) and for urinary urgency/pain with urination
Bupropion (WELLBUTRIN, ZYBAN)	Selective serotonin uptake inhibitor (SSRI)—induced sexual dysfunction*	Depression, seasonal affective disorder, smoking cessation
Testosterone†	Hypoactive sexual desire disorder (low libido) usually when low testosterone is present*	Not approved for use in women in the United States INTRINSA (transdermal testosterone patch) is approved in the European Union for treatment of hypoactive sexual desire disorder in women with surgically induced menopause receiving estrogen therapy

Information in this table is from the United States Product Circulars for the medications listed and from the EU Summary of Product Characteristics for INTRINSA. Information about possible side effects can be found in the "Patient Information" for each drug, and the "Important Safety Information" which are available on each product's website.

*Off label use in the United States SSRIs include fluoxetine, sertraline, paroxetine, escitalopram, citalopram.

†Preparations approved in the United States for men include injectable testosterone, gels, patches, buccal tablets (absorbed through the gums), implantable pellets.

in women have found a direct correlation between testosterone levels, sexual desire, and frequency of sexual intercourse (21).

To date efforts to gain regulatory approval for testosterone use in postmenopausal women have been unsuccessful in the United States, but more successful in Europe. A testosterone patch, INTRINSA, for surgically menopausal women (women who had had their ovaries and uterus surgically removed) with hypoactive sexual disorder (low libido) was rejected by the FDA in 2005, and subsequently approved by regulatory authorities in the European Union in 2006 for specific use in surgically menopausal women with hypoactive sexual desire disorder who were also taking estrogen therapy. In the United States, some experts had concerns over the cardiovascular safety of this medication, because heart attacks in men occur at a much younger age than in women. However, it should be pointed out that in women who use the testosterone patch, blood levels of testosterone increase only to levels seen in pre-menopausal women (22), which are far lower than testosterone levels in men (22). In a recent review of potential safety issues in women taking testosterone because of symptoms of testosterone deficiency, Mathur and Braunstein found no good evidence for adverse cardiovascular effects, nor for increased risk of breast cancer (21).

The testosterone patch was subsequently studied in naturally menopausal women with hypoactive sexual desire disorder, showing benefit both in women taking estrogen and in women not taking estrogen (23). Use of the testosterone patch in naturally menopausal women has not as yet been approved by regulatory authorities in the United States or Europe. Nevertheless, despite the fact that in the United States, testosterone is not approved for use in women, about 2 million prescriptions of testosterone annually are written for women (24). Unfortunately, some of these preparations are prepared by pharmacies that mix testosterone with other ingredients to create topical creams, lozenges, oral gels, and drops. The standardization of such therapies is in question and therefore experts in the field do not encourage their general use (21).

However, some physicians with expertise in reproductive endocrinology (the study of hormones as it relates to fertility and the menopause) prescribe low doses of testosterone (by gel applied to the skin) on a case by case basis to individual patients with decreased libido who are postmenopausal, have low testosterone levels, and have not responded satisfactorily to treatment with estrogens. For many of these patients, especially those who are in healthy relationships and have suffered from loss of libido and markedly diminished sexual satisfaction with aging, the benefits of testosterone supplementation are worth the potential risks. As with many medications there are as yet no long-term safety data for this treatment. The main adverse effects include acne, oily skin, and increased hair growth at the site of application of testosterone. Virilization (the development of unwanted male sex characteristics such as facial hair, baldness, deepened voice) is rare. Women who take testosterone should be made aware of the potential benefits and potential risks of therapy, and should be told that the treatment is not approved by the FDA at this time. Also, serum levels of total and free testosterone should be monitored to keep these levels in the normal range for young women.

One might ask whether testosterone would benefit younger premenopausal women with decreased sexual desire if such women had low levels of testosterone. There are few clinical trials evaluating this. However, one placebo-controlled study in 51 women of reproductive age with low testosterone levels due to pituitary gland disease found a positive effect of the testosterone patch on some but not all parameters of sexual function, including a positive effect on arousal (25).

Summary and Conclusions

Sexual dysfunction is a common problem of men and women and may have both organic and psychological components. Abnormalities such as vascular or neurologic disease in men with erectile dysfunction, low levels of testosterone in men and some women with decreased sexual desire (hypoactive sexual desire disorder), and possibly alterations in neurotransmitters in women with low desire and low arousal may be the initial cause of the problem. The evaluation of patients with sexual problems should take into account organic and psychological factors, and treatment should combine medical and psychosocial therapies, as appropriate for the individual patient. The introduction of VIAGRA for men with erectile dysfunction, which is often due to vascular or neurogenic causes, has dramatically improved the prognosis of men with erectile dysfunction. Nevertheless psychological factors may still need to be addressed in patients who respond to VIAGRA and similar treatments. When choosing a medicine for an individual patient, as with any treatment, the benefit/risk balance must be taken into account and the patient should be fully informed about potential benefits as well as potential side effects. When there are no medications approved for use for a sexual disorder, such as premature or early ejaculation, the doctor and patient may sometimes cautiously use medications that are approved for other uses, but have been found effective in that particular sexual disorder.

There are very few medicines for sexual dysfunction in women. For women with low libido (hypoactive sexual disorder) and low levels of testosterone, the testosterone preparations that are available for men are not approved for use in women in the United States. Yet, physicians may prescribe testosterone in some women because the clinical trial data support the effectiveness of testosterone replacement, and both physician and patient perceive that the benefit/risk balance is acceptable. The lack of approved medications for women with sexual problems is of concern and argues for more research to understand the appropriate drug targets for women with sexual problems such as low desire, low arousal and difficulties with orgasm.

References

1. Goldbeck-Wood, S. (2010). Commentary: Female sexual dysfunction is a real but complex problem. *BMJ, 341*, p. c5336.
2. Moynihan, R. (2010). Merging of marketing and medical science: female sexual dysfunction. *BMJ, 341*, p. c5050.
3. Bhasin, S. and Basson, R. (2008). Sexual dysfunction in men and women. In: Kronenberg H, Melmed, S, Polonsky, K, Larsen, PR ed. *Williams Textbook of Endocrinology,* 11th ed. Philadelphia: Saunders Elsevier; pp. 701–737.
4. Basson, R. (2006). Clinical practice. Sexual desire and arousal disorders in women. *N. Engl J. Med, 354,* pp. 1497–1506.

5. McCall, K. and Meston, C. (2007). Differences between pre- and postmenopausal women in cues for sexual desire. *J Sex Med, 4*, pp. 364–371.

6. Segraves, R.T. (2010). Considerations for diagnostic criteria for erectile dysfunction in DSM V. *J Sex Med, 7*, pp. 654–660.

7. Feldman, H.A, Goldstein, I., Hatzichristou, D.G., Krane, R.J., McKinlay, J.B. (1994). Impotence and its medical and psychosocial correlates: results of the Massachusetts Male Aging Study. *J Urol, 151*, pp. 54–61.

8. Johannes, C.B., Araujo, A.B., Feldman, H.A., Derby, C.A., Kleinman, K.P., McKinlay, J.B. (2000). Incidence of erectile dysfunction in men 40 to 69 years old: longitudinal results from the Massachusetts male aging study. *J Urol, 163*, pp. 460–463.

9. Laumann, E.O., Paik, A., Rosen, R.C. (1999). Sexual dysfunction in the United States: prevalence and predictors. *JAMA, 281*, pp. 537–544.

10. Lindau, S.T., Schumm, L.P., Laumann, E.O., Levinson, W., O'Muircheartaigh C.A., Waite, L.J. (2007). A study of sexuality and health among older adults in the United States. *N Engl J Med, 357*, pp. 762–774.

11. Shifren, J.L., Monz, B.U., Russo, P.A., Segreti, A., Johannes, C.B. (2008). Sexual problems and distress in United States women: prevalence and correlates. *Obstet Gynecol, 112*, 970–978.

12. Segraves, R.T. (2010). Considerations for an evidence-based definition of premature ejaculation in the DSM-V. *J Sex Med, 7*, pp. 672–679.

13. Masters, W., Johnson, V. (1970). *Human Sexual Inadequacy*. Boston: Little, Brown, and Company.

14. Waldinger, M.D., Olivier, B. (2004). Utility of selective serotonin reuptake inhibitors in premature ejaculation. *Curr Opin Investig Drugs, 5*, pp. 743–747.

15. Waldinger, M.D., Zwinderman, A.H., Olivier, B. (2003). Antidepressants and ejaculation: a double-blind, randomized, fixed-dose study with mirtazapine and paroxetine. *J Clin Psychopharmacol, 23*, pp. 467–470.

16. Diaz, V.A. Jr., Close, J.D. (2010). Male sexual dysfunction. *Prim Care, 37*, pp. 473–489, vii–viii.

17. Bhasin, S., Cunningham, G.R., Hayes, F.J., Matsumoto, A.M., Snyder, P.J., Swerdloff, R.S., Montori, V.M. (2010). Testosterone therapy in men with androgen deficiency syndromes: an Endocrine Society clinical practice guideline. *J Clin Endocrinol Metab, 95*, pp. 2536–2559.

18. Heiman, J.R. (2002). Psychologic treatments for female sexual dysfunction: are they effective and do we need them? *Arch Sex Behav, 31*, pp. 445–450.

19. Pfaus, J.G. (2009). Pathways of sexual desire. *J Sex Med, 6*, pp.1506–1533.

20. Nappi, R.E., Martini, E., Terreno, E., Albani, F, Santamaria, V., Tonani, S., Chiovato, L., Polatti, F. (2010). Management of hypoactive sexual desire disorder in women: current and emerging therapies. *Int J Womens Health, 2*, pp. 167–175.

21. Mathur, R., Braunstein, G.D. (2010). Androgen deficiency and therapy in women. *Curr Opin Endocrinol Diabetes Obes, 17*, pp. 342–349.

22. FDA. (2004). Transcript, FDA Advisory Committee for Reproductive Health Drugs, December 2, 2004.

23. Davis, S.R., Moreau, M., Kroll, R., Bouchard, C., Panay, N., Gass, M., Braunstein, G.D., Hirschberg, A.L., Rodenberg, C., Pack, S., Koch, H., Moufarege, A., Studd, J. (2008).Testosterone for low libido in postmenopausal women not taking estrogen. *N Engl J Med, 359*, pp. 2005–2017.

24. Snabes, M.C., Simes, S.M. (2009). Approved hormonal treatments for HSDD: an unmet medical need. *J Sex Med, 6*, pp.1846–1849.

25. Miller, K.K., Biller, B.M., Beauregard, C., Lipman, J.G., Jones, J., Schoenfeld, D., Sherman, J.C., Swearingen, B., Loeffler, J., Klibanski, A. (2006). Effects of testosterone replacement in androgen-deficient women with hypopituitarism: a randomized, double-blind, placebo-controlled study. *J Clin Endocrinol Metab, 91*, pp. 1683–1690.

CONNIE B. NEWMAN is an endocrinologist and adjunct associate professor of medicine at New York University School of Medicine, New York, New York.

Anita P. Hoffer

 **NO**

The Hidden Costs of the Medicalization of Female Sexuality—How Did We Get Here? An Overview

Medicalization in our society wields enormous socio-economic influence and this influence is underestimated, particularly as it pertains to female sexuality. Medicalization has traditionally referred to a "process whereby non-medical problems become defined and treated as medical problems, usually in terms of illnesses or disorders" (Conrad, 1992; Farrell and Cacchioni, 2012) or a process wherein "more and more areas of everyday life have come under medical dominion, influence and supervision" (Zola, 1983). Especially in the arena of women's health, Tiefer (2012) and Starr (1982) have pointed out that the expanding cultural and institutional authority of medicine in the 20th century has been responsible for medicalization becoming a defining social process that places sexual problems and their treatments in an authoritarian framework of diagnoses and therapies that is overseen by healthcare providers (medical and non-medical) with expertise in the field of sexuality. The result is a system which favors a traditional medical approach and offers women as well as the doctors who care for them biomedical interventions in preference to other possible sexuality therapies. In addition, all too often, unfortunately, a system so deeply embedded in the fabric of our society leads to an ideal of sexual normalcy which in turn fosters market demand for "solutions"—products, pills, procedures and potions which will cure the illness and enable a captive population of consumers to experience improved, aka "normal," sex that conforms to social norms. The quest for female sexual "normalcy" results in a very large market which benefits the biomedical and biopharmaceutical industries that sell these remedies. But it also has costs that include personal and psychological harm, theoretical distortions in the way we conceptualize health and well-being, and political as well as socioeconomic impact.

An excellent example of this phenomenon is the disease entity known as "female sexual dysfunction," or FSD, which is listed in the *Diagnostic and Statistical Manual of Mental Disorders-IV* (hereafter, 'the DSM'). For those unfamiliar with this publication, the DSM is published by the American Psychiatric Association and is used in the United States and to various degrees around the world. It provides a common language and standard criteria for the classification of mental disorders. Because it is relied upon by clinicians, researchers, psychiatric drug regulation agencies, health insurance companies, pharmaceutical companies, and policy makers, its sphere of influence is very wide and it has played a significant role in how the healthcare industry deals with female sexuality as well as other medical issues.

In the middle of the 20th century, medical experts commonly used the term "frigid" to describe women who were unable to experience "normal sex," as the word "normal" was being defined by the medical, mostly male, establishment. Kroger and Freed (1950) wrote an article in a leading medical journal stating that frigidity was a common gynecological problem that affected 75% of American women. Heading into the 21st century, the label of frigidity has morphed into female sexual dysfunction or "FSD." This is a new illness which may be used to describe any woman who has experienced ordinary, run-of-the-mill sexual problems and is bothered by them. The notion of a sexual "dysfunction" is relatively recent, appearing for the first time in the DSM in the 1980s. Since then, the definition of FSD has changed many times. In simplest terms, the condition is currently described as consisting of four sub-disorders: desire, arousal, orgasm, and pain (*Diagnostic and Statistical Manual of Mental Disorders-IV-TR*, 2000). Arousal disorder, also known as FSAD (female sexual arousal disorder) is defined as inadequate genital lubrication and swelling in response to sexual excitement. Female orgasmic disorder describes a condition in which a woman is unable to reach orgasm or is delayed in having one. A disinterest in sexual activity or lack of fantasies is called low desire or hypoactive sexual desire disorder (HSDD). Pain disorder is also known as dyspareunia or vaginismus, the experience of pain during sexual intercourse.

One problem with the aforementioned definition of FSD is that it is focused so narrowly on "function," such that experiences or difficulties once considered to be a common part of women's day-to-day experience have come to be labeled as the symptoms of a dysfunction (Leiblum, in Goldstein et al. 2006). Given that definition, it is not surprising that research protocols, surveys and psychometric questionnaires (often written by the drug companies or the medical experts whom they hire as consultants) that explore and document these common experiences and sub-disorders have "revealed" that nearly one in two women in the USA suffers from this "new" medical disease. Findings of this sort, which are increasingly common (Laumann et al. 1999; Laumann et al. 2005), are being widely publicized and incorporated into corporate-sponsored marketing campaigns for new drugs. But wait . . . red flags should be going up here. If roughly half of a study population has a condition and the other half does not, who's to say which half is "abnormal"? Indeed the distinction between a "difficulty" and a "disorder" has become seriously blurred. If left unchecked, the long-term impact of this trend on women (as well as their partners), and how they experience their sexuality, is potentially disastrous—not only as it applies to FSD but also as it applies to how they feel about themselves.

In order to understand some of the factors that have contributed to such a sweeping definition of FSD, it is necessary to explain how the academic and corporate worlds interact around the subject of research and development. The nature of this complex and co-dependent relationship is clearly laid out in the excellent book, *Sex, Lies and Pharmaceuticals* (Moynihan and Mintzes, 2010). Basic research is traditionally the province of academia whereas development is typically left to biomedical and pharmaceutical companies ("Big Pharma") which have the vast resources needed to conduct huge lengthy clinical trials navigate and comply with endless Food and Drug Administration (FDA) requirements and, once regulatory approval by the FDA is gained, market and sell the product. Historically, there has been a close collaboration between the drug companies and the thought leaders in academic medicine and psychology. Many of the academics that have played a fundamental role in helping Big Pharma ferret out "symptom patterns" end up shaping companies' assumptions about women's sexual problems. Often they have been paid by companies with a vested interest in seeing the scope of a new disease entity broadened as much as possible. At the heart of the matter is the question of whether common sexual ailments should be interpreted and treated as aspects or fluctuations of normal female sexuality, or as the symptoms of widespread medical conditions that are treatable with some sort of biomedical intervention. The potential for financially driven conflict-of-interest is significant and rarely acknowledged. On the one hand, it is understandable, and indeed part of their fiduciary responsibility to their shareholders, for drug companies to grow their markets and develop medications that can be marketed to the broadest range of people possible. On the other hand, some healthy skepticism may be warranted when we are exposed to messages that FSD is so highly prevalent, affecting anywhere from 20–50% of women (Moynihan and Mintzes, 2010).

Once armed with a functional definition of a "new disease," a biomedical company can then move ahead to gather together large groups of women and conduct surveys that are designed to evaluate the scope of the problem they have identified and defined. By designing and scoring these surveys so that an affirmative answer to any one of several questions places the respondent in the category of the condition under examination, women who don't necessarily feel sick may end up being told that they are. This is what is called "selling sickness to the wealthy healthy" (Moynihan and Mintzes, 2010). The data collected from these surveys is used to substantiate the claim that there is a huge unmet need for new treatments, including the drugs or procedures made by the company that conducted the survey in the first place. To facilitate these studies further, corporate employees move ahead with development of new devices and tools to measure and diagnose the symptoms their company identified. The availability of these tools tends to influence the problems that get investigated in the sense that if you have a ruler, you are probably going to be engaged in measuring length. By using these tools, countless numbers of women (the ones who did not feel sick in the first place) come to be labeled as suffering from the "condition" and thus become eligible to receive the sponsor's drug.

The USA is one of the very few countries in the world where direct-to-consumer (DTC) advertising in healthcare is legal. This allows the American consumer, male *or* female, to be directly targeted with information on TV and other media that allegedly is essential to their well-being. Even though DTC is regulated by the FDA if a pharmaceutical company is promoting their own drug, destructive or unhealthy stereotypes still often manage to find their way into these advertisements. The drug companies are eager to help potential patients recognize that they have a treatable illness so that they will consult their doctors for a remedy. Patients naturally take the information they hear from the media, and questions engendered by it, to their doctors. The local medical doctors (LMD's) are genuinely eager to provide the latest and best possible care for their patients. They may be eager to attend free, industry-sponsored educational programs, held during professional meetings or at corporate conferences and industrial centers. There the doctors are exposed to "cutting-edge" thinking about new clinical problems/conditions and the solutions that the company has developed for them. Prestigious thought leaders often serve as faculty at these educational programs, and it probably won't come as a big surprise that the speakers who are given the honor of lecturing to their peers very often are the same experts who were the consultants who have worked all along with the company to study, identify and define the clinical problem (Angell, 2004). While there is increasing scrutiny and legislation recently that addresses the tight relationship between biomedical marketing and the medical community, it is neither uniform nor universal and much of this activity is still permitted in most states. (Exceptions which restrict or prohibit some activities, as of this writing, include Massachusetts, Vermont, California, Minnesota, New Hampshire, West Virginia and Washington, DC.) It is worth noting that the above-described system operates to showcase the work of the thought leaders whose perspectives coincide with those of Big Pharma. These individuals are thus the ones who gain visibility among their peers. By contrast, dissenting voices, or alternative treatment approaches to these ailments are less likely to get comparable high-profile publicity. A potential result over time may be a trend toward a pro-drug bias which thus becomes the status quo in the medical community as well as in the wider public arena of debate about sex (Caplan and Cosgrove, 2004).

So far we have examined the forces that have allowed "more and more areas of everyday life in general to fall under medical dominion, influence and supervision" (Zola, 1983) and we have seen one example of this process of medicalization at work—namely the creation of FSD, an entirely new woman's sexual disease and its carefully defined sub-disorders (Moynihan and Mintzes, 2009).

What are the opportunity costs of the medicalization of female sexuality? In the business world, an opportunity cost is defined as the value of the next best choice that one gives up when making a decision—in other words, "what you would have done if you didn't make the choice that you did." What then are these costs, or what is the harm, if any, that results from a system which, according to some, favors a traditional medical approach and offers women as well as the doctors who care for them biomedical interventions in preference to other possible sexuality therapies?

Leonore Tiefer, the founder of the global grassroots campaign known as the New View (www.newviewcampaign.org), is a leading researcher, New York University psychology professor, sex therapist and renowned global activist who advocates for women's health and sexual rights. While she acknowledges that the conventional medical perspective does take non-biomedical interventions into account, she argues that the DSM definition of FSD and its four sub-types is much too focused on functional problems and too often leaves the whole patient out of the equation. Rather than the four *sub-disorders* of sexual illness, Dr. Tiefer proposes four *causes* of women's sexual difficulties: (i) psychological factors such as depression or abuse, (ii) relationship challenges including discrepant desire problems, (iii) broad societal factors that impact sexuality (e.g., religious taboos that leave us feeling ashamed of our bodies, economic factors that leave us exhausted from struggling to meet work and family responsibilities, and sex-negative cultures that help create our inhibitions), and finally, (iv) medical causes like surgical damage to nerves or adverse side effects (ASE's) from drugs (including but not necessarily limited to antidepressants) which can interfere with sexual desire or the ability to climax (Kaschak and Tiefer, 2001).

In the author's opinion, Dr. Tiefer's approach embodies a wiser and more thoughtful, holistic perspective. It leaves room for the whole person and doesn't force an individual into a mold constructed by external "experts." Sadly, constraining definitions in the field of sexuality are not new and they are not limited to FSD. In fact, they creep into other models of women's sexual behavior as well. For example, in Masters and Johnson's classic model of the sexual response cycle published nearly 50 years ago,

four stages of response were defined: excitement, plateau, orgasm, and resolution (Masters and Johnson, 1966). But this linear model is desire-driven and postulates the arousal pattern is the same for men and women. As sexuality educators, we now know that many women do not move through all these phases sequentially and many do not even experience all of these phases. The Masters and Johnson biologic model ignores context, pleasure, satisfaction, and relationship. It sets up expectations that leave many women who don't experience it feeling like they have failed or may be doing something wrong. A few years ago, a Canadian researcher published a less biologically focused model of female sexual response; she named it the circular or "non-linear model of female sexual response" which runs on triggered or responsive sexual desire (Basson, 2001). Like Dr. Tiefer's consideration of female sexual problems, Dr. Basson also leaves room for the individual . . . ALL of her . . . and much less room for self-criticism, shame and depression.

There are additional downsides, or opportunity costs, to classifying the normal fluctuations of everyday sexual life as a medical dysfunction and using pills, potions or procedures to treat them. Not only is it expensive (and potentially dangerous) to take medicines that are not really needed, or that are ineffective, but also it places an additional financial burden on a healthcare system that is already struggling to keep its head above water. Equally important is the ever-present potential for the new "wonder drug" to cause direct ASEs or cross-reactivity with other medicines that a patient may already be taking. For example, a man who is taking nitroglycerin for angina or amyl nitrates ("poppers") for recreational use should *not* be taking Viagra because it can cause a precipitous drop in blood pressure and even a heart attack. In addition, treating a symptom without knowing its cause may gloss over a deeper medical problem which does indeed require a medical intervention. Here again, Viagra is a useful case in point because it is well-documented that erectile difficulties can be a predictor of cardiovascular problems or predisposition to stroke (Banks et al. 2013; Hall et al. 2010). If the Viagra appears to solve the problem temporarily by enabling an erection, the underlying circulatory issues may go undetected until they become dangerously severe. Alternatively, the erectile difficulty may have nothing at all to do with a physiological problem and rather be an expression of relationship problems or other psychosocial pressures (Rosen, 2007). This is not an anti-Viagra admonition . . . it is merely a recommendation that pills be used when the etiology of the problem is clearly understood. And finally, there are no pills or procedures that can be prescribed to deal with psychosocial or cultural components of sexual difficulties. The quest to find them can siphon off energy from doing a different kind of research, namely taking psychological and emotional inventory and uncovering non-biological contributors to the problem.

In addition to the above-described opportunity costs, there are also examples of potentially harmful procedures that have emerged recently and are available to women who have concluded, or been convinced, that their dissatisfaction with their vulvas can best be addressed by creation of designer-vaginas through surgical intervention. Female cosmetic genital surgery (FCGS) includes the practices of labiaplasty, re-virginization (tightening and/or hymen restoration), and other vaginal rejuvenation protocols.

Notwithstanding warnings from the American College of Obstetricians and Gynecologists about severe complications that may arise from these procedures (ACOG, 2007), FCGS is one of the fastest growing fields of surgery in the country and is "increasingly affordable, available and normative" (Tiefer, 2010). FCGS has moved from insurance-reimbursed procedures to "cash-only" with private financing plans offered by the individual surgeon in his (or her) office. This obsession with genital beauty is now embraced by doctors who are members of the International Society of Cosmetogynecology (ISCG; information available at www.iscg.com). The ISCG is exploiting the body insecurity issues of their patients and promoting the impression that so-called aberrations are abnormal by failing to inform them that genitals are as diverse as faces or fingerprints. It has even gone so far as to be on record as promoting, marketing and even national franchising of cosmetic genital procedures . . . all this despite documented potential consequences of this surgery such as infection, altered sensation, pain, adhesions, severe hemorrhaging, scarring and even obstetric risks! Surely there must be a "next best choice" for resolving sexual dissatisfaction that is better than opting for a procedure as extreme and potentially harmful as this one.

Perhaps the most subtle and insidious of all of the opportunity costs arising from this troubling trend toward creating diseases is how the focus on the quick fix can distract us from recognizing that conscious reframing of the meaning of sexual satisfaction throughout the life cycle is a gradual but rich, ongoing opportunity for personal growth. This growth process is disrupted by the crippling sexual stereotypes that abound in our society. It starts early with the sexualization of our children. Then, preconceived notions of how we should feel about sex, how much of it we should want and have in order to be "real women," whether we should shave, wax, color (www.mynewpinkbutton.com), pierce, be-jewel (www.themodernsavage.com/2010/03/06/theart-of-vajazzling) or surgically alter our genitals in order to be considered young and attractive, and how (or if) we should continue to perform sexually as we age (Marshall, 2012) are all expectations that women (and men) are saddled with in American society. It is most assuredly unfair to blame Big Pharma and the biomedical establishment in general for these cultural issues. But to the extent that they capitalize on these trends and exploit these messages to persuade women they have newly defined "diseases" for which they need products, medications, and services, the phenomenon of medicalization of sexuality is contributing to collective sexual angst and depriving women of becoming their own unique sexual selves.

In closing, balance is important. It is crucial to emphasize that many of the medical advances that have come about as the result of collaboration between corporate and academic medical researchers are vitally important; our health would be sorely compromised without the fruits of their efforts. The author, who was trained in academic medicine, was privileged to work for several years in the field of women's health in one of the world's leading pharmaceutical companies. It would be difficult to find a more sincere, dedicated, intelligent group of professionals. Not all are as cynical as sometimes portrayed in discussions of this topic. There are professionals of unimpeachable integrity in both worlds.

Being skeptical about medical approaches and pharmaceutical solutions does not mean losing all trust in the value of these contributions. Critical analysis of the phenomenon of medicalization is not a rejection of medicine; rather it highlights the potential for unnecessary pathologization, biological reductionism, the downplaying of social factors and the prioritizing of profit and career expansion over health and well-being (Farrell and Cacchioni, 2012). As Moynihan and Mintzes (2009) point out, we all need to take a little more time to sort out the fake hype from the genuine hope. The milder a problem is, the smaller the benefit that can come from a medical label and a pill, and the bigger the risk of doing more harm than good. But there are medical and physiological components to all behavior, including sexual behavior. There are many women and their partners whose sexual difficulties cause real suffering and in whom real medical problems are affecting their ability to experience sexual pleasure. Psychosocial approaches may not work for, or may not be available to, all of these people. Therefore, innovative companies that may be able to offer drugs, devices, or procedures for these women have the potential to make a needed contribution, *provided* that their remedies are proven to be necessary, safe, and effective (Hoffer, 2011).

References

1. ACOG (American College of Obstetricians and Gynecologists), Committee on Gynecologic Practice. (2007). ACOG Committee Opinion No. 378: Vaginal 'rejuvenation' and cosmetic vaginal procedures. *Obstet Gynecol.,110*(3), 737–738.
2. Angell, M. (2004). *The Truth About the Drug Companies: How They Deceive Us and What to Do About It.* New York and Canada: Random House.
3. Banks, E., Joshy, G., Abhayaratna, W. P., Kritharides, L., Macdonald, P. S., Korda, R. J., et al. (2013). Erectile Dysfunction Severity as a Risk Marker for Cardiovascular Disease Hospitalization and All-Cause Mortality: A Prospective Cohort Study. *PLoS Med 10*(1).
4. Basson, R. (2001). Human Sex-Response Cycles. *Journal of Sex & Marital Therapy 27,* 33–43.

5. Caplan, P. J., & Cosgrove, L. (Eds.). (2004). *Bias in Psychiatric Diagnosis* [Hardcover]. Oxford, UK: Rowman and Littlefield Publishers.

6. Conrad, P. (1992). Medicalization and Social Control. *Annual Review of Sociology, 18,* 209–232.

7. *Diagnostic and Statistical Manual of Mental Disorders-IV-TR* (2000). American Psychiatric Association, Arlington, VA, http://psych.org/MainMenu/Research/DSMIV.aspx

8. Farrell, J., & Cacchioni, T. (2012). The Medicalization of Women's Sexual Pain. *Journal of Sex Research, 49*(4), 328–336.

9. Goldstein, I., Meston, C., Davis, S., & Traish, A. (Eds.). (2006). *Women's Sexual Function and Dysfunction: Study, Diagnosis and Treatment.* Boca Raton: Taylor and Francis. P. 263

10. Hall, S. A., Shackelton, R., Rosen, R. C., & Araujo, A. B. (2010). Sexual Activity, Erectile Dysfunction, and Incident Cardiovascular Events. *American Journal of Cardiology, 105*(2), 192–197.

11. Hoffer, A. P. (2011). A Review of ORGASM INC.: The Strange Science of Female Pleasure. *American Journal of Sexuality Education, 6,* 317–322.

12. Kaschak, E., & Tiefer, L. (Eds.). (2001). *A New View of Women's Sexual Problems. Part I, 1–8.* New York: The Haworth Press, Inc.

13. Kroger, W., & Freed, C. (1950). Psychosomatic Aspects of Frigidity. *Journal of the American Medical Association (JAMA), 143,* 526–532.

14. Laumann, E., Paik, A., & Rosen, R. (1999). Sexual dysfunction in the United States: prevalence and predictors. *JAMA, 281,* 537–544.

15. Laumann, E. O., Nicolosi, A., Glasser, D. B., Paik, A., Gingell, C., Moreira, E., et al. (2005). Sexual problems among Women and Men Aged 40–80 Years: Prevalence and Correlates Identified in the Global Study of Sexual Attitudes and Behaviors. *International Journal of Impotence Research, 17*(1), 39–57.

16. Marshall, B. (2012). Medicalization and the Refashioning of Age-Related Limits on Sexuality. *Journal of Sex Research, 49*(4), 337–343.

17. Masters, W. H., & Johnson, V. E. (1966). *Human Sexual Response.* New York: Bantam Books.

18. Moynihan, R., & Mintzes, B. (2010). *Sex, Lies and Pharmaceuticals: How Drug Companies Plan to Profit from Female Sexual Dysfunction.* Vancouver, BC: Greystone Books.

19. Rosen, R. C. (2007). Erectile Dysfunction: Integration of Medical and Psychological Approaches. In S. R. Leiblum (Ed.), *Principles and Practices of Sex Therapy - 4th edition.* New York: The Guilford Press.

20. Tiefer, L. (2010). Female Genital Cosmetic Surgery. Paper presented at Framing the Vulva: Genital Cosmetic Surgery and Genital Diversity, Las Vegas.

21. Tiefer, L. (2012). Medicalization and Demedicalization of Sexuality Therapies. *Journal of Sex Research, 49*(4), 311–318.

ANITA P. HOFFER, PhD, EdD, a clinical sexologist and sexuality educator, originally worked at Harvard Medical School in the field of male reproductive biology and chemical male contraceptives before moving into the pharmaceutical industry to work in women's health. She now lectures at universities, medical schools, and nonprofit organizations, and presents at national and regional conferences on sexuality and aging.

EXPLORING THE ISSUE

Should Sexual Problems Be Treated Pharmaceutically?

Critical Thinking and Reflection

1. What are the main causes of sexual problems?
2. Do you think most Americans would prefer a pharmaceutical treatment for sexual problems or psychological treatment? Why?
3. Is there potential for an integrated approach for addressing sexual problems? Explain.
4. Why do you think there are so many more medicinal treatments available to men?

Is There Common Ground?

Advocates both for and against sexual medicine express concern for patients suffering from sexual difficulties. The disagreements between them center around understanding—and treating—the root causes of sexual problems. Are sexual difficulties biologically, psychologically, or socially constructed? Or, are they the result of a combination of these factors?

Connie Newman explains that "sexual dysfunction is a common problem of men and women and may have both organic and psychological components." Since it is not only a psychological problem, it shouldn't be treated only with psychosexual therapy. Treatment needs to combine medical and psychosexual therapies "as appropriate for the individual patient." She also notes that men have a variety of medications available to treat sexual dysfunctions, but that there are few such medical options for women. More research is needed to develop safe and effective sexual medicines for women. Why do you think there are fewer medical treatments available for women?

In citing activist and psychology professor Leonore Tiefer, Hoffer outlines four root causes of sexual difficulties: psychological factors, such as depression and abuse; relationship problems, including problems with desire; societal factors, such as sexual shame imparted by religious messages; and medical causes. What overlap do you observe between these two authors with respect to the causes of sexual problems?

One of the most interesting, yet least discussed, aspects of the controversy over the medicalization of sexuality is the future of sex therapy. If people are able to have their sexual issues treated chemically by their general practitioners, OB-GYNs, and urologists, what role will the therapist fill? Newman suggests that pharmacological and psychological treatments can co-exist, and even used together. Hoffer similarly says that skepticism of sexual medicine does not mean an outright rejection of it. It may, indeed, have its right uses for the right people. How comfortable would you be taking medications for sexual problems? Would you rather deal with these issues through counseling first? Or would you be more comfortable raising the issue in doctor's office than on a therapist's couch?

In their new book, *Older, Wiser, Sexually Smarter*, sexuality educator Peggy Brick and her colleagues argue that many of the physical changes that people experience related to their sexuality as they grow older are not inherently problematic and may not necessarily require medication or therapy. Rather, they necessitate a new understanding of one's sexuality and, perhaps, new sexual behaviors that may not be quite the same as when they were age 18. What do you think of this viewpoint? Can sexuality be experienced differently as one grows older? What adjustments might a person need to their sexual expectations and behaviors as they grow older?

Create Central

www.mhhe.com/createcentral

Reference

(1) Laumann, E., Paik, A., & Rosen, R. (1999). Sexual dysfunctions in the United States. *Journal of the American Medical Association, 281*: 537–544.

Additional Resources

Brick, P., Lunquist, J. Sandak, A., & Taverner (2009). *Older, Wiser, Sexually Smarter: 30 Sex Ed Lessons for Adults Only*. Morristown, NJ: The Center for Family Life Education.

Frank, J.E., Mistretta, P., & Will, J. (2008). Diagnosis and treatment of female sexual dysfunction. *American Family Physician, 77*(5): 635–642.

Green, B. The quick fix: *Orgasm Inc.* examines the treatment of female sexuality. *Honolulu Weekly*, May 4, 2011.

Katz, S. Return of desire: Fighting myths about female sexuality. *AlterNet,* July 23, 2008.

Tiefer, L. (2008). *Sex Is Not a Natural Act & Other Essays.* New York, NY: Westview Press.

Internet References . . .

International Society for Sexual Medicine (ISSM)

Established in 1982 to promote erectile dysfunction research, the ISSM today encourages research and education across a broad spectrum of human sexual functioning. The ISSM publishes the *Journal of Sexual Medicine.*

www.issm.info

New View Campaign

The New View Campaign is an educational campaign that challenges myths promoted by the pharmaceutical industry and calls for research on the causes of women's sexual problems. Visitors will find developing information on Intrinsa at this website.

www.NewViewCampaign.org

World Association for Sexual Health

The World Association for Sexual Health (WAS) promotes sexual health throughout the lifespan and through the world by developing, promoting, and supporting sexology and sexual rights for all. WAS accomplishes this by advocacy actions, networking, facilitating the exchange of information, ideas, and experiences, and advancing scientifically based sexuality research, sexuality education, and clinical sexology, with a transdisciplinary approach.

www.WorldSexology.org

Selected, Edited, and with Issue Framing Material by:
Ryan W. McKee, *Widener University*
and
William J. Taverner, *Center for Family Life Education*

ISSUE

Should Prostitution Be Legal?

YES: Susan A. Milstein, from "Want a Safer Community? Legalize Prostitution," Original essay for this edition (2009)

NO: Donna M. Hughes, from "The Demand: Where Sex Trafficking Begins," *A Call to Action: Joining the Fight against Trafficking in Persons Conference,* Rome, Italy (2004)

Learning Outcomes
After reading this issue, you should be able to: • Distinguish between legalization, criminalization, decriminalization, and regulation of prostitution. • Distinguish between the terms *prostitution, sex work,* and *sex trafficking.* • Describe the benefits of legalizing and regulating prostitution, as outlined by Susan A. Milstein. • Outline the negative impacts of sex trafficking, as described by Donna M. Hughes.

ISSUE SUMMARY

YES: Susan A. Milstein, EdD, CHES, associate professor in the Health Department at Montgomery College and advisory board member Men's Health Network, argues that while the legalization of prostitution will not stop all of the social problems associated with the institution, the benefits of legalization make it the best option.

NO: Donna M. Hughes, PhD, professor at the University of Rhode Island and leading international researcher on trafficking of women and children, counters that the criminalization of prostitution not only reduces demand, but also slows the spread of international sex trafficking.

Prostitution is often referred to as the "oldest profession in the world." Despite the fact that prostitution is illegal in many places of the world, both female and male prostitutes can be found in every city, of every country of the world. Prostitution, often referred to as "sex work," ranges from solicitation in outdoor settings like parks or the street, to brothels and high-end escort services, to the trafficking of unwilling individuals. There exists an ongoing debate about whether prostitution should be criminalized, decriminalized, or legalized.

It may be helpful when examining this issue to gain clarity about the distinction between criminalization, decriminalization, and legalization. Those who seek to end the practice through the criminalization of prostitution would take an abolitionist perspective, meaning that all aspects of prostitution would be illegal and punishable by law. The decriminalization of prostitution would remove any criminal penalties associated with the trade, and allow prostitutes to operate in a similar manner to independent contractors or other independently licensed businesses.

The third option, the legalization of prostitution, would call for state licensing and regulations, including the possibility of mandated testing for sexually transmitted infections. According to the U.S. Department of State Bureau of Democracy, Human Rights, and Labor the legality of prostitution varies across the world with it being illegal in many countries, legalized and regulated in others, while in some parts of the world, the act of prostitution itself is legal, though other activities related to it are illegal, such as soliciting sex in a public place.

In the United States, Nevada is well known for being the only state in which prostitution is legal. (In recent history, prostitution was also allowed in Rhode Island, though a 2009 law made it a misdemeanor in that state.) Nevada legalized prostitution in 1971 and has 28 legal brothels and about 300 licensed female prostitutes. Brothels in Nevada are allowed in counties that have fewer than 400,000 residents, which excludes major metropolitan areas, including the county where Las Vegas is located. However, research has indicated that 90 percent of prostitution in Nevada takes place in Las Vegas and Reno, where it is in fact illegal. Legalized brothels are highly regulated and state law requires that brothel prostitutes receive weekly tests for chlamydia and gonorrhea and monthly tests for HIV and syphilis. Condom use is also required. In fact, research has shown that condom use is higher during sexual activity between a prostitute and a client, compared to sexual activity between a prostitute and a nonpaying sex partner. Such regulations exist as a public health measure, to reduce the rates of sexually transmitted infections (STIs). They seem to be working. Among prostitutes affiliated with Nevada brothels studied, there have been no cases of HIV infection and the positive gonorrhea rate is about 1 percent. One study found that the prevalence of STIs among illegal street prostitutes in Australia, working outside of the legalized and regulated system, was drastically higher (80 times greater) than their brothel counterparts.

In the past few years, prostitution and sex work have also found their place on the Internet, where prostitutes and clients arrange meetings on websites such as Craigslist, even though such websites don't condone the behavior. Websites have also cropped up offering other Internet-based sex work, such as adult web camera video chat hosting, or "chat hosts." Chat hosts use their cameras to broadcast erotic acts live to viewers, often in private chat rooms, where a viewer may communicate with a chat host via text-based chat, audio, or audio–visual chat, depending on preferences and the capabilities of the website. Another notable example of virtual sex work can be found in the game, Second Life, a three-dimensional online virtual world where users log on to learn, explore, shop for virtual items, and conduct business, including virtual prostitution, all carried out by customizable avatars.

Different views about prostitution may depend on the context in which it takes place. Organizations such as the Coalition Against Trafficking in Women (CATW) considers prostitution to be sexual exploitation and focuses on abolishing sex trafficking of women and girls. According to the U.S. Department of State, "Where prostitution is legalized or tolerated, there is a greater demand for human trafficking victims and nearly always an increase in the number of women and children trafficked into commercial sex slavery. Of the estimated 600,000 to 800,000 people trafficked across international borders annually, 80 percent of victims are female, and up to 50 percent are minors. Hundreds of thousands of these women and children are used in prostitution each year."

Some sex worker activist organizations such as Call Off Your Old Tired Ethics (COYOTE) and the North American Task Force on Prostitution view prostitution as a choice and support the decriminalization of prostitution, but oppose the regulations that come with legalization such as in Nevada.

In the following selections, Dr. Susan A. Milstein presents a rationale for legalizing prostitution, outlining the benefits of doing so, including financial and public health benefits, while Dr. Donna M. Hughes asserts that prostitution is a violation of human rights, leads to the dehumanization of women and children, and should not be legalized.

YES ↵

Susan A. Milstein

Want a Safer Community?
Legalize Prostitution

Prostitution is a reality in the United States, regardless of its legal status. If it becomes legal, then outreach services, like drug and mental health counseling, can be provided. This will not only improve the prostitute's quality of life, it may encourage them to leave the profession. Legalization means that measures could be taken to protect prostitutes from becoming victims of rape and other forms of violence, while mandatory condom use, and STI and HIV testing, will help decrease disease transmission. There is also the benefit of the government being able to make money by imposing taxes. It's in society's best interest to make prostitution as safe as possible, which can be accomplished through legalization.

Legalize it, decriminalize it, or keep it illegal, the fact remains that prostitution is going to happen regardless of what the law says. Once we come to accept that as fact, the question then becomes, what is the best way to approach it?

So What Is Prostitution?

When you say "prostitute" people automatically get an image in their head. That image may be of a streetwalker, a call girl or a male escort. It may be of Heidi Fleiss or Deborah Jeane Palfrey, the DC Madam. It may even be of Elliott Spitzer. But what is prostitution? It's the exchange of sex for money. With this definition in mind, let's change how we look at prostitution. Instead of thinking of a streetwalker and pimp, imagine a woman who sleeps with a man in exchange for rent money and gifts. Is this prostitution? Some might say no, others might say yes.

Change the scenario again. Imagine a woman who is engaging in a specific behavior in exchange for money. Is that prostitution, or is it a job? It may be difficult to think of prostitution as just another job, but why? Is it because prostitution is seen as demeaning and degrading? What's the difference between working as a prostitute, and being locked into a Wal-Mart overnight and being forced to clean (Greenhouse, 2005)? It may be difficult to separate prostitution out from what may seem like other degrading and dehumanizing jobs simply because it involves sex. But if we can look past the sexual aspect, if we can stop looking at prostitution as being inherently immoral or unacceptable, if we can start to look at it as an industry, then we can start to see the benefits of legalizing it.

Benefits of Legalizing Prostitution

There are multiple benefits to legalizing prostitution, the first of which is improving the health of the prostitute. If the United Sates were to legalize prostitution then there could be legislation that would mandate regular STI and HIV testing. This is currently how it works in Nevada, the only state in the United States that has legalized prostitution. In addition to STI and HIV testing, using condoms for every sex act could also be made mandatory. Both of these types of mandates would help to prevent disease transmission among the prostitutes, their clients, and their clients' other sexual partners. But decreasing the risk of disease transmission, while important, is not the only health benefit of legalizing prostitution.

A study done in New York City found that the majority of prostitutes were addicted to drugs. Many continue to work as prostitutes as a way of making money so that they can feed their addiction. If prostitution were legalized, it would be easier to do drug outreach and education for the prostitutes. This might decrease the amount of drug use that is seen amongst prostitutes, and it may also help to decrease the number of people who are engaging in sex for money. Once sober, they may look to other professions for a steady source of income.

In addition to drug use, another problem facing many prostitutes is that of violence. Many prostitutes are raped by their clients. One study found that 80% of prostitutes had either been threatened with violence, or had been victims of violence. Violence, and threats of, may come from clients, pimps or the police. Currently, if a prostitute is raped or otherwise victimized, he or she has little to no legal recourse. But if prostitution were to be legalized, a sex worker who is raped would have the ability to go to the police and report it without fear of being arrested.

Legalizing prostitution may also make the work safer in that precautions can be put into place ahead of time to try and prevent violence from occurring. Many of these types of strategies have already been implemented in Nevada, where prostitution is legal in selected counties. Installing panic buttons in rooms may help to save a prostitute from harm if a client does get violent. Additionally, if violence occurs, the brothel owners can call the police without fear of being arrested.

A safer working environment, counseling services to help deal with drug use and being victims of violence, and reducing the disease transmission rates all create a safer environment for the prostitutes and their customers, but what about the community?

Benefits to the Community

What kind of community are we creating if we legalize prostitution? Perhaps we can create a safer one. If we pass legislation mandating STI and HIV testing, and condom use during each sex act, we can also pass legislation that restricts where prostitutes can work. Since men and women won't be out be on the street trying to attract customers, the streets will see fewer streetwalkers, and fewer people trolling for prostitutes. Combine this with a decrease in the amount of violence and drugs that surround the profession, and all of this is a benefit to the community. There is also the financial benefit.

If we require a prostitute to register so that we can monitor his or her STI and HIV testing, then that will create jobs. There will be a need for more people to work in the labs that will be doing the testing, as well as a need to staff an office that deals with regulation and record maintenance. Increases in social service programs, like crisis counseling and drug programs, will provide even more jobs. And if it's legalized, it can be taxed.

Sin taxes are taxes that are imposed on activities that are considered immoral, yet are still legal. These taxes may be imposed on drugs, like nicotine and alcohol, or on specific activities like gambling. With this kind of precedent, there is no reason why prostitution couldn't be legalized, and then taxed. The revenue generated by a prostitution tax could be used to help benefit a myriad of different government programs. This could in turn lead to an increase in the quality of life for thousands of United States citizens.

Rethinking Prostitution in the United States

Some may wonder why it is that Americans say they live in a free society, yet an individual does not have the right to decide to have consensual sex for money. If the country, outside of Nevada, is so anti-prostitution, why do we punish the sex worker, and not the person who is paying for sex? The majority of laws in the United States actually trap a person in a life of prostitution. It may be that one way to decrease the number of people who work as prostitutes, is to legalize it.

When someone gets arrested for prostitution, they have a criminal record that will follow him or her. What jobs are available to someone who has been arrested for prostitution? If we don't make it a crime, a prostitute may be able to get the job training, health care, and mental and legal counseling that would enable them to leave the world of prostitution. Perhaps the answer is to change the way we deal with prostitution and arrest the people who are paying for sex, which is the law in Sweden. Or perhaps the United States can do what many other countries are doing, and either decriminalize or legalize prostitution.

The fact is that the United States has already taken a step towards legalization. Depending on the population of the county, prostitution is legal in Nevada. Prostitutes must register to work, must use condoms for all sex acts, and must be tested for STIs and HIV on a regular basis. Some countries have chosen to decriminalize prostitution. Since changing the law in 2003, New Zealand has found no major increase in the number of prostitutes in the country, and there has been a positive change in the lives of many sex workers. Other countries, including England, Argentina, Canada, Germany, Greece, Scotland, and more than twenty others, have chosen to legalize prostitution (Procorn.org, 2008).

Bottom Line. . . . Prostitution Happens

Legalizing prostitution will not make the industry perfectly safe. False negatives can occur on STI and HIV tests, and condoms can break, which means disease transmission is always a possibility. Panic buttons and good working relationships with police won't guarantee a prostitute's safety. Make eighteen the minimum working age for a prostitute, and you will find people younger than that selling their bodies for sex, and others who are more than willing to pay for it. Legalization is not a cure for all the issues surrounding sex work in the United States.

The bottom line is that regardless of the law, prostitution is going to happen. By legalizing it we can make it safer, for the prostitutes, the clients, their significant others, and society at large.

Susan A. Milstein is a professor in the Department of Health Enhancement, Exercise Science, and Physical Education at the Rockville Campus of Montgomery College and is the founder and lead consultant of Milstein Health Consulting. She is a master certified health education specialist and a certified sexuality educator.

Donna M. Hughes

 **NO**

The Demand: Where Sex Trafficking Begins

In light of shared moral responsibility to help the millions of people who are bought, sold, transported and held against their will in slave-like condition, a conference entitled "A Call to Action: Joining the Fight Against Trafficking in Persons" was held at the Pontifical Gregorian University in Rome on June 17, 2004. The event was part of the 20th anniversary celebration of full diplomatic relations between the United States and the Holy See, and their shared work to promote human dignity, liberty, justice, and peace. The following is the text of my speech.

The Trafficking Process: The Dynamics of Supply and Demand

The transnational sex trafficking of women and children is based on a balance between the supply of victims from sending countries and the demand for victims in receiving countries. Sending countries are those from which victims can be relatively easily recruited, usually with false promises of jobs. Receiving or destination countries are those with sex industries that create the demand for victims. Where prostitution is flourishing, pimps cannot recruit enough local women to fill up the brothels, so they have to bring in victims from other places.

Until recently, the supply side of trafficking and the conditions in sending countries have received most of the attention of researchers, NGOs, and policy makers, and little attention was paid to the demand side of trafficking.

The trafficking process begins with the demand for women to be used in prostitution. It begins when pimps place orders for women. Interviews I have done with pimps and police from organized crime units say that when pimps need new women and girls, they contact someone who can deliver them. This is what initiates the chain of events of sex trafficking.

The crucial factor in determining where trafficking will occur is the presence and activity of traffickers, pimps, and collaborating officials running criminal operations. Poverty, unemployment, and lack of opportunities are compelling factors that facilitate the ease with which traffickers recruit women, but they are not the cause of trafficking. Many regions of the world are poor and chaotic, but not every region becomes a center for the recruitment or exploitation of women and children. Trafficking occurs because criminals take advantage of poverty, unemployment, and a desire for better opportunities.

Corruption of government officials and police is necessary for trafficking and exploitation of large numbers of women and children. In sending countries, large-scale operations require the collaboration of officials to obtain travel documents and facilitate the exit of women from the country.

In destination countries, corruption is an enabler for prostitution and trafficking. The operation of brothels requires the collaboration of officials and police, who must be willing to ignore or work with pimps and traffickers. Prostitution operations depend on attracting men. Pimps and brothel owners have to advertise to men that women and children are available for commercial sex acts. Officials have to ignore this blatant advertising.

Components of the Demand

There are four components that make-up the demand: 1) the men who buy commercial sex acts, 2) the exploiters who make up the sex industry, 3) the states that are destination countries, and 4) the culture that tolerates or promotes sexual exploitation.

The Men

The men, the buyers of commercial sex acts, are the ultimate consumers of trafficked and prostituted women and children. They use them for entertainment, sexual gratification, and acts of violence. It is men who create the demand, and women and children who are the supply.

I recently completed a report for the TIP Office, United States Department of State on the demand side of sex trafficking that focuses on the men who purchase sex acts. Typically, when prostitution and sex trafficking are discussed, the focus is on the women. The men who purchase the sex acts are faceless and nameless.

Research on men who purchase sex acts has found that many of the assumptions we make about them are myths. Seldom are the men lonely or have sexually unsatisfying relationships. In fact, men who purchase sex acts are more likely to have more sexual partners than those who do not purchase sex acts. They often report that they are satisfied with their wives or partners. They say that they are searching for more—sex acts that their wives will not do or excitement that comes with the hunt for a woman they can buy for a short time. They are seeking sex without relationship responsibilities. A significant number of men say that the sex and interaction with the prostitute were unrewarding and they did not get what they were seeking; yet they compulsively repeat the act of buying sex. Researchers conclude that men are purchasing sex acts to meet emotional needs, not physical needs.

Men who purchase sex acts do not respect women, nor do they want to respect women. They are seeking control and sex in contexts in which they are not required to be polite or nice, and where they can humiliate, degrade, and hurt the woman or child, if they want.

The Exploiters

The exploiters, including traffickers, pimps, brothel owners, organized crime members, and corrupt officials make-up what is known as the sex industry. They make money from the sale of sex as a commodity. Traffickers and organized crime groups are the perpetrators that have received most of the attention in discussions about the sex trafficking.

The State

By tolerating or legalizing prostitution, the state, at least passively, is contributing to the demand for victims. The more states regulate prostitution and derive tax revenue from it, the more actively they become part of the demand for victims.

If we consider that the demand is the driving force of trafficking, then it is important to analyze the destination countries' laws and policies. Officials in destination countries do not want to admit responsibility for the problem of sex trafficking or be held accountable for creating the demand. At this point to a great extent, the wealthier destination countries control the debate on how trafficking and prostitution will be addressed. Sending countries are usually poorer, less powerful, and more likely to be influenced by corrupt officials and/or organized crime groups. They lack the power and the political will to insist that destination countries stop their demand for women for prostitution.

In destination countries, strategies are devised to protect the sex industries that generate hundreds of millions of dollars per year for the state where prostitution is legal, or for organized crime groups and corrupt officials where the sex industry is illegal.

In the destination countries, exploiters exert pressure on the lawmakers and officials to create conditions that allow them to operate. They use power and influence to shape laws and polices that maintain the flow of women to their sex industries. They do this through the normalization of prostitution and the corruption of civil society.

There has been a global movement to normalize and legalize the flow of foreign women into sex industries. It involves a shift from opposing the exploitation of women in prostitution to only opposing the worst violence and criminality. It involves redefining prostitution as "sex work," a form of labor for poor women, and redefining the transnational movement of women for prostitution as labor migration, called "migrant sex work." It involves legalizing prostitution, and changing the migration laws to allow a flow of women for prostitution from sending regions to sex industry centers. The normalization of prostitution is often recommended as a way to solve the problem of trafficking.

States protect their sex industries by preventing resistance to the flow of women to destination countries by silencing the voice of civil society. In many sending countries, civil society is weak and undeveloped. Governments of destination countries fund non-governmental organizations (NGOs) in sending countries to promote the destination country's views on prostitution and trafficking. Authentic voices of citizens who do not want their daughters and sisters to become "sex workers" in other countries are replaced by the voice of the destination country, which says that prostitution is good work for women. The result is a corruption of civil society.

In a number of countries, the largest anti-trafficking organizations are funded by states that have legalized prostitution. These funded NGOs often support legalized prostitution. They only speak about "forced prostitution" and movement of women by force, fraud, or coercion. They remain silence as thousands of victims leave their communities for "sex work" in destination countries. Effectively, these NGOs have abandoned the women and girls to the pimps and men who purchase sex acts.

When prostitution is illegal, but thriving, government officials often look jealously at the money being made by criminals, and think they are not getting their share. In countries that are considering the legalization of prostitution, the estimated amount of the future tax revenue is often used to argue for legalization.

Germany legalized brothels and prostitution in 2002. German lawmakers thought they were going to get hundreds of millions of euros in tax revenue. But the newly redefined "business owners" and "freelance staff" in brothels have not been turned into taxpayers. The Federal Audit Office estimates that the government has lost hundreds of millions of euros in unpaid tax revenue from the sex industry. Recently, lawmakers started to look for ways to increase collection of taxes from prostitutes. The state seems to be taking on the role of pimp by harassing prostitutes for not giving them enough money.

Although legalization has resulted in big legal profits for a few, other expected benefits have not materialized. Organized crime groups continue to traffic women and children and run illegal prostitution operations along side the legal businesses. Legalization has not reduced prostitution or trafficking; in fact, both activities increase as a result of men being able to legally buy sex acts and cities attracting foreign male sex tourists.

The promised benefits of legalization for women have not materialized in Germany or the Netherlands. In Germany, legalization was supposed to enable women to get health insurance and retirement benefits, and enable them to join unions, but few women have signed up for benefits or for unions. The reason has to do with the basic nature of prostitution. It is not work; it is not a job like any other. It is abuse and exploitation that women only engage in if forced to or when they have no other options. Even where prostitution is legal, a significant proportion of the women in brothels is trafficked. Women and children controlled by criminals cannot register with an authority or join a union. Women who are making a more or less free choice to be in prostitution do so out of immediate necessity—debt, unemployment, and poverty. They consider resorting to prostitution as a temporary means of making money, and assume as soon as a debt is paid or a certain sum of money is earned for poverty-stricken families, they will go home. They seldom tell friends or relatives how they earn money. They do not want to register with authorities and create a permanent record of being a prostitute.

The Culture

The culture, particular mass media, is playing a large role in normalizing prostitution by portraying prostitution as glamorous or a way to quickly make a lot of money. Within academia, "sex workers" are represented as being empowered, independent, liberated women.

To counter these harmful messages, there is an important role for churches to play in describing the harm of prostitution to women, children, families, and communities. In the United States, the Evangelical Christian churches are increasingly involved in the human rights struggle against sex trafficking and exploitation.

Unfortunately, in the battle against the global sex trade, the voice of moral authority that condemns all forms of sexual exploitation and abuse is being lost. Some churches are compromising on their mission and their vision. For example, in the Czech Republic, there is a government proposal to legalize and regulate prostitution, as a way to combat trafficking. Catholic Bishop Vaclav Maly, the Auxiliary Bishop of Prague, has made a statement in favor of legalization of prostitution. According to a *Radio Praha* report in April 2002, he has given up the moral battle saying, "The chances of eliminating it are practically nil. . . . Under those circumstances, it is better to keep it in check and under control by giving it a legal framework. This is not to say that I approve of brothels—but it seems to me that it would be better to have prostitution take place there—with medical checks-ups and prostitutes paying taxes. It would be the lesser of two evils."

More recently, Bishop Maly has been silent in the legalization debate in Czech Republic, but his original statement is posted on web sites supporting legalization, which gives the impression that the Catholic Church supports legalization. A voice of moral authority in support of human dignity and against the sexual exploitation and abuse of victims of prostitution and trafficking is needed in the Czech Republic. Bishop Maly could be this voice. He has a long history of supporting human rights. He was an original signer and spokesman for Charter 77, the petition calling for the communist government of Czechoslovakia to comply with international human rights agreements they had signed. He knows the importance of resisting abusive power and laws that enslave people instead of freeing them.

Faith communities, from the grassroots to the leadership, need to use their voice of authority to combat the increasing sexual exploitation of victims and its normalization.

Abolitionist Movement

There is a growing abolitionist movement around the world that seeks to provide assistance to victims and hold perpetrators accountable.

In Sweden, beginning in 1999, the purchasing of sexual services became a crime. The new law was passed as part of a new violence against women act that broadened the activities that qualified as criminal acts of violence. With this new approach, "prostitution is considered to be one of the most serious expressions of the oppression of and discrimination against women." The focus of the law is on "the demand" or the behavior of the purchasers of sex acts not the women.

The United States government has adopted an abolitionist approach at the federal level. In 2003, President George W. Bush issued a National Security Presidential Directive. It was the first United States opinion on the link between prostitution and trafficking: "Prostitution and related activities, which are inherently harmful and dehumanizing, contribute to the phenomenon of trafficking in persons . . . " This policy statement is important because it connects trafficking to prostitution and states that prostitution is harmful. This policy goes against attempts to delink prostitution and trafficking and redefine prostitution as a form of work for women.

As a result of this abolitionist approach, more attention is being focused on the demand side of sex trafficking. Destination countries, particularly those that legalize prostitution, are coming under new scrutiny.

Conclusion

I believe that only by going to the root causes, which are corruption and the demand in destination countries, will we end the trafficking of women and children.

We need to urge all governments, NGOs, and faith communities to focus on reducing the demand for victims of sex trafficking and prostitution. All the components of the demand need to be penalized—the men who purchase sex acts, the traffickers, the pimps, and others who profit, states that fund deceptive messages and act as pimp, and the culture that lies about the nature of prostitution.

We could greatly reduce the number of victims, if the demand for them was penalized. If there were no men seeking to buy sex acts, no women and children would be bought and sold. If there were no brothels waiting for victims, no victims would be recruited. If there were no states that profited from the sex trade, there would be no regulations that facilitated the flow of women from poor towns to wealthier sex industry centers. If there were no false messages about prostitution, no women or girls would be deceived into thinking prostitution is a glamorous or legitimate job.

DONNA M. HUGHES, PhD, is the Elanor M. and Oscar M. Carlson Endowed Chair at the University of Rhode Island, and is one of the world's leading researchers on human trafficking.

EXPLORING THE ISSUE

Should Prostitution Be Legal?

Critical Thinking and Reflection

1. Distinguish between *legalizing, criminalizing, decriminalizing,* and *regulating* prostitution.
2. What are the pros and cons of legalizing, decriminalizing, and regulating prostitution?
3. Distinguish between the terms *prostitution, sex work,* and *sex trafficking.* Why would advocates prefer to use one of these terms over another?
4. Do people who become involved in prostitution really have a "choice" about it? Explain.
5. Do commercial websites that allow a viewer to pay for a live "partner" to perform sexual acts constitute prostitution? Why or why not?
6. Why are there more female sex workers than male sex workers? Why are male sex workers often ignored in this debate?

Is There Common Ground?

The "oldest profession in the world" exists in most places of the world. What differs are the ways with which it is dealt in the communities where it occurs. These communities consider a variety of issues when trying to determine the legal state of prostitution.

The one major area in which Susan A. Milstein and Donna M. Hughes may agree is in their desire to help women avoid the negative outcomes often associated with commercial sex, such as violence against sex workers and sexually transmitted infections. However, they disagree on the means to avoid these outcomes. Milstein posits that if we are able to move beyond viewing prostitution as immoral or unacceptable, and begin seeing it as an industry, it is easier to understand the benefits of legalizing it. Legalization would lead to mandated STI and HIV testing, and condom use for all sex acts, dramatically reducing the spread of STIs among prostitutes and their nonpaying partners, as well as between clients and their partners. Violence against prostitutes, such as rape, typically comes from their clients, pimps, or the police, and the criminal penalties associated with prostitution often leave the prostitute with no ability to report the violence or take legal recourse against it. Milstein suggests that legalization, as in Nevada, would decrease violence against prostitutes through the installation of panic buttons in rooms and the ability to report violence without fear of arrest. Milstein also suggests that legalizing prostitution would facilitate more drug outreach and education for the prostitutes. Do you think that legalized prostitution would reduce violence against prostitutes and drug addiction among them? How would these protections work if prostitution were to occur outside of the confines of a brothel? How would a street prostitute be safe from violence, or access drug education and outreach? Are there ways to reduce violence and increase drug outreach and education to prostitutes without legalization?

Donna M. Hughes disagrees with proponents of legalized prostitution who argue that prostitution is a sexual choice and people have the right to choose what they do with their bodies. Hughes argues that prostitution is demoralizing, and that prostitutes, the majority of who are women, are not exerting personal choice, but are rather being subjected to criminal assault and kidnapping that arises from the exploitation of people from communities devastated by economic strife. Who do you think is in control in these types of relationships? Are women (and men) simply choosing to express their sexuality in this manner? Are the clients seeking their services exploiting or dehumanizing prostitutes in any way? Do the social, economic, and policy imbalances between men and women in our society influence the context in which the women's choices are being made? Do you think there is a distinction between women who knowingly enter prostitution and those who are forced into it through human trafficking? Do the women who choose to enter prostitution really have a choice? Hughes also posits that women may be coerced into prostitution because they find they have no other options for employment. Does this also stem from societal imbalances? Should we simply accept the lack of other viable jobs for women as an argument for legalized prostitution, or should we strive to create additional opportunities for women and a society where there are less structural imbalances based on sex and gender?

It is evident that the arguments for and against the legalization of prostitution are varied. Where do you stand on the issue? Will legalizing prostitution reduce rates of STIs? Will it lower violence toward prostitutes? Will it financially benefit our communities? Does it represent a core human right to be able to choose how to express one's sexuality? Does prostitution as it exists around the world today represent free choice or coercion? Does it support a patriarchal society?

Create Central

www.mhhe.com/createcentral

Additional Resources

"Craigslist Can't Stop Online Prostitution." Associated Press. *CBS News*, September 6, 2010.

Friess, S. "Brothels Ask to Be Taxed, but Official Sees a Catch," *The New York Times*, January 26, 2009.

Kaplan, K. "Climate Change Causes Prostitution? Rep. Barbara Lee Explains," *Los Angeles Times*, April 30, 2013.

Pearson, E. "Sex-Trafficking Operations Expand Outside of Queens into New York City Suburbs," *New York Daily News*, May 12, 2013.

Internet References . . .

Bound, not Gagged

A blog written by and for sex workers, this website provides an authentic voice and covers issues ranging from legal issues, media representation, sex trafficking, sex worker conventions, and more.

http://deepthroated.wordpress.com/

Children of the Night

This website describes the efforts of an organization dedicated to "rescuing America's children from the ravages of prostitution."

www.childrenofthenight.org

Stella

Stella is a legal support organization started in 1995 in Canada to provide legal and other assistance to sex workers.

www.chezstella.org

The Coalition against Trafficking in Women—International

This international organization focuses on ending sexual exploitation, including the sex trafficking of women and girls.

www.catwinternational.org

The Link between Prostitution and Sex Trafficking

Put out by the U.S. Department of State Bureau of Public Affairs, and reprinted by the Global Network of Sex Works Projects, this document outlines the U.S. government's position against legalized prostitution.

www.nswp.org/resource/fact-sheet-the-link-between-prostitution-and-sex-trafficking

Selected, Edited, and with Issue Framing Material by:
Ryan W. McKee, *Widener University*
and
William J. Taverner, *Center for Family Life Education*

ISSUE

Is Monogamy a More Sustainable Relationship Style than Polyamory?

YES: Jenna Gourdeau, from "What's So Wrong with Monogamy?" (February 13, 2012), www.forbes.com/sites/jennagoudreau/2012/02/13/monogamy-sexual-fidelity-marriage-relationships

NO: Jessica Bennett, from "Only You. And You. And You," *Newsweek* (July 28, 2009), www.thedailybeast.com/newsweek/2009/07/28/only-you-and-you-and-you.html

---

Learning Outcomes

After reading this issue, you should be able to:

- Define monogamy and nonmonogamy.
- Describe several nonmonogamous relationship styles (i.e., open relationships, "swinging," or polyamory).
- Describe the concept of "compersion" as it relates to polyamory.
- Describe some of the social and benefits of monogamous and nonmonogamous relationships.

ISSUE SUMMARY

YES: Jenna Gourdeau, a journalist and speaker on women's leadership, contrasts research and theory on monogamy and open relationship styles. She argues that monogamy is the best way to maintain emotional security and satisfaction in relationships.

NO: Jessica Bennett, a journalist who covers social trends, culture, and women's issues, examines polyamory, which she believes could be a shift in the relationship paradigm. She argues that, while challenging, polyamorous relationships not only can survive, but thrive in modern society.

Marriage is a popular tradition in American culture. More than 2 million Americans are married every year, and 97 percent of adults ages 70 and older have been married. Worldwide, 89 percent of people get married before age 49. For most, "Until death do us part" is a popular sentiment expressed in their wedding vows, with expectations that their marriage will be a lifelong romantic relationship with sexual exclusivity. The reality of American relationships, however, seldom matches these expectations. Pre-marital sex is common, despite the promotion of abstinence-only education. Divorce, remarriage, and serial monogamy (having one partner after another) are more common than lifelong sexual exclusivity to one spouse. And for those who do remain married, a portion will experience periods of known or unknown infidelity.

These challenges to the traditional ideal of marriage may be enough to make you rethink the sustainability of monogamous relationships. Indeed, for a new generation of people embracing the idea of nonmonogamy, it has. While many consider themselves to be nonmonogamous while dating, the appeal of sexual or romantic "in-exclusivity" is becoming more popular among committed couples. Relationships that are committed but nonmonogamous can take many forms and are known by many names. The term *open relationship* is often used to describe them, but there are many different relationship styles that can occur.

Some committed couples open their relationships for occasional sexual experiences with others. Sometimes, but not always, these couples consider themselves to be part of the "Swinger" community. Others eschew labels and simply enjoy an occasional hook-up with another person. "Polyamorous" is a term used to describe those who engage in romantic, loving, and often (but not always) sexual relationships with more than one partner. Those who practice polyamory may have a "primary" partner, with whom the relationship is centered around, as well as "secondary," "tertiary," or even more partners whom they also date. In some cases, those in a polyamorous relationship may form a group relationship. In other cases, a person's primary, secondary, or tertiary partners may not interact. There are many different ways to structure relationships when one embraces nonmonogamy.

The concept of a committed, but sexually in-exclusive relationship, is not new. In fact, some evolutionary anthropologists and psychologists argue that nonmonogamy may be the "natural" relationship status of humans. In their book *Sex at Dawn,* Christopher Ryan and Cacilda Jetha, argue that, like our close genetic relative the bonobo ape, human sexual relationships are naturally egalitarian and non-exclusive. As societies grew larger and more complex, sex and relationships became tied to economic stability. Egalitarian hunter-gatherer cultures gave way to patriarchal societies in which men had multiple wives. Eventually, western religious leaders and politicians began supporting the idea of sexually exclusive monogamy as the highest level of social evolution, and the only acceptable form of marriage. However, history and anthropology indicate that each human society adapts the structure of marriage to meet its particular social environment, with its varied economic, political, and religious needs. When this environment changes, whether rapidly or slowly, the structure of relationships and marriage changes as well.

The twentieth and twenty-first centuries have certainly seen their share of social, economic, and political changes. These shifts may be causing many to rethink the structure of their sexual and romantic relationships. Many are experimenting with alternatives to traditional monogamy in hopes of finding intimacy, pleasure, love, and happiness. But can a person really experience close, intimate bonds with multiple partners in an open relationship? Could one raise a family in a polyamorous household? Is sexually monogamous marriage still a realistic relationship style in today's world? In the following selections, Jenna Gourdeau examines the increasing popularity of nonmonogamy, as well as research on the benefits of monogamous marriage. She concludes that monogamy is the relationship structure in which emotional security and satisfaction are most likely to thrive. Jessica Bennett finds that polyamory can be a successful relationship and family structure. The freedom, intimacy, and communication necessary in nonmonogamous relationships, she argues, allow for a person's emotional and sexual needs to be safely met by several partners.

YES ⬅

Jenna Gourdeau

What's So Wrong with Monogamy?

I must have my rose-colored glasses on again.

The city streets are painted red and pink, and the windows dressed for love. Yet this year as Valentine's Day approaches, with its standard fare of flowers, chocolates and candlelit romance, quite another sentiment looms. Increasingly, people are asking the question: First comes love, then comes marriage, then comes a lifetime of fulfilling fidelity?

It's not too surprising that monogamy is under the microscope. Divorce rates have skyrocketed, marriage is on the decline, and there's no end of cheating scandals among the power and political elite. Last summer, the *New York Times* magazine devoted nearly 6,000 words to sex-advice columnist Dan Savage's belief that monogamy is harder than we admit and may not work for many couples. And this year the news of Newt Gingrich's alleged request for an open marriage with his second wife Marianne brought the concept of sexual openness back to the forefront, so much so that the *Times* style section questioned whether open marriage is showing signs of a second life.

Meanwhile, researchers are increasingly investigating the institution of love, and many may be unsettled by their conclusions. In his new book *The Monogamy Gap: Men, Love, and the Reality of Cheating*, sociologist Eric Anderson argues that "monogamy fails both men and women" and believes we need to have more honest conversations about love and sex.

Is monogamy unattainable? I decided to dig into the institution's biological and cultural history, and take a closer look at the arguments for and against our romantic ideal.

Monogamy. "Mono" means one, and "gamy" means spouse. "It does not mean sexual fidelity," says biological anthropologist Helen Fisher, a professor at Rutgers University in New York and author of several works on monogamy. Humans are among just 3% of mammals that form pair bonds, she says. Species like beetles, beavers and most birds share the instinct to partner up to rear their young.

It is a reproductive strategy, which Fisher posits evolved in humans because they walked upright. Unlike chimpanzees who carried their young on their backs, a human woman carried a child in her arms and thus likely desired a mate to protect and provide for her. Fisher notes that today, divorce commonly occurs in the fourth year of marriage, or about the length of human infancy. "Maybe a woman needed a man to raise a child through infancy," she speculates.

Human pair-bonding is not a new or negative trend. Fisher points to a recent fossil discovery that suggests partnering had already evolved some 4.4 million years ago. Committing to one person also has a host of social advantages. Research shows that monogamous marriage has been culturally favored for its "group-beneficial effects," namely decreasing crime rates (including rape, murder, assault, robbery, fraud and personal abuses), the spousal age gap, fertility and gender inequality. The theory goes that by shifting male attention from "seeking wives" (polygamy) to "paternal investment," monogamy boosts child investment and economic productivity and reduces household conflict and child neglect.

However, this definition doesn't include fidelity. "We've never found a species that's sexually faithful," Fisher says. In fact, she believes humans developed a dual-reproductive strategy, in which cheating had benefits too. It created more variety in the woman's family line, doubled a man's potential offspring, and served as an insurance policy against a spouse's death. "Through millions of years of both strategies, what we have today is a tremendous drive for social monogamy and also a drive to cheat."

Cue Anderson's controversial thesis that by-and-large sexual monogamy doesn't work. The American sociologist and professor of gender and sexuality at The University of Winchester in England reviewed existing research on love, sex and cheating and also interviewed 120 undergraduate men. Some 78% of the pool had cheated on their partners, which Anderson defines as a sexual interaction that would make the other person uncomfortable.

He believes that because we live in a "pornified culture," in which pornography is widely available, sexual experience begins at an earlier age and sex is easier to obtain, monogamy is becoming more and more difficult to uphold.

Essentially, he says today's young people will become habituated (bored) with their partner faster and experience an increased desire to seek sex with others. Anderson speaks of technology as a new gateway to cheating, insisting that easy exposure to pornography reduces the interest in and frequency of sex with a partner and can quickly lead to cyber sex and 3-D affairs. Website AshleyMadison connects individuals looking for an affair and currently counts 12.7 million members.

Anderson doesn't view the increased availability of sex as a problem. Instead, he sees the "restriction of sex to one person," what I'd call "faithfulness," as the issue. "It's a morality stance, and without evidence, that having sex with others hinders your primary relationship," he says. "The men I interviewed say 'cheating is proof that I love her—if I wasn't in love with her, I'd leave her.'"

"The real question is," Anderson poses, "Is our desire for monogamy serving our culture as best as it can?" He says no, and suggests we remove the stigma from open relationships in order to save partnerships. Then, he believes men and women would be more comfortable asking for what they "need," they'd be more likely to use protection with others, and relationships would be less likely to end over a "slip up."

Intellectually, it's a compelling perspective. But, be it my naiveté or six-year long (and counting) fulfilling relationship, I'm not convinced. Here's why.

Anderson interviewed a small, rarified group—unmarried, young men in a narrow demographic—that were chosen specifically for their increased opportunity to cheat. (His research on women is in progress.) He even admits that sexual fidelity is the best protection against sexually transmitted diseases and unwanted pregnancies. Besides health and financial concerns, both would at least complicate, and probably damage, the partnership.

Monogamy is likely the best way to maintain the emotional security and satisfaction in the primary relationship. "Open relationships have been tried for centuries and do not work for most people," says Fisher. "They're being decent by not wanting to sneak around, but they spend a huge amount of time discussing their jealousies. The human brain is not well built for sharing."

To this point, many men in Anderson's study expressed a desire to openly have sex with others, but they refused to consider allowing their partners the same freedom, saying they would be too jealous. Anderson argues that monogamy enforces "jealousy scripts," which fade over time in open relationships.

Sex with others is also certain to create emotional attachments that undermine the primary relationship—and the dignity of others. Logically, it would increase the likelihood of infatuation, and thus increase the chance of leaving the primary relationship. Anderson says the (cheating) men he interviewed said, "I wanted her and then I had her and now I'm over her"—that it's just a "matter of business." While exceedingly unromantic, these sentiments don't even consider the "her" that's been "had." The potential for hurt feelings and unkindness seems astronomic.

Furthermore, even if humans *want* sex with multiple people it doesn't mean they need it or that it's in their best interests. Let's be honest: Some weeks my desire to sit by a pool and eat brownies all day is incredibly strong. However, I ultimately conclude that the resulting fatness, sunburn and job loss [aren't] worth it. Blindly following our animal desires may lead to ills like obesity, excessive drug use and debt crises. When I point this out to Anderson, he counters that a person can satisfy their craving for a hamburger by balancing it out with a salad the next day. Of course, one can also have sex *with their partner*.

Finally, the argument that men will inevitably cheat is insulting at best. "We're all spending our lives balancing these drives," says Fisher. "There are an awful lot of myths about men in America." Surveys show that men are more romantic than we give them credit for. They're generally quicker to fall in love than women, the first to say "I love you," and more likely to express the desire for a family. Women, too, are more sexual than often believed. In a recent survey, 75% of married women said sex is "very important" to them.

I believe for most people, monogamy will likely reinforce the relationship, and research shows that good marriages boost your health and happiness and add years to your life. "I wouldn't be surprised that men in these long-term commitments have come to terms with their relationships and see the payoffs of fidelity," agrees Fisher.

Jenna Gourdeau is an associate editor at entrepreneuer .com and is a writer and speaker on women's leadership.

Jessica Bennett

 **NO**

Only You. And You. And You

Terisa Greenan and her boyfriend, Matt, are enjoying a rare day of Seattle sun, sharing a beet carpaccio on the patio of a local restaurant. Matt holds Terisa's hand, as his 6-year-old son squeezes in between the couple to give Terisa a kiss. His mother, Vera, looks over and smiles; she's there with her boyfriend, Larry. Suddenly it starts to rain, and the group must move inside. In the process, they rearrange themselves: Matt's hand touches Vera's leg. Terisa gives Larry a kiss. The child, seemingly unconcerned, puts his arms around his mother and digs into his meal.

Terisa and Matt and Vera and Larry—along with Scott, who's also at this dinner—are not swingers, per se; they aren't pursuing casual sex. Nor are they polygamists of the sort portrayed on HBO's *Big Love*; they aren't religious, and they don't have multiple wives. But they do believe in "ethical nonmonogamy," or engaging in loving, intimate relationships with more than one person—based upon the knowledge and consent of everyone involved. They are polyamorous, to use the term of art applied to multiple-partner families like theirs, and they wouldn't want to live any other way.

Terisa, 41, is at the center of this particular polyamorous cluster. A filmmaker and actress, she is well-spoken, slender and attractive, with dark, shoulder-length hair, porcelain skin—and a powerful need for attention. Twelve years ago, she started dating Scott, a writer and classical-album merchant. A couple years later, Scott introduced her to Larry, a software developer at Microsoft, and the two quickly fell in love, with Scott's assent. The three have been living together for a decade now, but continue to date others casually on the side. Recently, Terisa decided to add Matt, a London transplant to Seattle, to the mix. Matt's wife, Vera, was OK with that; soon, she was dating Terisa's husband, Larry. If Scott starts feeling neglected, he can call the woman he's been dating casually on the side. Everyone in this group is heterosexual, and they insist they never sleep with more than one person at a time.

It's enough to make any monogamist's head spin. But traditionalists had better get used to it.

Researchers are just beginning to study the phenomenon, but the few who do estimate that openly polyamorous families in the United States number more than half a million, with thriving contingents in nearly every major city. Over the past year, books like *Open*, by journalist Jenny Block; *Opening Up*, by sex columnist Tristan Taormino; and an updated version of *The Ethical Slut*—

widely considered the modern "poly" Bible—have helped publicize the concept. Today there are poly blogs and podcasts, local get-togethers, and an online polyamory magazine called Loving More with 15,000 regular readers. Celebrities like actress Tilda Swinton and Carla Bruni, the first lady of France, have voiced support for nonmonogamy, while Greenan herself has become somewhat of an unofficial spokesperson, as the creator of a comic Web series about the practice—called "Family"—that's loosely based on her life. "There have always been some loudmouthed ironclads talking about the labors of monogamy and multiple-partner relationships," says Ken Haslam, a retired anesthesiologist who curates a polyamory library at the Indiana University-based Kinsey Institute for Research in Sex, Gender and Reproduction. "But finally, with the Internet, the thing has really come about."

With polyamorists' higher profile has come some growing pains. The majority of them don't seem particularly interested in pressing a political agenda; the joke in the community is that the complexities of their relationships leave little time for activism. But they are beginning to show up on the radar screen of the religious right, some of whose leaders have publicly condemned polyamory as one of a host of deviant behaviors sure to become normalized if gay marriage wins federal sanction. "This group is really rising up from the underground, emboldened by the success of the gay-marriage movement," says Glenn Stanton, the director of family studies for Focus on the Family, an evangelical Christian group. "And while there's part of me that says, 'Oh, my goodness, I don't think I could see them make grounds,' there's another part of me that says, 'Well, just watch them.'"

Conservatives are not alone in watching warily. Gay-marriage advocates have become leery of public association with the poly cause—lest it give their enemies ammunition. As Andrew Sullivan, the *Atlantic* columnist, wrote recently, "I believe that someone's sexual orientation is a deeper issue than the number of people they want to express that orientation with." In other words, polyamory is a choice; homosexuality is not. It's these dynamics that have made polyamory, as longtime poly advocate Anita Wagner puts it, "the political football in the culture war as it relates to same-sex marriage."

Polys themselves are not visibly crusading for their civil rights. But there is one policy issue rousing concern: legal precedents concerning their ability to parent. Custody battles among poly parents are not uncommon; the most public of them was a 1999 case in which a 22-year-old Tennessee woman lost rights to parent her daughter after outing herself on an MTV documentary. Anecdotally, research shows that children can do well in poly families—as long as they're in a stable home with loving parents, says Elisabeth Sheff, a sociologist at Georgia State University, who is conducting the first large-scale study of children of poly parents, which has been ongoing for a decade. But because academia is only beginning to study the phenomenon—Sheff's study is too recent to have drawn conclusions about the children's well-being over time—there is little data to support that notion in court. Today, the nonprofit Polyamory Society posts a warning to parents on its Web site: *If your PolyFamily has children, please do not put your children and family at risk by coming out to the public or by being interviewed [by] the press!*

The notion of multiple-partner relationships is as old as the human race itself. But polyamorists trace the foundation of their movement to the utopian Oneida commune of upstate New York, founded in 1848 by Yale theologian John Humphrey Noyes. Noyes believed in a kind of communalism he hoped would fix relations between men and women; both genders had equal voice in community governance, and every man was considered to be married to every woman. But it wasn't until the late-1960s and 1970s "free love" movement that polyamory truly came into vogue; when books like *Open Marriage* topped best-seller lists and groups like the North American Swingers Club began experimenting with the concept. The term "polyamory," coined in the 1990s, popped up in both the Merriam-Webster and Oxford English dictionaries in 2006.

Polyamory might sound like heaven to some: a variety of partners, adding spice and a respite from the familiarity and boredom that's doomed many a traditional couple. But humans are hard-wired to be jealous, and though it may be possible to overcome it, polyamorous couples are "fighting Mother Nature" when they try, says biological anthropologist Helen Fisher, a professor at Rutgers University who has long studied the chemistry of love. Polys say they aren't so much denying their biological instincts as insisting they can work around them—through open communication, patience, and honesty. Polys call this process "compersion"—or learning to find personal fulfillment in the emotional and sexual satisfaction of your partner, even if you're not the one doing the satisfying. "It's about making sure that *everybody's* needs are met, including your own," says Terisa. "And that's not always easy, but it's part of the fun."

It's complicated, to say the least: tending to the needs of multiple partners, figuring out what to tell the kids, making sure that nobody's feelings are hurt. "I like to call it poly*agony*," jokes Haslam, the Kinsey researcher, who is himself polyamorous. "It works for some perfectly, and for others it's a f--king disaster." Some polyamorists are married with multiple love interests, while others practice informal group marriage. Some have group sex—and many are bisexual—while those like Greenan have a series of hetero-

sexual, one-on-one relationships. Still others don't identify as poly but live a recognizably poly lifestyle. Terisa describes her particular cluster as a "triad," for the number of people involved, and a "vee" for its organization, with Terisa at the center (the point of the V) and her two primary partners, Scott and Larry (who are not intimate with each other) as the tips of each arm. Other poly vocabulary exists, too: "spice" is the plural of "spouse"; "polygeometry" is how a polyamorous group describes their connections; "polyfidelitous" refers to folks who don't date outside their menage; and a "quad" is a four-member poly group.

It's easy to dismiss polyamory as a kind of frat-house fantasy gone wild. But in truth, the community has a decidedly feminist bent: women have been central to its creation, and "gender equality" is a publicly recognized tenet of the practice. Terisa herself is proof of that proposition, as the center of her cluster. She, Scott, and Larry have all been polyamorous since meeting in the Bay Area in the '90s, where they were all involved with the same theater community.

Terisa and Scott started dating first. Both were getting out of long-term monogamous relationships—Terisa had been married for six years—and knew they wanted something different. They fell in love, and though they were committed, they began dating around. Two years in, Scott introduced her to Larry, a pit violinist and mutual acquaintance. When Larry was offered the Microsoft job in Seattle, he asked Terisa and Scott to go with him. "We were like, 'Wow, are we really going to do this?' Terisa remembers. 'And we sort of just said, 'Well let's jump in!"

It wasn't long before they realized there was a thriving community of Seattleites living the same way. There were local outings, monthly poly potlucks, and a Sea-Poly e-mail list that served to keep everyone informed. Larry even found a poly club for Microsoft employees—listed openly on the company's internal Web site. (Microsoft declined to comment on the message board, or whether it still exists.) The trio has been together ever since, and they share a lakeside home in Seattle's Mt. Baker neighborhood, where they have a vegetable garden and three dogs. They often go on walks along the lake, hand in hand in hand. "I think if we were all given a choice, everyone would choose some form of open relationship," Scott explains, sitting in the family's hillside gazebo overlooking Lake Washington. "And I just like variety," Terisa chimes in, laughing. "I get bored!"

The trio have had emotional moments. Scott had a hard time the first time he heard Larry called Terisa "sweetie" nine years ago. Larry was nervous when Terisa began semiseriously dating somebody outside the group. There are times when Scott has had to put up with hearing his girlfriend have sex with someone else in the home they share. And there have been moments when each of them [has] felt neglected in their own way. But they agreed early on that they weren't going to be sexually monogamous, and they are open about their affairs. "So it's not as if anybody is betraying anybody else's trust," says Larry.

There are, of course, some things that are personal. "Terisa doesn't tell me a lot of the private stuff between her and Matt, and I respect that," says Scott. When there are twinges of jealousy, they talk them out—by getting to the root of what's causing the feeling. "It's one of those things that sounds really basic, but I think a lot of people in conventional relationships don't take the time to actually tell their partner when they're feeling dissatisfied in some way," says Terisa. "And sometimes it's as simple as saying, 'Hey, Larry,' or 'Hey, Scott, I really want to have dinner alone with you tonight—I'm feeling neglected.' We really don't let anything go unsaid." As Haslam puts it: "It's all very straight forward if everybody is just honest about what's going on in their brains—and between their legs."

Larry and Terisa married last year—with Scott's permission—in part for tax purposes. Larry owns the house they all live in, and Scott pays rent. Household expenses require a complicated spreadsheet. Terisa, Larry, and Scott all have their own bedrooms, but sleeping arrangements must be discussed. Larry snores, so Terisa spends most nights with Scott—which means she must be mindful of making up for lost time with Larry. Terisa and Larry only recently began dating Matt and Vera, after meeting on Facebook, and now every Friday, the couple bring their son over to the house and the three of them stay all weekend. Matt will usually sleep with Terisa, and Vera with Larry, or they'll switch it up, depending on how everyone feels.

The child, meanwhile, has his own room. And he's clearly the most delicate part of the equation. Matt and Vera have asked NEWSWEEK not to use their last names— or the name of their child—for fear, even in liberal Seattle, they might draw unwanted attention. Though Terisa doesn't have children—and doesn't want them—she adores Matt and Vera's son, who calls her Auntie. Recently, the child asked his father who he loved more: Mommy or

Terisa. "I said, 'Of course I love momma more,' because that's the answer he needed to hear," Matt says. He and Vera say they are honest with him, in an age-appropriate way. "We don't do anything any regular parents of a 6-year-old wouldn't do," he says. For the moment, it seems to be working. The child is happy, and there are two extra people to help him with his homework, or to pick him up or drop him off at school. They expect the questions to increase with age, but in the long run, "what's healthy for children is stability," says Fischer, the anthropologist.

It's a new paradigm, certainly—and it does break some rules. "Polyamory scares people—it shakes up their world view," says Allena Gabosch, the director of the Seattle-based Center for Sex Positive Culture. But perhaps the practice is more natural than we think: a response to the challenges of monogamous relationships, whose shortcomings—in a culture where divorce has become a commonplace—are clear. Everyone in a relationship wrestles at some point with an eternal question: *can one person really satisfy every need?* Polyamorists think the answer is obvious—and that it's only a matter of time before the monogamous world sees there's more than one way to live and love. "The people I feel sorry for are the ones who don't ever realize they have any other choices beyond the traditional options society presents," says Scott. "To look at an option like polyamory and say 'That's not for me' is fine. To look at it and not realize you can choose it is just sad."

JESSICA BENNETT is a freelance journalist and an editor for LeanIn.org. Formerly, she was a senior writer and editor at *Newsweek* and the *Daily Beast,* covering social trends, culture, and women's issues.

EXPLORING THE ISSUE

Is Monogamy a More Sustainable Relationship Style than Polyamory?

Critical Thinking and Reflection

1. What modern social and economic factors may be causing people to reconsider sexually monogamous marriage as a viable relationship style?
2. What are the social, health, and economic benefits of monogamy and monogamous marriage?
3. What might the challenges be to a sexually exclusive, lifetime, monogamous relationship?
4. What are the benefits and challenges of sexually or emotionally nonmonogamous relationships?
5. What role might jealousy play in nonmonogamous relationships? How might the practice of "compersion" counteract feelings of jealousy?

Is There Common Ground?

For 2,000 years proponents of sexual exclusivity have cited ducks, swans, and other animals that mate for life and are sexually faithful as models of the true nature of marriage. However, biologists have recently used DNA "fingerprinting" to prove that most animal species assumed to be monogamous do not live up to those expectations. For example, when scientists checked the DNA of the offspring of a variety of birds against the DNA of the mothers' mates, they found that about one-third of the offspring were fathered by birds other than the mates.

Considering all the species that engage in sex outside the pair-bond, can we ask whether the natural selection processes of evolution might have given humans a gene that makes us inclined toward monogamous behavior? Or are we hard-wired for non-monogamy? Is monogamy a choice?

Gourdeau implies that, while humans may have evolved as nonmonogamous beings, monogamy has allowed us to thrive as a species. She cites numerous health and relationship benefits to monogamy as proof. Do you agree that monogamy is the healthiest and most sustainable long-term relationship style? Bennett argues that sexual exclusivity is, and has always been, a challenge for humans. Rather than denying our nature, she proposes, we should restructure our relationships in ways that allow us to be more authentic. Do you think open relationships are sustainable in the long

term? Could polyamory become the norm in American society? What changes in American society over the last century might have led a reevaluation of monogamy as a cultural ideal? To what extent can and should we adapt our style or styles of marriage to radical changes in the social, economic, and political environment?

Create Central

www.mhhe.com/createcentral

Additional Resources

Anapol, D.T. "Mixed Marriages: Polyamory vs. Monogamy," *The Canadian National Newspaper*, November 8, 2011.

Anderson, E. (2011). *The Monogamy Gap: Men, Loving, and the Reality of Cheating.* New York, NY: Oxford University Press.

Antalffy, N. (2011). "Polyamory and the Media," *Journal of Media Arts Culture*, 8(11).

Oppenheimer, M. (2011). "Married, with Infidelities," *New York Times Magazine,* June 30, 2011.

Ryan, C. & Jetha, C. (2010). *Sex at Dawn: How We Mate, Why We Stray, and What It Means for Modern Relationships.* New York, NY: Harper.

Internet References . . .

5 Myths about Polyamory Debunked

This article, by Stephanie Pappas, challenges common assumptions about polyamory.

www.livescience.com/27128-polyamory-myths-debunked.html

Loving More

A nonprofit organization in support of polyamory and relationship choices.

www.lovemore.com

Number, Timing, and Duration of Marriage and Divorces: 2009

A summary report by the U.S. Census of the most recent data available on marriage and divorce.

www.census.gov/prod/2011pubs/p70-125.pdf

Why Neither Monogamy nor Polyamory Are More Natural

This article explores the monogamy/polyamory debate, and exposes flaws in each argument.

www.mindfulconstruct.com/2009/02/14/why-neither-monogamy-nor-polyamory-are-more-natural

Selected, Edited, and with Issue Framing Material by:
Ryan W. McKee, *Widener University*
and
William J. Taverner, *Center for Family Life Education*

ISSUE

Is There a Valid Reason for Routine Infant Male Circumcision?

YES: Hanna Rosin, from "The Case Against the Case Against Circumcision; Why One Mother Heard All of the Opposing Arguments, Then Circumcised Her Sons Anyway," *New York Magazine* (October 26, 2009)

NO: Michael Idov, from "Would You Circumcise This Baby? Why a Growing Number of Parents, Especially in New York and Other Cities, Are Saying No to the Procedure," *New York Magazine* (October 26, 2009)

Learning Outcomes

After reading this issue, you should be able to:

- Explain the cultural importance of circumcision rituals throughout history.
- Explain the decline in male circumcision rates in the United States.
- Describe the impact circumcision may or may not have on the transmission of HIV and other sexually transmitted infections.
- Describe the potential sexual side effects of male circumcision.

ISSUE SUMMARY

YES: Hanna Rosin, author of *The End of Men* and senior editor at *The Atlantic,* describes the public health benefits of male circumcision. As a mother who had her sons circumcised, she states that, though the practice seems "barbaric," it is a procedure she supports.

NO: Michael Idov, a novelist and contributing editor at *New York Magazine,* explores the history of circumcision and explains why a movement to end the practice is gaining popularity.

Circumcision, a practice in which the foreskin of the penis is cut and removed to expose the glans, is one of the most common surgical procedures in the United States. It is typically performed when a child is an infant, and it is carried out for a variety of reasons. Jewish parents, as well as those who practice a number of other religious traditions, perform the procedure as a religious rite. For some, there are presumed health benefits that make the practice worthwhile. Several studies have shown that circumcision reduces the risk of urinary tract and sexually transmitted infections, including HIV. Other parents simply do it because the child's father was circumcised.

Despite these reasons, the number of newborn males being circumcised in the United States is declining. Many parents choosing not to circumcise their sons have begun to question the perceived health benefits, pointing to inconclusive studies on the procedure. They question if the practice is really necessary in contemporary society. These questions, combined with the pain felt by infants during the surgery and recovery, have caused some to not

only question the necessity, but also to argue that the practice is a violation of a child's human rights. Many of these anti-circumcision activists compare male circumcision to the practice of female genital mutilation (FGM), sometimes called female circumcision, which is condemned by organizations like the World Health Organization. While FGM can vary in severity from culture to culture, the practice often involves cutting genital tissue like the clitoris from infant or adolescent girls as a religious or cultural ritual. Both FGM and male circumcision, opponents argue, are based on tradition and religious belief rather than medical science.

Though circumcision is still widely accepted, opponents have made great strides in raising awareness about their stance on the issue. In 2012, anti-circumcision activists in San Francisco, California, succeeded in placing a measure on the ballot for the November elections. Passage of the ballot would have banned male circumcision within the city, and imposed fines or even jail sentences on doctors who performed the procedure. The measure was widely criticized by the medical and religious communities. To ban the procedure outright, medical groups argued, could pose risks to public health and infringe upon a family's right to make medical decisions for their children. Members of the Jewish community, along with other religious groups and the American Civil Liberties Union, argued that a ban would infringe on religious freedom. Many considered the measure an outright expression of anti-Semitism, pointing to Internet comics featuring an anti-circumcision super hero named "Foreskin Man." In one comic the caped crusader, with blonde hair and blue eyes, "rescued" Jewish infants from Jewish rabbis who were drawn as "sinister-looking" villains (1). Several groups, including the Anti-Defamation League, sued the government to have the measure stricken from the ballot.

In July 2012, several months before the November elections, a Superior Court Judge did just that, removing the measure and noting that the regulation of medical services falls to the state, rather than individual cities. Despite the setback, anti-circumcision advocates promised to continue their efforts. While they have had little success in stopping the practice through legal means, circumcision rates continue to fall, indicating that there is, indeed, an evolving view of the practice.

Adding to the conversation, Hanna Rosin describes research pointing to the public health benefits of routine male circumcision. She remarks on the conflict she felt when having her own sons circumcised, but states that any temporary pain felt is worth the future health benefits. Michael Idov provides a historical perspective on male circumcision and explains why shifts in cultural and religious norms have led to a decline in the popularity of the procedure.

YES

Hanna Rosin

The Case Against the Case Against Circumcision; Why One Mother Heard All of the Opposing Arguments, Then Circumcised Her Sons Anyway

Anyone with a heart would agree that the Jewish bris is a barbaric event. Grown-ups sit chatting politely, wiping the cream cheese off their lips, while some religious guy with minimal medical training prepares to slice up a new-born's penis. The helpless thing wakes up from a womb-slumber howling with pain. I felt near hysterical at both of my sons' brisses. Pumped up with newmother hormones, I dug my nails into my palms to keep from clawing the rabbi. For a few days afterward, I cursed my God and everyone else for creating the bloody mess in the diaper. But then the penis healed and assumed its familiar heart shape and I promptly forgot about the whole trauma. Apparently some people never do.

I am Jewish enough that I never considered not circumcising my sons. I did not search the web or call a panel of doctors to fact-check the health benefits, as a growing number of wary Americans now do. Despite my momentary panic, the words "genital mutilation" did not enter my head. But now that I have done my homework, I'm sure I would do it again—even if I were not Jewish, didn't believe in ritual, and judged only by cold, secular science.

Every year, it seems, a new study confirms that the foreskin is pretty much like the appendix or the wisdom tooth—it is an evolutionary footnote that serves no purpose other than to incubate infections. There's no single overwhelming health reason to remove it, but there are a lot of smaller health reasons that add up. It's not critical that any individual boy get circumcised. For the growing number of people who feel hysterical at the thought, just don't do it. But don't ruin it for the rest of us. It's perfectly clear that on a grand public-health level, the more boys who get circumcised, the better it is for everyone.

Twenty years ago, this would have been a boring, obvious thing to say, like feed your baby rice cereal before bananas, or don't smoke while pregnant. These days, in certain newly enlightened circles on the East and West Coasts, it puts you in league with Josef Mengele. Late this summer, when *The New York Times* reported that the U.S. Centers for Disease Control might consider promoting routine circumcision as a tool in the fight against AIDS, the vicious comments that ensued included references to mass genocide.

There's no use arguing with the anti-circ activists, who only got through the headline of this story before hunting down my e-mail and offering to pay for me to be genitally mutilated. But for those in the nervous middle, here is my best case for why you should do it. Biologists think the foreskin plays a critical role in the womb, protecting the penis as it is growing during the third month of gestation. Outside the womb, the best guess is that it once kept the penis safe from, say, low-hanging thorny branches. Nowadays, we have pants for that.

Circumcision dates back some 6,000 years and was mostly associated with religious rituals, especially for Jews and Muslims. In the nineteenth century, moralists concocted some unfortunate theories about the connection between the foreskin and masturbation and other such degenerate impulses. The genuinely useful medical rationales came later. During the World War II campaign in North Africa, tens of thousands of American GIs fell short on their hygiene routines. Many of them came down with a host of painful and annoying infections, such as phimosis, where the foreskin gets too tight to retract over the glans. Doctors already knew about the connection to sexually transmitted diseases and began recommending routine circumcision.

In the late eighties, researchers began to suspect a relationship between circumcision and transmission of HIV, the virus that causes AIDS. One researcher wondered why certain Kenyan men who see prostitutes get infected and others don't. The answer, it turned out, was that the ones who don't were circumcised. Three separate trials in Uganda, Kenya, and South Africa involving over 10,000 men turned up the same finding again and again. Circumcision, it turns out, could reduce the risk of HIV transmission by at least 60 percent, which, in Africa, adds up to 3 million lives saved over the next twenty years. The governments of Uganda and Kenya recently started mass-circumcision campaigns.

These studies are not entirely relevant to the U.S. They apply only to female-to-male transmission, which is relatively rare here. But the results are so dramatic that people who work in AIDS prevention can't ignore them. Daniel Halperin, an AIDS expert at the Harvard School of Public Health, has compared various countries, and the patterns are obvious. In a study of 28 nations, he found that low circumcision rates (fewer than 20 percent) match up with high HIV rates, and vice versa. Similar patterns are turning up in the U.S. as well. A team of researchers from the CDC and Johns Hopkins analyzed records of over 26,000 heterosexual African-American men who showed up at a Baltimore clinic for HIV testing and denied any drug use or homosexual contact. Among those with known HIV exposure, the ones who did turn out to be HIV-positive were twice as likely to be uncircumcised. There's no causal relationship here; foreskin does not cause HIV transmission. But researchers guess that foreskins are more susceptible to sores, and also have a high concentration of certain immune cells that are the main portals for HIV infection.

Then there are a host of other diseases that range from rare and deadly to ruin your life to annoying. Australian physicians give a decent summary: "STIs such as carcinogenic types of human papillomavirus (HPV), genital herpes, HIV, syphilis and chancroid, thrush, cancer of the penis, and most likely cancer of the prostate, phimosis, paraphimosis, inflammatory skin conditions such as balanoposthitis, inferior hygiene, sexual problems, especially with age and diabetes, and, in the female partners, HPV, cervical cancer, HSV-2, and chlamydia, which is an important cause of infertility." The percentages vary in each case, but it's clear that the foreskin is a public-health menace.

Edgar Schoen, now a professor emeritus of pediatrics at the University of California San Francisco, has been pushing the pro-circumcision case since 1989, when he chaired an American Academy of Pediatrics Task Force on the practice. The committee later found insufficient evidence to recommend routine circumcision, but to Schoen, this is the "narrow thinking of neonatologists" who sit on the panels. All they see is a screaming baby, not a lifetime of complications. In the meantime, sixteen states have eliminated Medicaid coverage for circumcision, causing the rates among Hispanics, for one, to plummet. For Schoen and Halperin and others, this issue has become primarily a question of "health-care parity for the poor." The people whom circumcision could help the most are now the least likely to get it.

This mundane march of health statistics has a hard time competing with the opposite side, which is fighting for something they see as fundamental: a right not to be messed with, a freedom from control, and a general sense of wholeness. For many circumcision opponents,

preventive surgery is a bizarre, dystopian disruption. I can only say that in public health, preventive surgery is pretty common—appendix and wisdom teeth, for example. "If we could remove the appendix in a three- or four-minute operation without cutting into the abdomen, we would," says Schoen. Anesthesia is routine now, so the infants don't suffer the way they used to. My babies didn't seem to howl more than they did in their early vaccines, particularly the one where they "milk" the heel for blood.

Sexual pleasure comes up a lot. Opponents of circumcision often mention studies of "penile sensitivity regions," showing the foreskin to be the most sensitive. But erotic experience is a rich and complicated affair, and surely can't be summed up by nerve endings or friction or "sensitivity regions." More nuanced studies have shown that men who were circumcised as adults report a decrease in sexual satisfaction when they were forced into it, because of an illness, and an increase when they did it of their own will. In a study of Kenyan men who volunteered for circumcision, 64 percent reported their penis to be "much more sensitive" and their ease of reaching orgasm much greater two years after the operation. In a similar study, Ugandan women reported a 40 percent increase in sexual satisfaction after their partners were circumcised. Go figure. Surely this is more psychology than science.

People who oppose circumcision are animated by a kind of rage and longing that seems larger than the thing itself. Websites are filled with testimonies from men who believe their lives were ruined by the operation they had as an infant. I can only conclude that it wasn't the cutting alone that did the ruining. An East Bay doctor who came out for circumcision recently wrote about having visions of tiny foreskins rising up in revenge at him, clogging the freeways. I see what he means. The foreskin is the new fetus—the object that has been imbued with magical powers to halt a merciless, violent world—a world that is particularly callous to children. The notion resonates in a moment when parents are especially overprotective, and fantasy death panels loom. It's all very visual and compelling—like the sight of your own newborn son with the scalpel looming over him. But it isn't the whole truth.

HANNA ROSIN, author of the book *The End of Men,* is a senior editor at *The Atlantic,* and the founder and editor of *DoubleX.*

Michael Idov

 **NO**

Would You Circumcise This Baby? Why a Growing Number of Parents, Especially in New York and Other Cities, Are Saying No to the Procedure

To cut or not to cut. The choice loomed the moment New Yorkers Rob and Deanna Morea found out, three months into Deanna's pregnancy, that their first child was going to be a boy. Both had grown up with the view of circumcision as something automatic, like severing the umbilical cord. To Rob—white, Catholic, and circumcised—an intact foreskin seemed vaguely un-American. Deanna, African-American and also Catholic, dismissed the parents who don't circumcise their children as a "granola-eating, Birkenstock-wearing type of crowd." But that was before they knew they were having a son.

Circumcision is still, as it has been for decades, one of the most routinely performed surgical procedures in the United States—a million of the operations are performed every year. Yet more Americans are beginning to ask themselves the same question the Moreas did: Why, exactly, are we doing this? Having peaked at a staggering 85 percent in the sixties and seventies, the U.S. newborn-circumcision rate dropped to 65 percent in 1999 and to 56 percent in 2006. Give or take a hiccup here and there, the trend is remarkably clear: Over the past 30 years, the circumcision rate has fallen 30 percent. All evidence suggests that we are nearing the moment (2014?) when the year's crop of circumcised newborns will be in the minority.

Opposition to circumcision isn't new, of course. What is new are the opponents. What was once mostly a fringe movement has been flowing steadily into the mainstream. Today's anti-circumcision crowd are people like the Moreas—people whose religious and ideological passions don't run high either way and who arrive at their decision through a kind of personal cost-benefit analysis involving health concerns, pain, and other factors. At the same time, new evidence that circumcision can help prevent the spread of AIDS, coupled with centuries-old sentiments supporting the practice, are touching off a backlash to the backlash. Lately, arguments pro and con have grown fierce, flaring with the contentious intensity of our time.

The idea of separating the prepuce from the penis is older than the Old Testament. The first depiction of the procedure exists on the walls of an Egyptian tomb built in 2400 B.C.—a relief complete with hieroglyphics that read, "Hold him and do not allow him to faint." The notion appears to have occurred to several disparate cultures, for reasons unknown. "It is far easier to imagine the impulse behind Neolithic cave painting than to guess what inspired the ancients to cut their genitals," writes David L. Gollaher in his definitive tome *Circumcision: A History of the World's Most Controversial Surgery.* One theory suggests that the ritual's original goal was to simply draw blood from the sexual organ—to serve as the male equivalent of menstruation, in other words, and thus a rite of passage into adulthood. The Jews took their enslavers' practice and turned it into a sign of their own covenant with God; 2,000 years later, Muslims followed suit.

Medical concerns didn't enter the picture until the late-nineteenth century, when science began competing with religious belief. America took its first step toward universal secular circumcision, writes Gollaher, on "the rainy morning of February 9, 1870." Lewis Sayre, a leading Manhattan surgeon, was treating an anemic 5-year-old boy with partially paralyzed leg muscles when he noticed that the boy's penis was encased in an unusually tight foreskin, causing chronic pain. Going on intuition, Sayre drove the boy to Bellevue and circumcised him, improvising on the spot with scissors and his fingernails. The boy felt better almost immediately and fully recovered the use of his legs within weeks. Sayre began to perform circumcisions to treat paralysis—and, in at least five cases, his strange inspiration worked. When Sayre published the results in the *Transactions of the American Medical Association,* the floodgates swung open. Before long, surgeons were using circumcision to treat all manner of ailments.

There was another, half-hidden appeal to the procedure. Ever since the twelfth-century Jewish scholar and physician Maimonides, doctors realized that circumcision dulls the sensation in the glans, supposedly discouraging promiscuity. The idea was especially attractive to the Victorians, famously obsessed with the perils of masturbation. From therapeutic circumcision as a cure for insomnia there was only a short step toward circumcision as a way to dull the "out of control" libido.

In the thirties, another argument for routine circumcision presented itself. Research suggested a link between circumcision and reduced risk of penile and cervical cancer. In addition to the obvious health implications, the finding strengthened the idea of the foreskin as unclean. On par with deodorant and a daily shower, circumcision became a means of assimilating the immigrant and urbanizing the country bumpkin—a civilizing cut. And so at the century's midpoint, just as the rest of the English-speaking world began souring on the practice (the British National Health Service stopped covering it in 1949), the U.S. settled into its status as the planet's one bastion of routine neonatal circumcision—second only to Israel.

That belief held sway for decades. Men had it done to their sons because it was done to them. Generations of women came to think of the uncircumcised penis as odd. To leave your son uncircumcised was to expose him to ostracism in the locker room and the bedroom. No amount of debunking seemed to alter that. As far back as 1971, the American Academy of Pediatrics declared that there were "no valid medical indications for circumcision in the neonatal period." The following year, some 80 percent of Americans circumcised their newborns.

What changed? The shift away from circumcision is driven by a mass of converging trends. For one, we live in an age of child-centric parenting. New research suggests that the babies feel and process more than previously thought, including physical pain (see "How Much Does It Hurt?"). In a survey conducted for this story, every respondent who decided against circumcision cited "unwillingness to inflict pain on the baby" as the main reason. The movement toward healthier living is another factor. Just as people have grown increasingly wary of the impact of artificial foods in their diets and chemical products in the environment, so too have they become more suspicious of the routine use of preventive medical procedures. We've already rejected tonsillectomy and appendectomy as bad ideas. The new holistically minded consensus seems to be that if something is there, it's there for a reason: Leave it alone. Globalization plays a part too. As more U.S. women have sex with foreign-born men, the American perception of the uncut penis as exotic has begun to fade. The decline in the number of practicing Jews contributes as well. Perhaps as a reflection of all of these typically urban-minded ideas, circumcision rates are dropping in big coastal cities at a faster rate than in the heartland. In 2006, for example, a minority of male New York City newborns were circumcised—43.4 percent. In Minnesota, the rate was 70 percent. Circumcision, you could say, is becoming a blue-state-red-state issue.

The Moreas considered all of this and more, having imbibed more information about both the pros and cons of circumcision during the last four months of Deanna's pregnancy than they care to recall. They still hadn't decided what to do until the day after their son, Anderson, was born. Then, when a nurse came to take the boy to be circumcised, the decision came clear to them. "We didn't want to put him through that—we didn't want to cut him," says Deanna. "It's mutilation. They do it to girls in Africa. No matter how accepted it is, it's mutilation."

And yet, the pendulum is already swinging back. Earlier this year, *The New York Times* published a front-page story noting that the Centers for Disease Control was considering recommending routine circumcision to help stop the spread of AIDS. The idea was based largely on studies done in Africa indicating that circumcised heterosexual men were at least 60 percent less susceptible to HIV than uncircumcised ones. The story promptly touched off a firestorm, with pro- and anti-circumcision commenters exchanging angry barbs. The CDC will now say only that it's in the process of determining a recommendation.

Caught at the crossroads of religion and science, circumcision has proved to be a free-floating symbol, attaching itself to whatever orthodoxy captures a society's imagination. Its history is driven by wildly shifting rationales: from tribal rite of passage to covenant with God to chastity guarantor to paralysis cure to cancer guard to unnecessary, painful surgery to a Hail Mary pass in the struggle with the AIDS pandemic. There's no reason to think a new rationale won't come down the pike when we least expect it. Our millennia-long quest to justify one of civilization's most curious habits continues.

MICHAEL IDOV is a novelist and contributing editor at *New York Magazine*.

EXPLORING THE ISSUE

Is There a Valid Reason for Routine Infant Male Circumcision?

Critical Thinking and Reflection

1. What does scientific research tell us about the impact of male infant circumcision?
2. What are the perceived health benefits of the practice?
3. In what ways do religion and cultural norms influence the popularity of the practice?
4. Are comparisons between male circumcision and FGM valid?
5. If you have a son, would you have him circumcised? Why or why not?

Is There Common Ground?

Rosin, who is Jewish and supports male circumcision, begins her selection stating "Anyone with a heart would agree that the Jewish bris is a barbaric event." Terms like "barbaric" have often been used when arguing against female circumcision, or FGM, and have also been used recently by anti-male-circumcision activists. Comparisons of male circumcision to FGM often draw stern reprimands from critics, as FGM is seen as far more invasive. However, underlying arguments of tradition and culture versus health risks and bodily autonomy are comparable. In what ways do terms like "barbaric" add or subtract value to arguments over the practice?

Idov takes a historical perspective when examining the cultural practice of circumcision. Can you think of other common medical procedures that have fallen out of favor over the years? What caused their decline in popularity? Idov also notes the medical community's shifting stance on circumcision over the years. Does this make you more or less likely to support infant male circumcision?

Lastly, it is clear that infants cannot consent to a procedure such as circumcision and that, ultimately, parents must make the best decision possible with the information they have. After comparing the YES and NO selections, are you more or less likely to support the routine circumcision of male infants?

Create Central

www.mhhe.com/createcentral

Reference

(1) Watson, J. "Ánti-Circumcision Comic Hero Called Anti-Semitic," *Huffington Post*, June 18, 2011, www.huffingtonpost.com/2011/06/18/anticircumcision-comic-he_n_879739.html

Additional Resources

Barkham, P. "Circumcision: The Cruellest Cut?" *The Guardian*, August 28, 2012.

Bristol, N. "Male Circumcision Debate Blares in the USA," *The Lancet*, November 26, 2011.

Park, M. "San Francisco Judge Removes Circumcision Ban from Ballot," www.cnn.com/2011/HEALTH/07/28/circumcision.ban.voting/index.html (July 28, 2011).

Tobian, A. & Gray, R. (October 5, 2011). "The Medical Benefits of Male Circumcision," *The Journal of the American Medical Association*," 306(13).

Internet References . . .

National Organization of Circumcision Information Resource Centers (NOCIRC)

NOCIRC is an advocacy organization, founded by health professionals, who seek to prevent all forms of nonconsensual genital cutting and protect the human rights of those at risk.

www.nocirc.org

American Academy of Pediatrics Circumcision Policy Statement

This statement outlines the most recent changes to the American Academy of Pediatrics Circumcision Policy.

http://pediatrics.aappublications.org/content/103/3/686.full.pdf+html

World Health Organization (WHO)

This page compiles the latest updates on the worldwide impact of male circumcision and presents the WHO's current stance on the practice.

www.who.int/hiv/topics/malecircumcision/en/

Unit 2

Gender and Sexual Orientation

*F*ew issues have undergone such swift and dramatic change in recent American history than our understanding of and attitudes toward the diversity of sexual orientation and gender identity. Public opinion on same-sex marriage has changed dramatically over the last decade, with a majority now supporting marriage equality. In 2012, President Barack Obama became the first sitting president to support same-sex marriage. Increasingly, states, locales, and businesses are adding gender identity and expression to their nondiscrimination policies. Vice President Joe Biden called violence and discrimination against the transgender community "the civil rights issue of our time." In this unit, we will examine several issues concerning gender and sexual orientation.

Selected, Edited, and with Issue Framing Material by:
Ryan W. McKee, *Widener University*
and
William J. Taverner, *Center for Family Life Education*

ISSUE

Are Puberty-Blocking Drugs the Best Treatment Option for Transgender Children?

YES: S. Giordano, from "Lives in a Chiaroscuro. Should We Suspend the Puberty of Children with Gender Identity Disorder," *Journal of Medical Ethics* (August 2008)

NO: Emi Koyama, from "Thoughts on the Timing of Puberty and the 'Treatment' of Gender Dysphoria," Original essay for this edition (2013)

Learning Outcomes

After reading this issue, you should be able to:

- Define the terms "transgender," "cisgender," "gender identity disorder (GID)," and "gender dysphoria."
- Describe the physical and emotional benefits of suppressing puberty for transgender youth through hormonal treatments.
- Describe the benefits/risks of the hormonal induction of cross-sex puberty for transgender youth at an age similar to the pubertal onset of their cisgender peers.
- Summarize the ethical questions the suppression of puberty for transgender youth raises for parents and the medical community.

ISSUE SUMMARY

YES: S. Giordano, reader in bioethics at the School of Law at the University of Manchester, advocates for the hormonal suspension of puberty in transgender youth, arguing that to withhold this treatment is medically irresponsible.

NO: Emi Koyama, writer and activist, argues that while delaying puberty in transgender youth can have benefits, *inducing cross-sex* puberty at an age consistent with pubertal development of a child's cisgender peers may be even more beneficial.

For many people, the terms "sex" and "gender" are synonymous. The two terms, however, describe distinct concepts. Biological sex is determined by a combination of a person's sex chromosomes and their gonadal and genital anatomy. Depending on our sex, there are certain societal expectations of how society tells us we should feel or behave. In the United States, men, for example, are expected to be less emotional than women. Women are expected to be less aggressive than men. These expectations are called gender roles. Gender identity, to go a step further, is how one feels about and identifies with their biological sex and the role expectations that come along with it. Most people would say that their gender identity is congruent with their anatomical sex. While some males may feel more (or less) masculine than others, the majority would strongly identify as men. The same could be said for most females—regardless of how feminine they feel (or don't feel), the majority identify as women. These men and women, whose gender identities are in-line with social expectations of their biological sex would be considered "cisgender" ("Cis" is a prefix with Latin origins, meaning "on the same side"). These individuals enjoy the privilege of never having to give much thought to their gender or how they present it to the world.

But what about those who have gender identities incongruent with their birth sex? For those whose feeling of maleness or femaleness doesn't fall in line with the social expectations of their anatomical sex, gender identity can be hard to ignore. Their gender identities may not fit the binary gender system (a person is assumed to be *either* a man *or* a woman) seen as standard in the United States. Many (but not all) people who feel this way may identify as transgender or transsexual and, according to the fourth edition of the American Psychiatric Association's (APA) *Diagnostic and Statistical Manual of Mental Disorders* (DSM), have a condition known as gender identity disorder (GID).

This diagnosis is controversial and debated among mental health care providers and transgender activists alike. In the upcoming fifth edition of the DSM, the diagnosis will be changed to a condition labeled *gender dysphoria*, one that many feel removes the stigma of "disorder" and more accurately represents the lived experience of transgender children and adults. Gender nonconformity, the APA states, "is not in itself a mental disorder. The critical element of gender dysphoria is the presence of clinically significant distress or impairment in social, occupational, or other important areas of functioning" (1).

Adults with gender dysphoria, with the guidance of their mental health care providers and medical doctors, may elect to take hormones or undergo surgical sex-reassignment procedures in order to facilitate their gender transition. When a child, however, is diagnosed with gender dysphoria, the support of parents or legal guardians is crucial in securing appropriate treatment. Even with a support team that includes therapists and doctors, decisions about treatment can be stressful. Parents are likely to wonder if their children's dysphoria is "just a phase." Indeed, the World Professional Association for Transgender Health (WPATH) notes that childhood gender dysphoria persists into adulthood in only 12–27 percent of cases. Still, a childhood diagnosis must not simply be ignored. Early treatment options, according to WPATH, include counseling and therapy for the child, as well as counseling and support for family members. Some children may desire a "social transition," during which they begin to express a different gender by dressing in different clothing or going by a different name or pronouns. As adolescence approaches, the child's dysphoria, as noted above, may disappear.

For those in whom it does not subside, the onset of puberty presents new challenges. The development of secondary sex characteristics can be deeply troubling to adolescents who do not identify with their bodies. Treatments like counseling and a continuation a social transi-tion are recommended, but it is at this time that a variety of medical or physical interventions can be considered. For some, this may include the suspension of puberty through the use of hormones. While the treatment is considered "fully reversible" by WPATH, it is not without controversy. According to WPATH, there are two reasons for this intervention:

(i) Their use gives adolescents more time to explore their gender nonconformity and other developmental issues.
(ii) Their use may facilitate transition by preventing the development of sex characteristics that are difficult or impossible to reverse if adolescents continue on to pursue sex reassignment.

If gender dysphoria subsides during adolescence, and no further treatments have been undertaken, discontinuing the puberty blocking hormones will lead to the onset of puberty typical of a child of that sex.

Some debate the "fully reversible" claims, citing potential issues with bone density and height, as well as social disadvantages a child who delays puberty, but ceases treatment, may face (i.e., developing in their birth sex, but later than their peers). But there is no doubt that puberty suppression can help to reduce the negative social and emotional factors transgender adolescents face when confronted by puberty.

In the YES selection, S. Giordano argues in favor of the use of puberty suspension for children with GID (now referred to as gender dysphoria). She details the social prejudice and physical violence directed at the transgender community and, in particular, transgender adolescents. After weighing the benefits and risks of the puberty suspension, she argues that, for those adolescents who may be harmed by puberty, *denying* the treatment would be unethical and lead to unnecessary suffering. Writer and activist Emi Koyama argues that, rather than simply delaying a transgender adolescent's "natural" puberty, the hormonal induction of puberty consistent with the child's gender identity—at the same time as their peers—should be considered.

YES ↵

S. Giordano

Lives in a Chiaroscuro. Should We Suspend the Puberty of Children with Gender Identity Disorder?

Abstract

Transgender children who are not treated for their condition are at high risk of violence and suicide. As a matter of survival, many are willing to take whatever help is available, even if this is offered by illegal sources, and this often traps them into the juvenile criminal system and exposes them to various threats. Endocrinology offers a revolutionary instrument to help children/adolescents with gender identity disorder: suspension of puberty. Suspension of puberty raises many ethical issues, and experts dissent as to when treatment should be commenced and how children should be followed up. This paper argues that suspension of puberty is not only not unethical: if it is likely to improve the child's quality of life and even save his or her life, then it is indeed unethical to defer treatment.

A boy of 12 is believed to have become the world's youngest sex change patient after convincing doctors that he wanted to live the rest of his life as a female . . . The therapy involves artificially arresting male puberty, with a series of potent hormone injections . . .

—(Telegraph)[1]

In 2004 Alex,[2] another trans-gender child, convinced the Australian Courts to allow her treatment for gender identity disorder. At the age of 13, her puberty was suspended.[i]

Both these children suffer from Gender Identity Disorder (GID). This is a "condition in which individuals experience their 'gender identity' as being incongruent with their phenotype."[3] Their condition could also be described as a *chiaroscuro,* a term generally used in arts to describe figures painted in both light and shadow.

Children with GID can be treated with puberty suppressant drugs at the beginning of puberty or soon afterwards, when the first sex characteristics begin to appear. Physical development is thus arrested temporarily, in view of administering cross-sex hormones at a later stage (normally around the age of 16).

The main advantage of this approach is that these children gain time to reflect over their gender identity, without becoming trapped in a body that is experienced as alien.

While under puberty suppressant drugs, the child is assisted with psychotherapy and monitored medically, to verify any effects of medication, and may be encouraged to have what is called "a real life experience," that is, to dress and behave as a person of the other gender. This allows the child to explore the other gender and verify whether transition is what s/he really wants.[4] After a period on puberty suppressant drugs, the child will decide whether s/he wants to go on with transition or not. Not all children with GID will become transsexual adults: some will change sex later in life, some might not, and some will continue to participate to both genders, feeling that their identity is not unequivocally male or female. If the child does not wish to transition, puberty suppressant drugs can be withheld and development restarts as normal.[ii] If the child decides to change sex, transition is much smoother if puberty has been arrested. Starting cross-sex hormones on a body that has not developed the "wrong" sex characteristics allows achievement of a much more "normal" and satisfactory appearance. Every later cross-sex intervention on a person whose puberty has been allowed to progress is much more invasive: cross-sex hormones will act on a body that has already developed. The result is an ambiguous appearance. Some characters (height, size), once they have developed, cannot be reversed with hormonal therapy. Others (breasts, for example) can only be removed with surgery. Cross-sex surgery, for transgender people whose puberty has not been suppressed, is going to be much more invasive.

Suspending puberty can also be used as a part of diagnosis, as it helps to identify children who really want to transition[4]; it also decreases the risk of treating false positives (children who will seek cross-sex surgery once they are adult but who, later, will regret the choice).

Whereas suspension of puberty (SP) is regarded as a normal part of care in many countries, it can be very difficult to receive this treatment in England.

SP raises important ethical questions: can it be right to interfere with spontaneous development? Can children be capable of a judgment that can have long-term consequences? Is it ethical to offer this treatment, given that its risks have not been fully established within a research protocol?

I argue that SP should be offered when the long-term consequences of delaying treatment are likely to be worse than the likely long-term consequences of treatment. "Likely consequences" include long-term physical, psychological and relational/social results of treatment *versus* non-treatment, and thus the *overall welfare* of the child, and not just the potential risks and benefits *of medications*.

Physical, Psychological and Social Dimensions of Gender Identity Disorder

GID is a severe medical condition, associated with strong disgust for the body and profound uncertainty over the sense of the self. Invariably, growing in a chiaroscuro causes great distress. Once they start puberty, trans-boys may develop female secondary sex characteristics, such as breasts, may even start to menstruate and remain shorter in stature than average, whereas trans-girls may grow beards and prominent Adam's apples, experience erections and became taller than average.

Social adaptation can be very difficult.[5] Children with GID typically wish to engage in plays that are distinctive of the other gender and identify themselves with the other gender.[6] Once at school, they may feel uncomfortable in taking part in activities in which they are expected to share environments (changing rooms, dormitories) with their peers. Even going to the bathroom can become a major issue. For example, in *Alex* the school principal reported that Alex would wear nappies and refuse to drink for the whole duration of the school day, in order to avoid the bathroom.[2]

Moreover, the social response to GID is often one of rejection, discrimination and abuse.[7] Homophobic bullying in schools is common in the UK[8]: 89.2% of lesbian/gay/bisexual/transgender youth experience verbal bullying and 17.6% are physically assaulted for reasons related to their gender/sexual orientation.[9] There have been cases of children killed by their peers by reason of their gender ambiguity.[10]

A 16-year-old male-to-female patient reports:

> Many [. . .] are ignorant and cruel and they shout out things like, "Girl with a cock", 'There's the he/she/it", "Tranny boy" and other names. On my way to school, people shout similar comments from their cars, because of the way I look. [. . .] When I leave school, to go to University, or to get a job, I want to be able to keep my private life private; this is nobody else's business.

—(Personal communication, published with the kind permission of the patient and her parents)

This type of social response has negative long term consequences. Children who are victims of homophobic bullying are five times more likely than other students to fail to attend schools, and twice as likely not to pursue further education.[11] Substance abuse, homelessness, prostitu-

tion, HIV infection, self-harm, depression, anxiety[12] and suicide[13] are also included among the results of homophobic bullying.[14]

The Need for Medical Treatment

Given the severity of the condition, obtaining medical help is for many a matter of survival. If they are refused treatment, many might try to obtain medication off the illegal market. Injecting drugs at unregulated dosages and without medical supervision exposes them to dissatisfactory physical development and to life threatening conditions, such as HIV, AIDS and hepatitis. Involvement with illegal sources often also entangles these youth in the juvenile justice system, and "[once] a young person enters the juvenile justice system, the stigma of delinquency usually follows them throughout life and they often cycle into the adult criminal justice system upon maturity."[15]

Those who come from areas of the world where early treatment and change-sex surgery are unavailable need to emigrate in order to obtain proper medical care. Often they have to raise enough money for privately paid healthcare assistance, and given that sometimes clandestine immigration is the only way into countries where they can receive medical help, criminalised behaviour, such as prostitution, might become the only available option.[16]

It cannot be claimed that these people *freely* choose risky life styles: those who do not receive treatment are left without recourse, and "people without recourse are not free."[17]

Of course, many transsexual people do not have a similar fate, and are well integrated in society. However, research shows that delayed treatment is associated with poor outcome[4] and ill physical, psychological and relational/social health (p121).[5] Many would rather take their life than grow in the "alien" body(p3).[12]

It could be objected that we should not respond with *biological treatment* to a problem that is to an important extent *social*. If society responds in the wrong way to transgender children, we should not change their body, we should change society.

However, GID is not purely a *social problem*: it is a medical condition, whose causes seem to be genetic, hormonal and neuro-developmental.[3] The appropriate response to a serious medical condition is medical treatment. Early treatment prevents these children from growing in an unwanted body, in a body that they would change anyway at a later stage, at much higher costs. Social education might be necessary, but this is a different matter.

Suspension of Puberty: When Should It Start?

The first stage of hormonal treatment for GID is the administration of puberty suppressant drugs.[18]

These drugs, sometimes called "blockers," by acting on the pituitary gland, block the hormone secretion[iii] (oestrogen in girls and testosterone in boys). The most effective "blockers" are *gonadotropin-releasing hormone analogues* (GnRHa). After a period on "blockers," if the child persists in his/her desire to transition to the other gender, cross-sex hormones, and then surgery, will be offered.

The Harry Benjamin International Standards of Care[19] recommend that these medications be given when the child has had *some experience* of his/her biological gender.[iv]

The reason for this is that only about a quarter of children with gender dysphoria under the age of 12 will become transsexual adults,[18] whereas *the majority* of those who *continue to experience transgenderism in adolescence* become transsexual adults.[20] Once puberty has been experienced, if the disorder is still strong and persistent, treatment can start. The stage at which the adolescent begins his puberty is known as Tanner Stage II and III.[21, v] At these stages, testes and breasts begin to grow and pubic hair begins to appear (for a fuller description see ["Tanner Stages"]). In many countries, such as Germany, the USA, Canada, Australia, The Netherlands and Belgium, SP can be offered at this stage of pubertal development. In England, instead, it could be very difficult to obtain treatment at this early stage.

The UK Situation

In 2005, the British Society of Paediatric Endocrinology and Diabetes (BSPED)[22] stated that treatment for GID should not start until puberty is complete. This means that the child should be left to grow in the biological (unwanted) body. The effects of the puberty suppressant drugs are thus severely curtailed. It is in fact clear that puberty *cannot be suppressed if it has completed its course*. This exposes the child not only to the anguish and terror of growing in a body that is experienced as alien; and to the relational/social risks associated with this, but also to the ill effects of having to commence cross-sex treatment over a body that is already fully formed, and to much more invasive surgery, should s/he decide to transition.

The BSPED guidelines have now been withdrawn, but their publication brought to light a dissent about the appropriateness of SP and contributed to a climate of concern among professionals. The guidelines, published anonymously, were written by specialists in adolescent endocrinology at the University College of London Hospitals NHS Trust, which, in partnership with the Tavistock and Portman NHS Trust, provides the first and only Child and Adolescent GID Unit in the UK, one of the few units of this kind in the world. In practice, this means if a British resident was referred to the clinic, and the experts refused to treat him/her (based on application of the BSPED guidelines), it would have been extremely difficult for him/her to obtain another referral to a different service/specialist, and likewise difficult for other professionals in the UK to offer desired treatment, even if that treatment appeared to them to be in the patient's best interests.[23] One result of this, is medical tourism: US specialists report having to treat several children who have been turned down at UK clinics.[24] Those who cannot afford privately paid healthcare abroad are left in the UK to suffer.[v]

What are the reasons against SP?[vi]

Unknown Risks

Hormone suppressant drugs are routinely administered to prostate cancer patients[27,vii] and to children who experience precocious puberty. These drugs are administered to children with GID in an experimental way. The long-term effects on bone mass development and sitting height, metabolism and on the brain, are not entirely clear.[21] Additional concerns regard the effect of blockers on reproductive capability.[25]

It could be argued that experimenting on children/adolescents is irresponsible; that they cannot be competent to engage in experimental therapy; that it is impossible to give genuine consent to a therapy whose long-term risks are not entirely clear, and that therefore this form of therapy is necessarily unethical.

A Response

There is no ground for presuming that a child/adolescent with GID cannot be competent to make a judgment upon SP.[25]

Moreover, if it was impossible to give valid consent to treatment whose side-effects are unclear, it would follow that no-one (including adults) could consent to medical research. This is obviously not true. In order to give valid consent, applicants need to receive honest information about known and potential risks and benefits of the treatment. In the balance, the applicant (often with the help of his/her parents) will weigh the known and potential risks and benefits of treatment with the known psychological and physical effects of non-treatment. There is no reason to regard consent thus obtained as invalid.

It is not necessarily unethical to treat children within an experimental monitored programme. Indeed, it might be unethical to deny what is for many the only possible cure.

If this cure was likely to cause significant harm to the child, it would be appropriate to question its legitimacy even in the face of the child's competence and informed consent, but research shows that SP appears to have no hideous or non-controllable side effects.[4] After a period of GnRHa the child/adolescent might decide to revert to the biological sex; interrupt therapy and development is thought to restart as normal. For this reason, blockers are considered as "both temporary and reversible."[28]

However, Dr Russell Viner, one of the UK leading specialists in the field, stated that the claim that blockers are reversible is misleading.[29]

Viner's Argument on Reversibility

Viner argued that blockers have the *irreversible* outcome of denying the child the experience of puberty in the natural phenotype, and although puberty can be restored, it is *irreversible* that development has been interrupted at that particular point in time. Therefore, concludes Viner, blockers are not properly "reversible treatment."

This argument is "pseudo-philosophical argument."[30] Aristotle would call it "an apparent deduction."[31] Of course, when something has happened, nobody can undo reality. It does not follow that blockers are an irreversible treatment. It is irreversible that they have been given (*or not given*) but they are not for this reason *irreversible medications*. The adjective, in Viner's argument, is predicated of the wrong subject: irreversible is *the fact* that blockers have been administered, but not *blockers* themselves. If Viner's argument was correct, even lipstick should be regarded as an irreversible intervention. If I wear lipstick today, in fact, I cannot make it un-happened. Instead, it is clear that, although it is "irreversible" that I have worn lipstick today, this does not make lipstick irreversible in the same way as cosmetic surgery, for example, is. To claim that lipsticks are irreversible interventions because, once I have worn them, it cannot happen that I have not worn them, is to display gross conceptual confusion between the ineluctability of the events (I have worn lipstick today) and the quality of things (lipstick *is washable* and does not become *un-washable* only because the past is ineluctable).

Moreover, with this argument Viner shoots himself in the foot: if Viner's argument was valid, it would follow that *not suppressing puberty* would equally be an irreversible intervention (any clinician who understood the implications of this conclusion would find it threatening). Viner's argument, thus, demonstrates the opposite of what it is meant to demonstrate: failing to treat is at least as irreversible as treating.

Maybe the sense of Viner's argument is different. Maybe he is suggesting that if we subvert endogenous hormone production, we might be unable to understand what the child really wants and the degree of his/her disorder. SP, in other words, might create confusion and impinge upon the clarity of the diagnosis.

Tanner Stages[26]

Pubic hair (both male and female)
Tanner I: no pubic hair at all (typically age 10 and under)

Tanner II: small amount of long, downy hair with slight pigmentation at the base of the penis and scrotum (males) or on the labia majora (females) (10–11)

Tanner III: hair becomes more coarse and curly, and begins to extend laterally (12–14)

Tanner IV: adult-like hair quality, extending across pubis but sparing medial thighs (13–15)

Tanner V: hair extends to medial surface of the thighs (16+)

Genitals (male)
Tanner I: prepubertal (testicular volume less than 1.5 ml; small penis of 3 cm or less)

Tanner II: testicular volume between 1.6 and 6 ml; skin on scrotum thins, reddens and enlarges; penis length unchanged

Tanner III: testicular volume between 6 and 12 ml; scrotum enlarges further; penis begins to lengthen to about 6 cm

Tanner IV: testicular volume between 12 and 20 ml; scrotum enlarges further and darkens; penis increases in length to 10 cm and circumference

Tanner V: testicular volume greater than 20 ml; adult scrotum and penis of 15 cm in length

Breasts (female)
Tanner I: no glandular tissue; areola follows the skin contours of the chest (prepubertal)

Tanner II: breast bud forms, with small area of surrounding glandular tissue; areola begins to widen

Tanner III: breast begins to become more elevated, and extends beyond the borders of the areola, which continues to widen but remains in contour with surrounding breast

Tanner IV: increased breast size and elevation; areola and papilla form a secondary mound projecting from the contour of the surrounding breast

Tanner V: breast reaches final adult size; areola returns to contour of the surrounding breast, with a projecting central papilla.

Indeed, it can be difficult to make a correct diagnosis, and to determine the right time to commence treatment. This is, however, not a good reason to allow pubertal development in all cases, to the detriment of the child's welfare. Moreover, as SP combined with psychotherapy improves the precision of the diagnosis, it could prevent the risk of treating false positives.[4]

Conclusions

The following epitaph was published, with many more, by a non-profit charity in a website. It concerns a prostitute, murdered in Italy in 2003.

> My name was Adrian Torres de Assuncao. I was a Brazilian woman aged 24. I lived in Brescia, in Italy. One night a client hit me in the face with a hammer. Despite the pain I kept working and I didn't go to hospital because I feared they would send me back home (I was a clandestine immigrant). When I agreed to go to hospital it was too late. I died on the 7th of October.

This epitaph illustrates the fate of many of those who are left alone to deal with GID. Sufferers who are not helped in a timely manner, as a matter of survival, will take any chance to obtain the desired gender, even if this exposes them to serious risks, because anything is better than life in an alien body. In 2003, 38 similar murders have been reported across the world. Many of these victims were transgender adolescents or young adults, and it is well possible that, if early treatment was more largely available, many of them would still be alive.

If allowing puberty to progress appears likely to harm the child, puberty should be suspended. There is nothing unethical with interfering with spontaneous development, when spontaneous development causes great harm to the child. Indeed, it is unethical to let children suffer, when their suffering can be alleviated.

This is not responding with medicine to a problem that is social in nature. This is responding with medicine to a serious medical problem that causes enormous distress to the sufferers and makes them prefer unqualified help, street life and even death, to life with GID.

Whether or not the administration of puberty suppressant drugs is ethical depends not only on the net balance of *clinical* risks and benefits of *treatment,* but also on what is likely to happen to the child if s/he is not treated at the early stages of puberty. On balance, healthcare providers should include future physical risks (invasiveness of future surgery), and the psychological and relational/social risks (disgust for the self; social integration; risk of suicide).

Healthcare providers are ethically (and to some extent legally) responsible for what is likely to happen to the applicant as a consequence of the fact that treatment has been withheld.[32] Thus a decision on SP should involve a judgment on the overall quality of life and welfare of the child.

This implies that healthcare professionals should retain the freedom to assess their patients' condition, their competence and their best interests. No healthcare professional should find him/herself at risk of disciplinary action, if s/he acts in the patient's best interests and in line with established competent authorities, just because one professional body, however authoritative, considers SP clinically and ethically wrong, in stern and scarcely supported opposition to other well respected international authorities.

References

1. Pancevski B. Unhappy as a boy, Kim became youngest ever transsexual at 12. *Telegraph,* 2 Feb 2007. http://www.telegraph.co.uk/news/main.jhtml7xml = /news/2007/01/28/wkim28.xml (accessed 10 June 2008).
2. Re Alex [2004] FamCA 297.
3. GIRES. Atypical Gender Development—A Review. *Int J Transgenderism* 2006:9:29–44.
4. Cohen-Kettenis TP. Pubertal delay as an aid in diagnosis and treatment of a transsexual adolescent. *Eur Child Adolesc Psychiatry* 1998:7:246–8.
5. Cohen-Kettenis TP, Pfäfflin F. Transgenderism and intersexuality in childhood and adolescence. Making choices. London: Sage Publications, 2003.
6. Kotula D Jerry. In: Kotula D, Parker WE, eds. *The Phallus Palace.* Los Angeles: Alyson Publications, 2002:92–4.
7. GIRES 2007. Transphobic Bullying in Schools, http://www.gires.org.uk/medpros.php (accessed 10 June 2008).
8. Warwick I, Chase E, Aggleton P. Homophobia, sexual orientation and schools: a review and implications for action. University of London, 2004, Research Report No 594. Available at www.dfes.gov.uk/research/data/uploadfiles/RR594 .pdf (accessed 10 June 2008).
9. GLSEN's 2005. National school climate survey sheds new light on experiences of lesbian, gay, bisexual and transgender (LGBT) students, available online at http://glsen.org/cgi-bin/iowa/all/library/record/1927.html (accessed 10 June 2008).
10. Di Ceglie D. Gender identity disorder in young people. *Adv Psychiatr Treat* 2000:6:458–66.
11. Hall Horace R. Teach to reach: addressing lesbian, gay, bisexual and transgender youth issues in the classroom. *New Educator* 2006:2:149–157:150.
12. Department of Health. Stand up for us: challenging homophobia in schools, 2007. Available at http://www.wiredforhealth.gov.uk/PDF/stand_up_for_us_04.pdf (accessed 10 June 2008).
13. Di Ceglie D, Freedman D, McPherson S, *et al.* Children and adolescents referred to a specialist gender identity development service: clinical features and demographic characteristics. *Int J Transgenderism* 2002;6. Online at http://www.symposion .com/ijt/ijtvo06noO 1_01.htm (accessed 10 June 2008).
14. Whittle S, Turner L, AI-Alami M. Engendered penalties: transgender and transsexual people's experiences of inequality and discrimination. *Equality Reviews* 2007, Available at http://www.theequalitiesreview.org.uk/upload/assets/www .theequalitiesreview.org.uk/transgender.pdf (accessed 10 June 2008).
15. Fenner B, Mananzala R. Letter to the hormonal medication for adolescent guidelines drafting team. Oral presentation at the conference *Endocrine treatment of atypical gender identity development in adolescents.* London, 19–20 May 2005.
16. Fernanda de Albuquerque F, Janelli M. *Princesa.* Rome: Sensibili alle Foglie, 1994.
17. Korsgaard C. Capability and Well Being. In: Nussbaum M and Sen A, eds. *The Quality of life.* Oxford: Oxford University Press, 1999:59.
18. Royal College of Psychiatrists. *Gender identity disorders in children and adolescents, guidance for management, Council Report CR63.* January 1998. Online at http://www.symposion.com/ijVijtc0402.htm (accessed 10 June 2008).
19. Harry Benjamin International Gender Dysphoria Association's Standards of care for gender identity disorders. 6th Version, February 2001. Online at www.hbigda.org/Documents2/socv6.pdf (accessed 10 June 2008).
20. Wren B. Early physical intervention for young people with atypical gender identity development. *Clin Child Psychol Psychiatry* 2000:5:220–31.

21. Delemarre-van de Waal AH, Cohen-Kettenis TP. Clinical management of gender identity disorder in adolescents: a protocol on psychological and paediatric endocrinology aspects. *Eur J Endocrinol* 2006;*155*(suppl 1):131–7. online at: http://www.eje-online.org/cgi/content/full/155/suppl_1/S131#F2 (accessed 10 June 2008).

22. British Society of Paediatric Endocrinology & Diabetes. *Guidelines for the management of Gender Identity Disorder (GID) in adolescents and children, specific endocrinological recommendations.* Previously published at http://www.bsped.org.uk/professional/guidelines/docs/BSPEDGIDguidelines.pdf:2. Currently removed from website.

23. See the case of Russell Reid. *Guardian* 25 May 2007. http://www.guardian.co.uk/medicine/story/0,,2088289,00.html www.guardian.co.uk/print/0,,329615991-103701,00.html.

24. Personal communication.

25. Giordano S. Gender Atypical Organisation in Children and Adolescents: Ethico-legal Issues and a Proposal for New Guidelines. *International Journal of Children's Rights* 2007:*15*:365–90.

26. Tanner Stages. http://en.wikipedia.org/wiki/Tanner_stage

27. Stein R. *Prostate Cancer Drugs May Pose Danger.* Washington Post 19 Sept 2006. http://www.washingtonpost.com/wp-dyn/content/article/2006/09/18/AR2006091801167.html?nav = rss_print/asection (accessed 10 June 2008).

28. Lee P, Houk C. Diagnosis and care of transsexual children and adolescents: a pediatric endocrinologists' perspective. *J Pediatr Endocrinol Metab* 2006:*19*:103–9.

29. Dr R Viner oral presentation at the Royal Society of Medicine, 10 October 2006.

30. Platone. *Rebubblica (Republic).* Roma: Laterza, 2003, VI, 495a. My translation.

31. Aristotele. *Topici (Topics).* Napoli: Loffredo, 1974, VIII, 12,162b 3–5. My translation.

32. Gillick v West Norfolk and Wisbech Area Health Authority [1985] 3 All ER 402 at 409 e–h per Lord Fraser.

Notes

i. Suspension of puberty can also be used for other conditions. In 2004 it was used in the "Ashley case." See http://www.telegraph.co.uk.

ii. Administration of hormones facilitate[s] the restoration of puberty and return to the biological phenotype.[4]

iii. These are sometimes called *hypothalamic blockers*. I am grateful to Mike Besser for clarifying the real nature of these hormone suppressant drugs. I owe the specifications contained in these lines to him.

iv. The Royal College of Psychiatrists guidelines also recommend that adolescents have some "experience of themselves in the post-pubertal state of their biological sex," before any treatment commences, but contemplate the possibility that "for clinical reasons, it is [. . .] in the patient's interest to intervene before this [time]."[18]

v. It is possible to determine pubertal development accurately by measuring testicular and breast growth as well as the levels of circulating hormones.[21]

vi. I do not discuss arguments that say that SP is wrong because it is a violation of nature, or arguments that appeal to God's plans and the sanctity of suffering. I have dismissed them elsewhere.[25]

vii. It has been suggested that prostate cancer drugs may increase the risk of heart diseases. Experts in the field of paediatric endocrinology comment that similar risks cannot be found in the adolescent transgender population, for a number of reasons, one of which is that while testosterone is inhibited in this population, other hormones, like oestradiol, in males, are administered.[27]

S. GIORDANO, PhD, is a reader in bioethics at the School of Law at the University of Manchester. Additionally, she is director of medical ethics teaching at the Medical School in Manchester.

Emi Koyama

NO

Thoughts on the Timing of Puberty and the "Treatment" of Gender Dysphoria

For the purpose of this discussion, let us set aside questions such as whether or not "gender identity disorder," which has been characterized as a "severe medical condition" (Giordano, 2008), is an appropriate frame to understand and treat gender non-conformity and cross-gender identification in children and adults (I have questions), or if the production of socially defined "normal" characteristics and the elimination of "abnormal" ones are the proper goals of medical intervention (I have serious concerns, though not enough to unilaterally oppose this particular treatment. For the purpose of this discussion, I start from the assumption that having "abnormally" sexed or non-passing physical characteristics can make life extremely difficult for transgender people, in large part though not necessarily entirely due to the rampant transphobic violence, discrimination, and prejudice in our society, and that medicine can help improve their quality of life by enabling the development of more socially desirable or "normal" appearances for the gender they live as.

I recognize that cross-gender identification or gender identity disorder has both social and bio-medical aspects. While gender identity disorder/dysphoria may have "genetic, hormonal, and neuro-developmental"(Giordano, 2008) roots, many of the harms associated with gender identity disorder that make it a "severe medical condition" leading to increased risks of "substance abuse, homelessness, prostitution, HIV infection, self-harm, depression, anxiety, and suicide"(Giordano, 2008) are clearly social.

Given that the lack of biomedical intervention exacerbates these risks, and that medically induced suspension of puberty at an early age can alleviate many of these risks over the course of a transgender person's life, many have argued that this is the appropriate approach (Cohen-Kettinis, Delemarre-van de Waal, & Gooren, 2008; Hembree, et al, 2009), with others going so far as to say that it deferring such treatment would be unethical (Giordano, 2008). In order to reach this conclusion, Giornado (2008) asks us to consider not just the benefits and risks of the medical intervention itself, but also the "long-term consequences of delaying treatment." This is an important consideration, because of the vast likelihood of extremely negative social and psychological harms to transgender individuals when they are forced to live through irreversible physical changes brought on by "natural" puberty and adolescence predicated by their biological sex that is incongruent with their gender identity. Those who advocate for the delayed puberty approach typically suggest administering cross-sex hormones around the age of 16 (Cohen-Kettinis, Delemarre-van de Waal, & Gooren, 2008; Hembree, et al, 2009).

If we truly believe that we must assess benefits and risks of withholding medical intervention as well as those of going forward with it, however, I find it curious that proponents of puberty blocking hormones fail to consider another possible approach to treating transgender children and youth. That unexplored option is, along with blocking their "natural" puberty, to provide transgender teens with cross-sex hormones that can help them experience physical development similar to, and along with, those who are of the same age and gender identity, rather keeping them artificially underdeveloped compared to their peers. A host of psychosocial issues are associated with cisgender (or non-transgender) teens who are "off time (earlier or later) in their pubertal development" (Susman & Rogol, 2004). While there are obvious differences in the psychological and social development of cis- and transgender teens, going through puberty later than peers is not risk-free. I am not arguing that the use of cross-sex hormone is always a superior approach than suspension of puberty, but I am pointing out that many may have not considered the long-term consequences of withholding medical treatment that could enable age- and gender-appropriate development alongside cisgender peers.

Giornado (2008) does respond to Viner's (2006) claim that the impact of puberty blockers are, to a degree, "irreversible." I concur with Giornado's counter-argument that Viner's use of the term "irreversible" is confusing and different from what we normally mean when we discuss if a particular medical treatment is reversible or not, but Viner nonetheless has a point: a child whose puberty was suspended might experience a unique and potentially harmful interruption of their pubertal development at the time his or her peers are going through theirs, such as social anxiety and isolation. The administration of cross-sex hormones may not be an ideal option in every case, but it is most certainly what many transgender adults wish was offered to them when they were growing up.

As for potential risks of administering cross-sex hormones, this approach does entail bona fide *irreversible* consequences, not Vinerian hyperbole. In addition to the (desired) pubertal development consistent with their age and gender identity, the intervention could impact fertility. Because of the eugenic history of involuntary sterilization of people with physical and psychiatric disabilities, women of color, poor women, and others in our society, there are legal as well as ethical hurdles that must be satisfied before any treatment that causes, even as a side-effect, sterilization of a minor. However, my understanding is that this hurdle is not absolute if the treatment is desired by the child as well as by his or her family after they are properly informed, and there are overriding benefits to the individual, in many jurisdictions as determined by a judge.

This proposal may seem extreme and too risky, since there is always the risk that the child's gender dysphoria diagnosis might change during adolescence, but it is more coherent than it may appear initially. To endorse suspension of puberty instead of allowing young people to go through pubertal development consistent with their gender identity at the same as time their peers would imply that we cannot, as some people believe, make a definitive diagnosis of gender identity disorder at that age. Gender identity is still in the process of oscillating and consolidating at that stage, some might say, and it is too dangerous to prescribe irreversible medical treatment for children that young, even if they desperately demand it.

But if we are to believe that gender identity is still fluctuating at that stage and therefore we cannot help transgender children go through pubertal development appropriate for their age and gender identity, what is the justification for *not* suspending puberty for *all* children? There is an unspoken double-standard here: we take for granted that gender identity is solid and fully established when the child's gender identity appears to be consistent with his or her biological sex, and only question its validity or permanence when it is not. This double standard is consistent with the society's prejudicial treatment of transgender people's identities as up for debate, whereas cisgender identities are accepted as stable, natural, and normal without question.

There is of course a risk that a transgender adolescent who receives cross-sex hormones would realize that he or she is not transgender and regret it later. But this is a risk that we routinely accept whenever we assume that any given child who does not unambiguously manifest gender identity disorder is not transgender and therefore do not suspend their puberty. We accept the risk that *any* child could go through "natural" puberty and later regret it, and yet believe that the risk is too grave when it comes to transgender children that even the more "progressive," trans-friendly individuals can only advocate for puberty-delaying treatment.

I suspect that our society's unwillingness to consider the administration of cross-sex hormones is motivated not just by the acknowledgement that not every child who meets the diagnostic criteria for gender identity disorder grow up to become a transgender adult (after all, not every child who does not meet the same diagnostic criteria grow up to become a non-transgender adult either), but by our deeply held belief that being transgender is inherently abnormal and tragic. We find consequences of false positives (non-transgender children who are misidentified as transgender and given irreversible cross-sex hormones) completely unacceptable, while routinely tolerating the equally debilitating consequences of false negatives (transgender children who are not identified as such in time and experience irreversible "natural" pubertal development).

Perhaps suspension of puberty for transgender children is the most politically realistic or palatable approach to "treatment" in a world that is extremely hostile to transgender people. But the medical community's refusal to go one step further and consider the use of cross-sex hormones instead of puberty blockers in at least some cases is predicated on the double standard that inherently places more value on non-transgender bodies and lives over transgender ones.

We need to keep pushing the conversation to center the voices and needs of transgender individuals rather than treating them as voiceless sufferers of a "severe medical condition," and also continue addressing violence and discrimination against transgender children and adults that comprise a large part of harms that suspension of puberty is designed to circumvent.

References

Giordano, S. (2008). Lives in a Chiaroscuro. Should We Suspend the Puberty of Children with Gender Identity Disorder?" *Journal of Medical Ethics, 34* (8), pp. 580–584.

Cohen-Kettenis, P.T., Delemarre-van de Wall, H.A., & Gooren, L.J.G. (2008). The treatment of adolescent transsexuals: Changing insights. *The Journal of Sexual Medicine, 5*(8), pp. 1892–1897. doi: 10.1111/j.1743-6109.2008.00870.x

Hembree, W.C., Cohen-Kettenis, P., Delemarre-van de Wall, H.A., Gooren, L.J., Meyer III, W.J,, Spack, N.P., Tangpricha, V., & Montori, V.M, (2009). Endocrine treatment of transsexual lpersons: An endocrine society clinical practice guideline. *The Journal of Clinical Endocrinology & Metabolism,* (94)9, pp3132–3154. doi:10.1210/jc.2009-0345

Susman, E.J., & Rogol, A. (2004). Puberty and psychological development. In R.M. Lerner & L. Steinberg (Eds.), *Handbook of adolescent psychology,* (pp. 15–44). Hoboken, NJ: Wiley and Sons.

Viner, R. "Oral Presentation at the Royal Society of Medicine," October 10, 2006.

EMI KOYAMA is an activist and writer. Her work can be found at http://eminism.org/

EXPLORING THE ISSUE

Are Puberty-Blocking Drugs the Best Treatment Option for Transgender Children?

Critical Thinking and Reflection

1. When treating transgender youth, what does it mean to suspend puberty? How is this accomplished?
2. What are the physical benefits and risks to the suspension of puberty?
3. What are some social and emotional benefits to suppressing puberty for transgender youth?

Is There Common Ground?

Giordano and Koyama agree that gender identity disorder (GID), or gender dysphoria, is an issue with important biological and social considerations that make treatment a complex issue. The prejudice, discrimination, and physical violence felt by members of the transgender community make support and treatment for those with gender dysphoria, when possible, a time-sensitive decision. Many feel that the earlier treatment begins, the better the health outcomes in transitioning a person from their biological sex to their desired gender identity and presentation.

To this end, Giordano argues that the suspension of puberty for adolescents with gender dysphoria is the best treatment option. Furthermore, to deny such treatment would be unethical, she continues, because the onset of puberty could cause unnecessary suffering as the child begins developing secondary sex characteristics of their birth sex.

Koyama argues that, rather than simply delaying "natural" puberty, cross-sex hormone treatments should be introduced so that these teens can experience puberty in a way that is age-appropriate and in line with their gender identity. Koyama acknowledges that this may be seen as "extreme." Do you agree? What logic does she give for making this argument?

Organizations like WPATH present "Standards of Care" aimed at providing transgender children and adults, and their health care providers, treatment options that are in line with the most recent research available. At this point

in time, it is believed that gender dysphoria will persist into adulthood in only 12–27 percent of children diagnosed with the condition. For those diagnosed during adolescence, however, the persistence rate appears to be higher. Do these numbers influence your opinion on the use of puberty-blocking drugs? Since the effects of puberty blockers appear to be fully reversible, do the potential benefits of this treatment outweigh any risks? Why or why not?

Create Central

www.mhhe.com/createcentral

Additional Resources

Coleman, E., et al. (2012) "Standards of Care for the Health of Transsexual,Transgender, and Gender-Nonconforming People, Version 7," www.wpath .org/documents/SOC%20V7%2003-17-12.pdf

Gorman, A. "Transgender Kids Get Help Navigating a Difficult Path," *Los Angeles Times,* June 15, 2012.

Morgan, G. "Duke University Press' Transgender Studies Quarterly to Publish in 2014," *Huffington Post,* May 16, 2013, www.huffingtonpost.com/2013/05/16/duke-university-transgender-studies-_n_3285181.html

Moss, M. "Puberty Blockers: My Son's Life Preserver," (April 21, 2013), http://blog.timesunion.com/transgender/puberty-blockers-my-sons-life-perserver/466/

Internet References . . .

Injustice at Every Turn: A Report of the National Transgender Discrimination Survey

A survey conducted by the National Gay and Lesbian Task Force and the National Center for Transgender

Equality, this report addresses the level of discrimination transgender individuals face in many everyday areas of life. It was published in February 2011.

www.thetaskforce.org/reports_and_research/ntds

Oregon's Grant High School Creates Gender-Neutral Restrooms for Transgender Students

This article discusses the issues that transgender students face in schools regarding the necessary choice between bathrooms. It includes an interview with the school and a list of 15 things to know about being transgender.

www.huffingtonpost.com/2013/03/25/oregon-high-school-transgender-bathrooms_n_2949598.html

TransKids Purple Rainbow Foundation

Founded by the parents of a transgender girl named Jazz, this foundation seeks to enhance the lives of "TransKids" through educating schools and other social institutions about the needs of transgender young people. Jazz and her family have been profiled by a number of media outlets including 20/20, 60 Minutes, and were the subject of a documentary shown on the Oprah Winfrey Network.

www.transkidspurplerainbow.org

World Professional Association for Transgender Health (WPATH)

WPATH, formerly known as the Harry Benjamin International Gender Dysphoria Association, promotes the understanding and treatment of gender identity disorders through research, education, advocacy, and public policy. They are the publishers of the *Standards of Care for the Health of Transsexual, Transgender, and Gender Nonconforming People.*

www.wpath.org

Selected, Edited, and with Issue Framing Material by:
Ryan W. McKee, *Widener University*
and
William J. Taverner, *Center for Family Life Education*

ISSUE

Is Sexual Orientation Biologically Based?

YES: Qazi Rahman, from "The Neurodevelopment of Human Sexual Orientation," *Neuroscience & Biobehavioral Reviews* (October 2005)

NO: Stanton L. Jones and Alex W. Kwee, from "Scientific Research, Homosexuality, and the Church's Moral Debate: An Update," *Journal of Psychology and Christianity* (Winter 2005)

Learning Outcomes

After reading this issue, you should be able to:

- Explain the complexity in defining sexual orientation and describe the difference between identity, attraction, and behavior.
- Compare and evaluate research suggesting biological roots of sexual orientation with studies suggesting orientations are socially learned or chosen.
- Discuss the implications for public policy if researchers determine a biological or social origin of sexual orientation.

ISSUE SUMMARY

YES: Qazi Rahman, professor of psychology at Kings College, highlights research supporting a biological foundation of sexual orientation.

NO: Stanton L. Jones, professor of psychology at Wheaton College, and **Alex W. Kwee**, clinical psychologist, argue that scientific evidence for a biological origin of homosexuality is scant and suffers from research bias.

Research on the origins of our sexual orientations is a controversial area of scholarship. This should come as no surprise, given the personal, political, and often spiritual nature of the national dialogue on gay rights. At the heart of this research is a debate raised in countless psychology classrooms: "nature v. nurture." If sexual orientation is rooted in "nature," being caused by genetics or hormones, it would be an inborn trait. Everyone, be they gay, lesbian, straight, or bisexual, would be, as Lady Gaga famously sang, "born this way." If, on the other hand, our sexual orientations are developed through social learning, or "nurture," they could potentially be "unlearned" or somehow changed.

Researchers who take on this challenging question, regardless of their findings, often find their work used as evidence to support various claims by advocacy groups on both sides of the debate on gay rights. National and state policymakers on subjects like same-sex marriage, adoption, and military service have all presented such academic research in support of their arguments. Recently, a therapeutic practice known as sexual orientation conversion therapy, often called "reparative therapy," has been

at the center of a controversy among mental health care providers. Advocates for and against the practice have turned to research on the origins of sexual orientations to support their positions. On one side are counselors and therapists who believe that people can change their sexual orientations through counseling and other therapeutic interventions. Many who practice this form of therapy hold religious views that see homosexuality as "sinful" or prohibited. For these therapists, heterosexuality is the "norm" or default sexual orientation, and they believe that a bisexual or homosexual person can, over time, "heal" their "abnormal" orientation (hence the name "reparative therapy"). These practitioners often point to studies highlighting the possible influence of social learning as proof that a person's sexual orientation could be changed.

Opponents of reparative therapy point to studies suggesting strong links to biological determinants, such as genetics and birth order. These mental health care providers feel that homosexuality and bisexuality, while less common than heterosexuality, are a normal and healthy representation of the diversity of human sexuality. They see reparative therapy as harmful to clients and question the very nature of "reparative therapy," as the term assumes there is something to repair. A person who is uncomfortable with their same-sex attractions or behaviors can't change their orientation, they would argue. Their discomfort is a symptom of a society that stigmatizes nonheterosexual orientations. Reparative therapy, they believe, adds to that stigmatization.

Critics of reparative therapy note that the practice has been condemned by the American Psychiatric Association and argue that any change in a person's orientation is simply temporary behavior modifications in which people stop having sex with same-sex partners. The underlying attraction, that is, their sexual orientation, is still there. Some forms of reparative therapy encourage gay and bisexual individuals to alter their gender presentation by "acting" more in line with traditional gender roles. This conflation of gender and sexual orientation, the critics argue, is part of the problem and not based on research. Meanwhile, supporters of reparative therapy, such as the National Association for Research and Therapy of Homosexuality, maintain that therapy is necessary for those who "struggle with unwanted homosexuality."

Another important question to consider is how, precisely, do researchers define sexual orientation? People identify as a variety of sexual orientations, from heterosexual, to gay or lesbian, to bisexual, asexual, queer, and beyond. So what is sexual orientation, exactly? Is it defined by the sexual behaviors in which people engage? Or is it the motivations behind those behaviors? Is it simply a matter of our attractions to, and desires or fantasies about, people of a particular sex or gender? Is it the way a person

identifies themselves? Or is sexual orientation a complex combination of many variables? Further, nuances in language also reflect attitudes, assumptions, and biases that people hold with respect to the formation of sexual orientation. "Sexual preference," for instance, is a term favored by people who believe that sexual orientation is a choice. That is, one chooses the gender of the people they prefer to fall in love with, much the same way as one might exhibit other preferences in life. "Sexual orientation," on the other hand, might be seen as reflecting an assumption about the innate, biological nature of attraction.

Is sexual orientation an innate, or biological, trait? Or is it something that is learned or chosen? Uncovering the origins of our sexual orientations has proven to be a challenge for researchers studying the potential biological and social roots. In the YES selection, psychology professor Qazi Rahman examines several areas of research in neurodevelopment surrounding sexual orientation, including genetics, birth order, and neural circuitry. His summary reveals strong evidence for biological determinants of sexual orientation. Also included in his argument is a criticism of research highlighting the role of social learning in the development of sexual orientation. Psychology professor Stanton Jones and psychologist Alex Kwee take issue with many of the studies cited by Rahman as being biased or methodologically deficient. They argue that correlations between biological factors and sexual orientation do not prove causation. Therefore, they believe that social learning may indeed be at the root of the development of homosexuality.

YES ↵

Qazi Rahman

The Neurodevelopment of Human Sexual Orientation

1. Introduction

Sexual orientation refers to a dispositional sexual attraction towards persons of the opposite sex or same sex. Sexual orientation appears 'dispositional' in that it comprises a target selection and preference mechanism sensitive to gender, motivational approach behaviours towards the preferred target, and internal cognitive processes biased towards the preferred target (such as sexual fantasies). In contrast, sexual orientation does not appear to be a matter of conscious self-labelling or past sexual activity because these are subject to contingent social pressures, such as the presence of linguistic descriptors and visible sexual minorities within an individual's culture, and the availability of preferred sexual partners. Therefore, in human investigations, sexual orientation is often assessed using self-report measures of 'sexual feelings' (i.e. sexual attraction and sexual fantasies) rather than self-labelling or past hetero- or homosexual activity.

Sexual orientation appears to be a dichotomous trait in males, with very few individuals demonstrating an intermediate (i.e. 'bisexual') preference. This is borne out by fine-grained analyses of self-reported heterosexual and homosexual orientation prevalence rates (using measures of sexual feelings) in population-level samples, and work on physiological genital arousal patterns (e.g. using penile plethysmography) in response to viewing preferred and non-preferred sexual imagery. Both lines of evidence consistently demonstrate a bimodal sexual orientation among men—heterosexual or homosexual, but rarely 'bisexual'. This is less so in the case among women. For example, Chivers et al. demonstrated a 'bisexual' genital arousal pattern among both heterosexual and lesbian women, suggesting a decoupling of self-reported sexual feelings (which appears broadly bimodal) from peripheral sexual arousal in women.

If sexual orientation among humans is a mostly bimodal trait, this implicates a canalization of development along a sex-typical route (heterosexual) or a sex-atypical (homosexual) route. Statistical taxometric procedures have confirmed this by demonstrating that latent taxa (i.e. non-arbitrary natural classes) underlie an opposite-sex, or same-sex, orientation in both men and women. Less well established are the factors that may be responsible for this 'shunting' of sexual orientation along two routes (the edges of which are fuzzier in women). These factors are the subject of the remaining discussion and it is suggested that they probably operate neurodevelopmentally before birth.

2. Behavioural and Molecular Genetics

A natural starting point for the neurodevelopment of physiological and behavioural traits must begin with the genetic level of investigation. Several family and twin studies provide clear evidence for a genetic component to both male and female sexual orientation. Family studies, using a range of ascertainment strategies, show increased rate of homosexuality among relatives of homosexual probands. There is also evidence for elevated maternal line transmission of male homosexuality, suggestive of X linkage, but other studies have not found such elevation relative to paternal transmission. Among females, transmission is complex, comprising autosomal and sex-linked routes. Twin studies in both community and population-level samples report moderate heritability estimates, the remaining variance being mopped up by non-shared environmental factors. Early attempts to map specific genetic loci responsible for sexual orientation using family pedigree linkage methods led to the discovery of markers on the Xq28 chromosomal region, with one subsequent replication limiting the effect to males only. However, there is at least one independent study which produced null findings, while a recent genome wide scan revealed no Xq28 linkage in a new sample of families but identified putative additional chromosomal sites (on 7q36, 8p12 and 10q26) which now require denser mapping investigations. These studies are limited by factors such as the unclear maternal versus paternal line transmission effects, possible autosomal transmission and measurement issues. Two candidate gene studies which explored the putative hormonal pathways in the neurodevelopment of sexual orientation (see Section 3): one on the androgen receptor gene and another on aromatase (CYP19A1) both produced null findings. . . .

Rahman, Qazi. From *Neuroscience & Biobehavioral Reviews*, vol. 29, no. 7, October 2005, pp. 1057–1058, 1060, 1062, 1063 (excerpts). Copyright © 2005 by Elsevier Ltd. Reprinted by permission via Rightslink.

3. The Fraternal Birth Order Effect and Maternal Immunity

The maternal immunity hypothesis is certainly the most revolutionary neurodevelopmental model of human sexual orientation. Empirically, it rests on one very reliable finding—the fraternal birth order effect (FBO): that is, homosexual men have a greater number of older brothers than heterosexual men do (and relative to any other category of sibling), in diverse community and po pulation-level samples, and as early as they can be reliably surveyed. The estimated odds of being homosexual increase by around 33% with each older brother, and statistical modelling using epidemiological procedures suggest that approximately 1 in 7 homosexual men may owe their sexual orientation to the FBO effect. It has been suggested that the remaining proportions of homosexual men may owe their sexual orientation to other causes, such as differential prenatal androgen levels. Homosexual and heterosexual women do not differ in sibling sex composition or their birth order, thus any neurodevelopmental explanation for the FBO effect is limited to males. Importantly, recent work has demonstrated that homosexual males with older brothers have significantly lower birth weights compared to heterosexual males with older brothers. As birth weight is undeniably prenatally determined, some common developmental factor operating before birth must underlie FBO and sexual orientation among human males.

Specifically, investigators have proposed a role for the progressive immunization of some mothers to male-linked antigens produced by carrying each succeeding male foetus. That is, the maternal immune system 'sees' male- specific antigens as 'non-self' and begins producing antibodies against them. One possible group of antigens are the Y-linked minor histocompatibility antigens, specifically H–Y. The accumulating H–Y antibodies may divert male-typical sexual differentiation of the foetal brain, leading the individual to be sexually attracted to males. For example, male-specific antibodies may bind to, and inactivate, male-differentiating receptors located on the surface of foetal neurons thus preventing the morphogenesis of masculinized sexual preferences.

The maternal immunity theory is consistent with a number of observations: the number of older sisters is irrelevant to sexual orientation in later born males; the H–Y antigen is expressed by male foetuses only and thus the maternal immune system 'remembers' the number of males carried previously and may modulate its response; and H–Y antigens are strongly represented in neural tissue. Nonetheless, there is no data specifying a role for these particular antigens in sexual preferences among humans. There are several alternative candidate antigens to H–Y, including the distinct Y-linked protein families' *protocadherin* and *neuroligin*, both of which have been found in humans. These cell adhesion proteins are thought to influence cell–cell communication during early male-specific brain morphogenesis and may have male-typical behav-ioural consequences. Consistent with these studies is neurogenetic evidence for the direct transcription of Y-linked sex determination genes *SRY* and *ZFY* in the male human brain (including hypothalamus). The maternal immunity model may also explain the link between birth weight and sexual preferences: mouse models show that maternal immunization to male-derived antigens can affect foetal weight. Furthermore, male mice whose mothers are immunized to H–Y prior to pregnancy show reduced male-typical consummatory sexual behaviour towards receptive females.

The maternal immunity model implicitly relies on a non-hormonal immunologic neurodevelopmental explanation and thus cannot immediately explain the hypermale features (e.g. 2D:4D and AEPs) associated with male homosexuality. It is possible that male-specific antibodies may interact with sexual differentiation processes controlled by sex hormones or be completely independent of them—this is unknown as yet. . . .

4. Neural Circuitry

Neurodevelopmental mechanisms must wire neural circuits differently in those with same-sex attractions from those with opposite-sex attractions, but we still know very little about this circuitry. The first indication for neural correlates of sexual partner preference came from Simon LeVay autopsy study of the third interstitial nucleus of the anterior hypothalamus (INAH-3) which he found to be smaller in homosexual men than in presumed heterosexual men, and indistinguishable from presumed heterosexual women. Another study found a non-significant trend for a femaletypical INAH-3 among homosexual men (and confirmed the heterosexual sex difference), but this was not evidenced the main sexually dimorphic parameter reported by this study (the total number of neurons). This preceding finding is noteworthy as a prediction from the prenatal androgen theory would be that a parameter which shows significant sexual dimorphism should also demonstrate within-sex variation attributable to sexual orientation. A conservative conclusion regarding these data is that while INAH-3 is larger in heterosexual men than in heterosexual women, and possibly smaller in homosexual men, structurally speaking this within-sex difference may not be very large at all.

One recent positron emission tomography study has demonstrated stronger hypothalamic response to serotonergic challenge in heterosexual than in homosexual men, and neuroimaging studies comparing heterosexual men and women while viewing preferred sexual imagery show significantly greater hypothalamic activation in heterosexual men. These findings, coupled with the anatomical findings described earlier, could be taken to suggest that there is a functionally distinct anterior hypothalamic substrate to sexual attraction towards women. This supposition is further supported by mammalian lesion models of the preoptic area (POA) of the anterior hypothalamus showing reduced appetitive responses towards female by male animals. Nevertheless, investigations comparing heterosexual and homosexual women are needed to support a role for this region in sexual preference towards females among humans.

While animal models point to a role for prenatal androgens in producing sexual variation in hypothalamic regions, a similar relationship in humans is unclear. One study found no sexual-orientation-related differences in the distribution of androgen receptors in sexually dimorphic hypothalamic regions. However, one animal model often overlooked by scientists may provide some guidance. Some males of certain species of sheep show an exclusive same-sex preference, and also how reduced aromatase activity and smaller ovine sexually dimorphic nuclei (a possible homolog to the human INAH-3) compared to female-oriented sheep. A role for aromatized metabolites of testosterone in underscoring possible hypothalamic variation related to human sexual orientation requires further study in light of these findings. Moreover, putative sexual orientation differences in aromatase activity in human males may go some way to explaining the 'mosaic' profile of hypo-and hyper-masculinized traits described earlier. For example, a reduction in aromatase activity in homosexual compared to heterosexual men (predicted from the Roselli findings) may lead to reduced availability of aromatized testosterone (i.e. estradiol) which typically masculinizes the male mammalian brain. This may lead to hypo-masculinized hypothalamic circuitry and yet leave excess non-aromatized testosterone to hyper-masculinize additional androgen sensitive traits (e.g. 2D:4D) through other metabolic pathways, such as 5-alpha reductase. Note, one mitigating piece of evidence with respect to these suggestions is the null finding of DuPree et al. regarding sexual-orientation-related variation in the aromatase gene. . . .

5. Is There a Role for Learning in the Development of Human Sexual Orientation?

The role of learning in the development of human sexual orientation has been the subject of much debate and controversy, most likely because it is erroneously believed to result in particular socio-political consequences associated with homosexuality. While data are a little thin on the ground, several lines of evidence mitigate the involvement of learning mechanisms. In animal models, there are documented effects of conditioning on sexual arousal, approach behaviour, sexual performance and strength of sexual preference towards opposite-sex targets, but no robust demonstrations of learning in the organization of same-sex preferences among males. Interestingly, one study in female rats demonstrated that the volume of the sexually dimorphic nucleus of the preoptic region was increased (male-typical) by testosterone administration coupled with same-sex sexual experience. This suggests that sexual experience may interact with steroid exposure to shape sexual partner preferences in females.

In humans, the extent of childhood or adolescent homosexual versus heterosexual activity does not appear to relate to eventual adult sexual orientation. Documented evidence regarding the situational or cultural 'initiation' of juvenile males into extensive same-sex experience (for example, in single-sex public schools in Britain or the obligatory homosexual activity required of young males in the Sambia tribe of New Guinea) does not result in elevated homosexuality in adulthood.

An alternative explanation for the FBO effect is that sexual interaction with older brothers during critical windows of sexual development predisposes towards a homosexual orientation. Studies in national probability samples show that sibling sex-play does not underscore the link between FBO and male sexual orientation, and that the sexual attraction component of sexual orientation, but not sexual activity, are best predicted by frequency of older brothers. In further support, same-sex play between pairs of gay brothers is also unrelated to adult homosexual attraction.

Perhaps parent–child interactions influence the sexual orientation of children? An informative test here is to examine the sexuality of children of homosexual parents because this type of familial dynamic could promote same-sex preferences through observational learning mechanisms. However, evidence from retrospective and prospective studies provides no support for this supposition. Nonetheless, one must bear in mind that if parental behaviour does determine offspring sexual orientation, it could be equally common in homosexual and heterosexual parents.

While a role for learning factors can never be entirely omitted, it is perplexing that several of the key routes by which these could have their effect, such as through sexual experience during childhood or adolescence, or through parental socialization, are not supported. Almost certainly the expression of homosexual *behaviour* has varied over time and across cultures, but there is little reason to think that dispositional homosexuality varies greatly cross-culturally or even historically. . . .

Qazi Rahman, PhD, is a senior lecturer at the Institute of Psychiatry, Kings College London. His research focuses on sexual orientations and the biology of sexuality.

**Stanton L. Jones and
Alex W. Kwee**

Scientific Research, Homosexuality, and the Church's Moral Debate: An Update

Etiological Research

Significant new research on etiology has emerged in six areas: 1) behavioral genetics; 2) genetic scanning, 3) human brain structure studies, 4) studies of "gay sheep" and "gay fruit flies," 5) fraternal birth order research, and 6) familial structure impact.

Behavioral Genetics

Bailey's behavioral genetics studies of sexual orientation in twins and other siblings seemed to provide solid evidence of a substantial degree of genetic influence on formation of homosexual orientation. Jones and Yarhouse criticized these studies severely, most importantly on the grounds that both studies were making population estimates of the degree of genetic influence on sexual orientation on *potentially biased samples,* samples recruited from advertisements in gay publications and hence potentially biased by differential volunteerism by subjects inclined to favor a genetic hypothesis for the causation of their orientation. Later research by Bailey and other associates with a truly representative sample of twins drawn from the Australian Twin Registry in fact refuted the earlier findings by failing to find a significant genetic effect in the causation of homosexual orientation.

Not included in our review was a major behavioral genetics study paralleling the work of Bailey: Kendler, Thornton, Gilman, and Kessler. This study is remarkable in two ways. First, it replicates almost exactly the findings of the earlier Bailey studies in reporting relatively strong probandwise concordances for homosexual monozygotic twins. Kendler et al. report their findings as pairwise concordances, but when the simple conversions to probandwise concordances are done, Kendler et al.'s 48% proband-wise concordance for males and females together (reported as a 31.6% pairwise concordance) is remarkably similar to Bailey's reports of probandwise concordances of 52% for men and 48% for women.

Second, the Kendler et al. study is also remarkably similar to the earlier Bailey studies in its methodological weaknesses. Trumpeted as a study correcting the "unrepresentative and potentially biased samples" of the Bailey studies by using a "more representative sample," specifically a "U. S. national probability sample" (p. 1843), this

study appears actually to suffer all of the original problems of volunteer sample bias of the 1991 and 1993 Bailey studies. Further, the methodological problems give every sign of compounding one upon the next. The description of the methodology is confusing: Kendler et al. state that their sample comes from a MacArthur Foundation study of 3,032 representatively chosen respondents, but then they note that since this sample produced too few twins and almost no homosexual twins (as would be expected), they turned to a different sample of 50,000 households that searched for twins, and here the clear sampling problems begin: 14.8% of the households reported a twin among the siblings, but only 60% gave permission to contact the twin. There was further erosion of the sample as only 20.6% of the twins agreed to participate if the initial contact was with another family member, compared to 60.4% if the initial contact was a twin him- or herself (and given the lower likelihood of an initial contact being with a twin, this suggests a low response rate for twins overall). Yet further erosion may have occurred at the next step of seeking contact information of all siblings in the family; the write-up is confusing on this point. With all these potential sampling problems, it is then quite striking that the absolute number of identical/monozygotic twin pairs concordant for homosexuality were only 6 (out of a total of 19 pairs where at least one twin was "non-heterosexual"). With such a small absolute number of monozygotic twin pairs concordant for homosexuality, the smallest bias in the assembly of the sample would introduce problems in data interpretation; loss of just two concordant twin pairs would have wiped out the findings. It is remarkable that Kendler et al. give no explicit attention to these problems. Thus, we must regard this new study, promoted by some as a replication of Bailey's original 1991 and 1993 studies, as having the same fatal flaws as those earlier studies and as rightly superseded by Bailey's report in 2000 that there is no statistically significant indication of genetic influence on sexual orientation.

Genetic Scanning

Mustanski et al. reported on a "full genome scan of sexual orientation in men" (p. 272). This is the third study of genetics and homosexuality to emerge from

Jones, Stanton L.; Kwee, Alex W. From *Journal of Psychology and Christianity (JPC)*, vol. 24, no. 4, Winter 2005, pp. 304–307, 308–312 (excerpts). Copyright © 2005 by Christian Association for Psychological Studies, Inc – CAPS. Reprinted by permission.

the laboratory of the associates of Dean Hamer, and this study utilized 146 families; 73 families previously studied by either Hamer, Hu, Magnuson, Hu, and Pattatucci or Hu et al., and 73 new families not previously studied. The same sample limitations are present in these studies as were discussed in Jones and Yarhouse (pp. 79–83). If these studies were attempting to establish population estimates, these would constitute biased samples, but because they explicitly state that they are looking for genetic factors in a subpopulation of homosexual men predetermined to be more likely to manifest genetic factors, these are limitations and not methodological weaknesses. They obtained their sample through "advertisements in local and national homophile publications" and the "sole inclusion criterion was the presence of at least two self-acknowledged gay male siblings" (p. 273), a rare occurrence indeed.

Two findings are worth noting. First, the Mustanski et al. study continued the pattern of failing to replicate the original 1993 Hamer finding of an Xq28 region of the X chromosome being linked to male homosexuality, this despite somewhat heroic statistical focus in this study. This is yet another blow to the credibility of their original findings.

Second, while media outlets headlined the Mustanski et al. study as having found genes linked to homosexuality on chromosomes 7, 8, and 10, this is precisely what they did *not* find, but rather "we found one region of near significance and two regions close to the criteria for suggestive linkage" (p. 273). None of their findings, in other words, achieved statistical significance. It is hard to tell whether these findings represent a cluster of near false positives that will fail future replication, or clues that will lead to more fine-grained and statistically significant findings. If the latter, these genetic segments may be neither necessary nor sufficient to cause homo sexual orientation, and may either contribute to the causation of the orientation directly or indirectly. This is an intriguing but ambiguous report.

Human Brain Structure Studies

New brain research allows us to expand the reported findings on the relationship of brain structure to sexual orientation, and to correct one element of our prior presentation of the data in this complex field. We duplicate [here] . . . (Table 1) part of the table summarizing brain findings from pages 68–69 of Jones and Yarhouse.

Table 1

Summary of Brain Differences by Biological Sex and Sexual Orientation

Study	INAH1	Brain INAH2	Region INAH3	INAH4
Swaab & Fliers (1985)	HetM > HetF			
Swaab & Hoffman (1988)	HetM = HomM; (HetM & HomM) > HetF			
Allen et al. (1989)	HetM = HetF	HetM > HetF	HetM > HetF	HetM = HetF
LeVay (1991)	HetM = HetF	HetM = HetF	HetM > (HetF & HomM)	HetM = HetF
Byne et al. (2000)	HetM = HetF	HetM = HetF	HetM > HetF	HetM = HetF
Byne et al. (2001)	HetM = HetF	HetM = HetF	HetM > HetF	HetM = HetF
			HetM = HomM in number of neurons	

HetM = heterosexual males; HetF = heterosexual females; HomM = homosexual males.

Our correction is to recategorize in Table 1 the findings of Swaab and Hoffman from our listing, following the original report, as from the SDNH or sexually differentiated nucleus of the hypothalamus to a finding reporting on the INAH1 or interstitial nucleus of the hypothalamus, area 1. The review of Byne et al. pointed out that the SDNH is the INAH1; Swaab's 1988 report was an extension of his earlier work and not an exploration of a new area. The new work of Byne et al. continued the pattern of refuting Swaab's reported findings.

The new findings reporting on brain structure and sexual orientation (summarized in Table 1) come from the respected laboratory of William Byne and his colleagues. We cited Byne heavily in our critique of the famous Simon LeVay studies of brain differences in the INAH3 region. Byne et al. replicated the previous findings of sexual dimorphism (male-female differences) in INAH3, and thus it is now safe to say that this is a stable finding. Further, Byne and his team have refined the analysis to be able to say, based on their 2000 study, that the INAH3 size difference by sex "was attributable to a sex difference in neuronal number and not in neuronal size or density." Simply put, the INAH3 area in women is, on average, smaller than it is in men, and this is because women have fewer neurons in this area, and *not* because their neurons are smaller or less dense.

This makes the findings of Byne et al. on sexual orientation yet more curious; they found the size (specifically, volume) of the INAH3s of homosexual males to be intermediate (to a statistically nonsignificant degree) between heterosexual males and heterosexual females. In other words, the volume of the INAH3s was, on average, between the average volumes of heterosexual males and heterosexual females such that the differences did not achieve statistical significance in comparison to either heterosexual males or females. Hence, "sexual orientation cannot be reliably predicted on the basis of INAH3 volume alone." Further, and to complicate things more, they found that the nonsignificant difference noted between homosexual and heterosexual males was *not* attributable (as it was for the male-female difference) to numbers of neurons, as homosexual and heterosexual males were found to have comparable neuronal counts. So, there may be a difference between homosexual and heterosexual males, but if there is, it is not the same type of difference as that between males and females.

To complicate the analysis even further, Byne et al. point out that these differences, if they exist, are not proof of prenatal, biological determination of sexual orientation. While it is possible that differences in INHA3 may be strongly influenced by prenatal hormones, "In addition, sex related differences may also emerge later in development as the neurons that survive become part of functional circuits" (p. 91). Specifically, the difference in volume could be attributed to "a reduction in neuropil within the INAH3 in the homosexual group" (p. 91) as a result of "postnatal experience." In other words, if there are brain structure differences between homosexuals and heterosexuals, they could as well be the result rather than the cause of sexual behavior and sexual preference. (The same conclusion about directionality of causation can be drawn about the new study showing activation of sexual brain centers in response to female pheromones by male heterosexuals, and to male pheromones by female heterosexuals *and* male homosexuals. The authors themselves point out that these brain activations could be the result of learning as well as evidence of the "hard-wiring" of the brain.) . . .

Second, and in a rare admission for those advancing biological explanations of sexual orientation, Roselli et al. admit that the direction of causation is at this time

completely unclear, in the process echoing the possible causal role of postnatal experience mentioned by Byne et al. above:

> However, the existing data do not reveal which is established first—oSDN size or mate preference. One might assume that the neural structure is determined first and that this, in turn, guides the development of sexual partner preference. However, it is equally possible that some other factors(s), including social influences or learned associations, might shape sexual partner preference first. Then, once a sexual partner preference is established, the continued experiences and/or behaviors associated with a given preference might affect the size of the oSDN. (p. 241)

A new study released in June, 2005 has ignited the latest frenzy about biological causation of sexual orientation. In response to this study, the president of the Human Rights Campaign ("the largest national lesbian, gay, bisexual and transgender political organization") stated that "Science is closing the door on right-wing distortions. . . . The growing body of scientific evidence continues to refute the opponents of equality who maintain that sexual orientation is a 'choice.'" Chairman of the Case Western Reserve University Department of Biochemistry Michael Weiss expressed for the *New York Times* his hope that this study "will take the discussion about sexual preferences out of the realm of morality and put it into the realm of science." Both quotes epitomize the over-interpretation and illogic of those anxious to press findings from science to moral conclusions.

The new study appears to be a strong piece of scientific research that will have important implications for our understanding of the biological bases of sexual behavior. The researchers generated a gene fragment (the *"fruitless (fru)"* allele) that was "constitutively spliced in either the male or the female mode" in the chromosomes of the opposite sex (i.e., male fruit flies had the allele inserted in a female mode and female fruit flies had the allele inserted in a male mode) with dramatic effects: "Forcing female splicing in the male results in a loss of male courtship behavior and orientation, confirming that male-specific splicing of *fru* is indeed essential for male behavior. More dramatically, females in which *fru* is spliced in the male mode behave as if they were males: they court other females" (p. 786). The results reported were indeed powerful; the behavioral distinctions in the modified fruit flies were almost unequivocal.

The authors of this study were reasonably circumspect in their report of the implications of their findings, though others were not as noted before. Three issues deserve attention. First, as in our discussion of "gay sheep," the differences between human and animal (or insect) mating patterns are enormous, and those differences limit application to the human situation. Demir and Dickson noted that male courtship of the female fruit fly is highly scripted, "largely a fixed-action pattern" (p. 785). The finding that the normal, almost robotic mating patterns of this creature are hard-wired is hardly surprising; in contrast, the enormous complexity of human sexual and romantic response indicates that such a finding will be challenging to apply to the human condition. Further, the interpretation that this study establishes a genetic base for "sexual orientation" in fruit flies is careless; the study rather finds genetic determination (to some degree) of an entire pattern of mating/reproductive behavior. The genetic control of mating behavior in this study is of something both more and less than sexual orientation as experienced by humans.

Second, we have plenty of existing data to indicate that no such encompassing genetic determination of sexual behavior exists in humans. The behavior genetics evidence of sexual orientation (see the earlier discussion of the Kendler et al. study) provides strong evidence that genetic factors provide (at most) incomplete determination of sexual orientation, even if genetic factors are part of a multivariant causal array.

Third, we must question the following claim of the authors:

> Thus, male-specific splicing of *fru* is both necessary and *sufficient* [emphasis added] to specify male courtship behavior and sexual orientation. A complex innate behavior is thus specified by the action of a single gene, demonstrating that behavioral switch genes do indeed exist and identifying fru as one such gene.

Strictly understood, the authors appear to be claiming that the presence of *fru* elicits, *necessarily and sufficiently,* stereotypical male courtship by males of female fruit flies, but a famous study from a decade before falsifies the sufficiency of *fru* causation. Zhang and Odenwald reported on genetic alterations in male fruit flies which produced "homosexual behavior" in the altered fruit flies. This study too resulted in many tabloid headlines heralding the creation of a "homosexual gene." Media reports failed to cite the other curious finding of the study: when genetically normal or "straight" fruit flies were introduced into the habitat of the "gay" flies without females present, the normal (genetically unaltered) male flies began engaging in the same type of "homosexual" behavior as the genetically altered flies. In other words, genetically normal ("straight") flies began to act like homosexual flies because of their *social environment*. Thus, in a most biological experiment, evidence of environmental ("psychological") influence emerged once again. So if the authors of the 2005 study are claiming that the presence of *fru* elicits (is sufficient to produce) stereotypical male courtship, that claim was falsified a decade before by the finding that normal male fruit flies (presumably with intact *fru* alleles), when exposed to certain social contexts ("gay" flies), engage in behavior that violates the stereotypical male courtship of females; other conditions—specifically,

social conditions—are also sufficient to elicit homosexual behavior in fruit flies.

Together, these three issues suggest that, as powerful as the recent findings about fruit flies are, interpretive caution in application to humans is indicated.

Fraternal Birth Order Research

The fraternal birth order studies by Ray Blanchard, Anthony Bogaert, and various other researchers purport to show that sexual orientation in men correlates with an individual's number of older brothers. Specifically, it is claimed that male homosexuals tend to be born later in their sibships than male heterosexuals, and that male homosexuality is statistically (and causally) related to the number of older biological brothers (but not sisters) in the family. This purported relationship within the fraternal birth order is such that each additional older brother, it is claimed, increases the odds of homosexuality by 33%, and for gay men with approximately 2.5 older brothers, older brothers equal all the other causes of homosexuality combined.

Blanchard, Bogaert, and others advance the so-called maternal immune hypothesis to explain the fraternal birth order effect. According to this hypothesis, some mothers progressively produce, in response to each succeeding male fetus, antibodies to a substance called the H-Y antigen, which is produced by male fetuses and foreign to female bodies. The maternally produced anti-H-Y antibodies are thought to be passed on to the male fetus, preventing the fetal brain from developing in a male typical pattern, thereby causing the affected sons to develop homosexual orientations in later life. So much hyperbole surrounds the maternal immune causal hypothesis that it appears the assumption is simply being made that the fraternal birth order effect itself is indisputable when, in fact, it is not. We will direct the bulk of our critical attention to the birth order phenomenon. The maternal immune theory underlying the phenomenon can be quite readily dispatched at this point by stating that no direct evidence has ever been found for it, and so it remains purely speculative.

The major flaw of the fraternal birth order research is that the main studies were conducted on nonrepresentative samples. For example, one of the "landmark" studies that demonstrated the birth order effect recruited its sample from the 1994 Toronto Gay Pride Parade and several LGBT community organizations. Nonrepresentative samples are known to be vulnerable to a variety of selection biases. For instance, perhaps later-born gay men were overrepresented in this sample because they were more apt to be "out and proud," participate in Gay Pride events, and affiliate with overtly LGBT groups. If later born siblings tend to be less conventional and more rebellious as some research shows, later-born gay men, accordingly, may be less gender conforming and more likely to flaunt their sexual orientation. This may have resulted in an overrepresentation of later-born gay men and an underrepresentation of earlier-born gay men at Gay Pride events and within LGBT groups, which naturally exaggerated the fraternal birth order effect in this sample. This is just one of several possible selection biases which may have flawed Blanchard and Bogaert's sample.

To his credit, Bogaert attempted to correct for the methodological flaw of selection bias by examining national probability samples in the United States and Britain respectively. His study yielded a finding of fraternal birth order effects in both samples. While this may appear to replicate initial research results, we must question the size of the effects given the large samples involved—over 1,700 subjects in each of the samples. Bogaert did not clearly report the effect sizes he found. It is well known that using large enough samples, even small differences can be found to be statistically significant. Since statistical significance is a function of both sample size and effect size, and we really care about the effect size (and not merely that it is non-zero), Bogaert's findings are quite unhelpful.

In an even more recent study, Bogaert and Cairney attempted to answer the question of whether there is a fraternal birth order and parental age interaction effect in the prediction of sexual orientation. The researchers examined two samples—a U.S. national probability sample, and the flawed Canadian sample which we discussed above. The study based on the U.S. sample found an interaction, but the data was so flawed—and acknowledged to be so by the authors themselves—that we cannot possibly take its conclusion seriously. Specifically, the preexisting U.S. data allowed for only an examination of absolute (not fraternal) birth order, surmised sexual orientation from behavior alone, and did not separate biological from non-biological siblings. The conclusion was counterintuitive in that while a positive association between (absolute) birth order and the likelihood of homosexuality was found, this association was weakened and in fact *reversed* with increasing maternal age. We believe that this conclusion highlights the problem of bias when researchers attempt to find putative phenomena in data to support a cherished theory. If one is trying to establish a link between maternal age and homosexuality, it seems counterintuitive that the likelihood of homosexuality weakens or is reversed with increasing maternal age. Of course, if there is no relationship between sexual orientation and maternal age (which we suspect), a finding of *any* relationship is probably spurious and a methodological artifact. The researchers acknowledge the counterintuitiveness of their result by stating that they "know of no evidence of a stronger maternal reaction [to the H-Y antigen] in younger (versus older) mothers" (p. 32), betraying their bias towards a theory for which no direct evidence has ever been established, and then calling for new research.

Turning to the Canadian sample, Bogaert and Cairney found a Parental Age x Birth Order interaction. Their weighted analysis (giving larger families a greater impact on the results) revealed that this interaction was carried by a Mother's Age x Older Sisters effect. This finding actually *undermines* the fraternal birth order theory

because it provides some evidence that homosexuality is independent of the fraternal birth order effect. The authors acknowledge but downplay this, calling instead for the gathering of new data.

Other studies have falsified the fraternal birth order effect or showed no support for the maternal immune hypothesis. Using an enormous and nationally representative sample of adolescents that we discuss fully below, Bearman and Brückner found "no evidence for a speculative evolutionary model of homosexual preference" (i.e., the older-brother findings; p. 1199).

Despite various methodological problems with the fraternal birth order research, we concede that the evidence as a whole points to some sort of relationship between the number of older brothers and homosexuality. As responsible scientists, we should approach this body of research critically but not ignore the fact that it consistently shows some link between sexual orientation and fraternal but not sororal birth order. Research may well identify some pathway by which some men develop a stable same-sex attraction that is linked to their placement in the birth order. However, those who argue that the maternal immunosensitivity theory explains the fraternal birth order effect run into the problem of having to show that the same hypothesis does not underlie pedophilia, sexual violence, and other forms of sexual deviancy. While Blanchard, Bogaert, and other researchers deny any link between fraternal birth order and pedophilia, or they believe that any such link exists only for pedophiles who are homosexual, other studies have demonstrated a link between fraternal birth order and general (pedophilic and non-pedophilic) sexual offending, raising the possibility that homosexuality shares a common pathway with some forms of sexual deviance.

Research has not clearly established what this pathway is. One of the most natural but politically divisive speculations, which cautiously raises its head in the literature now and then, is that childhood sexualization and abuse has some causative relationship to homosexuality and pedophilia. This speculation is logical in relation to the fraternal birth order effect because younger brothers with higher fraternal birth order indices may have a higher probability of being victimized sexually by older brothers or otherwise experiencing same-sex sexualization. Preadolescent sexualization and abuse underlie the post-natal learning theory of homosexuality and pedophilia, which most recently has been supported by James in his review of several major studies. However plausible this theory appears, it is based on inferences from other studies and the direct empirical evidence for it is extremely weak.

Familial Structure Impact

A particularly powerful study challenging all of the major paradigms asserting biological determination of sexual orientation, and of the claim that there is no meaningful evidence of psychological/experiential causation of orientation, was recently published. Bearman and Brückner reported on analyses of an enormous database of almost 30,000 sexuality interviews with adolescents, with fascinating findings on the determinants of same-sex attraction for males (they found no evidence of significant determinants for females). Their summary of their findings merits citation in full:

> The findings presented here confirm some findings from previous research and stand in marked contrast to most previous research in a number of respects. First, we find no evidence for intrauterine transfer of hormone effects on social behavior. Second, we find no support for genetic influences on same-sex preference net of social structural constraints. Third, we find no evidence for a speculative evolutionary model of homosexual preference. Finally, we find substantial indirect evidence in support of a socialization model at the individual level. (p. 1199)

Table 2

Core Findings of Bearman & Brückner

Relationship (Subject is a . . .)	% Reporting Same-Sex Attraction	N (all males)
Opposite Sex Dizygotic Twin	16.8%	185
Same Sex Dizygotic Twin	9.8%	276
Same Sex Monozygotic Twin	9.9%	262
Opposite Sex Full Sibling	7.3%	427
Same Sex Full Sibling	7.9%	596
Other (adopted non-related; half-sibling)	10.6%	832

Their second conclusion is a direct reference to the types of genetic influence posited by Bailey and others; the third conclusion a direct reference to the "older-brother" findings of Blanchard, Bogaert and others. But not only do their findings contradict other research, a new finding of socialization effects on same-sex attraction emerge from their data (see Table 2).

Bearman and Brückner found a single family constellation arrangement that significantly increased the likelihood that an adolescent male would report same-sex attraction, and that was when the adolescent male was a dizygotic (fraternal) twin whose co-twin is a sister (what they call "male opposite-sex twins"); in this arrangement, occurrence of same-sex attraction more than doubled over the base-rate of 7% to 8%: "we show that adolescent male opposite-sex twins are *twice as likely* as expected to report same-sex attraction, and that the pattern of concordance (similarity across pairs) of same-sex preference for sibling pairs does not suggest genetic influence independent of the social context" (p. 1181). They advance a socialization hypothesis to explain this finding, specifically proposing that sexual attraction is an outgrowth of gender socialization, and that no arrangement presents as much a challenge to parents to gender socialization than for a boy to be born simultaneous with a girl co-twin. In other words, they suggest that the parental task of accomplishing effective solidification of male sexual identity is challenged by parents having to handle a mixed-sex twin pair. The result of the diminished effectiveness of sexual identity formation in boys on average is the increased probability of same-sex attraction in the group of boys with twin sisters.

Bearman and Brückner go on to explore in their data the possibility that there could be a hormonal explanation for this finding: "Our data falsify the hormonal transfer hypothesis [i.e., the hypothesis posited to explain the fraternal birth order phenomenon], by isolating a single condition that eliminates the OS effect we observe—the presence of an older same-sex sibling" (p. 1181). Put simply, they found their effect disappeared when the boy with the twin sister was born into a family where there was already an older brother, an effect they attributed to the family already having grown accustomed to the process of establishing the sexual identity of a boy child; parents appear to be able to better handle the special challenges of a mixed-sex twin pair when they have already had some practice with an older brother. They firmly suggest that their "results support the hypothesis that less gendered socialization in early childhood and preadolescence shapes subsequent same-sex romantic preferences" (p. 1181). At a moment in time when it is common for many to deny that any firm evidence exists for the influence of non-biological causes on sexual orientation, these are remarkable findings (perhaps especially when the presence of an older brother decreases rather than increases the likelihood of homosexual orientation). . . .

STANTON L. JONES, PhD, is provost and professor of psychology at Wheaton College.

ALEX W. KWEE is a licensed clinical psychologist providing Christian-faith affirming psychological care to clients.

EXPLORING THE ISSUE

Is Sexual Orientation Biologically Based?

Critical Thinking and Reflection

1. How does Rahman define sexual orientation in his review of the literature? How do you define sexual orientation?
2. Why are studies of twins important to understanding the possible genetic or biological roots of sexual orientation?
3. What criticisms of social learning theories of sexual orientation does Rahman have?
4. What criticisms of genetic or biological theories of sexual orientation do Jones and Kwee present?
5. How might research on the biological or socially learned origins of sexual orientation impact public debate on social issues such as "reparative therapy" or marriage equality?

Is There Common Ground?

Recently, former "Sex and the City" star Cynthia Nixon sparked a controversy when discussing her sexual orientation in an interview. Nixon, who had been married to a man but is now partnered with a woman stated, "And for me, it is a choice. I understand for many people it's not, but for me it's a choice and you don't get to define my gayness for me."

The pushback from gay activists was strong. Writer Jon Aravosis predicted that Nixon's words would "do tremendous damage to our civil rights effort. Every religious right hatemonger is now going to quote this woman every single time they want to deny us our civil rights."

Several days later, Nixon released a statement to clarify her remarks. She stated "While I don't often use the word, the technically precise term for my orientation is bisexual. I believe bisexuality is not a choice, it is a fact. What I have 'chosen' is to be in a gay relationship."

Scenarios like this highlight the political, religious, and social contentions surrounding the origins of our sexual orientations. In the original interview, Nixon also noted that many are "concerned that it not be seen as a choice, because if it's a choice, then we could opt out. I say it doesn't matter if we flew here or we swam here, it matters that we are here and we are one group. . . ." In his response, Aravosis agreed with this statement, to an extent, saying "And finally, she's right. It shouldn't matter if it's a choice. . . . The entire reason we have a civil rights movement is because it shouldn't matter, but it does."

What is the importance of studies seeking to find the social or biological "cause" of our sexual orientations? Do you think sexual orientation is, as Qazi Rahman believes, a biological, or inborn, trait? Or is it a trait that is socially learned, as Jones and Kwee state? Another researcher, Lisa Diamond, believes in many cases sexual orientation can be "fluid," or caused by a complex combination of biological and environmental factors that may change over time? What do you think about this theory? Finally, does it matter how we obtain our sexual orientations? Why or why not?

Create Central

www.mhhe.com/createcentral

References

(1) A. Witchel, "Life After Sex," *New York Times*, January 19, 2012.
(2) J. Aravosis, "Actress Cynthia Nixon Says It's a Choice to Be Gay. And She's Wrong," *AmericaBlog* (January 23, 2012).

Additional Resources

Bagemihl, B. (1999). *Biological Exuberance: Animal Homosexuality and Natural Diversity.* New York, NY: Free Press.

Cook, A.T. (2004). *And God Loves Each One: A Resource for Dialogue about Sexual Orientation.* Washington, DC: ManyVoices.org.

Diamond, L. (2009). *Sexual Fluidity: Understanding Women's Love and Desire.* Cambridge, MA: Harvard University Press.

Levine, S. (2012). *Gay, Straight and the Reason Why: The Science of Sexual Orientation.* New York, NY: Oxford University Press.

Internet References . . .

Psychiatry Giant Sorry for Backing Gay "Cure"

This article describes the evolving positions on reparative therapy held by one leading psychiatrist.

www.nytimes.com/2012/05/19/health/dr-robert-l-spitzer-noted-psychiatrist-apologizes-for-study-on-gay-cure.html

American Institute for Bisexuality

This organization encourages, supports, and assists research and education about bisexuality, through programs likely to make a material difference and enhance public knowledge, awareness, and understanding about bisexuality.

www.bisexual.org

National Association for Research and Therapy of Homosexuality

This organization promotes research and therapeutic treatment for individuals struggling with unwanted homosexuality.

www.narth.com

Sexual Orientation "Choice" is Irrelevant

This op-ed by James Castle in the *Minnesota Daily* proposes that the idea of sexual orientation being a choice should have no bearing on your support of same-sex marriage.

www.mndaily.com/opinion/columns/2013/03/10/sexual-orientation-%E2%80%98choice%E2%80%99-irrelevant

Selected, Edited, and with Issue Framing Material by:
Ryan W. McKee, *Widener University*
and
William J. Taverner, *Center for Family Life Education*

ISSUE

Should Same-Sex Marriage Be Legal?

YES: **Theodore B. Olson**, from "The Conservative Case for Gay Marriage: Why Same-Sex Marriage Is an American Value," *The Daily Beast* (January 8, 2010), www.thedailybeast.com/newsweek/2010/01/08/the-conservative-case-for-gay-marriage.html

NO: **Lyle Denniston**, from "Same-Sex Marriage III: The Arguments Against," (November 29, 2012), www.scotusblog.com/2012/11/same-sex-marriage-iii-the-arguments-against/

Learning Outcomes
After reading this issue, you should be able to:
• Explain the controversy surrounding California's Proposition 8 and the subsequent legal challenges.
• Compare conservative arguments both for and against same-sex marriage.
• Describe the Defense of Marriage Act (DOMA) and its impact on same-sex marriage.

ISSUE SUMMARY

YES: Theodore B. Olson, former U.S. solicitor general, explains that fighting for marriage equality for same-sex couples is an expression of true conservative values.

NO: Lyle Denniston, legal journalist and blogger for the award-winning SCOTUS blog, presents the arguments against same-sex marriage that are likely to be used in any legal attempts to marriage equality federal law.

On May 17, 2004, Massachusetts became the first state in the United States to grant marriage licenses to same-sex couples. The state acted under the direction of its supreme court, which had found that withholding marriage licenses from lesbian and gay couples violated the state constitution. More than 600 same-sex couples applied for marriage licenses that first day alone. The first same-sex couple to be issued a marriage license was Marcia Kadish and Tanya McClosky. That couple had waited over 18 years for the day to arrive.

Since that day, the legal battle over the same-sex marriage, otherwise known as "marriage equality," has been on the forefront of the American culture war. Same-sex marriage has been used as a "wedge issue" in American political elections, motivating voters on all sides to make their voices heard. In response, over 30 states enacted laws or state constitutional amendments prohibiting legal recognition of same-sex marriage (some even included restrictions on civil unions). These states were in addition to those who already had anti-marriage equality laws, and in addition to a *federal* law, known as the Defense of Marriage Act (DOMA), signed by President Clinton in 1996. DOMA defines marriage at the federal level as being between one man and one woman. It also prevents states

from having to recognize same-sex marriage licenses that may be granted in other states.

Despite these setbacks to the cause of marriage equality, proponents have been gaining ground. According to Washington Post/ABC News polls taken between 2004 and 2013, the percentage of Americans who think same-sex marriage should be legal has increased from 41 percent to an all-time high of 58 percent. During the same timeframe, those who believe it should be illegal decreased from 55 percent to 36 percent. The last decade has also seen an increase in the number of states passing marriage equality laws—at the time of this writing, 12 states, as well as Washington, D.C., gave same-sex couples the right to marry. Strangely, this tally does not include California, which has a unique place in the legal landscape.

In 2008, a California state supreme court ruling opened the door for same-sex couples to wed. In response, groups opposed to marriage equality sponsored a ballot initiative, known as Proposition 8, asking voters to weigh in on the issue. That November, a majority of California voters approved the measure, again making same-sex marriage illegal in the state. Opponents of Prop 8 challenged the law in court, but in May 2009 the law was upheld as constitutional by the California supreme court. To add another twist to the saga, the ruling did not invalidate the approximately 18,000 same-sex marriages that occurred during the brief window of opportunity. Those couples remain legally married. After several appeals by Prop 8 supporters, the legal challenge found its way to the U.S. Supreme Court. In June 2013 decisions were handed down on the legal standing of Prop 8 as well as on the constitutionality of DOMA, the law signed by President Clinton in 1996. In the Prop 8 case, the Supreme Court cleared the way for legal same-sex marriages to resume.

The case against DOMA centered around 83-year-old Edith Windsor. After her wife, Thea Spyer, died in 2009, Windsor inherited her estate but was levied an estate tax bill of over $300,000! Had Windsor been married to a man, she would have owed nothing. Since they were married in Canada and lived in New York, their marriage was legally recognized at the state level. DOMA, however, prevented federal recognition of their marriage, and thus the estate tax bill was issued. Windsor sued and, after a lengthy appeals process, the U.S. Supreme Court decided in her favor, striking down parts of DOMA.

Throughout this legal odyssey, popular rallying cries surrounding same-sex marriage have been framed largely through a lens of equality versus tradition, with activists on the side of the "wedge issue" arguing for loosening prohibitions on same-sex marriage and expanding personal freedoms. Love, they argue, is love—regardless of the sex of the couple. These arguments have typically been expressed by those who might be considered politically liberal. The politically conservative arguments against same-sex marriage have typically focused on Judeo-Christian religious teachings, and a desire not to overturn thousands of years of tradition. Marriage is marriage, and marriage is between one man and one woman.

But as debates occurred in courtrooms, living rooms, and legislatures across the country, many on both sides of the political spectrum found themselves exploring the gray areas of the issue. Could one be a conservative and support marriage equality? Could one be socially liberal in certain areas, but oppose same-sex marriage? As the Prop 8 and DOMA cases reached the Supreme Court, activists and organizations of all political stripes and ideologies made their voices heard.

Theodore Olson, a former U.S. solicitor general and an attorney who argued the case against Proposition 8 in federal court, argues in favor of same-sex marriage in the YES selection. Olson, who describes himself as "a politically active, lifelong Republican, a veteran of the Ronald Reagan and George W. Bush administrations" writes that marriage equality is a fundamentally conservative value and a constitutional right. Lyle Denniston, a journalist who has covered the Supreme Court for over 55 years, presents the legal arguments most likely to be used against the constitutionality of same-sex marriage.

YES ↙

Theodore B. Olson

The Conservative Case for Gay Marriage: Why Same-Sex Marriage Is an American Value

Together with my good friend and occasional courtroom adversary David Boies, I am attempting to persuade a federal court to invalidate California's Proposition 8—the voter-approved measure that overturned California's constitutional right to marry a person of the same sex.

My involvement in this case has generated a certain degree of consternation among conservatives. How could a politically active, lifelong Republican, a veteran of the Ronald Reagan and George W. Bush administrations, challenge the "traditional" definition of marriage and press for an "activist" interpretation of the Constitution to create another "new" constitutional right?

My answer to this seeming conundrum rests on a lifetime of exposure to persons of different backgrounds, histories, viewpoints, and intrinsic characteristics, and on my rejection of what I see as superficially appealing but ultimately false perceptions about our Constitution and its protection of equality and fundamental rights.

Many of my fellow conservatives have an almost knee-jerk hostility toward gay marriage. This does not make sense, because same-sex unions promote the values conservatives prize. Marriage is one of the basic building blocks of our neighborhoods and our nation. At its best, it is a stable bond between two individuals who work to create a loving household and a social and economic partnership. We encourage couples to marry because the commitments they make to one another provide benefits not only to themselves but also to their families and communities. Marriage requires thinking beyond one's own needs. It transforms two individuals into a union based on shared aspirations, and in doing so establishes a formal investment in the well-being of society. The fact that individuals who happen to be gay want to share in this vital social institution is evidence that conservative ideals enjoy widespread acceptance. Conservatives should celebrate this, rather than lament it.

Legalizing same-sex marriage would also be a recognition of basic American principles, and would represent the culmination of our nation's commitment to equal rights. It is, some have said, the last major civil-rights milestone yet to be surpassed in our two-century struggle to attain the goals we set for this nation at its formation.

This bedrock American principle of equality is central to the political and legal convictions of Republicans, Democrats, liberals, and conservatives alike. The dream that became America began with the revolutionary concept expressed in the Declaration of Independence in words that are among the most noble and elegant ever written: "We hold these truths to be self-evident, that all men are created equal, that they are endowed by their Creator with certain unalienable Rights, that among these are Life, Liberty and the pursuit of Happiness."

Sadly, our nation has taken a long time to live up to the promise of equality. In 1857, the Supreme Court held that an African-American could not be a citizen. During the ensuing Civil War, Abraham Lincoln eloquently reminded the nation of its founding principle: "our fathers brought forth on this continent, a new nation, conceived in liberty and dedicated to the proposition that all men are created equal."

At the end of the Civil War, to make the elusive promise of equality a reality, the 14th Amendment to the Constitution added the command that "no State . . . shall deprive any person of life, liberty or property, without due process of law; nor deny to any person . . . the equal protection of the laws."

Subsequent laws and court decisions have made clear that equality under the law extends to persons of all races, religions, and places of origin. What better way to make this national aspiration complete than applying the same protection to men and women who differ from others only on the basis of their sexual orientation? I cannot think of a single reason—and have not heard one since I undertook this venture—for continued discrimination against decent, hardworking members of our society on that basis.

Various federal and state laws have accorded certain rights and privileges to gay and lesbian couples, but these protections vary dramatically at the state level, and nearly universally deny true equality to gays and lesbians who wish to marry. The very idea of marriage is basic to recognition as equals in our society; any status sort of that is inferior, unjust, and unconstitutional.

The United States Supreme Court has repeatedly held that marriage is one of the most fundamental rights that we have as Americans under our Constitution. It is an expression of our desire to create a social partnership, to live and share life's joys and burdens with the person we love, and to form a lasting bond and a social identity. The Supreme Court has said that marriage is a part of the Constitution's protections of liberty, privacy, freedom of association, and spiritual identification. In short, the right to marry helps us to define ourselves and our place in a community. Without it, there can be no true equality under the law.

It is true that marriage in this nation traditionally has been regarded as a relationship exclusively between a man and a woman, and many of our nation's multiple religions define marriage in precisely those terms. But while the Supreme Court has always previously considered marriage in that context, the underlying rights and liberties that marriage embodies are not in any way confined to heterosexuals.

Marriage is a civil bond in this country as well as, in some (but hardly all) cases, a religious sacrament. It is a relationship recognized by governments as providing a privileged and respected status, entitled to the state's support and benefits. The California Supreme Court described marriage as a "union unreservedly approved and favored by the community." Where the state has accorded official sanction to a relationship and provided special benefits to those who enter into that relationship, our courts have insisted that withholding that status requires powerful justifications and may not be arbitrarily denied.

What, then, are the justifications for California's decision in Proposition 8 to withdraw access to the institution of marriage for some of its citizens on the basis of their sexual orientation? The reasons I have heard are not very persuasive.

The explanation mentioned most often is tradition. But simply because something has always been done a certain way does not mean that it must always remain that way. Otherwise we would still have segregated schools and debtors' prisons. Gays and lesbians have always been among us, forming a part of our society, and they have lived as couples in our neighborhoods and communities. For a long time, they have experienced discrimination and even persecution; but we, as a society, are starting to become more tolerant, accepting, and understanding. California and many other states have allowed gays and lesbians to form domestic partnerships (or civil unions) with most of the rights of married heterosexuals. Thus, gay and lesbian individuals are now permitted to live together in state-sanctioned relationships. It therefore seems anomalous to cite "tradition" as a justification for withholding the status of marriage and thus to continue to label those relationships as less worthy, less sanctioned, or less legitimate.

Simply because something has always been done a certain way does not mean that it must always remain that way. Otherwise we would still have segregated schools and debtors' prisons.

The second argument I often hear is that traditional marriage furthers the state's interest in procreation—and that opening marriage to same-sex couples would dilute, diminish, and devalue this goal. But that is plainly not the case. Preventing lesbians and gays from marrying does not cause more heterosexuals to marry and conceive more children. Likewise, allowing gays and lesbians to marry someone of the same sex will not discourage heterosexuals from marrying a person of the opposite sex. How, then, would allowing same-sex marriages reduce the number of children that heterosexual couples conceive?

This procreation argument cannot be taken seriously. We do not inquire whether heterosexual couples intend to bear children, or have the capacity to have children, before we allow them to marry. We permit marriage by the elderly, by prison inmates, and by persons who have no intention of having children. What's more, it is pernicious to think marriage should be limited to heterosexuals because of the state's desire to promote procreation. We would surely not accept as constitutional a ban on marriage if a state were to decide, as China has done, to discourage procreation.

Another argument, vaguer and even less persuasive, is that gay marriage somehow does harm to heterosexual marriage. I have yet to meet anyone who can explain to me what this means. In what way would allowing same-sex partners to marry diminish the marriages of heterosexual couples? Tellingly, when the judge in our case asked our opponent to identify the ways in which same-sex marriage would harm heterosexual marriage, to his credit he answered honestly: he could not think of any.

The simple fact is that there is no good reason why we should deny marriage to same-sex partners. On the other hand, there are many reasons why we should formally recognize these relationships and embrace the rights of gays and lesbians to marry and become full and equal members of our society.

No matter what you think of homosexuality, it is a fact that gays and lesbians are members of our families, clubs, and workplaces. They are our doctors, our teachers, our soldiers (whether we admit it or not), and our friends. They yearn for acceptance, stable relationships, and success in their lives, just like the rest of us.

Conservatives and liberals alike need to come together on principles that surely unite us. Certainly, we can agree on the value of strong families, lasting domestic relationships, and communities populated by persons with recognized and sanctioned bonds to one another. Confining some of our neighbors and friends who share these same values to an outlaw or second-class status undermines their sense of belonging and weakens their ties with the rest of us and what should be our common aspirations. Even those whose religious convictions preclude endorsement of what they may perceive as an unacceptable "lifestyle" should recognize that disapproval should not warrant stigmatization and unequal treatment.

When we refuse to accord this status to gays and lesbians, we discourage them from forming the same relationships we encourage for others. And we are also telling them, those who love them, and society as a whole that their relationships are less worthy, less legitimate, less permanent, and less valued. We demean their relationships and we demean them as individuals. I cannot imagine how we benefit as a society by doing so.

I understand, but reject, certain religious teachings that denounce homosexuality as morally wrong, illegitimate, or unnatural; and I take strong exception to those who argue that same-sex relationships should be discouraged by society and law. Science has taught us, even if history has not, that gays and lesbians do not choose to be homosexual any more than the rest of us choose to be heterosexual. To a very large extent, these characteristics are immutable, like being left-handed. And, while our Constitution guarantees the freedom to exercise our individual religious convictions, it equally prohibits us from forcing our beliefs on others. I do not believe that our society can ever live up to the promise of equality, and the fundamental rights to life, liberty, and the pursuit of happiness, until we stop invidious discrimination on the basis of sexual orientation.

If we are born heterosexual, it is not unusual for us to perceive those who are born homosexual as aberrational and threatening. Many religions and much of our social culture have reinforced those impulses. Too often, that has led to prejudice, hostility, and discrimination. The antidote is understanding, and reason. We once tolerated laws throughout this nation that prohibited marriage between persons of different races. California's Supreme Court was the first to find that discrimination unconstitutional. The U.S. Supreme Court unanimously agreed 20 years later, in 1967, in a case called *Loving v. Virginia.* It seems inconceivable today that only 40 years ago there were places in this country where a black woman could not legally marry a white man. And it was only 50 years ago that 17 states mandated segregated public education—until the Supreme Court unanimously struck down that practice in *Brown v. Board of Education.* Most Americans are proud of these decisions and the fact that the discriminatory state laws that spawned them have been discredited. I am convinced that Americans will be equally proud when we no longer discriminate against gays and lesbians and welcome them into our society.

It is inconceivable that only 40 years ago there were places in this country where a black woman could not legally marry a white man.

Reactions to our lawsuit have reinforced for me these essential truths. I have certainly heard anger, resentment, and hostility, and words like "betrayal" and other pointedly graphic criticism. But mostly I have been overwhelmed by expressions of gratitude and good will from persons in all walks of life, including, I might add, from many conservatives and libertarians whose names

might surprise. I have been particularly moved by many personal renditions of how lonely and personally destructive it is to be treated as an outcast and how meaningful it will be to be respected by our laws and civil institutions as an American, entitled to equality and dignity. I have no doubt that we are on the right side of this battle, the right side of the law, and the right side of history.

Some have suggested that we have brought this case too soon, and that neither the country nor the courts are "ready" to tackle this issue and remove this stigma. We disagree. We represent real clients—two wonderful couples in California who have longtime relationships. Our lesbian clients are raising four fine children who could not ask for better parents. Our clients wish to be married. They believe that they have that constitutional right. They wish to be represented in court to seek vindication of that right by mounting a challenge under the United States Constitution to the validity of Proposition 8 under the equal-protection and due-process clauses of the 14th Amendment. In fact, the California attorney general has conceded the unconstitutionality of Proposition 8, and the city of San Francisco has joined our case to defend the rights of gays and lesbians to be married. We do not tell persons who have a legitimate claim to wait until the time is "right" and the populace is "ready" to recognize their equality and equal dignity under the law.

Same-Sex Marriage Is Legal In:

Connecticut, District of Columbia*, Iowa, Massachusetts, New Hampshire, Vermont

*Pending Congressional Approval

Civil Union or Domestic Partnership Is Legal In:

California, Colorado, Hawaii, Maine, Maryland, Nevada, New Jersey, Oregon, Washington, Wisconsin

No State Laws Regarding Civil Unions, Domestic Partnerships, or Same-Sex Marriage In:

New Mexico, New York, Rhode Island

Same-Sex Marriage Is Illegal In:

Alabama, Alaska, Arizona, Arkansas, California, Colorado, Delaware, Florida, Georgia, Hawaii, Idaho, Illinois, Indiana, Kansas, Kentucky, Louisiana, Maine, Maryland, Michigan, Minnesota, Mississippi, Missouri, Montana, Nebraska, Nevada, North Carolina, North Dakota, Ohio, Oklahoma, Oregon, Pennsylvania, South Carolina, South Dakota, Tennessee, Texas, Utah, Virginia, Washington, West Virginia, Wisconsin, Wyoming

Citizens who have been denied equality are invariably told to "wait their turn" and to "be patient." Yet veterans of past civil-rights battles found that it was the act of insisting on equal rights that ultimately sped acceptance of those rights. As to whether the courts are "ready" for this case, just a few years ago, in *Romer v. Evans,* the United States Supreme Court struck down a popularly adopted Colorado constitutional amendment that withdrew the rights of gays and lesbians in that state to the protection of anti-discrimination laws. And seven years ago, in *Lawrence v. Texas,* the Supreme Court struck down, as lacking any rational basis, Texas laws prohibiting private, intimate sexual practices between persons of the same sex, overruling a contrary decision just 20 years earlier.

These decisions have generated controversy, of course, but they are decisions of the nation's highest court on which our clients are entitled to rely. If all citizens have a constitutional right to marry, if state laws that withdraw legal protections of gays and lesbians as a class are unconstitutional, and if private, intimate sexual conduct between persons of the same sex is protected by the Constitution, there is very little left on which opponents of same-sex marriage can rely. As Justice Antonin Scalia, who dissented in the *Lawrence* case, pointed out, "[W]hat [remaining] justification could there possibly be for denying the benefits of marriage to homosexual couples exercising '[t]he liberty protected by the Constitution'?" He is right, of course. One might agree or not with these decisions, but even Justice Scalia has acknowledged that they lead in only one direction.

California's Proposition 8 is particularly vulnerable to constitutional challenge, because that state has now enacted a crazy-quilt of marriage regulation that makes no sense to anyone. California recognizes marriage between men and women, including persons on death row, child abusers, and wife beaters. At the same time, California prohibits marriage by loving, caring, stable partners of the same sex, but tries to make up for it by giving them the alternative of "domestic partnerships" with virtually all of the rights of married persons except the official, state-approved status of marriage. Finally, California recognizes 18,000 same-sex marriages that took place in the months between the state Supreme Court's ruling that upheld gay-marriage rights and the decision of California's citizens to withdraw those rights by enacting Proposition 8.

California recognizes marriages involving persons on death row, child abusers, and wife beaters, but not loving, stable partners of the same sex.

So there are now three classes of Californians: heterosexual couples who can get married, divorced, and remarried, if they wish; same-sex couples who cannot get married but can live together in domestic partnerships; and same-sex couples who are now married but who, if they divorce, cannot remarry. This is an irrational system, it is discriminatory, and it cannot stand.

Americans who believe in the words of the Declaration of Independence, in Lincoln's Gettysburg Address, in the 14th Amendment, and in the Constitution's guarantees of equal protection and equal dignity before the law cannot sit by while this wrong continues. This is not a conservative or liberal issue; it is an American one, and it is time we, as Americans, embraced it.

Critical Thinking

1. Identify the current legal issues regarding gay marriage.
2. Where does gay marriage stand in the courts today?
3. Present arguments for and against gay marriage as a civil right.

THEODORE OLSON served as U.S. solicitor general from 2001 to 2004. He served under Presidents George W. Bush and Ronald Reagan, and was named one of *Time Magazine's* 100 *greatest thinkers* in 2010.

Lyle Denniston    **NO**

Same-Sex Marriage III: The Arguments Against

Marriage is an institution so valued in virtually every society, modern or ancient, that it always has been easy to rally public support against challenges to it. The fervor of that defense has been obvious, across the country, in recent years, especially since 1993, when the Hawaii Supreme Court signaled that same-sex couples in that state might soon gain a right to marry, under the state constitution. No state had previously even hinted at that, and the reaction of defenders of marriage was swift and widespread. As a result, the change did not happen in Hawaii, and would not, in any state, until Massachusetts' highest state court opened marriage to same-sex couples, nine years ago this month.

The Hawaiian hint, of course, ran counter to a traditional understanding about marriage. A state court in New York would remark later: "It was an accepted truth for almost everyone who ever lived, in any society in which marriage existed, that there could be marriages only between participants of different sex." Changing that understanding has been seen, in many quarters of society, as a threat to marriage itself, and, with it, a threat to society's capacity to renew itself generation after generation. Same-sex marriage, some would and did argue, was nothing less than a suicide pact for humanity.

That understanding had been so well established that, in 1972, it would be entirely unremarkable that the Supreme Court would conclude that a gay couple's challenge to a traditional marriage law did not even raise "a substantial federal question." That was the Justices' brief and apparently unanimous ruling in the case of *Baker v. Nelson*, and that ruling reverberates still, regularly cited by marriage defenders with the argument that it is the Court's binding last word on the subject.

In fact, if the Supreme Court were to conclude in one or more of the new same-sex marriage cases now on its docket that *Baker v. Nelson* did, indeed, settle the matter, that might well be the end of gay marriage equality as a constitutional matter—at least for the next several years, and perhaps longer. The current status of that precedent is thus one of the first questions the Court probably would need to answer before moving on to any other arguments, for or against same-sex marriage.

The *Baker* argument of marriage defenders is a simple one: that it is a precedent set by the Court, and it cannot be set aside unless the Court itself does so. As the lawyers for the Republican leaders of the U.S. House of Rep-

resentatives told the Justices in a filing in one of the new cases: "*Baker* controls this case. . . . *Baker* stands for the proposition that a state may use the traditional definition of marriage without violating equal protection. It necessarily follows that Congress may use the same traditional definition of marriage for federal purposes without violating equal protection."

Since the constitutional core of the argument of advocates of same-sex marriage is the guarantee of "equal protection," a new Supreme Court ruling interpreting *Baker* as broadly as the House GOP leaders do would undercut the legal foundation of the claim to marriage equality. Indeed, that is why federal courts that have struck down laws against same-sex marriage have done so only after first treating the *Baker* precedent as narrow in scope, and not binding in the new cases.

Marriage defenders have another basic point to make to the Justices: their argument that laws seeking to preserve the traditional concept of marriage should be judged by the most tolerant constitutional test, "rational basis." . . .

When the marriage defenders move beyond their point about *Baker's* force as controlling precedent, their arguments on constitutional questions go back to the same root: the Constitution, they contend, does not forbid the government, at any level, from taking steps to preserve marriage in its traditional form. Indeed, their lawyers insist that opposition to same-sex marriage has no source in discrimination, but rather is a positive effort to assure that the social values served by marriage go on being served by that institution. Those values depend, they insist, upon marriage being limited to one man and one woman.

The point that they emphasize most heavily, about opposite-sex marriage, is the necessary link they say exists between marriage and child-bearing and child-rearing. They quote the English philosopher and social critic Bertrand Russell: "But for children, there would be no need of any institution concerned with sex. . . . It is through children alone that sexual relations become of importance to society, and worthy to be taken cognizance of by a legal institution." That institution, of course, is marriage, opposite-sex marriage.

As recently as two years ago, marriage defenders' lawyers could say in court filings that "*every* appellate court decision, both state and federal, to address the validity of traditional opposite-sex marriage laws under the federal Constitution has upheld them as rationally related to the state's interest in responsible procreation and child-rearing." (Included among the courts making that connection was the Minnesota Supreme Court, in the decision left undisturbed by the Justices in *Baker v. Nelson* in 1972.) And, the defenders argue, more than three-fourths of the states still adhere to the traditional definition of marriage, confining same-sex marriages to the status of a novelty in little more than a handful of states.

Although more recent federal appeals court rulings at both the appeal and trial levels have struck down traditional marriage-definition laws, and similar laws have been set aside in a few more states recently, it remains true that there is a considerably longer list of decisions upholding such laws. That is likely to be among the arguments the defenders of marriage will be making to the Justices.

On the merits, though, the marriage–children link is still the heart of their argument against same-sex marriage. It is founded in historical, legal, scientific and cultural principles.

Marriage, the defenders contend, cannot possibly be treated as a "fundamental right" open to gays and lesbians because such a right must have a foundation in American history, legal traditions, and practices. It has, they say, none of those characteristics; it was unheard of in law until 2003, and can make no claim to being common even today. At the time the nation was founded, and at the time the Fourteenth Amendment was added to the Constitution in 1868, it was clearly understood that marriage was the union between one man and one woman, the defenders assert. Those historic foundations of the definition should count heavily today in interpreting what the Constitution permits or demands, they argue.

The "responsible procreation" branch of their marriage–children link is keyed to what they call "the undeniable biological reality" that opposite-sex unions, and only those, can produce children. It is better, they argue, that children be born into a stable union that only marriage can create, and it is marriage that is the foundation of America's—and the world's—enduring family units. Children, the marriage defenders contend, prosper better with parents of opposite sexes—a father and mother—because they derive unique values from such parents, and because marriage encourages the parents to remain together while the children mature.

Many laws, they argue, are enacted and enforced precisely to encourage the continuation of marriage and the fulfillment of its obligations. Such laws assure that marriages are between two, rather than several, individuals, that the commitment is meant to last for lifetimes, that the partners remain loyal to it, and that the father is presumed to be the father of the child whose mother is his wife. Those laws cannot even be understood, it is argued, unless they are seen as strengthening the responsible birth and rearing of children.

Marriage, its defenders concede, is not conditioned upon having children, because that by itself would be unconstitutional state coercion. But opposite-sex couples may, indeed, become parents by accident, and that is a potential that same-sex partners could never experience, they note.

To the argument that the Supreme Court's 1967 decision in *Loving v. Virginia* validated the idea that traditional marriage could not be limited to traditional marital partners, the marriage defenders counter that . . . ruling, too, promoted procreation by opening up the prospect of children of mixed-race being raised within a stable family unit. Moreover, they contend that the decision would have come out the other way, had the couple involved been of the same sex, since only five years later, the Supreme Court decided *Baker v. Nelson,* and the gay couple in that case had tried to claim the *Loving* decision as a precedent in their favor.

Whatever virtues the supporters of same-sex marriage can claim for such unions, the defenders of traditional marriage argue, those cannot compare with those that justify the protection and promotion of traditional marriage, and those who pass the laws of a state—including its citizens in voting on ballot measures—are clearly entitled to choose the definition of the institution that they find to be superior.

Further, the defenders say, it is essential—in a time when traditional cultural and moral values are being tested—that legislatures be allowed to proceed with caution before fundamental alterations are made in the institution of marriage. Such changes should await more scientific certainty about child-bearing and child-rearing outside of traditional marital unions, and also should await the development—if there is to be one—of a different public consensus about whether or not to protect marriage as it has been known for countless years. The defenders buttress this argument about caution with a fervent defense of the power of the individual states, the long-time source of laws about marriage, to make their own judgments about who can enter that institution.

Perhaps the most controversial argument that the defenders make is that the institution itself would be harmed if it were opened to same-sex couples. They have relied upon social science claims that, merely by altering the definition of marriage, such a change cannot help but alter its basic character. The public's conscious understanding of what marriage is, and is supposed to be, would surely be altered, the argument goes, if a new form of marriage were to have the official blessing of government. The reality that one cannot predict just what would happen to marriage if the popular perception of it were to change in a basic way, the defenders say, is reason enough not to risk that potential development.

Accelerating rates of divorce, the defenders add in another argument, have already begun the process of "deinstitutionalizing" marriage, so that marriage's standing among the social norms of America already is suffering, and would suffer further if its traditional character is compromised for those who remain in their legal unions.

To the argument that a string of Supreme Court rulings recognizing gay rights and providing constitutional protection for gays and lesbians bolsters the idea that the string should be extended to include marital rights, the marriage defenders argue that the Court has given no hint whatsoever that it is willing to take that much greater step constitutionally. Those decisions, the defenders of marriage contend, were about government intrusions into private lives, not about access to a state-conferred benefit that the legislature has chosen to limit for entirely valid social and cultural reasons.

And to the argument that excluding gays and lesbians from civil marriage is motivated by religious or moral reasons that legislators are not supposed to put into public laws, the marriage defenders respond that the mere fact that the traditional definition has, for some who support it, a religious or moral dimension does not make it constitutionally suspect. And, to make that point, their lawyers have recited quotations from President Obama, in a 2006 address, in which he said that "our law is by definition a codification of morality, much of it grounded in the Judeo-Christian tradition."

When marriage defenders turn to the federal law that is now at issue before the Court, the Defense of Marriage Act of 1996, they add arguments that Congress was entitled to craft a uniform definition to guide all government agencies to a common understanding, that Congress was free to express a moral judgment about the kind of marital unions it wished to support, and that Congress had it in its power to limit those who would qualify for federal benefits linked to marriage, in order to save federal funds.

A final argument, one that marriage defenders hope might ultimately be persuasive for the Supreme Court, is that the issue of same-sex marriage should be left, as much as possible, to be worked out in the democratic process. It is there, they contend, that the people of America can best make a judgment about something so fundamental to their lives.

Lyle Denniston is a journalist who has covered the Supreme Court for over 55 years.

EXPLORING THE ISSUE

Should Same-Sex Marriage Be Legal?

Critical Thinking and Reflection

1. What are three arguments in favor of, and against, marriage equality?
2. What are benefits that marriage brings on an interpersonal relationship level? On a societal level?
3. Why might legally recognized relationships like civil unions or domestic partnerships be considered "second class" according to marriage equality advocates?
4. Should the legality of same-sex marriage be decided by the federal government, or left up to individual states?

Is There Common Ground?

In 2012 President Obama became the first sitting American president to support marriage equality. A host of other politicians, including several conservatives, followed suit. As of this writing, 13 states recognize same-sex marriages, along with the District of Columbia. A few others recognize some rights for same-sex couples. In several of these states, couples may enter into civil unions or domestic partnerships, but may not marry in the traditional (or legal) sense of the word. None of the relationships, including same-sex marriages, are afforded the same federal rights and benefits as heterosexual marriages.

Many, including Theodore Olson, argue that anything less than marriage equality is a violation of the Equal Protection Clause of the Constitution. Opponents of same-sex marriage argue, however, that same-sex relationships are not protected by the Constitution, and that marriage has been defined as being between one man and one woman for thousands of years. To alter that definition would be to challenge one of the fundamental pillars of society. Some opponents of marriage equality, often arguing from a conservative religious viewpoint, argue that same-sex relationships are not entitled to any legal recognition. The institution of marriage, they believe, would be weakened by any alterations to its definition. Do you agree? Why or why not?

Other opponents simply argue that civil unions or domestic partnerships are suitable for granting the same legal protections and benefits available to heterosexual married couples. Do you believe civil unions are a just substitution? Why or why not?

How do you view the arguments to legalize same-sex marriage? What potential benefits or difficulties do you foresee resulting from this action? Finally, what do you believe is the *purpose* of marriage? Is marriage primarily about love? Rights? Children and family? Monogamy? Do you regard it as primarily a religious institution or a legal institution? Is there any *single, predominant* purpose of marriage, or are there many purposes worthy of consideration?

Create Central

www.mhhe.com/createcentral

Additional Resources

Alpert, E. "Salt Lake City Has the Highest Rate of Same-Sex Couples Raising Kids," *Los Angeles Times*, May 21, 2013.

Bash, D. "One Conservative's Dramatic Reversal on Gay Marriage" (March 15, 2013), www.cnn .com/2013/03/15/politics/portman-gay-marriage.

Calmes, J. & Baker, P. "Obama Says Same-Sex Marriage Should Be Legal," *New York Times*, May 9, 2012.

Cornyn, J. "In Defense of Marriage," *National Review*, July 2004.

Von Drehle, D. "How Gay Marriage Won," *Time Magazine*, March 28, 2013.

Internet References . . .

Health Benefits of Marriage

A public health perspective on the health benefits of marriage.

www.humanimpact.org/from-the-hip/item/17-the-health-benefits-of-marriage-equality

How the Court Could Rule on Same-Sex Marriage

A graphic flow chart representation of the potential ways the Supreme Court could rule regarding same-sex marriage and the resulting legal implications.

www.nytimes.com/interactive/2013/03/24/us/how-the-court-could-rule-on-same-sex-marriage.html?_r=0

Human Rights Campaign—Marriage Center

The Human Rights Campaign, America's largest LGBT organization provides current information on the state of marriage equality across the nation.

www.hrc.org/marriage-center

National Organization for Marriage

The National Organization for Marriage advocates for a traditional definition of marriage.

www.nationformarriage.org

Unit 3

UNIT

Sex and Reproduction

*S*ome of the most contentious modern debates about sexuality involve reproduction. Abortion, contraception, and reproductive technologies that are expanding the possibilities of human sexual reproduction are all issues that force us to consider our values amid a rapidly changing world. The ethical questions we must consider go far beyond our own families, as the decisions we make and stances we hold can have a strong influence on society. In this unit we examine contemporary issues that involve reproductive choice.

Selected, Edited, and with Issue Framing Material by:
Ryan W. McKee, *Widener University*
and
William J. Taverner, *Center for Family Life Education*

ISSUE

Is Abortion Moral?

YES: Jennifer Webster, from "Choosing Abortion Is Choosing Life," an original essay written for this volume (2009)

NO: Douglas Groothuis, from "Why I Am Pro-life: A Short, Nonsectarian Argument," adapted from http://theconstructivecurmudgeon.blogspot.com/2009/03/why-i-am-pro-life-short-nonsectarian.html(2009)

Learning Outcomes

After reading this issue, you should be able to:

- Describe the legal status of abortion in the United States, including at least two restrictions on access to abortion.
- Outline at least two reasons why some may consider abortion a moral decision.
- Describe at least two reasons why some may consider abortion an immoral decision.
- Distinguish between legal and moral reasons for the acceptability of abortion.

ISSUE SUMMARY

YES: Jennifer Webster, project coordinator for the Network for Reproductive Options, asserts that the choice of abortion is a multifactorial decision that always expresses a moral consideration.

NO: Douglas Groothuis, author and professor of philosophy at Denver Seminary, draws on the philosophical tradition to present his moral argument against abortion.

Women have abortions for a variety of reasons. Financial concerns, health issues, relationship problems, family responsibilities, and the desire to attend or remain in school or pursue a career path are but a few. Until the onset of modern surgical techniques, folk methods such as ingesting plant compounds or inserting chemicals or sharp objects into the vagina or uterus were used to induce abortion. Information about both contraception and abortion was passed through an oral history from woman to woman for generations, thanks in part to religious and legal prohibitions against transmitting written instructions or information.

Discussions about abortion are often framed as a matter of "rights," that is, a woman's right to reproductive autonomy (often termed the "right to choose") versus the right of the unborn to be born (i.e., the "right to life"). The right to an abortion is essentially determined by the laws in one's area. In the United States, the Comstock Laws formalized the illegal status of abortion in 1873. During the late 1960s and early 1970s, several states began to loosen their restrictions. In 1973 the cases of *Roe v. Wade* and *Doe v. Bolton* legalized abortion on the federal level. They established the "trimester framework," essentially legalizing first trimester abortions on demand, allowing states to regulate second trimester procedures with regard to the mother's health and allowing states to prohibit abortion during the third trimester, unless the mother's health is at risk.

As the legality of abortion changed over time, individual states enacted legislation to restrict access to abortion. In many states, antiabortion advocates have imparted restrictions on abortion rights through an array of tactics including restricting federal and state funding for abortion, requiring waiting periods (26 states), parental notification or consent for teens seeking abortion (38 states), and mandating counseling for those seeking abortions (17 states). Some states require that patients be told that abortion increases risk of breast cancer, causes fetal pain, or causes negative psychological effects, even though the research science has not found evidence to support any of these assertions. The most restrictive measure was signed into law in North Dakota in early 2013. This law forbids abortion once a fetal heartbeat is "detectable." Since this can be done as early as 6 weeks, the law effectively makes nearly all abortions illegal in

North Dakota. Legal experts say the new law is in conflict with the 1973 *Roe v. Wade* decision, and will need to be resolved by the U.S. Supreme Court.

According to the Guttmacher Institute, about 40 percent of unintended pregnancies are terminated. About one-third of women will have had an abortion by the age of 45. The number of abortions in 2008 was 1.21 million, down from 1.31 million in 2000. The number of abortions per 1,000 women ages 15–44, per year fell from 29.3 in the early 1980s to 19.4 in 2005 and remained steady through 2008. Nearly 50 percent of abortions are obtained by women over 25. Thirty-three percent are obtained by women between the ages of 20 and 24. Teenagers account for 18 percent of abortions. Almost 90 percent of abortions occur during the first 12 weeks of pregnancy.

For many, the decision of whether or not to have an abortion, or to support or deny access to abortion procedures has little to do with law or statistics. Certainly laws can make accessing an abortion easier or more difficult, but abortions still take place in countries where abortion is illegal. For many, the question often boils down to morality; and our concepts of morality are often based on our worldviews. For people with different worldviews, it can be hard to see eye to eye on any number of issues. Is abortion moral? If your worldview holds that abortion takes an innocent life, the answer is probably no. If your worldview emphasizes the autonomy of women, the answer may be yes. Many people have complex and nuanced beliefs that are based on a variety of factors that do not easily allow for an answer to the question, "Is abortion a moral or immoral decision?"

In the following selections, Jennifer Webster, project coordinator for the Network for Reproductive Options, asserts that choosing abortion is always a moral decision based on a multitude of factors. Douglas Groothuis, a professor of philosophy at Denver Seminary, presents the case for the immorality of abortion while arguing for the status of a fetus as a living human being.

YES ↩   Jennifer Webster

Choosing Abortion Is Choosing Life

I think it is a measure of how well the anti-abortion movement has been able to influence thinking and discussion of abortion in this country that when I sat down to write this essay I found myself confounded and conflicted on what I see as a fairly straightforward question. Can abortion be moral? Yes. Absolutely, without question, choosing an abortion is always a moral decision.

I say this and immediately I hear all the objections of the anti-abortion movement, what about the rights of the innocent baby, abortion is murder, women shouldn't be allowed to use abortion as birth control. Even I, who ought to know better, hear these voices and feel compelled to answer them. For nearly four decades we have allowed those most vehemently opposed to abortion to control the public debate and claim the moral high ground on abortion.

Women have abortions for lots of reasons.

- A senior in college has an abortion after one night celebrating with her boyfriend.
- A woman raped by her brother-in-law chooses to have an abortion, contrary to her Catholic upbringing, because she knows that this baby will cause her to re-live the the horror of the attack she suffered every day that she is pregnant and perhaps for the rest of her life.
- A young woman just moved to a new city with her husband who is finishing his master's degree and is overwhelmed by the needs of her 10-month-old baby; she chooses an abortion because she knows her son will suffer if she has a second baby so soon.
- A mother of three who lost her job, pregnant by the man who is divorcing her, chooses an abortion to enable her to care for the three kids she has.
- A woman trying to get out of an abusive relationship gets an abortion because she doesn't want to be tied to her abuser for the rest of her life and doesn't feel she is emotionally capable of caring for his child.

These are just a handful of stories that women seeking abortions tell everyday. They are by no means the only stories. Often a woman simply knows she does not have the emotional, social, or material resources to nurture and care for a child.

According to a study by the Guttmacher Institute,[1] approximately 3 million United States women become pregnant unintentionally every year. Nearly half of those women were using some form of birth control and of those 3 million pregnancies, about 1.3 million will end with an abortion. Among women choosing abortion, 60% are already mothers. By far, the most common reason women give for terminating pregnancies is they feel that now is not a good time for them to have a baby, because, for whatever reason, they are not able to provide for a child the way that child needs and deserves to be provided for. Women choose to have abortions because they want to be good mothers. Women who choose to have an abortion are making a moral decision for their own welfare and for the welfare of their children and family. As one young woman put it, "Choosing an abortion, for me, was choosing life. It was the first time I acted as if my life mattered."[2]

One reason abortion is not seen as a moral decision in our society is the historical discounting of women as moral agents. It is only recently that women have been recognized as capable of thinking, reasoning and making moral decisions. Take the story of a young married woman in the 1940s. She and her husband decided to postpone having children because of their limited income, need to finish school and no desire to live with their parents. They use a diaphragm to prevent conception, but it fails and she becomes pregnant. Her doctor tells her he can recommend someone who will perform a safe, although illegal, abortion but she must first get written permission from her husband and her father.[3] Is it even possible to imagine a medical procedure for which a man would need to get permission from his wife and mother?

There is a lot of complexity in the decision to terminate a pregnancy (as there is in virtually every moral decision we face in our lives). Abortion is the only moral deliberation that we, as a society, reduce to the black and white question of whose life is valued. It is only because women are the primary moral agents in abortion decisions that we allow it to be seen in such absolute terms.

When we collectively deliberate on the morality of any issue, we have to look at all the factors. The only way to look at abortion as an immoral decision is to see the unborn fetus as having an absolute right to life and to discount or erase the life of the woman faced with the decision. If you look at the preceding stories of women who have chosen abortion, who can say that those women made the wrong choice? Do those women deserve to be punished? No, those women made brave decisions to protect their welfare and to improve the welfare of their families. Women who choose abortions are making a moral decision by choosing to protect the lives of the already-born.

There are vast social and economic inequities in our society that impact on women's reproductive decision-making. Women living at or below the Federal Poverty Level are four times more likely to get an abortion than women who live at 300% above the Federal Poverty Level. Women in certain communities of color are more likely to choose to terminate a pregnancy, probably because they are more likely to be living in poverty. These women also tend to have less access to contraception, health care and educational opportunities. This lack of access is part of a larger system of social and economic inequality that abortion opponents rarely, if ever address. By ignoring a woman's life and circumstances, we erase her history, her autonomy and her right to self-determination.

In a society filled with racism, sexism, poverty, war and violence, in a country where half a million children live in foster care, four children die every day from abuse and 28 million children live in poverty,[4] we have much more pressing moral concerns than the question of when life begins and the rights of fetuses. It is the height of arrogance, or perhaps just misplaced priorities, to question the morality of abortion decisions, when so many members of our communities don't enjoy access to their basic human rights.

What is truly immoral and unjust are the attempts by courts and legislatures to restrict women's access to abortion. Everything from requiring parental notification/consent, mandatory waiting periods, mandated counseling with medically inaccurate information are all attempts to restrict abortion access and disproportionately impact young women, women of color, and low-income women.

These attempts at restricting women's access to abortion are particularly troublesome in light of a 2007 study by the Guttmacher Institute.[5] The study found that abortion rates were lowest in the countries in which abortion was the most accessible. In countries where abortion is legal, free, and available, such as the Netherlands, abortion rates are among the lowest in the world. Likewise, in countries as diverse as Peru, the Philippines, or Uganda, where abortion is illegal, abortion rates are only slightly higher than the United States. The countries with the lowest abortion rates were also the countries in which contraception is readily available and sexuality education is comprehensive and evidence-based, two things that the anti-abortion movement also generally opposes.

The Guttmacher study clearly indicates that the best way to reduce the number of abortions performed was to reduce the need for abortion. The history of abortion in the United States vividly illustrates that restricting access to abortion does little to stop abortions. Despite this overwhelming evidence, the anti-abortion movement continues to seek to restrict women's access to abortion, which raises a lot of questions about the motivations and true purpose of the anti-abortion movement.

The abortion debate in the United States is a tiring one. For decades now, both sides have argued for their position and given little ground. Life is pitted against choice and there seems to be no way to move forward. What gets lost in this endless debate is the reality of women's lives. The decision of what to do with an unintended pregnancy is a morally complex one and women faced with the decision weigh their responsibilities carefully to examine what they have to offer to a new child. The issue is not so much a woman's right to choose to have an abortion, as a woman's right to choose her life.

Until women are seen as equal to men, with full complement of human rights, discussing the morality of abortion is specious. If we truly believed in women's autonomy, moral authority and right to self-determination, if we believed that only women can rightly make the decisions that will shape their lives, then we would recognize abortion for what it is: a safe medical procedure that is sometimes necessary for some women. If we lived in a society that valued women and women's lives this debate would go away. We would all work to prevent unintended pregnancy, to support women and the children they choose to have, recognizing that a woman's fundamental right to choose her own life is the first step to creating a morally just society.

Notes

1. Heather Boonstra, Rachel Benson Gold, Cory Richards and Lawrence Finer, *Abortion in Women's Lives* (Guttmacher Institute, 2006).
2. Anne Eggebroten, *Abortion: My Choice, God's Grace, Christian Women Tell Their Stories* (New Paradigm Books, 1994, p. 32).
3. From Helen Forelle, *If Men Got Pregnant, Abortion Would Be a Sacrament* (Canton, SD: Tesseract Publications, 1991).
4. Child Welfare Information Gateway. . . .
5. "Induced Abortion: Rates and Trends Worldwide," a study by the Guttmacher Institute and the World Health Organization authored by Gilda Sedgh, Stanley Hensha, Susheela Singh, Elisabeth Aahman and Iqbal Shah, published in *The Lancet*, October 13, 2007.

JENNIFER WEBSTER is the project coordinator for the Network for Reproductive Options, a grassroots feminist organization seeking to ensure reproductive justice for the women of the world.

Douglas Groothuis

 **NO**

Why I Am Pro-life:
A Short, Nonsectarian Argument

Abortion is the intentional killing of a human fetus by chemical and/or surgical means. It should not be confused with miscarriage (which involves no human intention) or contraception (which uses various technologies to prohibit sperm and egg from producing a fertilized ovum after sexual intercourse). Miscarriages are natural (if sad) occurrences, which raise no deep moral issues regarding human conduct—unless the woman was careless in her pregnancy. Contraception is officially opposed by Roman Catholics and some other Christians, but I take it to be in a moral category entirely separate from abortion (since it does not involve the killing of a fetus); therefore, it will not be addressed here.[1]

Rather than taking up the legal reasoning and history of abortion in America (especially concerning *Roe vs. Wade*), this essay makes a simple, straightforward moral argument against abortion. Sadly, real arguments (reasoned defenses of a thesis or claim) are too rarely made on this issue. Instead, propaganda is exchanged. Given that the Obama administration is the most pro-abortion administration in the history of the United States, some clear moral reasoning is called for at this time.

The first premise of the argument is that human beings have unique and incomparable value in the world. Christians and Jews believe this is the case because we are made in God's image and likeness. But anyone who holds that humans are special and worthy of unique moral consideration can grant this thesis (even if their worldview does not ultimately support it). Of course, those like Peter Singer who do not grant humans any special status will not be moved by this.[2] We cannot help that. Many true and justified beliefs (concerning human beings and other matters) are denied by otherwise intelligent people.

Second, the *burden of proof* should always be on the one taking a human life and the *benefit of doubt* should always be given to the human life. This is not to say that human life should never be taken. In an often cruel and unfair world, sometimes life-taking is necessary, as many people will grant. Cases include self-defense, the prosecution of a just war, and capital punishment. Yet all unnecessary and intentional life-taking is murder, a deeply evil and repugnant offense against human beings. (This would also be acknowledged by those, such as absolute pacifists, who believe that it is never justifiable to take a human life.)

Third, abortion nearly always takes a human life intentionally and gratuitously and is, therefore, morally unjustified, deeply evil, and repugnant—given what we have said about human beings. The fetus is, without question, a *human being*. Biologically, an entity joins its parents' species at conception. Like produces like: apes procreate apes, rabbits procreate rabbits, and humans procreate humans. If the fetus is not human, what else could it possibly be? Could it be an ape or a rabbit? Of course not.

Some philosophers, such as Mary Anne Warren, have tried to drive a wedge between *personhood and humanity*. That is, there may be persons who are not human (such as God, angels, ETs—if they exist), and there may be humans that are not persons (fetuses or those who lose certain functions after having possessed them). While it is true that there may be persons who are not humans, it does not logically follow that there are humans who are not persons. The fetus is best regarded as a person with potential, not a potential person or nonperson.[3]

When we separate personhood from humanity, we make personhood an achievement based on the possession of certain qualities. But what are these person-constituting qualities? Some say a basic level of consciousness; others assert viability outside the womb; still others say a sense of self-interest (which probably does not obtain until after birth). All of these criteria would take away humanity from those in comas or other physically compromised situations.[4] Humans can lose levels of consciousness through injuries, and even infants are not viable without intense and sustained human support. Moreover, who are we to say just what qualities make for membership in the moral community of persons?[5] The stakes are very high in this question. If we are wrong in our identification of what qualities are sufficient for personhood and we allow a person to be killed, we have allowed the wrongful killing of nothing less than a person. Therefore, I argue that personhood should be viewed as a substance or essence that is given at conception. The fetus is not a lifeless *mechanism* that only becomes what it is after several parts are put together—as is the case with a watch or an automobile. Rather, the fetus is a living human *organism*, whose future unfolds from within itself according to internal principles. For example, the fertilized ovum contains a complete genetic code that is distinct from that of the mother or father. But this is not a mere inert blueprint (which is separable from the building it describes); this is a living blueprint that becomes what its human nature demands.

Yet even if one is not sure when personhood becomes a reality, one should err on the side of being conservative simply because so much is at stake. That is, if one aborts a fetus who is already a person, one commits a deep moral wrong by wrongfully killing an innocent human life. Just as we do not shoot target practice when we are told there may be children playing behind the targets, we should not abortion fetuses if they may be persons with the right not to be killed. As I have argued, it cannot be disputed that abortion kills a living, human being.

Many argue that outside considerations experienced by the mother should overrule the moral value of the human embryo. If a woman does not want a pregnancy, she may abort. But these quality of life considerations always involve issues of lesser moral weight than that of the conservation and protection of a unique human life (which considers the sanctity or innate and intrinsic value of a human life).[6] An unwanted pregnancy is difficult, but the answer is not to kill a human being in order to end that pregnancy. Moreover, a baby can be put up for adoption and bring joy to others. There are many others who do want the child and would give him or her great love and support. Furthermore, it is not uncommon for women to experience deep regrets after aborting their offspring.

The only exemption to giving priority to the life of the fetus would be if there were a real threat to the life of the mother were the pregnancy to continue. In this case, the fetus functions as a kind of intruder that threatens the woman's life. To abort the pregnancy would be tragic but allowable in this imperfect world. Some mothers will nonetheless choose to continue the pregnancy to their own risk, but this is not morally required. It should be noted that these life-threatening situations are extremely rare.

This pro-life argument does not rely on any uniquely religious assumptions, although some religious people will find it compelling. I take it to be an item of natural law (what can be known about morality by virtue of being human) that human life has unique value. A case can be made against abortion by using the Bible (only the Hebrew Bible or both the Hebrew Bible and New Testament combined) as the main moral source, but I have not given that argument here.[7] Rather, this essay has given an argument on the basis of generally agreed upon moral principles. If the argument is to be refuted, one or more of those principles or the reasoning employed needs to be refuted.

Although at the beginning of this essay I claimed I would not take up the legal reasoning related to abortion, one simple point follows from my argument. In nearly every case, abortion should be illegal simply because the Constitution requires that innocent human life be protected from killing.[8] Anti-abortion laws are not an intrusion of the state into the family any more than laws against murdering one's parents are an intrusion into the family.

Notes

1. See Scott Rae, *Moral Choices,* 3rd ed. (Grand Rapids, MI: Zondervan, 2009), 288–291.
2. For an exposition and critique of Singer's thought, see Gordon R. Preece, ed., *Rethinking Peter Singer* (Downers Grove, IL: InterVarsity Press, 2002).
3. See Clifford Bajema, *Abortion and the Meaning of Personhood* (Grand Rapids, MI: Baker Books, 1974). This book is on line. . . .
4. On the dangerous implications of his perspective, see Francis A. Schaeffer and C. Everett Koop, *Whatever Happened to the Human Race?,* revised ed. (Wheaton, IL: Crossway Books, 1983).
5. For a developed philosophical and legal case for including the unborn in the moral community of human beings, see Francis Beckwith, *Defending Life: A Moral and Legal Case Against Abortion Choice* (Cambridge University Press, 2007); and Robert P. George and Christopher Tollefsen, *Embryo: A Defense of Human Life* (New York: Doubleday, 2008).
6. On the distinction between a quality of life ethic and a sanctity of life ethic, see Ronald Reagan, "Abortion and the Conscience of a Nation." . . . This was originally an article in the Spring 1983 issue of *The Human Life Review.*
7. See Rae, 129133.
8. See Beckwith, Chapter 2.

DOUGLAS GROOTHUIS is a professor of philosophy at Denver Seminary and the author of over 10 books, including *Truth Decay.*

EXPLORING THE ISSUE

Is Abortion Moral?

Critical Thinking and Reflection

1. How can the use of certain terms, such as "pro-choice," "anti-choice," "pro-abortion," "antiabortion," and "pro-life" affect debates and public discourse about abortion? Which terms do the authors rely on, and why?
2. What are reasons a woman might choose to have an abortion?
3. Why do different states restrict abortion in different ways?
4. How much say, if any, should a woman's partner have in the decision to terminate a pregnancy?

Is There Common Ground?

There are few issues as divisive in the United States as abortion. Perhaps the strongest consensus is that 78 percent of Americans say that abortion should be legal in at least some circumstances, while only 20 percent say it should always be illegal. (Two percent said they had no opinion.) Attitudes toward abortion have shifted in recent years. A 2012 Gallup poll found that 47 percent of Americans considered themselves "pro-choice" on abortion, compared with 46 percent who described themselves as "pro-life." The results of this poll marked a substantial change compared to 1996 when this question was asked, when the figures were 56 and 37 percent, respectively. How would you define the terms "pro-life" and "pro-choice"? How do these terms differ with alternate descriptors, such as "pro-abortion," "anti-abortion," and "anti-choice"? With respect to the question of morality, in 2013, 49 percent of Americans said that abortion was morally unacceptable, while 42 percent said it was morally acceptable, and 8 percent said it depended on the circumstances. Do you think abortion is morally acceptable? Under what circumstances, if any, do you think abortion should be legal?

Despite the mostly divisive nature of abortion, there may be other common ground. President Barack Obama has stated publicly that he would "like to reduce the number of unwanted pregnancies that result in women feeling compelled to get an abortion or at least considering getting an abortion." Reducing the number of unwanted pregnancies may be a goal shared by both supporters and opponents of abortion rights.

Create Central

www.mhhe.com/createcentral

Additional Resources

Eckholm, E. "North Dakota's Sole Abortion Clinic Sues to Block New Law," *The New York Times*, May 15, 2013.

Johnston, M. (2009). *Pregnancy options workbook.* Binghamton, NY : Ferre Institute.

Waddington, L. "American Pendulum Swings Back in Favor of a Woman's Right to Make Reproductive Choices," *The Iowa Independent*, May 23, 2011.

Wetzstein, C. "Murder: Gosnell Guilty Verdict Hailed on Both Sides of Abortion Debate," *Washington Times*, May 13, 2013.

Wicklund, S. & Kessleheim, A. (2008). *This common secret: my journey as an abortion doctor.* New York: Public Affairs.

Internet References . . .

Abortion Conversation Project

An organization that envisions a world where abortion is considered a moral decision and the removal of the abortion stigma.

www.abortionconversation.com

An Overview of Abortion Laws

This chart by the Guttmacher Institute summarizes state-by-state laws on abortion in the United States.

www.guttmacher.org/statecenter/spibs/spib_OAL.pdf

Methods of Abortion

A description of in-clinic abortion procedures and the abortion pill; this website also includes frequently asked questions about each.

www.plannedparenthood.org/health-topics/abortion-4260.asp

Pro-Life Action League

This organization works to end abortion for the benefit of both women and fetuses through peaceful direct action.

www.prolifeaction.org

Selected, Edited, and with Issue Framing Material by:
Ryan W. McKee, *Widener University*
and
William J. Taverner, *Center for Family Life Education*

ISSUE

Should Pharmacists Have the Right to Refuse Contraceptive Prescriptions?

YES: Eileen P. Kelly, from "Morally Objectionable Work Assignments: Catholic Social Teaching and Public Policy Perspectives," *The Catholic Social Science Review* (vol. 12, 2007)

NO: National Women's Law Center, from "Pharmacy Refusals 101" (May 2011), www.nwlc.org

Learning Outcomes
After reading this issue, you should be able to:
• Define "conscience clauses" and explain their purpose.
• Discuss the impact of contraceptive refusals on women's health.
• Discuss the protection of religious expression in the workplace.
• Explain what to do if you are refused contraceptives by a pharmacist.

ISSUE SUMMARY

YES: Eileen P. Kelly, a professor of management at Ithaca College, argues that conscience clauses are necessary to protect the religious liberty and rights of pharmacists and others in the workplace.

NO: The National Women's Law Center, a national organization that works to promote issues that impact the lives of women and girls, highlights laws and public opinion while stressing that free and unrestricted access to contraception is in the best interest of women's health.

Imagine, for a moment, that you (or your partner or friend) have just received a prescription for hormonal contraceptives. You take the prescription to your local pharmacy and hand it to the pharmacist on duty. Now imagine the pharmacist handing the slip of paper back to you and stating that they will not fill your prescription, because doing so would violate their religious or ethical beliefs. When you ask them to call the other local pharmacy, which is about a 30 minute drive across town, and they again refuse, citing their right under state or federal law, how would you feel?

Now, picture yourself as a pharmacist in another state. Your religious beliefs are such that you feel any attempt to prevent pregnancy goes against God's will. However, you fear that refusing to fill prescriptions for contraception could cost you your job. You like your job and your short commute, which allows you to spend more time with your family. If you lost your job, you'd have to try your luck with another pharmacy, and there would be no guarantee that they would support your religious beliefs either. How would you feel if your manager insisted you either fill prescriptions for birth control or risk being fired?

In 1973 the U.S. Supreme Court legalized abortion in the landmark *Roe v. Wade* decision. Soon after, Congress passed the Church Amendment in response. The amendment, deemed a "conscience clause," was seen as a way to protect health care providers from being required to take part in medical procedures they objected to on religious grounds. Essentially the Church Amendment "prevents the government (as a condition of a federal grant) from requiring health care providers or institutions to perform or assist in abortion or sterilization procedures against their moral or religious convictions. It also prevents institutions receiving certain federal funds from taking action against personnel because of their participation, nonparticipation or beliefs about abortion or sterilization" (1).

Over the years, additional federal conscience clauses have been enacted that deal not only with abortion services, but also with education and training on abortion or sterilization procedures. Additionally, nearly all states have enacted their own "conscience clauses." Most states allow individuals the right to refuse to participate in abortion services. Others protect objectors from participating in sterilization and contraceptive services as well. Recently, more attention has been given to involving pharmacists who refuse to fill prescriptions for birth control and emergency contraception based on their religious beliefs. State laws differ on how much protection is provided for pharmacists who object. In some cases, they must offer to transfer the prescription to a willing pharmacy. In other states, there is no such requirement—a patient could simply be denied.

In the final days of his second term as president, George W. Bush expanded the reach of federal "conscience clauses" through the Provider Refusal Rule. Supporters, including the U.S. Conference of Catholic Bishops and the group Pharmacists for Life, praised the president for protecting the religious freedom of those who work in the health care fields, from surgeons to ambulance drivers. Opponents, including the American Medical Association and Planned Parenthood, stressed that ideology should not trump patient care. In February 2011, President Barack Obama partially rescinded the Provider Refusal Rule, asserting that contraception cannot be equated with abortion and clarifying language that could have denied service to individuals based on "lifestyle." The issue became more problematic for opponents of contraception when, in 2013, the U.S. Department of Health and Human Services decided that emergency contraception (medication used up to five days *after* unprotected intercourse) should be available over the counter to young women 15 and older.

In the last few years, the debate extended beyond the local pharmacy. The Affordable Health Care for America Act (also known as "Health Care Reform") requires employers to provide contraceptive coverage for their employees. Exemptions were made for churches and other houses of worship that hold moral objections to contraception; however, some religious institutions said that the

exemptions did not go far enough. Religiously affiliated hospitals, schools, and nonprofit agencies should also be exempt, they reasoned. They claim that the mandate infringes on their religious liberties. More recently, Hobby Lobby, a chain of arts and crafts stores unaffiliated with a religious institution, but holding strong religious beliefs, has challenged the requirement to provide emergency contraceptive coverage for their employees by bringing their case to a federal appeals court. At the time this goes to press, the court has not yet ruled.

How far should conscience clauses be allowed to reach? Is pharmacy refusal without a referral to another pharmacy acceptable? Or should those who oppose contraception be forced to refer a customer to a pharmacist who doesn't share their values? Is part of being a doctor or pharmacist providing the best services and information available regardless of belief? If a medication is approved by the Food and Drug Administration (FDA), should a licensed pharmacist, trained and licensed to dispense these medications, be able to pick and choose which prescriptions they fill? Should companies have a say in the medications their insurance coverage provides?

Supporters of the conscience clauses stress that they are simply living their ethics, and that they should not be punished for their religious beliefs. Opponents warn that such laws interfere with women's access to health care, and that refusal to fill a prescription can be used as an attempt to shame and humiliate.

In the YES selection, Eileen P. Kelly argues that conscience clauses are a necessary protection of civil rights. In the NO selection, the National Women's Law center zeros in on the effects of such refusals on women's health and what can be done to prevent them.

YES ↵   Eileen P. Kelly

Morally Objectionable Work Assignments: Catholic Social Teaching and Public Policy Perspectives

This article examines the increasing problem of health care employees other than physicians and nurses, especially pharmacists, facing discipline or termination for refusing to engage in immoral practices such as dispensing contraceptives. The article considers the limitations of current anti-discrimination statutes in protecting such employees, and believes that "conscience laws"—which so far only a minority of states have enacted, but many are considering—afford the best possibility for protection.

In Ohio, a pharmacist is fired for refusing to fill a prescription for birth control pills. In Wisconsin, another pharmacist faces a similar fate plus sanctions from the state licensing board for refusing to fill a prescription for emergency contraceptives. In Illinois, an emergency medical technician is terminated for refusing to drive a woman to an abortion clinic. In each instance, the employee is placed in the untenable position of having to choose between providing services that are contrary to their deeply held religious beliefs or facing discipline and discharge for refusing to do so.

In the last several years, there has been a notable increase in the number of incidences of employees placed in such nightmarish dilemmas. Not coincidentally, most of the employees receiving media scrutiny are health care workers, particularly pharmacists. While doctors and nurses have long had the right to refuse morally objectionable work under state statutes, pharmacists and other health care workers have not. The statutory right of refusal has only recently been extended by a minority of states to other categories of health care employees.

Catholic Social Teaching

A vigorous and contentious national debate is now occurring over whether health care professionals have the right to withhold services for procedures they find morally objectionable. Advances in medical technology, coupled with the overall decline in morality in society, make the outcome of this debate critical for society's long term welfare. Morally objectionable procedures and practices that were unthought-of in previous generations are now commonplace and either legally sanctioned or conceivably will be in the not too distant future.

Embryonic stem cell research, euthanasia, physician assisted suicide, abortion, abortifacients, artificial birth control, sterilization and artificial insemination are just a few of the procedures and practices that contribute to the "culture of death" enveloping society. The Catholic Church has consistently upheld the value and dignity of each human life and taught that life must be unequivocally protected in all its various stages. John Paul II persuasively articulated the gospel of life in *Evangelium Vitae*. In doing so, he underscored long-standing Church teaching. As the *Catechism* notes, abortion has been condemned by the Church since the first century.

Rational employees do not accept jobs or undertake professions that are opposed to their religious beliefs. In short, no morally upright person is going to voluntarily work for Don Corleone or become an abortionist. More commonly, employees enter into employment relationships that subsequently force them to make choices in morally compromising situations. In extreme scenarios, the employee may be compelled to leave a job to maintain his or her moral integrity. What is particularly pernicious with the current moral crisis facing the health care professions is that most employees enter into those professions with the understanding that they are embarking on a noble and moral career to help others. In most instances, the employee invests a great deal of time and expense getting an education for his or her profession. Increasingly, Catholic health care workers are now being confronted with having to choose between their jobs or their religious beliefs. In some cases, they may even have to leave their profession.

Existing public policy is somewhat muddled in both protecting and encroaching on the employee's right to refuse morally objectionable work. While there is some legal protection for an employee's right of refusal, that protection is very limited. Employees who refuse to perform morally objectionable work have essentially two legal avenues of recourse open to them. First, they can seek protection under existing federal and state discrimination laws. Second, if they live in a state with a "conscience law" covering their particular job, they can seek protection under it. On the other hand, there is a movement afoot to pass state statutes requiring certain health care providers to provide morally objectionable services.

Kelly, Eileen P. From *The Catholic Social Science Review*, vol. 12, 2007, pp. 425–430. Copyright © 2007 by Society of Catholic Social Scientists. Reprinted by permission.

Anti-Discrimination Statutes

Title VII of the Civil Rights Act of 1964 makes it illegal for a non-sectarian employer to discriminate against an applicant or employee on the basis of religion. All fifty states have similar prohibitions in their respective state anti-discrimination laws, as well as some municipalities. In addition to prohibiting employers from discriminating on the basis of religion, Title VII and related statutes require that the employer reasonably accommodate the religious beliefs and practices of their employees to the extent that it does not create an undue hardship on the business. There are essentially three common types of accommodations that employees seek. The first is accommodation for religious observances or practices, such as asking time off for Sabbath observance. The second is grooming and dress code accommodation, such as a Muslim woman asking to wear a hijab. The third and most contentious is accommodation for conscientious objections to assigned work which is in opposition to an employee's religious beliefs, such as a pharmacist requesting not to dispense emergency contraceptives.

Notably, the employer's duty to accommodate the religious beliefs and practices of their employees is not an absolute one. Rather, the employer has only a duty to reasonably accommodate an employee's request to the extent that it does not create an undue hardship on the business. Unlike disability cases, the Supreme Court ruled in *TWA v. Hardison,* 432 U.S. 63 (1973) that the obligation to accommodate religious beliefs and practices is a *de minimis* one. The Supreme Court held in *Ansonia Board of Education v. Philbrook,* 55 USLW 4019 (1996) that once the employer offers any reasonable accommodation, they have met their statutory burden. Notably, that accommodation need not be the most optimal one or the employee's preferred one. The determination of undue hardship is at issue only when the employer claims that it is unable to offer any reasonable accommodation without such hardship. The definition of undue hardship is essentially any accommodation that would be unduly costly, extensive, substantial, disruptive, or that would fundamentally alter the nature or operation of the business. Factors that would be taken into account in assessing undue hardship would be the nature of the business, the cost of the accommodation, the nature of the job needing accommodation, and the effect of the accommodation on the employer's operations. No bright line rule exists to determine precisely what constitutes an undue hardship. Rather the determination is made on a case-by-case basis contingent upon the particular factual scenario of each situation.

The limited nature of an employer's *de minimis* legal obligation to accommodate an employee's religious beliefs and practices has serious implications for employees requesting to refrain from morally objectionable work assignments. In many instances, an employer could readily demonstrate undue hardship. For example, a pharmacist may request reasonable accommodation for his or her religious beliefs by being allowed not to fill customer prescriptions for emergency contraceptives. The employer can readily demonstrate undue hardship if the pharmacy normally has only one pharmacist on duty. It is impossible to foresee when a customer may appear at the counter with a prescription for emergency contraceptives. Thus only three practical accommodations could be made. First, the pharmacy could hire another pharmacist to be on site with the conscientious objector pharmacist. This obviously would entail extra expense. Second, the customer could be directed by the objecting pharmacist to another pharmacy. Third, the objecting pharmacist could direct the customer to return when a non-objecting pharmacist is on duty. The latter two alternatives would both entail possible lost revenue, customer alienation, bad publicity and lawsuits. Thus the employer could readily meet its *de minimis* obligation and demonstrate that it would create an undue hardship to accommodate the pharmacist with religious objections.

Because the bar is set so low for an employer to meet its duty of reasonable accommodation for religious beliefs and practices, existing federal and state anti-discrimination statutes provide inadequate legal protection for employees with moral and religious objections to assigned work. More often than not, such employees would find themselves disciplined or discharged with scant legal recourse. Because of this inadequate statutory protection, many observers believe that conscience laws are needed to provide more substantive protection to employees.

Conscience Laws

Conscience laws are laws that grant an employee a statutory right to refuse to perform work or provide services that violate their religious or moral beliefs (see: Dennis Rambaud, "Prescription Contraceptives and the Pharmacist's Right to Refuse: Examining the Efficacy of Conscience Laws," *Cardozo Public Law, Policy and Ethics Journal* (2006), 195–231). Conscience laws are also referred to as conscience clauses or right of refusal clauses. Conscience laws first appeared in the aftermath of *Roe v. Wade, 410 U.S. 113* (1973) when state laws were passed which permitted doctors and other direct providers of health care services the statutory right to refuse to provide or participate in abortions. In general, conscience laws would prevent an employer from taking coercive, adverse or discriminatory action against an employee who refuses to perform assigned work for reasons of conscience. Depending on the particular text of the statute, conscience clauses may additionally protect the worker from civil liability and from adverse action by licensing boards.

More recent conscience clauses have focused on pharmacists, although some have broader coverage. The impetus for the flurry in state legislative action was the FDA approval of the morning-after pill. In the wake of that approval, pharmacists who refused to dispense the drug on moral grounds increasingly faced discipline, discharge and confrontations with state licensing boards. The current status of state conscience laws and pending bills is constantly in flux as more legislatures consider such laws. According to the National Conference of State Legislatures at the time of this writing, Arkansas, Georgia, Mississippi and South Dakota have passed statutes which permit a pharmacist to refuse to dispense emergency contraception because of moral convictions. Four other states (Colorado, Florida, Maine and Tennessee) enacted conscience clauses that are broader in nature and do not specifically mention pharmacists. California has enacted a more restrictive conscience clause which permits a pharmacist to refuse to fill a prescription only if the employer approves the refusal and the customer can still have the prescription filled in a timely manner (see: National Conference of State Legislatures, "Pharmacist Conscience Clauses: Laws and Legislation," [October 2006] . . .). At least 18 states are contemplating some 36 bills with varying scope and protection. Among those, nine states are considering conscience clauses that cover a broad array of health care workers. A few states are even considering bills that would permit insurance companies to opt out of providing coverage for morally objectionable services (see: Rob Stein, "Health Workers' Choice Debated," *Washington Post* [January 30, 2006], A01).

Needless to say, the surfeit of proposed state protective legislation has created an outcry among pro-choice and Planned Parenthood proponents. Some of this backlash is being translated into state law. In Illinois for example, the governor passed an emergency rule that requires a pharmacist to fill prescriptions for FDA-approved contraception. Several Illinois pharmacists have been fired for refusing to fill such prescriptions.

On the federal level in 2004, President Bush signed into law the Weldon Amendment which bars federal funding of any government program that subjects any institutional or individual health care provider to discrimination on the basis that the health care provider does not provide, pay for, provide coverage of, or refer for abortions. The U.S. Conference of Catholic Bishops has gone on record supporting the amendment. The State of California has filed a lawsuit challenging the constitutionality of the amendment.

Conscience laws seek to provide a balance between protecting workers compelled to choose between their livelihood and their religious beliefs and the public welfare. Whether American society will support this compromise or instead insist on forcing compliance by employees with moral objections to work assignments remains to be played out in the legal system.

EILEEN P. KELLY, PhD, is a professor at Ithaca College and teaches courses in applied ethical issues in management, labor relations, strategic management, and employment law.

National Women's Law Center

 **NO**

Pharmacy Refusals 101

Prescription Contraception Is Basic Health Care for Women

- Family planning is central to good health care for women. Access to contraception is critical to preventing unintended pregnancies and to enabling women to control the timing and spacing of their pregnancies. Contraceptive use in the United States is virtually universal among women of reproductive age. A woman who wants only two children must use contraception for roughly three decades of her life. Also, women rely on prescription contraceptives for a range of medical purposes in addition to birth control, such as regulation of cycles and endometriosis.
- Emergency contraception (EC), also known as the morning after pill, is an FDA-approved form of contraception that prevents pregnancy after sexual intercourse. EC is a time-sensitive medication that has great potential to prevent unintended pregnancies. Currently, there are several options for emergency contraception available, one that requires a prescription and two that are available without a prescription for individuals 17 and older.

Refusals to Dispense Contraception Are Increasing

- Reports of pharmacist refusals to fill prescriptions for birth control—or provide EC to individuals who do not require a prescription—have surfaced in at least twenty-four states across the nation, including: AZ, CA, DC, GA, IL, LA, MA, MI, MN, MO, MT, NH, NY, NC, OH, OK, OR, RI, TN, TX, VA, WA, WV, WI.
- These refusals to dispense prescription contraceptives or provide EC are based on personal beliefs, not on legitimate medical or professional concerns. The same pharmacists who refuse to dispense contraceptives because of their personal beliefs often refuse to transfer a woman's prescription to another pharmacist or to refer her to another pharmacy. These refusals can have devastating consequences for women's health.
- Despite the fact that two brands of EC are available without a prescription to certain individuals, refusals based on personal beliefs are still a problem. Non-prescription EC must be kept behind

the counter, so individuals seeking it must interact with pharmacists or other pharmacy staff who may have personal beliefs against providing the drug.

- Some examples of refusals in the pharmacy:
  - November 2010: Adam Drake attempted to purchase non-prescription EC at a Walgreens in **Houston, Texas** and was turned away, despite the fact that the federal Food and Drug Administration (FDA) has approved that brand of EC for sale to *men and women* aged seventeen and older.
  - March 2010: A pro-life pharmacy refusing to stock or dispense contraceptives in **Chantilly, Virginia**, closed due to lack of business. When it opened in October 2008, staff at the pharmacy refused to provide referrals or help individuals find contraception elsewhere.
  - January 2010: A mother of two in **Montclair, California** went to her local CVS to purchase EC after she and her fiancé experienced a birth control failure. The pharmacist refused to dispense EC to her, even though it was in stock, and told her to "come back in two and a half days," at which point it would no longer be effective.
  - May 2007: In **Great Falls, Montana**, a 49-year-old woman who used birth control to treat a medical condition went to her local pharmacy to fill her latest prescription. She was given a slip of paper informing her that the pharmacy would no longer fill any prescriptions for birth control. When she called back to inquire about the policy change, the owner of the pharmacy told her that birth control was "dangerous" for women.
  - January 2007: In **Columbus, Ohio**, a 23-year-old mother went to her local Wal-Mart for EC. The pharmacist on staff "shook his head and laughed." She was told that even though the store stocked EC, no one on staff would sell it to her. She had to drive 45 miles to find another pharmacy that would provide her with EC.
  - December 2006: In **Seattle, Washington**, a 25-year-old woman went to her local Rite-Aid to get non-prescription EC after she and her fiancé experienced a birth control failure. The pharmacist told her that although EC was in stock, he would not give it to her because he thought it was wrong. The woman had to repeatedly insist

that the pharmacist find her another pharmacy in the area that would provide her with EC.

• January 2006: In **Northern California**, a married mother of a newborn baby experienced a birth control failure with her husband. Her physician called in a prescription for EC to her regular pharmacy, but when she went to pick it up, the pharmacist on duty not only refused to dispense the drug, which was in stock, but also refused to enter the prescription into the pharmacy's computer so that it could be transferred elsewhere.

• January 2005: In **Milwaukee, Wisconsin**, a mother of six went to her local Walgreens with a prescription for emergency contraception. The pharmacist refused to fill the prescription and berated the mother in the pharmacy's crowded waiting area, shouting "You're a murderer! I will not help you kill this baby. I will not have the blood on my hands." The mother left the pharmacy mortified and never had her prescription filled. She subsequently became pregnant and had an abortion.

• April 2004: In *North Richland Hills, Texas*, a 32-year-old mother of two went to her local CVS for her regular birth control prescription refill. The pharmacist refused to refill her prescription because of his personal beliefs. The pharmacist said he would not fill the prescription because oral contraceptives are "not right" and "cause cancer."

• January 2004: In *Denton, Texas*, a rape survivor seeking EC was turned away from an Eckerd pharmacy by three pharmacists, who refused to fill the time-sensitive prescription due to their religious beliefs. The pharmacists' refusal put the survivor in danger of becoming pregnant due to the rape.

The Legal Landscape: What Governs the Practice of Pharmacy?

• The laws governing pharmacists vary from state to state. Pharmacists must abide by state laws and regulations, which are written by the state legislature and the state Pharmacy Board.

• The laws and regulations in most states do not specifically speak to the issue of pharmacist refusals based on personal beliefs. States that provide general guidance about when pharmacists may refuse to dispense tend to limit the reasons for such a refusal to professional or medical considerations—such as potentially harmful contraindication, interactions with other drugs, improper dosage, and suspected drug abuse or misuse—as opposed to personal judgments.

• Many pharmacist associations that have considered this issue, including the American Pharmacists Association, have issued policies requiring that patient access to legally prescribed medications is not compromised—for example by either filling valid prescriptions or transferring them to another pharmacist who can. Although such policies are not legally binding, they encourage pharmacists to meet consumers' needs.

Legislative and Administrative Responses to Refusals in the Pharmacy

Fewer than half of the states in the country explicitly address the issue of refusals to provide medication to patients in the pharmacy.

Prohibiting or Limiting Refusals

• *Existing State Laws and Policies:*
  • **Eight states**—CA, IL, ME, MA, NV, NJ, WA, WI—explicitly require pharmacists or pharmacies to provide medication to patients. In April 2011, a court prevented the Illinois regulation from being enforced against two pharmacists and the pharmacies they own.
  • In **seven states**—AL, DE, NY, NC, OR, PA, TX—pharmacy boards have issued policy statements that allow refusals but prohibit pharmacists from obstructing patient access to medication.
• *State Legislation*: Thus far in the 2011 legislative session, **seven states** (AZ, IN, MO, NJ, NY, OK, and WV) have considered **eleven bills** to prohibit or limit refusals. These bills would prevent pharmacists or pharmacies from denying access to contraception based on personal beliefs, including **seven bills** that apply to non-prescription EC.

Permitting Refusals

• *Existing State Laws and Policies:* **Six states**—AZ, AR, GA, ID, MS, and SD—have laws or regulations that specifically allow pharmacies or pharmacists to refuse for religious or moral reasons without critical protections for patients, such as requirements to refer or transfer prescriptions. However, a state court prevented Arizona's law allowing pharmacy and pharmacist refusals from going into effect pending litigation and it is therefore not currently enforceable.
• *State Legislation:* Thus far in the 2011 legislative session, **three states** (IN, MO, and PA) have considered **three bills** that could permit pharmacists or pharmacies to refuse to dispense certain drugs and devices without protecting patient access. The Missouri bill incorrectly classifies EC as an abortifacient despite the fact that the FDA approved it as a form of birth control.

Public Opinion

• According to surveys, the public is overwhelmingly opposed to allowing refusals in the pharmacy that prevent women from obtaining contraception.

- A national survey of Republicans and Independent voters conducted in September and October 2008 on behalf of the National Women's Law Center and the YWCA found that 51% *strongly* favor legislation that requires pharmacies to ensure that patients get contraception at their pharmacy of choice, even if a particular pharmacist has a moral objection to contraceptives and refuses to provide it. That includes 42% of Republicans and 62% of Independents.
- In a national opinion survey released in July 2007, which was conducted for the National Women's Law Center and Planned Parenthood Federation of America by Peter D. Hart Research Associates, 71% of voters said that pharmacists should not be allowed to refuse to fill prescriptions on moral or religious grounds, including majorities of every voter demographic such as Republicans (56%), Catholics (73%), and evangelical Christians (53%). Even more respondents (73% overall) supported requiring pharmacies to dispense contraception to patients without discrimination or delay.
- A poll conducted in May 2007 by Lake Research Partners found that 82% of adults and registered voters believed that "pharmacies should be required to dispense birth control to patients without discrimination or delay."
- An August 2006 poll conducted by the Pew Research Center on People and the Press found that 80% of Americans believe that pharmacists should not be able to refuse to sell birth control based on their religious beliefs. This was true across party lines and religious affiliations.

Particularly notable was the poll's finding that "No political or religious groups express majority support for this type of conscience clause."
- A November 2004 *CBS/New York Times* poll showed that public opinion disfavoring pharmacist refusals was strong regardless of party affiliation. 78% of Americans believe that pharmacist refusals should not be permitted, including 85% of Democrat respondents and 70% of Republican respondents.

How to Respond to a Refusal in the Pharmacy

- File a complaint with your state's pharmacy board to get sanctions against the pharmacist or pharmacy.
- Communicate your story to the press.
- Ask the state pharmacy board or legislature to put in place policies that will ensure every consumer's right to access legal pharmaceuticals.
- Alert the pharmacy's corporate headquarters; some pharmacies have policies that protect women's right to receive contraception in store, without discrimination or delay.
- Get EC today, before you need it!

NATIONAL WOMEN'S LAW CENTER is a nonprofit organization that works to expand the possibilities for women and focuses on family economic security, education, employment opportunities, and health, with special attention given to the concerns of low-income women.

EXPLORING THE ISSUE

Should Pharmacists Have the Right to Refuse Contraceptive Prescriptions?

Critical Thinking and Reflection

1. Should health care providers be allowed to refuse certain treatments or medications based on their religious beliefs?
2. Why are medications like contraceptives at the forefront of this controversy?
3. What can you do if a pharmacist refuses to fill your contraceptive prescription?

Is There Common Ground?

The YES and NO selections present a compelling contrast between the rights of employees and the rights of patients. Both provide examples of scenarios with minor citations. Are these types of examples useful or does the lack of clear citation damage their effectiveness?

Kelly presents her side from the perspective of Catholic social teaching. It is important, however, to understand that followers of particular religions are not completely homogeneous in their beliefs and practices. While Christian organizations such as the U.S. Conference of Catholic Bishops and the Christian Medical and Dental Association support broadening the reach of conscience clauses, other religious organizations such as Catholics for Choice and the United Methodist General Board of Church and Society encouraged President Obama to reverse Bush's expansion of the clause. Similarly, not all who support the expansion of the "right of refusal" are religiously identified.

The National Women's Law Center provides a set of statistics showing widespread opposition to pharmacists' refusal of contraception. Were any of the statistics surprising? Why or why not? The group also provides a set of steps to take if a prescription is refused. Would you feel comfortable taking any of these steps? Why or why not?

Across the country, several "pro-life" pharmacies have opened—these pharmacies refuse to stock condoms, hormonal birth control, or emergency contraception. Is this an acceptable compromise? Should such pharmacies be required to inform potential customers that they do not stock such items by posting the information on the door?

Where do you stand on this issue? Most people agree that freedom of religion is a valuable part of a democratic society. But does that freedom have limits if someone's health or well-being is involved? If a pharmacist's religion adheres to the belief that antidepressants are not a suitable way to treat depression, should they be allowed the right of refusal? Why do you think much of the controversy over pharmacist refusals has focused on contraception and not other medications? The Provider Refusal Rule also covers other health care workers—should a pharmacy technician be allowed to refrain from ordering contraceptives during their routine inventory checks? Should an EMT be allowed to refuse to drive the ambulance to the hospital if he or she fears an abortion may be necessary in order to save the patient's life?

Create Central

www.mhhe.com/createcentral

References

1. Sonfield A. "Rights vs. Responsibilities: Professional Standards and Provider Refusals," *The Guttmacher Report on Public Policy,* August 2005, Volume 8 (3).

Additional Resources

Anonymous. "The Pontifical Commission and How Birth Control Became Known as Intrinsically Evil" *RH Reality Check,* February 21, 2012.

Chaput C. "Religous Freedom and the Need to Wake Up," *National Catholic Reporter* (May 24, 2013).

Jacobson, J. "Obama Administration Repeals Portions of Bush Provider Conscience Rules," *RH Reality Check,* February 18, 2011

Pear, R. "U.S. Clarifies Policy on Birth Control for Religious Groups," *New York Times,* March 16, 2012.

Stein, R. "Pro-Life Drugstores Market Beliefs," *The Washington Post,* June 2008.

Internet References . . .

Catholics for Choice

Catholics for Choice is "a voice for Catholics who believe that the Catholic tradition supports a woman's moral and legal right to follow her conscience in matters of sexuality and reproductive health."

www.catholicsforchoice.org

United States Council of Catholic Bishops

The United States Council of Catholic Bishops was a leading voice opposing the contraceptive mandate in Health Care Reform. This page summarizes its objections.

www.usccb.org/issues-and-action/human-life-and-dignity/contraception/fact-sheets/contraceptive-mandates.cfm

Guttmacher Institute

This page summarizes state laws regarding access to emergency contraception.

www.guttmacher.org/statecenter/spibs/spib_EC.pdf

The Heritage Foundation

This page summarizes conservative legal arguments opposing contraceptive mandates.

www.heritage.org/research/reports/2012/06/obama-religious-liberty-and-the-legal-challenges-to-the-hhs-contraceptive-mandate

The National Women's Law Center (NWLC)

The NWLC advocates for women and families through education and litigation. They advance issues of education, employment, family and economic security, and health and reproductive rights through changes in law and public policy. This page summarizes the legal chronology of pharmacy contraceptive refusals.

www.nwlc.org/resource/pharmacy-refusals-101

Selected, Edited, and with Issue Framing Material by:
Ryan W. McKee, *Widener University*
and
William J. Taverner, *Center for Family Life Education*

ISSUE

Should Parents Be Allowed to Select the Sex of Their Baby?

YES: **John A. Robertson**, from "Extending Preimplantation Genetic Diagnosis: Medical and Non-Medical Uses," *Journal of Medical Ethics* (vol. 29, 2003)

NO: **Marcy Darnovsky**, from "Revisiting Sex Selection: The Growing Popularity of New Sex Selection Methods Revives an Old Debate" (January/February 2004), www.gene-watch.org/genewatch/articles/17-1darnovsky.html

---

Learning Outcomes

After reading this issue, you should be able to:

- Describe the medical and nonmedical uses of preimplantation genetic diagnosis (PGD).
- Compare the process of PGD to other means of sex selection used throughout history.
- Describe the ethical issues surrounding the use of PGD for nonmedical purposes.
- Explain the "slippery slope" argument, and how it applies to PGD and sex selection.

ISSUE SUMMARY

YES: Law professor John A. Robertson argues that preimplantation genetic diagnosis (PGD), a new technique that allows parents-to-be to determine the sex of their embryo before implantation in the uterus, should be permissible. Robertson argues that it is not sexist to want a baby of a particular gender, and that the practice should not be restricted.

NO: Marcy Darnovsky, associate director of the Center for Genetics and Society, argues that by allowing PGD for sex selection, governments are starting down a slippery slope that could create an era of consumer eugenics.

T he practice of selecting the sex of a child is nothing new. Many cultures have folklore dictating which sexual positions are more likely to result in children of a particular sex. Some cultures even turn to herbal supplements to increase their chances of a boy or a girl. If those steps were ineffective, a child of a specific sex might be abandoned on the doorstep of a church or orphanage. Another method, though unpleasant to consider, involves infanticide by leaving an unwanted boy or girl in the wilderness.

While these practices still continue in some societies, sex selection has also changed in significant ways. The development of ultrasound technology, for example, has allowed expecting parents to know the sex of a baby before it is born. While sex-selective abortion is highly controversial, some parents might consider the procedure if an ultrasound reveals the child is not of their desired sex. Parents might feel additional pressure to make this decision in countries like China, which has a "one child" policy, whereby additional children receive no governmental

support—a critical consideration in a country that has traditionally placed a higher value on male infants than female infants.

For many Americans, the idea of sex selection by abandonment, abortion, or infanticide would be considered unethical, if not appalling. But in other areas of the world, the practices are carried out routinely to help parents meet strong cultural preferences to produce a male child. Such actions are based on the entrenched sexism of these male-dominated societies.

A seemingly more ethical technique that sorts sperm cells before conception has offered about a 50–85 percent effectiveness rate at predetermining sex for the past 30 years. More recently a new development in medical technology known as preimplantation genetic diagnosis (PGD), previously used to screen embryos for markers that may signal diseases like cystic fibrosis, now allows people using in vitro fertilization to select the sex of an embryo, with 99.9 percent accuracy. In this procedure, egg cells that have been fertilized in a laboratory are tested for specific markers before being implanted into the uterus. To many satisfied customers, this has provided the opportunity to "balance" a family by adding a child of the other sex, evening out the number of male and female children. In some cases, first-time parents simply desire a child of one sex or the other.

The practice is not without controversy. One ethical question, what to do with the embryos that aren't implanted, is related to the in vitro fertilization technique. Unused embryos can be donated, saved for later attempts at implantation, or simply destroyed. Some "pro-life" activists, who believe that life begins at fertilization, argue that the disposal of these unused embryos is akin to abortion. For this population, the potential fate of the embryos calls into question the ethical nature of many reproductive technologies. Despite the concerns of anti-abortion activists, in vitro fertilization and the medical use of PGD, such as screening for Down syndrome, are widely seen as acceptable. It is the nonmedical uses of PGD that raise ethical questions for a larger number of people.

By allowing parents to express a preference for—and choose—one sex over another, PGD for sex selection is, according to critics, by its very definition sexist. By allowing a societal preference for sons or daughters, gender stereotypes would be reinforced and promoted. Furthermore, if the ability to select other physical, intellectual, or personality traits is developed, the commodification of children could become the new normal.

Defenders of sex selection through PGD argue that the issue is one of reproductive freedom. Parents should have control over their reproductive futures. As technology improves, we become closer to a world in which every child born is one that is wanted. While selecting the sex of a firstborn child could be seen as sexist, the high cost is likely to keep that from happening in cultures where first-born sons are prized. It is more likely that the process could be used for "family balancing," or having a child a different sex than earlier children.

No matter the side you find yourself on, technological advancements like these bring up many ethical questions, both new and old. Is wanting to choose the sex of your child inherently sexist? Does the procedure reflect or perpetuate a gender bias in society? If selecting the sex of your unborn child is possible and legal, what about predetermination of other characteristics, such as eye color? Height? Musical ability? Sexual orientation?

In the following selections, John A. Robertson, professor at the University of Texas School of Law, argues that using PGD for sex selection in certain instances is not inherently sexist, and that it—and perhaps other nonmedical types of PGD—should not be regulated based on the fear of what could possibly happen at some future time. Marcy Darnovsky, executive director of the Center for Genetics and Society, argues that by allowing PGD for sex selection, governments are starting down a slippery slope that could create an era of consumer eugenics.

YES ↩

John A. Robertson

Extending Preimplantation Genetic Diagnosis: Medical and Non-Medical Uses

PGD and Its Prevalence

PGD has been available since 1990 for testing of aneuploidy in low prognosis in vitro fertilisation (IVF) patients, and for single gene and X linked diseases in at risk couples. One cell (blastomere) is removed from a cleaving embryo and tested for the genetic or chromosomal condition of concern. Some programmes analyse polar bodies extruded from oocytes during meiosis, rather than blastomeres.[1] Cells are then either karyotyped to identify chromosomal abnormalities, or analysed for single gene mutations and linked markers.

Physicians have performed more than 3000 clinical cycles of PGD since 1990, with more than 700 children born as a result. The overall pregnancy rate of 24% is comparable to assisted reproductive practices which do not involve embryo or polar body biopsy.[1] Four centres (Chicago, Livingston (New Jersey), Bologna, and Brussels) accounted for nearly all the reported cases. More than 40 centres worldwide offer the procedure, however, including other centres in the United States and Europe, four centres in London and centres in the eastern Mediterranean, Southeast Asia, and Australia.

More than two-thirds of PGD has occurred to screen out embryos with chromosomal abnormalities in older IVF patients and in patients with a history of miscarriage. About 1000 cycles have involved single gene mutational analysis.[1] Mutational analysis requires additional skills beyond karyotyping for aneuploidies, including the ability to conduct the multiplex polymerase chain reaction (PCR) of the gene of interest and related markers.

Several new indications for PGD single gene mutational analysis have recently been reported. New uses include PGD to detect mutations for susceptibility to cancer and for late onset disorders such as Alzheimer's disease.[2,3] In addition, parents with children needing hematopoietic stem cell transplants have used PGD to ensure that their next child is free of disease and a good tissue match for an existing child.[4] Some persons are also requesting PGD for gender selection for both first and later born children, and others have speculated that selection of embryos for a variety of non-medical traits is likely in the future.

PGD is ethically controversial because it involves the screening and likely destruction of embryos, and the selection of offspring on the basis of expected traits. While persons holding right to life views will probably object to PGD for any reason, those who view the early embryo as too rudimentary in development to have rights or interests see no principled objection to all PGD. They may disagree, however, over whether particular reasons for PGD show sufficient respect for embryos and potential offspring to justify intentional creation and selection of embryos. Donation of unwanted embryos to infertile couples reduces this problem somewhat, but there are too few such couples to accept all unwanted embryos, and in any event, the issue of selecting offspring traits remains.

Although ethical commentary frequently mentions PGD as a harbinger of a reproductive future of widespread genetic selection and alteration of prospective offspring, its actual impact is likely to be quite limited.[5,6] Even with increasing use the penetrance of PGD into reproductive practice is likely to remain a very small percentage of the 150,000 plus cycles of IVF performed annually throughout the world. Screening for susceptibility and late onset diseases is limited by the few diseases for which single gene predispositions are known. Relatively few parents will face the need to conceive another child to provide an existing child with matched stem cells. Nor are non-medical uses of PGD, other than for gender, likely to be practically feasible for at least a decade or more. Despite the limited reach of PGD, the ethical, legal, and policy issues that new uses raise, deserve attention.

New Medical Uses

New uses of PGD may be grouped into medical and non-medical categories. New medical uses include not only screening for rare Mendelian diseases, but also for susceptibility conditions, late onset diseases, and HLA matching for existing children.

Embryo screening for susceptibility and late onset conditions are logical extensions of screening for serious Mendelian diseases. For example, using PGD to screen out embryos carrying the p53 or BRCA1&2 mutations prevent the birth of children who would face a greatly increased lifetime risk of cancer, and hence require close monitoring, prophylactic surgery, or other preventive measures. PGD for highly penetrant adult disorders such as Alzheimer's or Huntington's disease prevents the birth of a child who will be healthy for many years, but who in her late 30s or early

40s will experience the onset of progressive neurological disease leading to an early death.

Although these indications do not involve diseases that manifest themselves in infancy or childhood, the conditions in question lead to substantial health problems for offspring in their thirties or forties.[7] Avoiding the birth of children with those conditions thus reflects the desire of parents to have offspring with good prospects for an average life span. If PGD is accepted to exclude offspring with early onset genetic diseases, it should be accepted for later onset conditions as well.

PGD for adult onset disorders does mean that a healthy child might then be born to a person with those conditions who is likely to die or become incompetent while the child is dependent on her.[8] But that risk has been tolerated in other cases of assisted reproduction, such as intrauterine insemination with sperm of a man who is HIV positive, IVF for women with cystic fibrosis, and use of gametes stored prior to cancer therapy. As long as competent caregivers will be available for the child, the likely death or disability of a parent does not justify condemning or stopping this use, anymore than that reproduction by men going off to war should be discouraged.

A third new medical indication—HLA matching to an existing child—enables a couple to have their next child serve as a matched hematopoietic stem cell donor for an existing sick child. It may also ensure that the new child does not also suffer from that same disease. The availability of PGD, however, should not hinge on that fact, as the Human Fertilisation and Embryology Authority, in the UK, now requires.[9] A couple that would coitally conceive a child to be a tissue donor should be free to use PGD to make sure that that child will be a suitable match, regardless of whether that child is also at risk for genetic disease. Parents who choose PGD for this purpose are likely to value the new child for its own sake, and not only for the stem cells that it will make available. They do not use the new child as a "mere means" simply because they have selected HLA matched embryos for transfer.[10, 11]

Non-Medical Uses of PGD

More ethically troubling has been the prospect of using PGD to screen embryos for genes that do not relate to the health of resulting children or others in the family. Many popular accounts of PGD assume that it will eventually be used to select for such non-medical traits as intelligence, height, sexual orientation, beauty, hair and eye colour, memory, and other factors.[5, 6] Because the genetic basis of those traits is unknown, and in any case is likely to involve many different genes, they may not be subject to easy mutational analysis, as Mendelian disease or susceptibility conditions are. Aside from gender, which is identifiable through karyotyping, it is unrealistic to think that non-medical screening for other traits, with the possible exception of perfect pitch, will occur anytime soon.

Still, it is useful to consider the methodology that ethical assessment of non-medical uses of PGD, if available, should follow. The relevant questions would be whether the proposed use serves valid reproductive or rearing interests; whether those interests are sufficient to justify creating and destroying embryos; whether selecting for a trait will harm resulting children; whether it will stigmatise existing persons, and whether it will create other social harms.

To analyse how these factors interact, I discuss PGD for sex selection and for children with perfect pitch. Similar issues would arise with PGD for sexual orientation, for hair and eye color, and for intelligence, size, and memory.

PGD for Gender Selection

The use of medical technology to select the sex of offspring is highly controversial because of the bias against females which it usually reflects or expresses, and the resulting social disruptions which it might cause. PGD for gender selection faces the additional problem of appearing to be a relatively weak reason for creating and selecting embryos for discard or transfer.

The greatest social effects of gender selection arise when the gender of the first child is chosen. Selection for first children will overwhelmingly favour males, particularly if one child per family population policies apply. If carried out on a large scale, it could lead to great disparities in the sex ratio of the population, as has occurred in China and India through the use of ultrasound screening and abortion.[12, 13] PGD, however, is too expensive and inaccessible to be used on a wide scale for sex selection purposes. Allowing it to be used for the first child is only marginally likely to contribute to societal sex ratio imbalances. But its use is likely to reflect cultural notions of male privilege and may reinforce entrenched sexism toward women.

The use of PGD to choose a gender opposite to that of an existing child or children is much less susceptible to a charge of sexism. Here a couple seeks variety or "balance" in the gender of offspring because of the different rearing experiences that come with rearing children of different genders. Psychologists now recognise many biologically based differences between male and female children, including different patterns of aggression, learning, and spatial recognition, as well as hormonal differences.[14, 15] It may not be sexist in itself to wish to have a child or children of each gender, particularly if one has two or more children of the same gender.

Some feminists, however, would argue that any attention to the gender of offspring is inherently sexist, particularly when social attitudes and expectations play such an important role in constructing sex role expectations and behaviours.[16] Other feminists find the choice of a child with a gender different from existing children to be morally defensible as long as "the intention and consequences of the practice are not sexist," which is plausibly the case when gender variety in children is sought.[17] Desiring the different rearing experiences with boys and girls does not mean that the parents, who have already had children of one gender, are sexists or likely to value unfairly one or the other gender.[18]

Based on this analysis the case is weak for allowing PGD for the first child, but may be acceptable for gender variety in a family. With regard to the first child, facilitating preferences for male firstborns carries a high risk of promoting sexist social mores. It may also strike many persons as too trivial a concern to meet shared notions of the special respect due preimplantation embryos. A proponent of gender selection, however, might argue that cultural preferences for firstborn males should be tolerated, unless a clearer case of harm has been shown. If PGD is not permitted, pregnancy and abortion might occur instead.

The case for PGD for gender variety is stronger because the risk of sexism is lessened. A couple would be selecting the gender of a second or subsequent children for variety in rearing experiences, and not out of a belief that one gender is privileged over another. Gender selection in that case would occur without running the risks of fostering sexism and hurting women.[18]

The question still arises whether the desire for gender variety in children, even if not sexist, is a strong enough reason to justify creating and discarding embryos. The answer depends on how strong an interest that is. No one has yet marshalled the evidence showing that the need or desire for gender variety in children is substantial and important, or whether many parents would refrain from having another child if PGD for gender variety were not possible. More evidence of the strength and prevalence of this need would help in reaching a conclusion. If that case is made, then PGD for gender variety might be acceptable as well.[19]

The ethics committee of the American Society of Reproductive Medicine (ASRM) has struggled with these issues in a series of recent opinions. It initially addressed the issue of PGD for gender selection generally, and found that it "should be discouraged" for couples not going through IVF, and "not encouraged" for couples who were, but made no distinction between PGD for gender selection of first and later children.[20] Subsequently, it found that preconception gender selection would be acceptable for purposes of gender variety but not for the first child.[18]

Perceiving these two positions to be inconsistent, a doctor who wanted to offer PGD for gender selection inquired of the ethics committee why preconception methods for gender variety, which lacked 100% certainty, were acceptable but PGD, which guaranteed that certainty, was not. Focusing only on the sexism and gender discrimination issue, the chair of the ethics committee, in a widely publicised letter, found that PGD for gender balancing would be acceptable.[21] When the full committee reconsidered the matter, it concluded that it had not yet received enough evidence that the need for gender variety was so important in families that it justified creating and discarding embryos for that purpose.[19] In the future if such evidence was forthcoming then PGD for gender variety might also be acceptable.

What might constitute such evidence? One source would be families with two or more children of one gender who very much would like to have another child but only if they could be sure that it would be a child of the gender opposite of existing children. Given the legitimacy of wanting to raise children of both genders, reasonable persons might find that this need outweighs the symbolic costs of creating and discarding embryos for that purpose.

Another instance would be a case in which a couple has had a girl, but now wants a boy in order to meet cultural norms of having a male heir or a male to perform funeral rituals or play other cultural roles. An IVF programme in India is now providing PGD to select male offspring as the second child of couples who have already had a daughter.[22] Because of the importance of a male heir in India, those couples might well consider having an abortion if pregnant with a female fetus (even though illegal in India for that purpose). In that setting PGD for gender selection for gender variety appears to be justified.

PGD for Perfect Pitch

Perfect or "absolute" pitch is the ability to identify and recall musical notes from memory.[23] Although not all great or successful musicians have perfect pitch, a large number of them do. Experts disagree over whether perfect pitch is solely inborn or may also be developed by early training, though most agree that a person either has it or does not. It also runs in families, apparently in an autosomal dominant pattern.[23] The gene or genes coding for this capacity have not, however, been mapped, much less sequenced. Because genes for perfect pitch may also relate to the genetic basis for language or other cognitive abilities, research to find that gene may be forthcoming.

Once the gene for perfect pitch or its linked markers are identified, it would be feasible to screen embryos for those alleles, and transfer only those embryos that test positive. The prevalence of those genes is quite low (perhaps three in 100) in the population, but high in certain families.[23] Thus only persons from those families who have a strong interest in the musical ability of their children would be potential candidates for PGD for perfect pitch. Many of them are likely to take their chances with coital conception and exposure of the child to music at an early age. Some couples, however, may be willing to undergo IVF and PGD to ensure musical ability in their child. Should their request be accepted or denied?

As noted, the answer to this question depends on the importance of the reproductive choice being asserted, the burdens of the selection procedure, its impact on offspring, and its implications for deselected groups and society generally. The strongest case for the parents is if they persuasively asserted that they would not reproduce unless they could select that trait, and they have a plausible explanation for that position. Although the preference might appear odd to some, it might also be quite understandable in highly musical families, particularly ones in which some members already have perfect pitch. Parents clearly have the right to instill or develop a child's musical ability after birth. They might reasonably argue that they should have that right before birth as well.

If so, then creating and discarding embryos for this purpose should also be acceptable. If embryos are too rudimentary in development to have inherent rights or interests, then no moral duty is violated by creating and destroying them.[24] Some persons might think that doing so for trivial or unimportant reasons debases the inherent dignity of all human life, but having a child with perfect pitch will not seem trivial to parents seeking this technique. Ultimately, the judgment of triviality or importance of the choice within a broad spectrum rests with the couple. If they have a strong enough preference to seek PGD for this purpose and that preference rationally relates to understandable reproductive goals, then they have demonstrated its great importance to them. Only in cases unsupported by a reasonable explanation of the need—for example, perhaps creating embryos to pick eye or hair colour, should a person's individual assessment of the importance of creating embryos be condemned or rejected.

A third relevant factor is whether musical trait selection is consistent with respect for the resulting child. Parents who are willing to undergo the costs and burdens of IVF and PGD to have a child with perfect pitch may be so overly invested in the child having a musical career that they will prevent it from developing its own personality and identity. Parents, however, are free to instill and develop musical ability once the child is born, just as they are entitled to instill particular religious views. It is difficult to say that they cross an impermissible moral line of risk to the welfare of their prospective child in screening embryos for this purpose. Parents are still obligated to provide their child with the basic education and care necessary for any life plan. Wanting a child to have perfect pitch is not inconsistent with parents also wanting their child to be well rounded and equipped for life in other contexts.

A fourth factor, impact on deselected groups, is much less likely to be an issue in the case of perfect pitch because there is no stigma or negative association tied to persons without that trait. Persons without perfect pitch suffer no stigma or opprobrium by the couple's choice or public acceptance of it, as is arguably the case with embryo selection on grounds of gender, sexual orientation, intelligence, strength, size, or other traits. Nor is PGD for perfect pitch likely to perpetuate unfair class advantages, as selection for intelligence, strength, size, or beauty might.

A final factor is the larger societal impact of permitting embryo screening for a non-medical condition such as perfect pitch. A valid concern is that such a practice might then legitimise embryo screening for other traits as well, thus moving us toward a future in which children are primarily valued according to the attractiveness of their expected characteristics. But that threat is too hypothetical to justify limiting what are otherwise valid exercises of parental choice. It is highly unlikely that many traits would be controlled by genes that could be easily tested in embryos. Gender is determined by the chromosome, and the gene for pefect pitch, if ever found, would be a rare exception to the multifactorial complexity of such traits. Screening embryos for perfect pitch, if otherwise acceptable, should not be stopped simply because of speculation about what might be possible several decades from now.

PGD for Other Non-Medical Traits

The discussion of PGD for perfect pitch illustrates the issues that would arise if single gene analysis became possible for other traits, such as sexual orientation, hair or eye colour, or height, intelligence, size, strength, and memory. In each case the ethical assessment depends on an evaluation of the importance of the choice to the parents and whether that choice plausibly falls within societal understandings of parental needs and choice in reproducing and raising children. If so, it should usually be a sufficient reason to create and screen embryos. The effect on resulting offspring would also be of key moral importance. Whether selection carries a public or social message about the worth of existing groups should also be addressed.

Applying this methodology might show that some instances of non-medical selection are justified, as we have seen with embryo selection for gender variety and perhaps for having a child with perfect pitch. The acceptability of PGD to select other non-medical traits will depend on a careful analysis of the relevant ethical factors, and social acceptance of much greater parental rights to control the genes of offspring than now exists.

Conclusion

Although new indications are emerging for PGD, it is likely to remain a small part of reproductive practice for some time to come. Most new indications serve legitimate medical purposes, such as screening for single gene mutations for late onset disorders or susceptibility to cancer. There is also ethical support for using PGD to assure that a child is an HLA match with an existing child.

More controversial is the use of PGD to select gender or other non-medical traits. As with medical uses, the acceptability of non-medical screening will depend upon the interests served and the effects of using PGD for those purposes. Speculations about potential future non-medical uses should not restrict new uses of PGD which are otherwise ethically acceptable.

References

1. International Working Group on Preimplantation Genetics. Preimplantation genetic diagnosis: experience of 3000 clinical cycles. Report of the 11th annual meeting, May 15, 2001. *Reprod Biomedicine Online* 2001;3:49–53.
2. Verlinsky Y, Rechitsky S, Verlinsky O, et al. Preimplantation diagnosis of P53 tumor suppressor gene mutations. *Reprod Biomedicine Online* 2001;2:102–5.

3. Verlinsky Y, Rechitsky S, Schoolcraft W, et al. Preimplantation diagnosis for fanconi anemia combined with HLA matching. *JAMA* 2001;285:3130–3.

4. Verlinsky Y, Rechitsky S, Verlinsky O, et al. Preimplantation diagnosis for early-onset alzheimer's disease caused by V717L mutation. *JAMA* 2002;283:1018–21.

5. Fukuyama F. *Our postmodern future: consequences of the biotechnology revolution.* New York: Farrar, Strauss, & Giroux, 2002.

6. Stock G. *Redesigning humans: our inevitable genetic future.* New York: Houghton Mifflin, 2002.

7. Simpson JL. Celebrating preimplantation genetic diagnosis of p53 mutations in Li-Fraumeni syndrome. *Reprod Biomedicine Online* 2001;3:2–3.

8. Towner D, Loewy RS. Ethics of preimplantation diagnosis for a woman destined to develop early-onset alzheimer disease. *JAMA* 2002;283:1038–40.

9. Human Fertilisation and Embryology Authority. Opinion of the ethics committee. Ethical issues in the creation and selection of preimplantation embryos to produce tissue donors. London: HFEA, 2001 Nov 22.

10. Pennings G, Schots S, Liebaers I. Ethical considerations on preimplantation genetic diagnosis for HLA typing to match a future child as a donor of haematopoietic stem cells to a sibling. *Hum Reprod* 2002;17:534–8.

11. Robertson JA, Kahn J, Wagner J. Conception to obtain hematopoietic stem cells. *Hastings Cent Rep* 2002;32:34–40.

12. Sen A. More than 100 million women are missing. *New York Review of Books* 1990;37:61–8.

13. Eckholm E. Desire for sons drives use of prenatal scans in China. *The New York Times* 2002 Jun 21: A3.

14. Jaccoby EE, Jacklin CN. *The psychology of sex differences.* Palo Alto: Stanford University Press, 1974.

15. Robertson JA. Preconception gender selection. *Am J Bioeth* 2001;1:2–9.

16. Grubb A, Walsh P. Gender-vending II. *Dispatches* 1994;1:1–3.

17. Mahowald MB. *Genes, women, equality.* New York: Oxford University Press, 2000: 121.

18. American Society of Reproductive Medicine, Ethics Committee. Preconception gender selection for nonmedical reasons. *Fertil Steril* 2001;75:861–4.

19. Robertson JA. Sex selection for gender variety by preimplantation genetic diagnosis. *Fert Steril* 2002;78:463.

20. American Society of Reproductive Medicine, Ethics Committee. Sex selection and preimplantation genetic diagnosis. *Fertil Steril* 1999;72:595–8.

21. Kolata G. Society approves embryo selection. *The New York Times* 2001 Sept 26: A14.

22. Malpani A, Malpani A, Modi D. Preimplantation sex selection for family balancing in India. *Hum Reprod* 2002;17:11–12.

23. Blakeslee S. Perfect pitch: the key may lie in the genes. *The New York Times* 1990 Nov 30: 1.

24. American Society of Reproductive Medicine, Ethics Committee. Ethical considerations of assisted reproductive technologies. *Fertil Steril* 1994; 62(suppl):32–7S.

JOHN A. ROBERTSON holds the Vinson and Elkins Chair at the University of Texas School of Law at Austin. Additionally, he is chair of the Ethics Committee of the American Society for Reproductive Medicine.

Marcy Darnovsky

 **NO**

Revisiting Sex Selection: The Growing Popularity of New Sex Selection Methods Revives an Old Debate

In the United States and a few other prosperous, technologically advanced nations, methods of sex selection that are less intrusive or more reliable than older practices are now coming into use. Unlike prenatal testing, these procedures generally are applied either before an embryo is implanted in a woman's body, or before an egg is fertilized. They do not require aborting a fetus of the "wrong" sex.

These pre-pregnancy sex selection methods are being rapidly commercialized—not, as before, with medical claims, but as a means of satisfying parental desires. For the assisted reproduction industry, social sex selection may be a business path toward a vastly expanded market. People who have no infertility or medical problems, but who can afford expensive out-of-pocket procedures, are an enticing new target.

For the first time, some fertility clinics are openly advertising sex selection for social reasons. Several times each month, for example, the *New York Times'* Sunday Styles section carries an ad from the Virginia-based Genetics & IVF (in-vitro fertilization) Institute, touting its patented sperm sorting method. Beside a smiling baby, its boldface headline asks, "Do You Want to Choose the Gender of Your Next Baby?"

Recent trends in consumer culture may warm prospective parents to such offers. We have become increasingly accepting of—if not enthusiastic about— "enhancements" of appearance (think face-lifts, collagen and Botox injections, and surgery to reshape women's feet for stiletto heels) and adjustments of behavior (antidepressants, Viagra, and the like). These drugs and procedures were initially developed for therapeutic uses, but are now being marketed and normalized in disturbing ways. When considering questions of right and wrong, of liberty and justice, it is well to remember that the state is not the only coercive force we encounter.

This constellation of technological, economic, cultural, and ideological developments has revived the issue of sex selection, relatively dormant for more than a decade. The concerns that have always accompanied sex selection debates are being reassessed and updated. These include the prospect that selection could reinforce misogyny, sexism, and gender stereotypes; undermine the well-

being of children by treating them as commodities and subjecting them to excessive parental expectations or disappointment; skew sex ratios in local populations; further the commercialization of reproduction; and open the door to a high-tech consumer eugenics.

Sex Selection Debates in the United States

Sex selection is not a new issue for U.S. feminists. In the 1980s and early 1990s, it was widely discussed and debated, especially by feminist bioethicists. This was the period when choosing a boy or girl was accomplished by undergoing prenatal diagnostic tests to determine the sex of a fetus, and then terminating the pregnancy if the fetus was of the undesired sex.

Ultrasound scanning and amniocentesis, which had been developed during the 1970s to detect, and usually to abort, fetuses with Down's syndrome and other conditions, were on their way to becoming routine in wealthier parts of the world. Soon they were also being openly promoted as tools for enabling sex-selective abortions in South and East Asian countries where the cultural preference for sons is pervasive. Opposition in these countries, especially strong in India, mounted in the early 1980s and remains vibrant today.

Throughout the 1980s and early 1990s, feminists and others in the U.S. who addressed the issue of sex selection were—almost universally—deeply uneasy about it. Not all opposed it equally, but none were enthusiastic or even supportive.

Some, like Helen Bequaert Holmes, pointed out that the deliberate selection of the traits of future generations is a form of eugenics.[1] Many deplored the practice as a symptom of a sexist society, in effect if not always in intent. In a book-length treatment of these concerns, published in 1985, philosopher Mary Anne Warren asked whether the practice should be considered an aspect of what she dubbed 'gendercide'—"no less a moral atrocity than genocide"—and published an entire book on the topic in 1985.[2]

But there was also broad consensus among feminists that any effort to limit sex-selective abortions, especially in the U.S., would threaten reproductive rights. Warren, despite her misgivings, argued that choosing the sex of one's child was sexist only if its intent or consequence was discrimination against women. She concluded that "there is great danger that the legal prohibition of sex selection would endanger other aspects of women's reproductive freedom," and considered even moral suasion against the practice to be unwarranted and counterproductive.

By the mid-1990s, the discussion had reached an impasse. No one liked sex selection, but few were willing to actively oppose it. Sex selection largely faded as an issue of concern for U.S. feminists, especially outside the circles of an increasingly professionalized bioethics discourse.

Separating Sex Selection from Abortion Politics

The new technologies of sex selection (and, perhaps, their potential profits) have prompted some bioethicists to argue in favor of allowing parents to choose their offspring's sex. As in past debates on other assisted reproductive procedures, they frame their advocacy in terms of "choice," "liberty," and "rights." John Robertson, a lawyer and bioethicist close to the fertility industry, is one of the leading proponents of this approach. In a lead article of the Winter 2001 issue of *American Journal of Bioethics,* Robertson wrote, "The risk that exercising rights of procreative liberty would hurt offspring or women—or contribute to sexism generally—is too speculative and uncertain to justify infringement of those rights."[3]

Robertson's claims are based on a world view that gives great weight to individual preferences and liberties, and little to social justice and the common good. As political scientist Diane Paul writes in a commentary on Robertson's recent defense of "preconception gender selection," "If you begin with libertarian premises, you will inevitably end up having to accept uses of reprogenetic technology that are even more worrisome" than sex selection.[4]

Definitions of procreative liberty like Robertson's are expansive—indeed, they often seem limitless. They are incapable, for example, of making a distinction between terminating an unwanted pregnancy—that is, deciding whether and when to bear children—and selecting the qualities and traits of a future child. However, sex selection and abortion are different matters, especially when a pregnancy is not involved.

Since new sex selection technologies are used before pregnancy, political discussions and policy initiatives which address them need not directly affect women's rights or access to abortion. In fact, many countries already prohibit "non-medical" sex selection, with no adverse impact on the availability or legality of abortion. One such nation is the United Kingdom, where, in November, 2003, after a comprehensive reconsideration of the issue, their Human Fertilization and Embryology Authority recommended that sex selection for social reasons continue to be prohibited, and that the Authority's purview be expanded to include regulation of sperm sorting technologies as well as other sex selection procedures. Even in the United States, where abortion rights are imminently threatened, the emergence of pre-pregnancy technologies should make it far easier than before, when sex determination meant selective abortion, to consider sex selection apart from abortion politics.

Eugenics: Is the Slope Becoming More Slippery?

When Mary Anne Warren considered sex selection in 1985, she summarily dismissed concerns of its contribution to a new eugenics as "implausible" on the grounds that "[t]here is at present no highly powerful interest group which is committed to the development and use of immoral forms of human genetic engineering."[5]

However, less than two decades later, a disturbing number of highly powerful figures are in fact committed to the development and use of a form of human genetic engineering that huge majorities here and abroad consider immoral—inheritable genetic modification, or manipulating the genes passed on to our children. These scientists, bioethicists, biotech entrepreneurs, and libertarians are actively advocating a new market-based, high-tech eugenics.

Princeton University molecular biologist Lee Silver, for example, positively anticipates the emergence of genetic castes and human sub-species. "[T]he GenRich class and the Natural class will become . . . entirely separate species," he writes, "with no ability to cross-breed, and with as much romantic interest in each other as a current human would have for a chimpanzee."[6] Nobel laureate James Watson promotes redesigning the genes of our children with statements such as, "People say it would be terrible if we made all girls pretty. I think it would be great."[7]

Silver's and Watson's remarks (and all too many similar ones) refer to technologies that are being used routinely in lab animals, but have not been applied to human beings. However, pre-implantation genetic diagnosis (PGD), the most common new sex selection method, is very much related to these technologies. It was introduced in 1990 as a way to identify and discard embryos affected by serious genetic conditions, and thus prevent the birth of children with particular traits. Though PGD is touted as a medical tool, disability advocates have pointed out that many people who have the conditions it targets live full and satisfying lives. PGD, they say, is already a eugenic technology.

In recent years, PGD has begun to be used to screen for more and more genetic attributes—late-onset conditions, tissue types suitable for matching those of a future child's sick sibling, and sex. Advocacy of even greater permissiveness in the use of PGD is beginning to pepper the professional literature. Bioethicist Edgar Dahl recently published an essay arguing that if a "safe and reliable genetic test" for sexual orientation were to become available, "parents should clearly be allowed" to use it, as long as they are permitted to select for homosexual as well as heterosexual children.[8] Bioethicist Julian Savulescu even baits disability advocates with the argument that we "should allow people deliberately to create disabled children."[9]

Concern about consumer eugenics and the commodification of children looms large for critics of social sex selection. As part of a recent campaign aimed at the Human Fertilization and Embryology Authority, the UK-based bioethics group Human Genetics Alert writes, "If we allow sex selection it will be impossible to oppose 'choice' of any other characteristics, such as appearance, height, intelligence, et cetera. The door to 'designer babies' will not have been opened a crack—it will have been thrown wide open."[10]

Another British NGO, Gene Watch UK [*no relation to* GeneWatch *magazine—ed.*] puts it this way: Allowing sex selection "would represent a significant shift towards treating children as commodities and [subjecting] the selection of a child's genetic make-up . . . to parental choice, exercised through paying a commercial company to provide this 'service'."[11]

Some researchers, bioethicists, and fertility practitioners have publicly opposed such uses of PGD, and expressed alarm at what the new push for social sex selection seems to portend. In September, 2001, Robertson, then acting chair of the Ethics Committee of the American Society for Reproductive Medicine (ASRM), issued an opinion that overturned the organization's opposition to PGD for social sex selection. The *New York Times* reported that this "stunned many leading fertility specialists." One fertility doctor asked, "What's the next step? . . . As we learn more about genetics, do we reject kids who do not have superior intelligence or who don't have the right color hair or eyes?"[12]

In the U.S., several women's organizations and other NGOs drafted a letter, signed by nearly a hundred groups and individuals, urging the ASRM not to loosen its recommendations on sex selection. Several months later, the ASRM affirmed its opposition to the use of PGD for "non-medical" sex selection. (The organization does not oppose sperm selection to select the sex of a child for "family balancing.") The spread of social sex selection and the ASRM episode were described in an *Atlantic Monthly* article titled "Jack or Jill? The era of consumer-driven eugenics has begun." Author Margaret Talbot concluded,

> [I]f we allow people to select a child's sex, then there really is no barrier to picking embryos—or, ultimately, genetically programming children—based on any whim, any faddish notion of what constitutes superior stock. . . . A world in which people (wealthy people, anyway) can custom-design human beings unhampered by law or social sanction is not a dystopian sci-fi fantasy any longer but a realistic scenario. It is not a world most of us would want to live in.[13]

A Transnational Issue and a Preference for Girls

In 1992, Nobel Prize-winning economist Amartya Sen estimated the number of "missing women" worldwide, lost to neglect, infanticide, and sex-specific abortions, at one hundred million. Similarly shocking figures were confirmed by others.

Many in the global North are distressed by the pervasiveness and persistence of sex-selective abortions in South and East Asia, and believe bans on sex selection procedures may be warranted there. At the same time, some of these people believe sex selection in countries without strong traditions of son preference may not be so bad.

This double standard rests on shaky grounds. The increased use and acceptance of sex selection in the U.S. would legitimize its practice in other countries, while undermining opposition by human rights and women's rights groups there. Even *Fortune* recognized this dynamic. "It is hard to overstate the outrage and indignation that MicroSort [a sperm sorting method] prompts in people who spend their lives trying to improve women's lot overseas," it noted in 2001.[14]

In addition, there are also large numbers of South Asians living in European and North American countries, and sex selection ads in *India Abroad* and the North American edition of *Indian Express* have specifically targeted them.[15] South Asian feminists in these communities fear that sex selection could take new hold among immigrants who retain a preference for sons. They decry the numerous ways it reinforces and exacerbates misogyny, including violence against women who fail to give birth to boys. If these practices are unacceptable—indeed, often illegal—in South Asia (and elsewhere), should they be allowed among Asian communities in the West?

In contrast to sex selection in South and East Asia, however, a preference for girls may be emerging in North America and Europe. Anecdotal evidence—based on reports from companies offering various methods for sex control and on perusal of the "Gender Determination" message board . . ., which has over a quarter million postings—tends to confirm that of North Americans trying to determine the sex of their next child, many are women who want daughters.

That North Americans may not use new technologies to produce huge numbers of "extra" boys does not, however, mean that sex selection and sexism are unrelated. One study, by Roberta Steinbacher at Cleveland State University, found that 81% of women and 94% of men who say they would use sex selection would want their firstborn to be a boy. Steinbacher notes that the research literature on birth order is clear: firstborns are more aggressive and higher-achieving than their siblings. "We'll be creating a nation of little sisters," she says.[16]

Observers of sex selection point to another discriminatory impact: its potential for reinforcing gender stereotyping. Parents who invest large amounts of money and effort in order to "get a girl" are likely to have a particular kind of girl in mind. As a mother of one of the first MicroSort babies recalled, "I wanted to have someone to play Barbies with and to go shopping with; I wanted the little girl with long hair and pink fingernails."[17]

There are many reasons people may wish for a daughter instead of a son, or a boy rather than a girl. In a sympathetic account, *New York Times* reporter and feminist Lisa Belkin described some of the motivations of U.S. women who are "going for the girl."

"They speak of Barbies and ballet and butterfly barrettes," she writes, but "they also describe the desire to rear strong young women. Some want to recreate their relationships with their own mothers; a few want to do better by their daughters than their mothers did by them. They want their sons to have sisters, so that they learn to respect women. They want their husbands to have little girls. But many of them want a daughter simply because they always thought they would have one."[18]

Wishes and Consequences

Compelling though some of these longings may be, sex selection cannot be completely understood or appropriately confronted by evaluating the rightness or wrongness of parental desires. The preferences of prospective parents are obviously relevant in child-bearing matters, but so are the well-being of future children, and the social consequences of technologies—especially those that are already being aggressively marketed.

Wishing for a girl, or for a boy, is cause for neither shame nor condemnation. But as legal scholar Dorothy Roberts points out, it is important to "scrutinize the legal and political context which helps to both create and give meaning to individuals' motivations."[19]

If wishes, choices, and preferences are to be appropriately balanced with social justice and the common good, they cannot be unthinkingly transformed into protected liberties, much less codified rights. Isolated from social consequences, both wishes and liberties are at best naïve.

Notes

1. Humber and Almeder, eds. "Sex Preselection: Eugenics for Everyone?" *Biomedical Ethics Reviews*, 1985

2. Mary Ann Warren. *Gendercide: The Implications of Sex Selection.* Rowman & Littlefield, 1985
3. John A. Robertson. "Preconception Gender Selection," *American Journal of Bioethics*, Winter 2001
4. Dian Paul. "Where Libertarian Premises Lead," *American Journal of Bioethics*, Winter 2001
5. Mary Ann Warren. *Gendercide: The Implications of Sex Selection.* Rowman & Littlefield, 1985
6. Lee Silver. *Remaking Eden.* Avon, 1997
7. Shaoni Bhattacharya. "Stupidity should be cured, says DNA discoverer," *New Scientist,* February 28, 2003 . . .
8. Edgar Dahl. "Ethical Issues in New Uses of Preimplantation Genetic Diagnosis," *Human Reproduction,* Vol. 18 No. 7
9. Julian Savunescu, from the title of a November 25, 2003 presentation in London. . . .
10. "The Case Against Sex Selection," December 2002 . . .
11. "GeneWatch UK Submission to the HFEA Consultation on Sex Selection," January 2003
12. Gina Kolata. "Fertility Ethics Authority Approves Sex Selection," *The New York Times,* September 28, 2001
13. Margaret Talbot. "Jack or Jill? The era of consumer-driven eugenics has begun," *The Atlantic Monthly,* March 2002
14. Meredith Wadman. "So You Want a Girl?," *Fortune,* February 2001
15. Susan Sachs. "Clinics' Pitch to Indian Émigrés," *New York Times,* August 15, 2001
16. Lisa Belkin. "Getting the Girl," *The New York Times Magazine,* July 25, 1999
17. "Choosing Your Baby's Gender," . . . November 7, 2002
18. Belkin.
19. Dorothy Roberts, *Killing the Black Body: Race, Reproduction, and the Meaning of Liberty,* New York: Vintage Books, 1997, p. 286

MARCY DARNOVSKY, PhD, is the executive director for the Center for Genetics and Society. She speaks and writes on the politics of human biotechnology.

EXPLORING THE ISSUE

Should Parents Be Allowed to Select the Sex of Their Baby?

Critical Thinking and Reflection

1. What is preimplantation genetic diagnosis (PGD), and what has it been traditionally used for? How can it be used for sex selection?
2. What, if any, ethical concerns do you have about reproductive technologies such as in vitro fertilization and PGD?
3. Robertson uses the term "gender" as a synonym for sex. Is there a difference between sex and gender? What do potential parents need to know about both sex and gender?
4. Robertson states that sex selection for a first child could be seen as problematic. Are there instances in which you find the practice more or less acceptable than others?
5. What is the slippery slope argument expressed by Darnovsky? Is the comparison she makes to the eugenics movement valid?

Is There Common Ground?

Imagine yourself in the position of being able to choose the sex of your future children. What would be the benefits of having a daughter as opposed to a son, or vice versa? How many of these benefits rest on your expectations of your future child's personality? Are these traits inherently tied to their sex? Can you be certain that the child's gender will "match" their sex?

Now imagine the way your future child looks. How tall are they? What color eyes do they have? What color is their hair? Is your child athletic? Artistic? Intelligent? In the near future, it may be possible to make your "dream family" come true—for a fee. If you had the economic means, would you consider purchasing certain characteristics for your child? Why or why not?

Is there something about yourself that you consider unique? Is it a physical ability or talent, or even a physical feature that sets you apart from the crowd? Did it come from your mother or father—or is it distinctive from all of your family members? Now imagine that your parents told you that they wanted you to have this feature so bad that they "selected" it while you were still an embryo. Would you feel any less unique? What if they simply said they wanted you to be a certain sex? Would that change the way you feel about yourself?

Do you consider it acceptable to use PGD (or other techniques) to predetermine the characteristics of your baby? Is it acceptable to screen for hereditary debilitating conditions and diseases? What did you make of Darnovsky

claim that allowing PGD for sex selection could pave the way for "designer babies"?

Robertson challenged the "slippery slope" argument by stating "Speculations about potential future nonmedical uses should not restrict new uses of PGD which are otherwise ethically acceptable." Do you agree? Is genetic sex selection medically ethical?

Create Central

www.mhhe.com/createcentral

Additional Resources

Colls, P., Silver, L., Olivera, G., Weirer, J., Escudero, T., Goodall, N., Tomkin, G., & Munne, S. (2009). "Preimplantation Genetic Diagnosis for Gender Selection in the USA," *Reproductive Biomedicine Online* (vol. 19 no. 2).

McGowan, M. & Sharp, R. (March 2013). "Justice in the Context of Family Balancing," *Science, Technology, and Human Values* (vol. 38, no. 2).

Puri, S. & Nachtigall, R.D. (May 2010). "The Ethics of Sex Selection: A Comparison of the Attitudes and Experiences of Physicians and Physician Providers of Clinical Sex Selection Services," *Fertility & Sterility* (vol. 93, no. 7).

Trivedi, B. "Boy or Girl? Embryo Tests Give Parents the Choice," *New Scientist*, September 30, 2006.

Internet References . . .

How to Buy a Daughter

This article, by Jasmeet Sidhu, details the financial and emotional struggle some parents go through to have a child of a specific sex through PGD.

www.slate.com/articles/health_and_science/medical_examiner/2012/09/sex_selection_in_babies_through_pgd_americans_are_paying_to_have_daughters_rather_than_sons_.single.html

The Center for Genetics and Society

The Center for Genetics and Society advocates for the responsible use of genetic and reproductive technologies, while opposing those who "commodify human life and threaten to divide human society."

www.geneticsandsociety.org

World Health Organization

The World Health Organization outlines the motivations behind and ethical issues raised by genetic sex selection.

www.who.int/genomics/gender/en/index4.html

Unit 4

UNIT

Understanding Sexual Expression

Robert T. Francoeur, author of the Complete Dictionary of Sexology, *called sexuality a "bio-psycho-socio and cultural phenomenon." Humans are sexual beings from birth through death, and our sexuality is shaped by our physical makeup (biological), our thoughts, feelings, and perceptions of our sexuality (psychological); and the way we interact with our environment (sociological and cultural). In many ways, sexuality may be as subjective as the individual who expresses it.*

Defining "sex" is no more universal. One of our favorite classroom activities is to ask students to take out their cell phones, call, or text a few friends and family members, and ask them what "sex" means. The varied responses illustrate many different viewpoints people have about the nature of sex.

This unit examines the very nature of sex by presenting debates on issues related to sexual definitions, how we understand sexual behavior, and how sexual problems are addressed.

Selected, Edited, and with Issue Framing Material by:
Ryan W. McKee, *Widener University*
and
William J. Taverner, *Center for Family Life Education*

ISSUE

Has Sex Become Too Casual?

YES: **Rebecca Hagelin,** from "Parents Should Raise the Bar for Their Kids," (March 10, 2009), http://townhall .com/columnists/RebeccaHagelin/2009/03/10/parents_should_raise_the_bar_for_their_kids

NO: **Lara Riscol,** from "Purity, Promiscuity or Pleasure?" An original essay written for this volume (2009)

Learning Outcomes

After reading this issue, you should be able to:

- Describe the role of personal, family, and cultural values in influencing sexual attitudes and behaviors.
- Define and discuss the concept of abstinence.
- Give examples of erotic performances from the 1800s, and compare them with modern pornographic materials.
- Describe how sexual double standards have been applied to men and women throughout American history.

ISSUE SUMMARY

YES: Rebecca Hagelin, author and public speaker on family and culture, argues that sex education promotes casual sex and that schools and parents should do more to protect children.

NO: Lara Riscol, an author who explores the connections between society and sexuality, counters that blaming sex education is an oversimplification while arguing that sexuality has always been openly expressed throughout human history.

It seems that every generation envisions the younger, emerging generation as more permissive than their own. This pattern of observation can be seen at least throughout the past few centuries. In the late 1800s, the mass production of the *bicycle* worried many adults who thought that they would allow young people to ride far away and engage in sexual trysts, free of the watchful eyes of their parents. Similarly, the growing automobile industry gave young people new opportunities to be alone and led to concerns among many adults that younger generations were becoming sexually permissive. In the "Roaring '20's," "flappers"—women who drank, danced, voted, and wore their hair short—were regarded by their elders as being especially permissive. In the 1930s through the 1950s, the growing number of movie theaters, dance halls, and coed universities made adults worry that sex was becoming more and more casual.[1]

When television invaded American living rooms, adults looked to the hip gyrations of Elvis Presley as a signal of emerging sexual permissiveness. In the 1960s and 1970s many adults did not know what to make of young people and the sexual revolution, particularly with its "Free Love" messages. It was during this era that hormonal contraceptives were introduced and popularized, disassociating sex from reproduction for those who were "on the pill." Some critics still point to the sexual revolution as being the originator of a "casual sex" mentality. Sociologist Ira Reiss refutes this notion by observing that it wasn't sexual *behaviors* that changed so much during this period; rather, the *attitudes* people expressed about sex began to change (1).

In the 1980s, the concept of "family values" emerged as a political and social rallying cry. According to social conservatives, the gains of the feminist movement had weakened the bonds of the family, and at the center of its demise were loosened restrictions on sex and sexuality. The HIV epidemic, for these critics, was a reminder of the consequences of unrestricted sexuality. "Safer sex," lauded by the MTV video stars of the 1990s, while reducing the risks of sexually transmitted infections, continued to keep sex outside of the realm of the family. Abstinence until marriage was held up as the cultural ideal by proponents of family values.

Today, modern commentators continue to describe sex as more casual than ever. Some have remarked on the high volume of sexual content on television, in the movies, and on the Internet—almost everywhere—which often has no marital or relationship context. Others point to the commitment-free "friends-with-benefits" status and the rise of "hook-up culture" as indicators of larger social problems. Concerns over teen sexting and apps such as "grindr" and "Bang With Friends," which allow people to arrange for discreet sexual encounters, have caused media uproar. But overlooked in these conversations is a serious discussion of the role of sex in the lives of Americans, and the ways our attitudes and values have (or have not) changed.

What are people's motivations for having sex? Is sex best saved for marriage? Should sex only occur within the bond of matrimony? Is it ok for unmarried couples to have sex only if they are monogamous? Are hook-ups and no-strings-attached sex the new normal? Do these kinds of encounters devalue sex? Or do they simply celebrate the pleasurable aspects of sex? Is there something inherently wrong with celebrating pleasure? Is sex more casual today? What do our attitudes about sex say about our values? What role does love play in sex and modern relationships?

In the following selections, author and commentator Rebecca Hagelin blames sex education for promoting casual sex and says that parents and schools should expect more of their children, instilling "concepts of self-worth," "basic morality," and abstinence education. Author Lara Riscol criticizes the Far Right for oversimplifying the issue, and responds by comparing the social and sexual norms today to those at other times in history, noting that in many instances the norms of today are better than norms of the past.

YES ↵

Rebecca Hagelin

Parents Should Raise the Bar for Their Kids

Spring break is in full swing for many college students across the country. And believe me, when I say "full swing," I mean full-rockin', rollin' party-hearty swinging!

But given that nearly all of these students' lifestyles are still funded by their parents, and that nearly all are still under the legal drinking age, it makes me wonder: What are their parents thinking?

As a mom of two college men I actually find it fairly easy to boldly proclaim: "If you are livin' on my dime, then you are livin' by my rules."

My rules for them as adults are actually filled with freedom, coupled with the principle of "self government." They were raised with this consistent theme, and they understand that my husband and I practice the "abuse and lose" approach. (I.e., they have both freedom and our full support as long as they follow basic rules that provide for their safety, moral development, and future.)

Of course, I can hear the naysayers now: "But they're adults. You can't tell adult children what to do." To this I simply answer, "BALONEY!"

I am a much older adult, and I understand that an employer can impose certain codes and expectations for my behavior on me. That's the deal in life—you work for someone, you have to play by their rules. (Of course, I know they can't trample your basic rights, deny civil liberties, etc. So don't go there. You know what I'm talking about.)

The young college men in my life—of whom I am so very proud and blessed to be called their "mom"—also know that my husband and I are fully committed to them as individuals and will provide plenty of opportunities for good, safe fun.

Let's get back to Spring Break as an example. Instead of shrugging our shoulders and letting them go off to some distant beach where mayhem, alcohol, and "Girls Gone Wild" abound, I booked a house at our favorite beach, which is located on a barrier island on Florida's Gulf Coast. With no bridge (you have to get here by boat) and no bars, this break is a lot safer and a lot more meaningful than what many are experiencing.

One of my dear friends has a house nearby and her daughter, also on Spring Break, has brought about nine of her "best friends" too. So, there's plenty of social activity, fun, and friendship without the nonsense. The kids go back and forth between our houses, so my friend and I both get to spend time with them and listen to their entertaining—and interesting—chatter.

Last night the gang was at my friend's house and the main topic of conversation proved an eye-opening, mind-numbing experience for her.

Most of the girls on this trip are freshmen, and somehow the conversation led to a shared humiliating experience now common at most college campuses: the mandatory co-ed, sex-ed course they all attended during their first few weeks on campus. They described the graphic nature of the class, and how embarrassed and outraged they were when they were shown how to put a condom on a banana.

But then it got worse—they were all encouraged to do the condom/banana exercise, too. The girls spoke of how a couple of their fellow students seemed to take great pride in demonstrating what seemed an all-too-familiar maneuver. However, my young friends said they were mortified and left the course feeling "trashy" and belittled by administration officials who expect them to all behave like wild animals in heat. "They seemed to be encouraging us to be sexually active," one member of the volleyball team said. "I was insulted and offended by the entire experience."

This particular young co-ed had gone to a private Christian high school, so she had managed to escape the low expectations that many educators bring to today's youth. She and her mom weren't aware that in today's public schools, millions of boys and girls are now, indeed, treated as if they are going to be sex-crazed creatures and, therefore, are actually encouraged to engage in risky behavior.

Face it: When an adult in authority stands in front of the classroom and directs graphic discussions of sex in every form, forces boys and girls to sit by each other throughout the humiliating lectures, and then further violates the child's natural tendencies to be private or modest, then you end up with kids who follow what they've been taught. On the other hand, when kids are treated with dignity, taught the value of abstinence, and how to avoid placing themselves in compromising situations in the first place, the research shows that more of them do, indeed, respond by adopting a lifestyle of self-control and more responsible behavior than those drowning in "sex ed." Also critical to the delayed on-set of sexual activity is parental involvement. I can not overstate the influence that loving, connected parents have on their teens and young adult children. You'll find loads of data and research on both points at www.abstinenceclearinghouse.com and www.familyfacts.org.

Which, once again, brings me back to the plethora of wild Spring Break "pah-tays" going on around the country as you read this. I wonder: If more public junior high and high schools joined hands with more parents in teaching abstinence education, the concepts of self-worth, and basic morality, wouldn't our nation's kids have a higher view of themselves and rise to meet the expectations?

And if colleges and parents expected better of our kids, wouldn't more of them choose the higher ground? If more parents took the effort to provide safer—but still "way fun"—supervised beach trips and other options for college kids, would more of them opt for something other than the drunken orgies that many Spring Break trips have become? In short, are older adults getting exactly the type of behavior from young adults that we expect?

Granted, my personal "focus group" is small. But the data, my experience, and the e-mails I receive from thousands of people tell me this: Young adults are still malleable, still looking for direction, and still crave to rise above the status quo. But they need help and encouragement. They need to be told that they can be self-controlled people of strong character, and they need to be provided with opportunities to thrive, have fun, and become men and women they can be proud of.

Young adults rise or fall to the expectation levels set for them. Will you help raise the bar?

REBECCA HAGELIN is a public speaker on family and culture and is the author of *30 Ways in 30 Days to Save Your Family*.

Lara Riscol

→ **NO**

Purity, Promiscuity or Pleasure?

"You would watch the girls give each other oral sex, do themselves with dildos, place cigars in their vaginas and rectums, suck on each others' breasts, and lick freshly poured beer off of one another's vulvas while their legs were tucked behind their necks." Often one fellow would get to have sex with one of the three performers directly before leering and cheering men.

No, this is not another spring break outrage making the latest round on cable news, but business as usual back in the good ol' days when live sex shows were easier to find than now. And I don't mean the '50s glory days of traditional values when *Ozzie and Harriet* reigned and the United States teen pregnancy rate hit an historic high, but in the prostitution heyday of the 1800s when feminists and medical experts warned against women riding bicycles lest the seat stir "libidinousness and immorality."

In the latest hot and seminal *Guide to Getting It On*, author Paul Joannides' longest chapter, "Sex in the 1800s," reminds us that the more things change, the more they stay the same. He compares the sexual contradictions of then "hardcore live sex shows and concerns about bicycle seats for adult women" to now "abstinence-only sex education and porn-filled Websites on the Internet." As today's technology flings sex front and center, in your face, round the clock, no escape, get me off of this d———n merry-go-round spinning ever faster into an erotic yawn of Girls Gone Wild, prostitots, MILFs, Bang Bus, booty call, and endless multimedia overexposures—America, "Land of the Free," remains stuck in a sexual schizophrenia of smut and sanctimony.

My first mental flash when reading about the famous centuries-ago sex show was VH1's latest season premiere of *Rock of Love Bus with Bret Michaels*, where Pamela Anderson wannabes vie for the lead singer of '80s hair band Poison. When one drunken contestant takes a vagina shot of booze from another, even a nonbeliever can fear the Apocalypse is near. Minus historical context and nuanced reasoning, I feel the appeal of Chicken Little conservatives crying the decline of Western civilization due to the sexual revolution and liberal moral relativism.

It's cheap and easy to dump hypersexualized floaties from our unfettered free market society on those who reject retro reactions to today's growing sexual, reproductive, gender, relationship, and family complexities. But could our nation's unmatched trouble with sex—runaway rates of teen and unplanned pregnancy, single parenthood, abortion, HIV and STDs, sexual "addiction," alienation and desire discrepancies, divorce—really be a black-and-white case of purity or promiscuity? How to reach the glorious human heights of pleasure—sacred to silly—when laden by potent conflicting forces intent on commercializing and politicizing sex?

Our dominantly Christian nation's schizophrenic approach to sex has deep roots. Likely former Governor Elliot Spitzer wouldn't have been so disgraced for feeding his costly call girl fetish in 1870, when New York City's second-largest economy was commercial sex. Yet America's prostitution-powered era wouldn't have tolerated a women's studies graduate auctioning off her virginity to finance her master's in family and marriage therapy, à la Natalie Dylan. Women weren't allowed the same transgressions as men. Of course women weren't allowed the same opportunities. Traditionalists argued that the intellectual rigors of higher education would shrink female reproductive organs and deny a real woman's one true calling: motherhood.

The God-fearing Victorian era of presumed moral restraint was nearly as sex segregated as Afghanistan today. Hooking up isn't so easy when you don't school, work, or socialize together. Young men routinely staved off masturbation at brothels where prepubescent virgins were in high demand; women were deemed unnatural if they displayed sexual desire, though ads for birth control abounded. Gender and sexuality has evolved along with technologies like automobiles, birth control, the Internet, economic shifts, and social equality. America, grounded in equality and plurality, rises from the right to life, liberty, and the pursuit of happiness. Our national stability and family honor doesn't rest on hypocritical sexual traditions like enforcing female virtue.

But that doesn't stop opportunistic purity posturing by family values conservatives, such as wedge-issue Republicans, the religious right, and Fox News, which airs so much B-roll of pulsating female flesh, while morally bloviating it inspired the NSFW FoxNewsPorn.com. The head of the "Biblically based" policy group Concerned Women for America says that proponents of sexual health education are financially motivated to encourage kids' having sexually transmitted diseases and abortions. A Morality in Media press release, "Connecting the Dots: The Link Between Gay Marriage and Mass Murders," links secular values, the sexual revolution, and the decline in morality to the gay rights movement, all sexual ills, including rape and the sexual abuse of children, and naturally the recent spate of mass murders.

Fox News megastar Bill O'Reilly, who a few years ago paid millions to make a sexual harassment suit go away, makes millions as lead culture-war bugle for traditional values against deviant secular progressives out to destroy America. In a recent column, "Kids Gone Wild," he decries the supposed sidelining of "Judeo-Christian principles of right and wrong" in policymaking. He shamelessly makes a slippery slope case against nuanced responses to sexual controversies by conflating child rape, unfettered abortion, gay marriage, and sexting—the latest shame name for teenagers and younger sharing provocative photos of themselves via cell phone, mostly girls sending and guys receiving.

But with child porn charges against juveniles now in at least five states, our sense of right and wrong can't be vindicated when we scar a kid as sex offender for a naughty consensual exchange. Some of the girls dragged into our criminal justice system posed in bikinis or thick, white bras. Flailing before budding sexuality and uncontainable technology, alleged adults lose all moral sense and lump the heinous crime of child pornography with a developing person's playful physical expression. Forget addressing the real potential harm to a child's well-being, such as high-tech bullying when a jerk "friend" recklessly or vindictively distributes private communication.

Yes, times are rapidly changing, and there's no going back to that elusive simpler time when men were predators and women gatekeepers, and anyone in between stayed in the closet. Despite hyperventilating sex-frenzied traditionalists, societal breakdowns go way beyond gay marriage, the hookup generation, Bill Clinton, or even Hugh Hefner. Although the "anything-goes, if it feels good do it" '60s is a tattered punching bag, liberalism not only ushered in free-love rebels, but also groundbreaking equality for women, queers, and ethnic minorities. Life can feel out of control as technology accelerates, rules of the game change, and our salacious 24/7 infotainment highway takes us to the edge of tolerance, but we face much graver threats today than friends with benefits, condoms on a banana, or two grooms in a tux.

With sexual debate stuck in such demonizing reductionism of traditional vs. secular, conservative vs. liberal, purity vs. perversion, abstinence vs. condoms, good vs. evil, no wonder we can't budge beyond nostalgia-fed moral panics to sane responses to modern challenges. A politically potent, multibillion-dollar industry of chastity crusaders seeks to save our national Gomorrah by corralling sex back into the procreative marital bedroom. But with virtually all of us doing some version of the dirty deed before, outside, between, or after marriage, America must expand the sexual conversation beyond purity balls or rainbow parties.

The two authors of the book, *Hooked: How Casual Sex Is Harming Our Kids*, recently lectured at a broadcast forum by the Christian-right Family Research Council,

the powerful lobbying arm of media empire Focus on the Family. Beyond the usual physical dire consequences, Joe McIlhaney and Freda Bush stated the irreparable emotional damage of one having multiple sex partners. Dr. Bush drove home their scientific claims by describing how adhesive tape loses its sticky power after pulling it apart more than once. Like used adhesive tape, the more you have sex with someone other than your spouse, the more you lose your ability to bond. Oh, and sex means anything that incites physical arousal; no word on masturbation. Bottom line is there are only two types of sex: married (good) and unmarried (bad).

Their conclusion supports the absolutist agenda of the synergistic family values, traditional marriage and abstinence-only movements that push the conservative ideal of sex confined to a heteronormative lifetime of marital fidelity, to the exclusion of all other sexual expressions. But hawking sexual purity as a salve for personal ills and tonic for a stronger America amounts to selling snake oil.

For many, a magic pill to make bad and scary things go away sounds nice. But if prescribing to dogmatic absolutes worked, then the most religious and conservative red states wouldn't have the highest rates of teen pregnancy, divorce, and porn consumption. And the fallen Colorado megachurch Pastor Ted Haggard, former head of the National Association of Evangelicals, frequent President George W. Bush confidant, and fierce opponent of same sex marriage, wouldn't have betrayed his family by spending three years with a male prostitute and crystal meth.

Ignoring the human frailties of adults and the capitalistic pornification of our public square, conservatives offer only one denial standard for all kids aged 8 to 28 if unmarried. Maybe in the Obama era, we're ready to grow up and stop making the most vulnerable ground zero in our lose–lose, sex-obsessed culture war. For the past eight years, we've been demonizing sexual science, distorting sex education, limiting access to information and health care services, and denying civil rights all for the sake of the children. Consequences be damned, we resist lessons of holistic sexual openness from our far sexually healthier Western allies. Instead we champion the A & B only of the "Abstinence, Be Faithful, Use Condoms" HIV campaign launched by war torn, polygamist Uganda, which now rewards virginal new brides with TV sets instead of goats.

Steeped in raunch culture that shames or sensationalizes young sex, we grasp onto Disney offerings of purity no matter how often or far our sexy virgins fall (Britney Spears, Jessica Simpson, Mandy Moore), and as long as new ones keep us afloat (Miley Cyrus, Jonas Brothers). But sustaining the virgin–whore dichotomy after all these centuries perverts smart decision making for all. You can't answer a high-tech free society's hypersexualized reality with fictionalized extremism? As I wrote in a 2001 column, "The Britney and Bob Challenge," about America's sexual schizophrenia and refusal to move beyond sexuality's marital ideal or commodified reality: neither excess nor repression develops into sexual intimacy or connection, let alone responsibility.

In *17 Again,* Disney's *High School Musical* heartthrob Zac Efron dresses down sexy cheerleaders, saying boys don't respect them, and rebukes a condom-distributing teacher with "abstinence is best," he knows. Well his character knows because he's really his dad who lost his basketball scholarship because he knocked up his high school sweetheart and chose teen marriage and fatherhood. So even though abstinence-only didn't work any more for him than for Bristol Palin, the lesson remains "no sex unless married," not responsible sexual choices like protection or non-coital play.

In real life, Zac Efron dates his HSM co-star Vanessa Hudgens, who suffered momentary embarrassment when earlier sexy photos surfaced online. But after celebrating her 20th birthday, she and Zac comfortably posed when shopping at a Los Angeles sex-toy shop.

The *Today Show* recently pitted the feminist author of *The Purity Myth: How America's Obsession with Virginity Is Hurting Young Women* against international abstinence advocate Lakita Garth, who promotes her success to staying a virgin until marriage at 36. Jessica Valenti points out that a women's worth is more than her hymen, and most fall between girls gone wild or chaste virgin. Like Zac and Vanessa versus their Disney image, most of us figure out how to achieve a full life *while* expressing our sexuality, married or not.

I saw Lakita Garth keynote an Abstinence Clearinghouse conference themed, "Abstinence: It's a Black and White Issue," as in "allowing no gray area between sexual integrity and irresponsibility." The flashy multimedia conference took me back to high school pep rallies and my cheerleader sentimentality. Watching a bejeweled and stylin' Garth flash photos of herself with President Bush as she bragged about her virginity-won "bling," I momentarily felt sexually inadequate for my life's choices before marrying at almost 32. After all, I don't have any photos with a United States president. But by Star Parker, a self-described former welfare queen and abortion regular, reducing all of America's problems to the denial of God's

sexual truth, I kept from getting further swept away by the idealism and heartfelt talent of the "Abstinence Idol" competition.

Though Kelly Clarkson, a self-proclaimed Christian virgin, won *American Idol's* first season, this year's likely winner, Adam Lambert, doesn't deny rumors of his being gay or bisexual. When Internet photos circulated of him kissing other men and dressed in drag, he responded, "I have nothing to hide. I am who I am." Other successful *American Idol* contestants include Clay Aiken, who finally came out as gay when he announced becoming a father with his male "friend," and Fantasia, a young single mom.

Oh, I like being an American and am glad my six-year-old son, husband, and I have so many more sexual and gender options today than in the 1800s or 1950s. The virginal ideal of the 1950s was beautiful, bubbly movie icon Sandra Dee, whose reality was as an incest survivor, divorced at 22, and with a lonely life of anorexia, alcoholism, and depression.

Because my son is so precious, I'll protect him by preparing him to make healthy sexual decisions throughout his life. I'm not going to feed him more of the same parental "do as I say, not as I do or did" crap, but will teach him moral reasoning over absolutes. I'll teach him to be is own moral agent, to value himself, to choose pleasure no matter how much purity or promiscuity extremes are forced upon him. I'll teach him that this is the United States of America and his sex does not belong to the church or state.

To reach humanity's highest ideals, permission trumps repression. With rights come responsibilities. My son may mess up, as I have, and will have to deal with consequences with respect and dignity. And I'll work for a world that uses all of its modern resources to ameliorate harm. As Mahatma Gandhi said, "Freedom is not worth having if it does not include the freedom to make mistakes."

Lara Riscol is a freelance writer who explores societal conflicts and controversies surrounding sexuality. Her writings have been published in *The Nation, Salon, Alter-Net,* and other national media outlets.

EXPLORING THE ISSUE

Has Sex Become Too Casual?

Critical Thinking and Reflection

1. What aspects of American life might be seen as promoting casual sex?
2. How have attitudes about sex shifted in American culture over the past several generations?
3. How do one's personal, family, and cultural values affect their sexual attitudes and behaviors?
4. How do societal sexual expectations differ for men and women?

Is There Common Ground?

In a study of college students, Meston and Buss (2) revealed some of the common motivations for having sex. Among the most popular reasons for both men and women were seemingly casual statements like "It's fun" and "I was horny." Also included among the most popular reasons were statements like "I wanted to show my affection to the person" and "I wanted to express my love for the person."

While the motivations behind sexual activity were not scientifically examined in the past, examples of both romantic love and casual sex can be found throughout many of history's greatest works of literature. Despite these examples, it still seems to many who would agree with Hagelin that today's society is more casual than ever about sex. What is it about modern day society that fosters these impressions?

Is Hagelin right that sex has become far too casual? Do parents and schools need to take greater responsibility in raising the bar of expectation for children? Is Riscol right that sexual values have been depraved at other times in history? How does Riscol's understanding of moral depravity differ from Hagelin's? With whom do you agree? After considering Hagelin's and Riscol's viewpoints, how would you describe the sexual norms at your college in comparison with what you know about other generations or other times in history?

Create Central

www.mhhe.com/createcentral

Note

1. Special thanks is owed to the late Dr. Robert T. Francoeur, co-editor of the *International Encyclopedia of Sexuality*, for his extensive notes on sexual customs in American history.

References

(1) Reiss, I.L. (2006). *An Insider's View of Sexual Science Since Kinsey*. Lanham, MD: Rowman & Littlefield.
(2) Meston, C. & Buss, D. (2007). "Why Humans Have Sex." *Archives of Sexual Behavior* (vol. 36, no. 4, pp. 477–507).

Additional Resources

Armstrong, E., England, P., & Fogarty, A. (2012). "Accounting for Women's Orgasm and Sexual Enjoyment in College Hookups and Relationships," *American Sociological Review* (vol. 77, no. 3, pp. 435–462).

Bailey, B. (1989). *From Front Porch to Back Seat: Courtship in Twentieth-Century America*. Baltimore, MD: The Johns Hopkins University Press.

Klein, M. (2012). *America's War on Sex: The Continuing Attack on Law, Lust, and Liberty*. Westport, CT: Praeger.

Stepp, L. (2008). *Unhooked*. New York, NY: Riverhead Trade.

Internet References . . .

Sexuality Information and Education Council of the United States (SIECUS)

SIECUS is an advocacy group dedicated to promoting and providing comprehensive sexuality education in order to increase sexual and reproductive health.

www.siecus.org

Abstinence Clearinghouse

The Abstinence Clearinghouse is a nonprofit organization that promotes abstinence-until-marriage education and events on national and international levels.

www.abstinence.net

Can Hookups Be More Fun?

This article, by Dr. Debbie Herbenick of the Kinsey Institute, addresses a study finding that women are less likely to orgasm during casual sexual encounters.

www.salon.com/2012/09/05/can_hookups_be_ more_fun/

Casual Sex-Tech?

Amanda Hess examines why women aren't showing much interest in apps designed to facilitate hookups. Is it because women don't desire casual sex? Or because the apps are designed by men?

www.slate.com/blogs/xx_factor/2013/01/30/bang_ with_friends_why_virtual_hook_up_apps_have_a_ woman_problem.html

Selected, Edited, and with Issue Framing Material by:
Ryan W. McKee, *Widener University*
and
William J. Taverner, *Center for Family Life Education*

ISSUE

Is Oral Sex Really Sex?

YES: Rhonda Chittenden, from "Oral Sex *Is* Sex: Ten Messages about Oral Sex to Communicate to Adolescents," *Sexing the Political* (May 2004)

NO: Nora Gelperin, from "Oral Sex and Young Adolescents: Insights from the 'Oral Sex Lady'," *Educator's Update* (September 2004)

Learning Outcomes

After reading this issue, you should be able to:

- Compare various reactions to teen sex and sexuality, including oral sex.
- Compare various definitions of "sex."
- Create your own definition of "sex."
- Explore the values that lead you to define sex the way you do.

ISSUE SUMMARY

YES: Sexuality educator Rhonda Chittenden says that it is important for young people to expand their narrow definitions of sex and understand that oral sex *is* sex. Chittenden offers additional educational messages about oral sex.

NO: Sexuality trainer Nora Gelperin argues that adult definitions of oral sex are out of touch with the meaning the behavior holds for young people. Rather than impose adult definitions of intimacy, educators should be seeking to help young people clarify and understand their own values.

It's been more than a decade since President Bill Clinton famously stated, "I did not have sexual relations with that woman, Miss Lewinsky." As it later became evident that the president, in fact, did have *oral* sex with intern Monica Lewinsky, a national debate raged over the meaning of sex. What, people asked, does "sexual relations" mean? What about "sex"? Do these terms refer to vaginal intercourse only, or are other sexual behaviors, like oral or anal sex, included?

Some welcomed this unprecedented opportunity to have an open, national discussion about sex in an otherwise erotophobic, sexually repressed culture. Sexuality education professionals lent their expertise, offering suggestions to help parents answer their children's questions about this "new" term they might hear on the evening news. Others feared such openness would inevitably lead to increased sexual activity among teens. Perhaps the media viewed this as a foregone conclusion when they began airing hyped reports indicating a rise in teen oral sex, based on anecdotal, rather than research-based evidence.

Many adults—parents, teachers, public health officials, and others—were concerned about what they felt was a new and risky trend. Their apprehension may have been rooted in the very meaning of sex. Since many people hold oral sex to be an intensely intimate act—one that may be even more intimate than vaginal intercourse—it was difficult for them to observe what they interpreted as casual attitudes toward this behavior. Others held religious or other moral objections. Additionally, there were concerns about the potential risk of sexually transmitted infections (STIs), which can be passed orally. Still others lamented the inequity of oral sex as young people reported experiencing it—with females *giving* oral sex far more than they *received* it.

In the 15 years since the Clinton scandal, media attention has shifted from one salacious-but-scantily-researched sex "trend" to the next. The media and parental concern expressed over oral sex is strikingly similar to the recent sexting phenomenon. Sending a nude picture of oneself may be seen by some as incredibly personal and intimate, requiring intense trust in the one receiving the image or message. New media reports, as they had with oral sex in the 1990s, exaggerate the popularity and risks of sexting, and often advocate harsh punishments to prevent what some view as the next step in the spread of thoughtless casual sex.

Many teens found the uproar over oral sex (and, more recently, over sexting) overblown. This reaction suggests a generational divide, indicating a shift in values. However, not all young people see eye to eye on the subject of oral sex. One of the editors of this Taking Sides book had the occasion to poll a class of American high school students on the question, "Is oral sex really sex?" Only a smattering of students raised their hands in agreement. When the same question was posed to a classroom of Swedish students, *every* hand was raised. One confused student asked, "Why would it *not* be sex?" It appears the divide over defining sexual behaviors can be cultural as well.

One of the reasons Americans—young and old—may find it difficult to define sex is that, as a culture, we find it quite difficult to have *any* serious discussions about sex. Many friends speak to each other euphemistically about sex, as if everyone has the same definition for "doing it" or "getting laid." Some parents, religious leaders, and educators teach young people to "just say no"—but not exactly what they should be saying "no" to. If a person has oral sex, are they still being abstinent? What about anal sex? Can they share nude images with each other and masturbate while texting? In reality, these euphemistic, cloudy discussions keep us from having a clear-cut idea of what, exactly, anyone means!

In the following selections, sexuality education professionals Rhonda Chittenden and Nora Gelperin examine the meaning of sex and oral sex in the context of giving young people helpful educational messages. Chittenden articulates several reasons why it is important for young people to know that oral sex is sex, and offers several other important messages for adults to convey to young people. Gelperin argues that it is not for adults to decide the meaning of such terms for young people. Rather, educators can help young people critically examine the meaning of such words and activities for themselves. She further argues against having overly dramatized media accounts dictate public health approaches.

YES ⬑

Rhonda Chittenden

Oral Sex *Is* Sex: Ten Messages about Oral Sex to Communicate to Adolescents

As a teen in the early-80s, I was very naïve about oral sex. I thought oral sex meant talking about sex with one's partner in a very sexy way. A friend and I, trying to practice the mechanics, would move our mouths in silent mock-talk as we suggestively switched our hips from left to right and flirted with our best bedroom eyes. We wondered aloud how anyone could engage in oral sex without breaking into hysterical laughter. In our naïveté, oral sex was not only hilarious, it was just plain stupid.

Twenty years later, I doubt most teens are as naïve as my friend and I were. Although the prevalence of oral sex among adolescents has yet to be comprehensively addressed by researchers,[1] any adult who interacts with teens will quickly learn that, far from being stupid or hilarious, oral sex is a common place activity in some adolescent crowds.

Some teens claim, as teens have always claimed about sex, that "everyone is doing it." They tell of parties—which they may or may not have attended—where oral sex is openly available. They describe using oral sex as a way to relieve the pressure to be sexual with a partner yet avoid the risk of pregnancy. Some believe oral sex is an altogether risk-free behavior that eliminates the worry of sexually transmitted infections. There is a casualness in many teens' attitudes towards oral sex revealed in the term "friends with benefits" to describe a non-dating relationship that includes oral sex. In fact, many teens argue that oral sex really isn't sex at all, logic that, try as we might, defies many adults. Most pointedly, teens' anecdotal experiences of oral sex reveal the continuing imbalance of power prevalent in heterosexual relationships where the boys receive most of the pleasure and the girls, predictably, give most of the pleasure.

Not willing to wait until research confirms what many of us already know, concerned adults want to address the issue of adolescent oral sex *now*. We know that young people long for straightforward and honest conversations about the realities and complexities of human sexuality, including the practice of oral sex. But where do we start with such an intimidating topic? The following ten messages may help caring and concerned adults to initiate authentic conversations about oral sex with young people.

1. Oral sex *is* sex. Regardless of how casual the behavior is for some young people, giving and receiving oral sex

are both sexual behaviors. This is made obvious simply by defining the act of oral sex: Oral sex is the stimulation of a person's genitals by another person's mouth to create sexual pleasure and, usually, orgasm for at least one of the partners. It's that straightforward.

Even so, many young people—and even some adults—believe that oral sex is not "real sex." Real sex, they say, is penis-vagina intercourse only. Any other sexual behavior is something "other" and certainly not *real* sex. This narrow definition of sex, rooted in heterosexist attitudes, is problematic for several reasons.

First, such a narrow definition is ahistorical. Art and literature reveal human beings, across human history and culture, consensually engaging their bodies in loving, pleasurable acts of sex beyond penis-vagina intercourse.[2] In Western culture, our notions of sex are still shackled by religious teachings that say the only acceptable sex—in society and the eyes of God—is procreative sex. Of course, the wide accessibility of contraceptives, among other influences, has dramatically shifted our understanding of this.[3] Even still, many people are unaware that across centuries and continents, human beings have enjoyed many kinds of sex and understood those acts to be sex whether or not they involved a penis and a vagina.

Next, by defining sex in such narrow terms, we perpetuate a dangerous ignorance that places people at risk for sexually transmitted infections (STIs), including HIV. Many people, including teens, who define sex in such narrow terms incorrectly reason that they are safe from HIV if they avoid penis-vagina intercourse. Because saliva tends to inhibit HIV, it's true that one's chances of contracting HIV through oral sex with an infected partner are considerably small, compared to the risk of unprotected vaginal or anal sex. Of course, this varies with the presence of other body fluids as well as the oral health of the giver. However, if one chooses to avoid "real sex" and instead has anal sex, the risk for HIV transmission increases.[4] In reality, regardless of what orifice the penis penetrates, all of these sex acts are real sex. In this regard, the narrow definition of sex is troubling because it ignores critical sexual health information that all people deserve, especially those who are sexually active or intend to be in the future.

Finally, this narrow definition of sex invalidates the sexual practices of many people who, for whatever reasons, do not engage in penis-vagina intercourse. Obviously, these people include those who partner with lovers of the same sex. They also include people who, regardless of the sex of their partners, are physically challenged due to illness, accident, or birth anomaly. To suggest to these individuals that oral sex—or any other primary mode of shared sexual expression—is not real sex invalidates the range of accessible and sensual ways they can and do share their bodies with their partners.

Clearly, we must educate young people that there are many ways to enjoy sex, including the sensual placement of one's mouth on another person's genitals. Oral sex may be practiced in casual, emotionally indifferent ways, but this does not disqualify it as a legitimate sex act. Oral sex *is* sex—and, in most states, the law agrees.

2. Without consent, oral sex may be considered sexual assault.

Adults who work with teens know that oral sex often takes place at parties where alcohol and other drugs are consumed. It's imperative, then, that when adults talk to teens about oral sex, we confront the legal realities of such situations. Of course, drinking and drug use are illegal for adolescents. In addition, according to Iowa law, if alcohol or drugs are used by either partner of any age, consent for oral sex (or any sex) cannot be given. Without consent, oral sex may be considered sexual assault.[5] Other states have similar laws.

While giving some adolescents reason to reflect on their substance use, this information may also help them to contextualize their past experiences of oral sex. It may affirm the often uneasy and unspoken feelings of some teens who feel they were pressured into oral sex, either as the giver or receiver. It may also illuminate other risks that often occur when sex and substance use are combined, especially the failure to use protection against pregnancy, and in the case of oral sex, sexually transmitted infections.

3. Practice safer oral sex to reduce the risk of sexually transmitted infections.

Because many young people don't consider oral sex to be real sex, they don't realize that sexually transmitted infections that are typically transmitted through genital-genital contact can also be transmitted through oral-genital contact. Although some are more easily transmitted through oral sex than others, these infections include chlamydia, gonorrhea, herpes, and, in some cases, even pubic lice. The lips, tongue, mouth cavity, and throat, are all vulnerable to various sexually transmitted bacteria and viruses.[6] With pubic lice, facial hair, including mustaches, beards and eyebrows, can be vulnerable.[7]

Aside from abstaining from oral sex, young people can protect themselves and their partners from the inconvenience, embarrassment, treatment costs, and health consequences of sexually transmitted infections by practicing safer oral sex. The correct and consistent use of latex condoms for fellatio (oral sex performed on a penis) and latex dental dams for cunnilingus (oral sex performed on a vulva) should be taught and encouraged. Manufacturers of condoms, dental dams, and pleasure-enhancing

lubricants offer these safer sex supplies in a variety of flavors—including mint, mango, and banana—to increase the likelihood that people will practice safer oral sex.[8] Certainly, adolescents who engage in oral sex should be taught about the correct, pleasure-enhancing uses of these products, informed of the location of stores and clinics that carry them, and strongly encouraged to have their own supply at hand.

4. Oral sex is a deeply intimate and sensual way to give sexual pleasure to a partner.

Although casual references to oral sex abound in popular music, movies and culture, many young people have never heard an honest, age-appropriate description of the profoundly intimate and sensual nature of oral sex. Especially for the giver of oral sex, the experience of pleasuring a partner's genitals may be far from casual. Unlike most other sex acts, oral sex acutely engages all five senses of the giver.

As is suggested by the availability of flavored safer sex supplies, for the giver of oral sex, the sense of taste is clearly engaged. If safer sex supplies are not used, the giver experiences the tastes of human body fluids—perhaps semen, vaginal fluids, and/or perspiration. In addition, the tongue and lips feel the varied textures of the partner's genitals, and, depending on the degree of body contact, other touch receptors located elsewhere on the body may be triggered. With the face so close to their partner's genitals, the giver's nose can easily smell intimate odors while the eyes, if opened, get a very cozy view of the partner's body. Lastly, during oral sex the ears not only pick up sounds of voice, moaning, and any music playing in the background, they also hear the delicate sounds of caressing another's body with one's mouth. Obviously, if one is mentally engaged in the experience, it can be quite intense! Honest conversations with adolescents about the intimate and sensual nature of oral sex acknowledge this incredibly unique way human beings share pleasure with one another and elevate it from the casual references of popular culture.

5. Boys do not have to accept oral sex (or any sex) just because it is offered.

As I talked with a group of teenagers at a local alternative high school, it became painfully clear to me that some teen girls offer oral sex to almost any guy they find attractive. As a consequence of such easy availability, these teen boys, although they did not find a girl attractive nor did they desire oral sex from her, felt pressured to accept it simply because it was offered. After all, what real man would turn down sex? Popular music videos, rife with shallow depictions of both men and women, show swaggering males getting play right and left from eager, nearly naked women. These same performances of exaggerated male sexual bravado are mirrored on the streets, in the hallways, and in the homes of many boys who may, for various reasons, lack other more balanced models of male sexuality.

When I told the boys that they were not obligated to accept oral sex from someone to whom they were not attracted, it was clearly a message they had never heard. I saw open expressions of surprise and relief on more than a few young faces. This experience taught me that adults must give young men explicit permission to turn down oral sex—and any sex—they do not want. We must teach them that their manhood is not hinged on the number of sex partners they amass.

6. Making informed decisions that respect others and one's self is a true mark of manhood. In May 2002, when Oprah Winfrey and Dr. Phil tried to tackle this subject on her afternoon talk show, they not only put the onus of curbing the trend of casual adolescent oral sex on the girls, they threw up their hands and said, "What do the guys have to lose in this situation? Nothing!"

Nothing? I would suggest otherwise. To leave teen boys off the hook in regard to oral sex fails them miserably as they prepare for responsible adult relationships. In doing so, we set up boys to miss out on developing skills that truly define manhood: healthy sexual decision making, setting and respecting personal boundaries, and being accountable for one's actions. We also leave them at risk for contracting sexually transmitted infections. In addition, although our culture rarely communicates this, men who accept oral sex whenever it is offered risk losing the respect of people who do not admire or appreciate men who have indiscriminate sex with large numbers of partners. Clearly, adults—and especially adult men—must be willing to teach boys, through words and actions, that authentic manhood is a complex identity that cannot be so simply attained as through casual sex, oral or otherwise.[9]

7. Giving oral sex is not an effective route to lasting respect, popularity or love. For some teen girls, giving oral sex is weighted with hopes of further attention, increased likeability, and perhaps even a loving relationship.[10] For them, giving oral sex becomes a deceptively easy, if not short-term, way to feel worthy and loved. Adults who care about girls must empower them to see beyond the present social situation and find other routes to a sense of belonging and love.

One essential route to a sense of belonging and love is the consistent experience of non-sexual, non-exploitive touch. Some adolescent girls seek sex as a way to find the sense of love and belonging conveyed by touch. If a girl's touch needs go unfilled by parents or other caregivers, sex is often the most available means for fulfilling them.[11] Adults who work with girls must acknowledge the deeply human need for touch experienced by some adolescent girls. Although outside the scope of this discussion, girl-serving professionals can provide creative ways for girls to experience safe, non-sexual touch as part of their participation in programs without violating program restrictions on physical touch between staff and clients.

On the other hand, it is possible—and developmentally normal—for teen girls to experience sexual desire. Although our cultural script of adolescent sexuality con-

tradicts this, it may be that some girls, especially older teens, authentically desire the kind of sensual and sexual intimacy oral sex affords. If this is the case, it is essential that adults do not shame girls away from these emergent desires. Instead, they should explore the ways oral sex may increase one's physical and emotional vulnerabilities and strategize ways that girls can stay healthy and safe while acknowledging their own sexual desires.

8. Girls can refuse to give oral sex. Unlike Oprah and Dr. Phil, I do not believe the onus for curbing casual adolescent oral sex rests solely or even primarily on teen girls. Teen boys can and should assert firmer boundaries around participating in oral sex. The cultural attitudes that make girls and women the gatekeepers of heterosexual male sexual behavior, deciding when and if sex will happen, are unduly biased and burdensome. By perpetuating these attitudes, Oprah and Dr. Phil missed a grand opportunity to teach the value of mutuality in sexual decision-making and relationships, a message many young people—and adults—desperately need to hear.

That said, it is disturbing to hear stories of adolescent girls offering casual oral sex to teen boys. Again, the models of a balanced female sexuality in the media and in the lives of many girls are often few and far between. This, coupled with the troubling rates of sexual abuse perpetrated against girls in childhood and adolescence, makes the establishment of healthy sexual boundaries a problem for many girls.

Therefore, adults must go beyond simply telling girls to avoid giving oral sex for reasons of reputation and health, as was stressed by Dr. Phil. We must empower girls, through encouragement, role plays, and repeated rehearsals, to establish and maintain healthy boundaries for loving touch in their friendships and dating relationships, an experience that may be new to some. Moreover, we must be frank about the sexual double-standards set up against girls and women that make them responsible for male sexual behavior. And, we must create safe spaces where girls can encourage and support each other in refusing to give boys oral sex, thus shifting the perceived norm that "everyone is doing it."

9. Young women may explore their own capacities for sexual pleasure rather than spending their energies pleasuring others. Some girls will argue that oral sex is just another exchange of friendship, something they do with their male friends as "friends with benefits." I would argue, however, that, in most cases, the benefits are rather one-sided. Rarely do the teen boys give oral sex to the teen girls in exchange. Neither research nor anecdotal evidence indicates a trend of boys offering casual oral sex to girls. It seems that the attention the girls get *en route* to oral sex make it a worthwhile exchange for them, even as they are shortchanged on other "benefits."

If, indeed, girls are fulfilling their valid need for attention and acceptance through giving oral sex, and if they don't consider what they are doing to be "real sex," it stands to reason that many girls engaged in oral sex may not be experiencing genuine sexual desire or pleasure at all. It wouldn't be surprising if they're not. After all, few girls receive a truly comprehensive sexuality education, one that acknowledges the tremendous life-enhancing capacities for desire and pleasure contained in the female body. Our sex education messages are often so consumed by trying to prevent girls from getting pregnant and abused that we fail to notice how we keep them as the objects of other people's sexual behaviors. In doing so, we keep girls mystified about their own bodies and thus fail to empower them as the sexual subjects of their own lives.[12]

Adults can affirm girls' emerging capacities for desire and pleasure by, first, teaching them the names and functions of all of their sexual anatomy, including the pleasure-giving clitoris and G-spot. When discussing the benefits of abstinence, adults can suggest to girls that their growing sexual curiosity and desires may be fulfilled by learning, alone in the privacy of one's room, about one's own body—what touch is pleasing, what is not, how sexual energy builds, and how it is released through their own female bodies. If girls could regard themselves as the sexual subjects of their own lives rather than spending vast energies on being desirable objects of others, perhaps they would make healthier, firmer, more deliberate decisions about the sexual experiences and behaviors they want as adolescents.[13] Not only might girls make better decisions around oral sex, they may feel more empowered to negotiate the use of contraception and safer sex supplies, a skill that would serve them well through their adult years.[14]

10. Seek the support and guidance of adults who have your best interests at heart. Young people do not have to figure it all out on their own. Human sexuality is complicated, and most of us, adults and adolescents, do better by sometimes seeking out the support, guidance, and caring of others who want to see us enjoy our sexualities in healthy, life-enhancing ways. Adults can let young people know we are willing to listen to their concerns around issues of oral sex. We can offer teens support and guidance in their struggles to decide what's right for their lives. We can become skilled and comfortable in addressing risk-reduction and the enhancement of sexual pleasure together, as companion topics. And, finally, adults can use the topic of oral sex as a catalyst to dispel myths, discuss gender roles, and communicate values that affirm the importance of mutuality, personal boundaries, and safety in the context of healthy relationships.

References

1. L. Remez, "Oral Sex Among Adolescents: Is It Sex or Is It Abstinence?" *Family Planning Perspectives,* Nov/Dec 2000, p. 298.
2. R. Tannahill, *Sex in History* (New York: Stein and Day, 1980), pp. 58–346.
3. M. Carrera, *Sex: The Facts, The Acts, and Your Feelings* (New York: Crown, 1981), pp. 49–51.
4. Centers for Disease Control and Prevention, "Preventing the Sexual Transmission of HIV, the Virus that Causes AIDS, What You Should Know about Oral Sex," Dec. 2000. . . .
5. Iowa Code, Section 709.1, Sexual abuse defined (1999). . . .
6. S. Edwards and C. Carne, "Oral Sex and the Transmission of Viral STIs," *Sexually Transmitted Infections,* April 1998, pp. 95–100.
7. Centers for Disease Control and Prevention, "Fact Sheet: Pubic Lice or 'Crabs'," June 2000. . . .
8. Several online retailers sell safer sex supplies, including flavored condoms and lubricants. . . .
9. P. Kivel, *Boys Will Be Men: Raising Our Sons for Courage, Caring and Community.* (Gabriola Island B.C., Canada: New Society, 1999), pp. 177–184.
10. S. Thompson, *Going All the Way: Teenage Girls' Tales of Sex, Romance, and Pregnancy* (New York: Hill & Wang, 1995), pp. 17–46.
11. P. Davis, *The Power of Touch* (Carlsbad, CA: Hay House, 1999), p. 71.
12. M. Fine, "Sexuality, Schooling, and Adolescent Females: The Missing Discourse of Desire," *Disruptive Voices: The Possibilities of Feminist Research,* Ann Arbor: University of Michigan, 1992), pp. 31–59.
13. M. Douglass & L. Douglass, *Are We Having Fun Yet? The Intelligent Woman's Guide to Sex* (New York: Hyperion, 1997), pp. 170–171.
14. TARSHI (Talking About Reproductive and Sexual Health Issues), *Common Ground Sexuality: Principles for Working on Sexuality* (New Dehli, India: TARSHI, 2001), p. 13.

RHONDA CHITTENDEN is a veteran executive and educator for several nonprofit organizations including EyesOpen-Iowa and Planned Parenthood of Greater Iowa.

Nora Gelperin

Oral Sex and Young Adolescents: Insights from the "Oral Sex Lady"

A Brief History

I've been the Director of Training at the Network for Family Life Education for three years, but recently I've become known as the "Oral Sex Lady." (My parents are so proud.) It all began when I started receiving more frequent calls from parents, teachers and the media concerning alleged incidents of 11–14-year-olds engaging in oral sex in school buses, empty classrooms or custodial closets, behind the gym bleachers and during "oral sex parties." People were beginning to panic that youth were "sexually out of control." Most people believe young teens should not engage in oral sex, but that's not our current reality. So in response, I developed a workshop about oral sex and young teens, which I have since delivered to hundreds of professionals throughout the country. This process has helped me refine my thinking about this so-called oral sex "problem." Now, when I arrive at a meeting or workshop I smile when I'm greeted with, "Hey, aren't you the Oral Sex Lady?!"

What's the "Problem"?

The 1999 documentary "The Lost Children of Rockdale County" first chronicled a syphilis outbreak in suburban Conyers, Georgia, due to a rash of sex parties. Since then, more anecdotal and media stories about middle school students having oral sex began to surface. Initially, a training participant would tell me about an isolated incident of a young girl caught performing oral sex on a boy in the back of the school bus. During a workshop in Minnesota, I was educated about "Rainbow Parties" in which girls wear different-colored lipstick and the goal for guys is to get as many different-colored rings on their penises by night's end. In Florida, there were stories of "chicken head" parties where girls supposedly gave oral sex to boys at the same time, thus bobbing their heads up and down like chickens. During a workshop in New Jersey, I learned that oral sex was becoming the ultimate bar mitzvah gift in one community, given under the table during the reception, hidden by long tablecloths. (At one synagogue, the caterer was ultimately asked to shorten the tablecloths as a method of prevention!) The media began to pick up on these stories and run cover stories in local and national newspapers and magazines. One could conclude from the media buzz that the majority of early adolescents are frequently having oral sex at sex parties around the country. But what was *really* going on and what can the research tell us?

What is missing from the buzz is any recent scientific data to support or refute the claims of early adolescents having oral sex at higher rates than in previous years. Due to parental rights, research restrictions, and lack of funding, there is no rigorous scientific data conducted on the behavior of early adolescents to establish the frequency or incidence of oral sex. So we are left with anecdotal evidence, research conducted on older adolescents, media reports and cultural hype about this "new" phenomenon. We don't know how frequent this behavior is, at what ages it might begin, how many partners a young teen might have, whether any safer sex techniques are utilized, or the reasoning behind a teen's decision to engage in oral sex. What is universal among the anecdotes is that girls are giving oral sex to boys without it generally being reciprocated and it's mostly the adults that find this problematic. But what can we learn from all this?

Major Questions to Consider

Is Oral Sex Really "Sex"?

One of the most common themes I hear during my workshop is that adults want to convince teens that oral sex is really "sex." The adult logic is that if we can just convince teens that oral sex is "really" sex, they will take it more seriously and stop engaging in it so recklessly. This perspective seeks to universally define oral sex from an adult perspective that is out of sync with how many teens may define it. Many teens view oral sex as a way to maintain their "virginity" and reduce their risk for pregnancy and infections. According to a recent Kaiser Family Foundation report, 33 percent of 15–17-year-old girls report having oral sex to avoid having intercourse. In the same report, 47 percent of 15–17-year-old girls and boys believe that oral sex is a form of safer sex. Most people believe that young adolescents should not engage in oral, anal, or vaginal sex. As a backup, we should make sure teens understand that if they are going to engage in sexual behaviors, oral sex is less risky for many infections than vaginal or anal sex if latex barriers like flavored condoms and sheer glyde dams[1] are used, and it cannot start a pregnancy.

If You've Only Had Oral Sex, Are You Still a Virgin?

From my experience facilitating workshops on oral sex, professionals really struggle with this question and many of the 32,000 teens per day who come to our *SEX, ETC.* Web site . . . do too. The concept of virginity, while troublesome to many adults, is still central to the identity of many teens, particularly girls. Many adults and teens define virginity as not having had vaginal intercourse, citing the presence or absence of the hymen. Some adults then wrestle with the idea of what constitutes actual intercourse—penetration of a penis into a vagina, orgasm by one or both partners, oral sex, anal sex, penetration of any body opening? For heterosexual couples, virginity is something girls are often pressured to "keep" and boys are pressured to "lose." The issue also becomes much more volatile when a teen may not have given consent to have intercourse the first time—does this mean that he/she is no longer a virgin? Gay and lesbian teens are also left out when virginity is tied to penis-vagina intercourse, possibly meaning that a gay or lesbian teen might always be a "virgin" if it's defined that way. Educators can help teens think more critically about their definitions of sex, intercourse, and virginity and the meanings of these words in their lives.

How Intimate Is Oral Sex?

Many adults in my workshops express their belief that oral sex is just as intimate as other types of penetrative sexual behaviors. Some adults believe oral sex is even *more* intimate than vaginal or anal intercourse because one partner is considered very vulnerable, it involves all of the senses (smell, taste, touch, sight, and sound) and requires a lot of trust. Many teens, although certainly not all teens, believe oral sex is *less* intimate than vaginal intercourse. Through my experience as an on-line expert for our *SEX, ETC.* Web site, I hear from hundreds of teens every month who submit their most personal sexual health questions. Some of these teens believe oral sex is very intimate and acknowledge the same issues that adults raise while others find it less intimate than vaginal intercourse. From a teen's perspective, it is less intimate because:

- oral sex doesn't require that both partners be nude;
- oral sex can be done in a short amount of time (particularly if performed on adolescent boys);
- oral sex can maintain virginity;
- oral sex doesn't involve eye contact with a partner;
- oral sex doesn't require a method of contraception;
- oral sex doesn't require a trip to the gynecologist; and
- most teens believe oral sex doesn't carry as much of a risk for sexually transmitted infections as vaginal or anal intercourse.

Some girls even feel empowered during oral sex as the only sexual behavior in which they have complete control of their partner's pleasure. Others feel pressured to engage in oral sex and exploited by the experience. So while many adults view oral sex as extremely intimate, some teens do not.

This dichotomy presents challenges for an educator in a group that may assign a different value to oral sex than the educator. Oral sex also requires a conversation about sexual pleasure and sexual response, topics that many educators are not able to address with young teens. The salient issue is how teens define behaviors, not how adults define behaviors, since we are operating in their world when we deliver sexuality education. I believe our definitions and values should be secondary to those of teens because ultimately teens need to be able to operate in a teen culture, not our adult world.

What Can an Educator Do?

As sexual health educators, our role is to provide medically accurate information and encourage all adolescents to think critically about decisions relating to their sexuality. We should ask middle school–age adolescents to sift through their own beliefs and hear from their peers, many of whom might not agree about oral sex, virginity, intimacy or the definition of sex. Finding ways to illuminate the variety of teens' opinions about oral sex will more accurately reflect the range of opinions instead of continuing to propagate the stereotype that "all teens are having oral sex." Additionally, instead of focusing exclusively on the ramifications of oral sex and infections, we should address the potential social consequences of having oral sex. Since early adolescents are not developmentally able to engage in long-term planning, focusing on the long-term consequences of untreated sexually transmitted infections (STIs) is not developmentally appropriate. Educators should be cognizant of what is developmentally appropriate for early adolescents and strive to include information about sexual coercion, correct latex condom and sheer glyde dam use, and infection prevention.

So Are They or Aren't They?

Without research, this question will remain unanswered and we must not rely on overly dramatized media accounts to dictate public health approaches. Instead we should focus on giving young adolescents developmentally appropriate information, consider their reasoning for wanting to engage in oral sex, explore their definitions of sex, virginity, and intimacy, and develop programs that incorporate all of these facets. We need to advocate for more research and reasoned media responses to what is likely a minority of early adolescents having oral sex before it becomes overly dramatized by our shock-culture media. Finally, we must not forget that the desire for early adolescents to feel sexual pleasure is normal and natural and should be celebrated, not censored. From my experience as the "Oral Sex Lady," teens are much more savvy than we adults think.

Note

1. Sheer glyde dams are squares of latex that are held in place on the vulva of a female during oral sex to help prevent sexually transmitted infections. They are the only brand of dental dam that is FDA approved for the prevention of infections.

NORA GELPERIN is director of Training and Education for Answer at Rutgers University, where she develops and conducts workshops for education professionals across the country.

EXPLORING THE ISSUE

Is Oral Sex Really Sex?

Critical Thinking and Reflection

1. What behaviors should be considered "sex"?
2. Why might it be useful to have a generally agreed upon societal definition of "sex"?
3. Why might it be important to have a personal definition of "sex"?
4. Which recommendations about oral sex given by the authors do you find most helpful?

Is There Common Ground?

Sex is more than sexual intercourse. This means teaching young people that there are many ways to be sexual with a partner besides intercourse and most of these behaviors are safer and healthier than intercourse. The word "sex" often has a vague meaning. When talking about intercourse, the word "intercourse" [should be] used.

This statement is taken from a list of principles for sexuality education developed by The Center for Family Life Education, included in the U.S. chapter of the *International Encyclopedia of Sexuality*. Do you agree or disagree with this principle? How does it compare with your own definition of "sex"? What kinds of sexual behaviors do you consider to be sex? What sexual behaviors "don't count" as sex? Does oral sex count? Anal sex? Showering together? Sexting? BDSM (Bondage Discipline Sadism and Masochism) behaviors? Do you agree with Chittenden that young people need to recognize oral sex as "really sex"? Or are you inclined to side with Gelperin as she asserts that adult values and definitions should be secondary, and that young people need to form their own meaning to oral sex?

Whereas Chittenden identifies specific messages that need to be articulated to young people, Gelperin seems more inclined to advocate a value clarification process and educational strategies based on the developmental needs of a given audience. What merits do these different approaches have? Would you advocate a combination of these approaches? Or would your own educational approach be very different?

Since both Chittenden and Gelperin are sexuality education professionals, you may have noticed several overlapping themes, such as the concern both expressed about condom use and protection from STIs. What other similarities did you observe?

Is it more important to have a uniform definition of "sex," which includes (or does not include) oral sex, or for people to create their own personal definitions that have meaning for themselves and/or their partners? Some reproductive health professionals have ascertained that if you cannot define "sex," then you cannot define its supposed opposite, "abstinence." In other words, one needs to understand what sex is before she or he can determine what it is they are being encouraged to abstain from. How has a culturally vague notion of "sex" and "abstinence" contributed to the widespread failure of abstinence-only education programs?

Create Central

www.mhhe.com/createcentral

Additional Resources

Brewster, K.L. & Tillman, K.H. (2008). "Who's Doing It? Patterns and Predictors of Youths' Oral Sexual Experiences," *Journal of Adolescent Health* (vol. 42, no. 1, pp. 73–80).

D'Souza, G., et al. (2009). "Oral Sexual Behaviors Associated with Prevalent Oral Human Papillomavirus Infection," *Journal of Infectious Diseases* (vol. 199, pp. 1263–1269).

Freeman, D.W. "Oral Sex Is Now Main Cause of Oral Cancer: Who Faces Biggest Risk?" *CBS News*, February 23, 2011.

Hans, J. & Kimberly, C. (2011). "Abstinence, Sex, and Virginity: Do They Mean What We Think They Mean?" *American Journal of Sexuality Education* (vol. 6, no. 4, pp. 329–342).

Lindberg, L.D., et al. (2008). "Noncoital Sexual Activities among Adolescents," *Journal of Adolescent Health* (vol. 43, no. 3, pp. 231–238).

Internet References . . .

Definition of Sex?

Go Ask Alice is an online advice repository for questions regarding sex and sexuality. The basic definition of "sex" is addressed in this article.

goaskalice.columbia.edu/definition-sex

Sexual Intercourse

This State of Connecticut website presents one potential legal definition of "sex" and outlines the legal implications. Other states may have other definitions.

www.jud.ct.gov/ji/criminal/glossary/sexualint.htm

What Is Sex?

This article presents potential definitions of the word sex, what acts may constitute sex, and outlines potential positive and negative physical outcomes.

www.plannedparenthood.org/info-for-teens/sex-masturbation/what-sex-33828.htm

Selected, Edited, and with Issue Framing Material by:
Ryan W. McKee, *Widener University*
and
William J. Taverner, *Center for Family Life Education*

ISSUE

Is Sexting a Form of Safer Sex?

YES: Brent A. Satterly, "Sexting, Not Infecting: A Sexological Perspective of Sexting as Safer Sex," Original essay written for this volume (2011)

NO: Donald A. Dyson, "Tweet This: Sexting Is NOT Safer Sex," Original essay written for this volume (2011)

Learning Outcomes

After reading this issue, you should be able to:

- Describe potential benefits and risks of sexting.
- Compare and contrast media depictions of sexting with the actual prevalence of sexting, according to contemporary research.
- Describe the harm reduction model as it relates to reducing the risks of sexting.
- Compare the World Health Organization's definition of sexual health to your own personal definition.

ISSUE SUMMARY

YES: Brent A. Satterly, associate professor and bachelor of Social Work Program Director at Widener University's Center for Social Work Education, acknowledges the risks involved in sexting while criticizing fear-based media coverage of the phenomenon. He argues in favor of harm-reduction strategies to reduce the risks associated with sexting rather than continuing the trend of panicked reactions to the expression of youth sexuality.

NO: Donald A. Dyson, director of the Center for Human Sexuality Studies and associate dean of the School of Human Services Professions at Widener University, examines sexting through the lens of the World Health Organization's definition of sexual health and determines that the risks inherent in the digital transmission of sext messages is not a form of safer sex.

The rise in cell phone and social media usage has given rise to a new outlet for sexual expression—sexting. Sexting is the nickname given to the sending of sexual messages or pictures via text or other electronic message. While engaging in steamy conversations is far from a new flirtation method, the ability to send, receive, and forward messages and images in an instant is a relatively new method.

Early media coverage of the phenomenon highlighted the perceived harm done to young victims of the sexting trend. Over the past several years, scandals involving underage teens snapping and sending nude pictures of themselves resulted in child pornography charges being filed against teens in several areas across the United States. In other cases, shared images or messages have been used to bully or embarrass the sender. Scandals involving adults, including professional athletes and entertainers, have caught the public's attention as well. Perhaps the most (in)famous sexting incident involved a politician.

In 2011, U.S. Congressman Anthony Weiner was forced to resign after sexually explicit images of him surfaced online. Weiner had been sending the photos, along with explicit messages, to female followers of his various social media accounts. Given the high-profile nature of those involved in the scandals, many felt sexting was a danger that had reached epidemic levels!

Research into sexting, however, tells a different story. A 2009 Pew Research study found that, while some young people text nude and semi-nude images for a variety of reasons, only 4 percent have actually sent an image of themselves to someone they know. Only 15 percent of young people report having received such an image via text (1). A study from 2012, which looked at cell phone and other electronic means of image sharing, found even lower percentages of young people participating. In this study only 2 and 1/2 percent of teens had appeared in nude or nearly nude images, and only 1 percent described the images as sexually explicit (showing breasts, genitals, or their buttocks) (2). These statistics present a different story than the sensational headlines and media coverage of the topic. Even in recent studies of young-adult populations, less than half of respondents report either sending or receiving sexts (3, 4).

If so few young people are actually sexting, why is the phenomenon so controversial? Many sexuality educators have questioned the fear-based response and challenged the assumption that sexting is always unhealthy. At its core, sexting is a form of communication, and communication about sexual thoughts and desires is not, in and of itself, a bad thing. Does the digital mode of communication change this? Does the history of messages stored in phones make sexual communication riskier than sharing feelings in face-to-face conversation? Do images need to be shared in order for a text message to become a sext message?

And what about the images themselves? How much skin needs to be shown for a flirtatious message to become a full-on sext? Does a male sharing a shirtless picture of himself, or female sharing a shot of herself in a bikini count as sexting? Or must there be exposed genitals in the frame? Is it safer for a person to snap and share an image of their genitals if their face (or other identifying features like tattoos) is not visible in the frame (5, 6)?

The controversy has presented sexologists an opportunity to question the "sext-panic" that has clouded the dialogue around sexting and examine what place, if any, the behavior has in sexuality education, and if sexting could be a form of safer sex. In the following selections, two professors in Widener University's Center for Education do just that. Brent A. Satterly argues that while sexting does not carry the same risks as exchanging bodily fluids, similar harm-reduction strategies applied to physical behaviors can reduce the risks involved in sexting and translate into dialogue and opportunities that will assist young people in navigating sexual scenarios in the future. Donald A. Dyson applies the definition of "healthy sexuality" developed by the World Health Organization to sexting and finds that qualities inherent in the behavior dictate that it is, in fact, unhealthy and therefore cannot be considered a form of safer sex.

YES ↵

Brent A. Satterly

Sexting, Not Infecting: A Sexological Perspective of Sexting as Safer Sex

According to the Pew Research Center (2009), the use of cell phones to text has become a primary mode of communication among adolescents. Over the course of the last few years, there has been a growing concern over how adolescents are using their texting capabilities around sexual expression. Sexting, the infamous phenomenon where individuals—usually assumed to be adolescents—share naked or partially naked pictures (a.k.a. "pics") or sexually explicit conversations with others, is often touted as a severely dangerous practice that can have far reaching negative outcomes for those who do so. The question of whether or not this practice is "safer sex" simply because it doesn't involve the exchange of bodily fluids is a misnomer. I would posit that it is indeed safe sex [not only] for that reason, but also because parents, educators, and public health officials can teach adolescents about how to reduce the potentially negative risks that sexting may involve.

Incidence

This practice has received wide public "sex-panic" oriented media coverage primarily focusing on adolescents (White, 2009). While this "kids these days" approach conveniently neglects to include the wide numbers of adults who engage in the same behavior, it still remains, however, primarily considered an adolescent phenomenon. The Pew Research Center conducted a 2009 survey citing that:

- 4% of 12–17 year olds who own cell phones have sent nude photos of themselves to someone;
- 15% of 12–17 year olds who own cell phones have received nude photos of someone;
- 8% of 17-year-olds who own cell phones have sent nude photos of themselves;
- 30% of 17-year-olds who own cell phones have received nude photos of someone.

Additionally, a MTV-Associated Press poll found that 1 out of 10 young adults between 14 and 24 have at some point shared nude photos of themselves with others (2009). Whether one considers a 24-year-old as an adolescent is another question entirely.

Is Sexting New?

"There's nothing new about using technology to get sex" (Joannides, 2009, p. 393). Sharing naked pictures or having sexually explicit conversations with others is not a new practice (Joannides, 2009). From naked Polaroids to dirty love letters to phone sex to lustful emails to dirty instant messaging, cell phones have made sexually explicit exchanges more accessible with their prominence (White, 2009).

Potential Negative Outcomes of Sexting?

Regardless of history and the populations who practice this behavior, there are potential negative outcomes for the sender based upon what the recipients of such photos or explicit texts do with it. In the immediate, this may include the public exposure of a nude picture by an angry ex who decides to send the picture to a number of other friends or post it online in an effort to humiliate the original sender. It can also have unintended legal consequences where the sender and/or receiver can be charged with various illegalities, including distribution or possession of child pornography and/or registration as a sex offender depending on state law (Ostrager, 2010).

For example, in the state of Pennsylvania, 17 students were threatened with being charged with child pornography possession or dissemination as a result of sending or receiving nude pictures of two female adolescents (Sexting Girls Facing Porn Charge Sue D.A.). The families of the two female teens countersued the local district attorney stating that since the pictures were distributed with their consent, they could not be charged accordingly. The potential far-reaching effects of this are evident.

While all of this is true, it nevertheless reinforces the quest to control American teen sexuality. Since this "sex-panic" effort to legislate and eliminate teen sexuality is fueled by such frightening incidents as the one previously mentioned, often parents or caregivers recount them as evidence for renewed efforts to squash teenage sexual expression. While this sex-panic bleeds over into how adult sexuality is viewed, ultimately the fear is for children. "Because not only are adults increasingly treated as children—incapable, where sex is concerned, of thinking with anything more elevated than their genitals: but the touchstone for policy in an adult world is increasingly 'what would happen if children got hold of this?'" (Fae, 2011, para. 6). A parental blog from America OnLine exemplifies such fear:

> The intention doesn't matter—even if a photo was taken and sent as a token of love, for example, the technology makes it possible for everyone to see your child's most intimate self. In the hands of teens, when revealing photos are made public, the subject almost always ends up feeling humiliated. Furthermore, sending sexual images to minors is against the law, and some states have begun prosecuting kids for child pornography or felony obscenity. There have been some high profile cases of sexting. (*Parentdish*, 2009, para 1.)

While one may assume that parents' desire here is to protect their adolescent, the result is the same as touting the fear-based abstinence-only message of sexuality education. "Just don't do it because bad things will happen to you" is an insufficient message for teens for behavior change.

Christopher White (2009) addresses such media-based sex-panic of sexting as blaming the victim. He reframes this fear-based reactivity as finger-pointing resulting in further harm:

> Sending photos out to friends and family members or posting them online without the consent of the other person is an assault on that individual in an attempt to cause them great harm and suffering and is where we should be focusing our greatest efforts at stopping a behavior, if that is the action most needed. Instead, certain groups are pointing their finger at the person whose photo was distributed without her permission and putting the blame on the victim. (2009, para. 3)

We cannot control adolescents; rather, we must understand adolescents and help adolescents understand themselves. Hence, the efforts public health officials and sexologists should be centered around is a developmentally appropriate comprehensive sexuality education approach starting from very young. Again, White (2009) poses a poignant solution by encouraging us to redirect our efforts toward working with adolescents around decision-making to safeguard themselves:

> Rather than focusing on how harmful and dangerous sexting is, we should be talking to young people about healthy sexual behaviors including the difference between consensual and nonconsensual acts. We should provide them with the truth about possible unintentional consequences and issues related to trust and dating in relationships. (2009, para. 5)

Is Sexting a Form of Safer Sex?

To frame sexting as a form of safer sex is a misleading question. Sexting, in and of itself, does not necessitate an exchange of bodily fluids. It is a digital exchange of pics and/or texts. The Pew Research Center states that sexting usually occurs within the context of three scenarios: (1) between romantic partners; (2) between partners that share the pics outside of the relationship, and (3) between individuals who aren't in relationship, but would like to be. Each context here carries its own risk of potential exploitation or harm, just as any kind of sexual behavior with another person carries a certain degree of risk, depending upon the variables. Many a sexuality educator has uttered the standard phrase, "What is the only 100% risk-free way to not get pregnant or [to not] get a sexually-transmitted infection?" The only acceptable answer is, of course, abstinence.

The same logic holds true for sexting. If an adolescent simply doesn't engage in the behavior, he or she is subsequently abstaining from sexting; therefore, the teen is free of risk of exploitation or harm from someone using a pic, the teen previously sent against them. (This does not account for those individuals who have pictures taken of them without their consent, of course.) If, however, the adolescent is engaging in some kind of sexting behavior, most typically within one of the three aforementioned contexts, she or he needs to consider reducing the risk of potential harm. Teaching healthy decision-making within a comprehensive sexuality education curriculum will aid the teen in considering the risks and benefits of such a behavior.

In the column *Go Ask Alice!*, a reader posed a question about how to become more comfortable with using sexting as a means of bridging the distance between she and her long-distance boyfriend. "Alice" responded with a series of both critical thinking questions and recommendations to reduce risks and increase sensuality. These included consideration of (1) who may view the sext, (2) the potential emotional outcomes should someone else see it, and (3) the level of trust of the recipient of the sext (Go Ask Alice!, para 3.). Alice continues, "If you're comfortable with the potential risks, sexting . . . [is a] great way to explore new and unique ways to sexual satisfaction. If you're not comfortable with the privacy concerns, you may want to let this sexual adaptation of technology slide"(para. 4). She adds some additional points to bear in mind:

- **Character limits.** Sexting a Shakespeare sonnet may callous your fingers and require 30 texts before you even get "there," so you may need to keep it short and sweet.
- **Different sense of time.** If one or both sexters are multitasking, response times may vary from seconds to days. If you're looking for more instant gratification from a distance, phone sex or cyber sex may be quicker. If you're looking for

something that fits into a busy schedule, this may be your sexual medium while you're physically away.

- **Beep beep!** If you're expecting a heavy flow of incoming sexts, you may want to switch your mobile device to vibrate or silent to not gather a crowd's attention or disturb bystanders.
- **Keep it discreet.** If you're in a public space, consider stepping aside as your face blushes, heart races, or breaths get deeper. Having a concerned stranger ask if you're hyperventilating may create some awkward moments.
- **Secure the messages.** Consider setting up the security and privacy features of your phone to minimize curious friends . . . and strangers from accessing your sexts. (Go Ask Alice!, para. 5)

Conclusion

Avoiding fear-based and controlling approaches to squashing teen sexuality is an important consideration by which to address the very real risks of sexting. In this rapidly changing world of technology, taking a comprehensive sexuality education-based approach to develop healthy decision-making skills for adolescents around sexting may just allow teens to apply such skills in their lives as a whole.

References

Go Ask Alice! (2010, October 15). *Sexting.* Retrieved from http://www.goaskalice.columbia.edu/11238.html.

Fae, J. (2011, February). *Sex is dangerous. Again.* Sexual Freedom, Retrieved February 24, 2011 from http://www.freedominapuritanage.co.uk/?p=1475.

Joannides, P. (2009). *The guide to getting it on* (6th ed.). Portland, OR: Goofy Foot Press.

MTV-AP Digital Abuse Study, Executive Summary. (September, 2009). AThinLine.org. http://www.athinline.org/MTV-AP Digital Abuse Study Executive Summary.pdf. Retrieved from Pewinternet.org.

Ostrager, B. (2010). SMS. OMG! LOL! TTYL: Translating the law to accommodate today's teens and the evolution from texting to sexting. *Family Court Review, 48*(4), 712.

Parentdish. (February 21). RE: Sexting and your kids [Web log message]. Retrieved from ProQuest Central. (Document ID:2272244681).

Sexting Girls Facing Porn Charge Sue D.A. (2009, March 27). CBS.com. Retrieved from http://www.cbsnews.com/stories/2009/03/27/earlyshow/main4896577.shtml

White, C. (May, 2009). Teen sex panic: Media still freaking out about "sexting". Retrieved from Alternet.org.

BRENT A. SATTERLY, PhD, LCSW, is an associate professor and bachelor of Social Work Program Director at Widener University's Center for Social Work Education.

Donald A. Dyson

➡ **NO**

Tweet This: Sexting Is NOT Safer Sex

In their publication Mobile Access 2010 (Smith, 2010), the Pew Internet and American Life Project identified the current trends in cell phone usage. At the time of the report, 82% of all adults (age 18+) in the United States owned a cell phone. Of those people, 76% used their cell phone to take pictures, 72% used text messaging, and 54% had sent photos or videos using their cell phone.

Leading the charge toward a fully wired populace, the 18–29 year olds in that survey scored higher across the board in their wireless technology utilization. In this age bracket, 90% of the overall population owned cell phones, with 93% of those individuals taking pictures, 95% texting, and 81% sending photos and videos.

Consider as well that the average age for young people to own their first cell phone has decreased dramatically. In the latest data available from Pew on adolescent cell phone use from 2009 (Lenhart, 2009), 58% of 12 year olds owned a cell phone. This number was up dramatically from 18% in 2004.

While ownership has increased, the available technology has moved ahead light years as well. Touch screens with incredible definition join with faster networks to easily facilitate the sharing of pictures and videos from phone to phone. Facetime features allow individuals to live video chat between similarly equipped smartphones. Add to this the increase of smartphone applications (apps) that connect random strangers for live video chat, and the implications are staggering.

For decades, professionals in the technology field have accepted the fact that pornography, in many ways, drives technological innovation (Johnson, 1996). This innovation, often moving faster than the development of ethical guidelines, creates new opportunities for sharing and expressing oneself, including one's sexual self. According to Coopersmith (2009), these technologies offer users the ability to create and share information with both a sense of privacy and with user-friendly interfaces. In essence, it is quick and easy to create and send sexual images in a way that feels, to the user, like it is safe from the judgment and oversight of others.

Out of this technological morass has come the phenomenon popularly referred to as "sexting," or the sending and receiving of sexually explicit text messages (including words, symbols, pictures and videos) using an individual's cell phone.

In the 2009 Pew data of teen cell phone users between 12 and 17, four percent (4%) had sent a sexual image (nude or nearly nude) of themselves to someone via text message and 15% had received such an image. In 17 year olds, those numbers literally doubled, with eight percent (8%) having sent and 30% having received such images (Lenhart, 2009).

Little research has been done on these patterns in adult users, but it is safe to assume that turning 18 years old does not immediately change an individual's behavior, and these trends are likely to continue as technology users get older. As a result, we must begin to acknowledge that sexting is a phenomenon that not only exists, but also exists with little or no oversight and little or no ethical study to guide its use.

Within this experience, some advocates for sexual freedom and expression along with some dedicated to the prevention of sexually transmitted infections, HIV, and unintended pregnancies have begun to consider whether or not sexting can be considered the new "safer sex." Consider the origin of the safer sex terminology. Rising out of the HIV pandemic, first as "safe sex" then as "safer sex," the term has come to be associated with sexual practices that do not risk spreading disease or creating an unintended pregnancy.

With this definition, sexting would certainly seem to be a natural fit. To date, it is not possible to pass human viruses or semen from one mobile device to another through a wireless network.

At issue here, though, is the narrow and reductionist view of sexuality that has too often been embraced as the guiding principle of sex in the current millennium. Ask most high-school sexuality educators for the core concepts of their curricula, and you are likely to get "safer sex" from almost every one. Lessons about condoms and contraception are surely included if allowed by the administration and school board.

In fact, the abstinence-only education movement succeeded in narrowing the debate about sexuality education to the extent that often, when advocates fight for "comprehensive sexuality education," what they are fighting for is the inclusion of medically accurate information about condoms and contraception (Collins, Alagiri & Summers, 2002).

It is important in this discussion, however, to consider a more holistic approach to sexuality. In response to the global need for a clear construction of what it means to be sexually healthy, the World Health Organization (WHO, 2002) created the following definition:

> A state of physical, emotional, mental and social wellbeing in relation to sexuality; it is not merely the absence of disease, dysfunction or infirmity. Sexual health requires a positive and respectful approach to sexuality and sexual relationships, as well as the possibility of having pleasurable and safe sexual experiences, free of coercion, discrimination and violence. (p. 10)

In this larger context, disease prevention is clearly a part of the physical wellbeing identified. As such, it is certainly an important consideration in sexual decision-making. However, it is far from the only consideration necessary. In fact the definition clearly defines health as beyond mere disease prevention. Using the WHO definition, in order to consider a behavior "safe," one would have to consider the emotional, mental, and social implications associated with the behavior as well.

Briefly consider the act of sexting in the framework provided by the WHO. To do this, one must remember that electronic images sent from one device to another have a few unique qualities. First, they have the potential to remain intact and available for years. Second, because of this longevity, they can be transferred from one device to another and can exist in multiple locations at the same time. Third, this potential for multiplication makes sending or showing them to people who were not the intended recipients remarkably easy.

Now, consider the WHO framework. Is sexting safe physically? Yes, from disease. And while images cannot physically harm an individual, a jealous lover in a fit of rage can certainly cause serious physical harm after seeing a sexual image of another person on a partner's cell phone or computer. Also consider the reality that in some municipalities in the United States, minors who are sending images of themselves, their friends, or their classmates are being charged with both creating and distributing child pornography. This offense can lead to incarceration as well as to inclusion in sex offender registries (Lenhart, 2009). Neither are "safe" locations.

Is sexting safer emotionally? This is a more difficult issue to parse out. Sexting can be flirtatious, fun, and bring an individual a great deal of emotional joy. It is also possible for those images to be kept over time, to be shown to unintended recipients, to be used to blackmail, bully, intimidate, and harass. Imagine the jilted lover who sends your seminude picture to your workplace, or the divorcee who uses stored sexts in a custody battle. The potential for emotional harm certainly needs to be acknowledged.

Is sexting safer mentally? While social networking has changed the nature of privacy in today's online world, sexual images of one's self are still generally considered to

be private, and shared with those with whom an individual chooses. The nature of digital communication removes the power of choice from the individual, allowing others the freedom to determine who does and does not have access to these very personal images. That powerlessness, combined with anxiety about the possible unintended recipients of the images, can certainly cause an individual mental anguish.

Finally, consider the "freedom from coercion, discrimination and violence" clause. It is clear that the images captured in sexting can be used for all of those things.

In short, sexting is not and cannot be the new "safer sex." In and of itself, it is NOT safe, and framing it as such teaches individuals to ignore the potential harm that may come from engaging in the behavior. Would you tell your 11-year-old niece that sexting was safe?

In the end, it is far wiser to consider sexting to be like most other sexual behaviors: a mixed bag. It can be fun, flirtatious, exciting, and contribute to some wonderful sexual experiences. It also has risks associated with it, and those risks are beyond mere disease transmission or pregnancy. The key is to educate people about the potential risks, help them to consider how those risks fit into their life, and to make individual choices about their willingness to accept those risks.

References

Collins, C., Alagiri, P., & Summers, T. (2002). Abstinence only vs. comprehensive sex education: What are the arguments? What is the evidence? AIDS Policy Research Center & Center for AIDS Prevention Studies, AIDS Research Institute, University of California, San Francisco. Retrieved April 1, 2011, from http://ari.ucsf.edu/pdf/abstinence.pdf

Coopersmith J. (2000). *Pornography, Technology and Progress,* ICON 4, 94–125.

Johnson, P (November 1996). *Pornography Drives Technology: Why Not to Censor the Internet.* Federal Communication Law Journal 49(1).

Lenhart, A. (2009). *Teens and Sexting.* Pew Internet & American Life. Retrieved from http://www.pewinternet.org/~/media//Files/Reports/2009/PIP_Teens_and_Sexting.pdf

Smith, A. 2010. *Mobile access 2010.* Washington, DC: Pew Internet & American Life Project.

World Health Organization. (2002). *Defining sexual health: report of a technical consultation on sexual health,* 28–31, January 2002, Geneva. Retrieved April 1, 2011, from www.who.int/reproductivehealth/publications/sexualhealth/defining_sh.pdf.

DONALD A. DYSON, PhD, is director of the Center for Human Sexuality Studies and associate dean of the School of Human Services Professions at Widener University.

EXPLORING THE ISSUE

Is Sexting a Form of Safer Sex?

Critical Thinking and Reflection

1. What are the risks involved in sexting for teens and adolescents? For young adults?
2. What strategies could be used by young people to reduce the risks of sexting?
3. Are there things that are easier for you to express via nonverbal communication like text messages? Why or why not?
4. In what ways could sexting be seen as a form of safer sex?
5. What other technologies, when first introduced, might have led to a "panic" similar to the controversies surrounding sexting?

Is There Common Ground?

In the YES selection, Satterly presents strategies for reducing the risks involved in sexting. Do you think these steps make sexting a safe practice? Or is it still too risky for teens to engage in the practice? Are there things that are easier to say via text than in person? Can sexting make communication about sexual desires or boundaries easier? Can sexting contribute to healthy sexual dialogue and expression of feelings? Or are the risks still too great? Dyson examines sexting through the World Health Organization's description of "healthy sexuality" and comes to the conclusion that it is not safe. Do you agree with his conclusions? Why or why not? What is your personal definition of sexual health? He states that describing sexting as a form of safer sex "teaches individuals to ignore the potential harm that may come from engaging in the behavior." Do you agree? Finally, Dyson asks "Would you tell your 11-year-old niece that sexting was safe?" What is your answer to this question?

Most of the attention given to sexting has focused on adolescents. But sexting is not limited to the keypad-savvy thumbs of teens. Adults also engage in the practice, and the high-profile sexting mishaps of celebrities and politicians have received media attention as well. Are there different risks for adults who sext as opposed to teens? Why might adults consider sexting a problem for youth while engaging in the practice themselves? What does this say about the risks, benefits, and meaning behind the practice?

Lastly, have you ever sent or received a sext message? What were the reasons behind your actions? How did you feel when you clicked the send button or opened the message? Did you consider both the risks and benefits involved? Did you talk with your partner about what should happen to the images or messages once the conversation (or relationship) has stopped? Do smartphone apps like "SnapChat," which deletes shared images within a few seconds of being viewed, reduce the risks of sexting? In the end, what shaped your final decision? Do you think

the conclusions you came to about sexting are the same conclusions everyone should come to? Should sexting be included in conversations of safer sex options?

Create Central

www.mhhe.com/createcentral

References

(1) Lenhart, A. (2009). "Teens and Sexting," www.pewinternet.org/~/media//Files/Reports/2009/PIP_Teens_and_Sexting.pdf

(2) Mitchel, K., Finkelhor, D., Jones, L., & Wolak, J. (2012). "Prevalence and Characteristics of Youth Sexting: A National Study," *Pediatrics* (vol. 129, no. 1, pp. 13–20).

(3) Benotsch, E., Snipes, D., Martin, A., & Bull, S. (2013). "Sexting, Substance Abuse, and Sexual Risk Behavior in Young Adults," *Journal of Adolescent Sexual Health* (vol. 52, pp. 307–313).

(4) Gordon-Messer, D. , Bauermeister, J., Grodzinski, A., & Zimmerman, M. (2013). "Sexting Among Young Adults," *Journal of Adolescent Sexual Health* (vol. 52, pp. 301–306).

(5) CBSnews.com "Girl, 15, Faces Porn Charges for Sexting" (February 20, 2009), www.cbsnews.com/stories/2009/02/20/national/main4816266.shtml

(6) Quaid, L. (December 3, 2009). "Think Your Kid Isn't Sexting? Think Again," www.msnbc.msn.com/id/34257556/ns/technology_and_science-tech_and_gadgets/

Additional Resources

Benotsch, E., Snipes, D., Martin, A, & Bull, S. (2013). "Sexting, Substance Abuse, and Sexual Risk Behavior in Young Adults," *Journal of Adolescent Sexual Health* (vol. 52 pp. 307–313).

Gordon–Messer, D., Bauermeister, J., Grodzinski, A., & Zimmerman, M. (2013). "Sexting Among Young Adults," *Journal of Adolescent Sexual Health* (vol. 52, 301–306).

Jaishankar, K. (2009). "Sexting: A New Form of Victimless Crime?" *International Journal of Cyber Criminology* (vol. 3, no. 1).

Lenhart, A. "Teens and Sexting" (2009), www.pewinternet.org/~/media//Files/Reports/2009/PIP_Teens_and_Sexting.pdf

Levine, D. "Sexting: A Terrifying Health Risk . . . or the New Normal for Young Adults?" *Journal of Adolescent Health* (vol. 52, no. 3, pp. 257–258).

Shafron-Perez, S. "Average Teenager or Sex Offender? Solutions to the Legal Dilemma Caused by Sexting," *The John Marshall Journal of Computer and Information Law* (February 2009).

Internet References . . .

MTV—A Thin Line Campaign

This page, from MTV's Thin Line Campaign, reports on research and lays out the risks of teen sexting.

www.athinline.org/facts/

Older Adults and Sexting

This article, from the American Association of Retired Persons (AARP) discusses trends in sexting among older adults.

www.aarp.org/relationships/love-sex/info-11-2009/sexting_not_just_for_kids.html

Sexting: Risky Actions and Overreactions

This is the FBI's infosheet on youth sexting. It addresses legal and other issues.

www.fbi.gov/stats-services/publications/law-enforcement-bulletin/july-2010/sexting

Youth+Tech+Health (YTH)

YTH, formerly known as ISIS, is an organization dedicated to advancing the health and wellness of youth through technology.

www.yth.org

Selected, Edited, and with Issue Framing Material by:
Ryan W. McKee, *Widener University*
and
William J. Taverner, *Center for Family Life Education*

ISSUE

Is BDSM a Healthy Form of Sexual Expression?

YES: **Wayne V. Pawlowski**, from "BDSM: The Ultimate Expression of Healthy Sexuality," Original essay for this volume (2009)

NO: **Rachel White**, from "The Story of 'No': S&M Clubs Sprout Up on Ivy Campuses, and Coercion Becomes an Issue," *The New York Observer* (November 16, 2012), http://observer.com/2012/11/the-story-of-no-sadomasochistic-sex-clubs-sprout-up-on-ivy-campuses-and-coercion-becomes-an-issue/

Learning Outcomes

After reading this issue, you should be able to:

- Describe the concept of consent and explain its importance.
- Explain the principles of "safe, sane, consensual" (SSC) and "risk aware consensual kink" (RACK).
- Describe several behaviors that could be included in sexual bondage, discipline, dominance, submission, sadism, and masochism.
- Discuss personal comfort levels with the spectrum of BDSM behaviors, from mild to extreme.
- Describe the importance of "community" as it relates to BDSM, and how it may increase both safety and risk.

ISSUE SUMMARY

YES: Sex educator Wayne V. Pawlowski provides an explanation of BDSM, and describes it as a normal, healthy expression of sexuality that includes a continuum of sexual behaviors.

NO: Journalist Rachel White details recent reports of alleged sexual assaults within the BDSM community, as well as the divisive responses from community members and leaders.

In 2012 the novel *50 Shades of Grey* (and its two sequels) took the publishing world by storm, selling a combined 70 million copies worldwide. The novels centered around lead characters Anastasia Steele, a sexually inexperienced college student, and Christian Grey, a wealthy business-man, who embark together on an erotic and romantic journey of sorts full of twists and turns. For seasoned romance novel readers, the setup will sound familiar. What set the *50 Shades* books apart, however, were the overt and explicit scenes involving BDSM-style sex play. BDSM stands for bondage, discipline, dominance/submission, and sadism/masochism.

BDSM involves the eroticization of the exchange of power. For some, like the dominant Christian Grey, there is no bigger turn on than taking control in a sexual encounter. For others, like submissive Anastasia Steele, surrendering power and being ordered to engage in certain behaviors may be thrilling. These actions may mani-fest in many different ways. Bondage play involves the restriction of movement by handcuffs, rope, or other more intricate devices. A sadist may enjoy striking a submissive partner with an object like a whip or cane. A masochist might revel in being on the receiving end of those strikes. These encounters, which can take on the form of elabo-rate role plays (with certain partners playing the dominant role and others the submissive), are called "scenes."

For many, questions about the nature and health of BDSM start with the behaviors and identities themselves. Is the couple who occasionally plays with pink fuzzy handcuffs necessarily "into" bondage? Does enjoying a smack on the behind make one a masochist, or must one be ritualistically paddled and scolded to carry that title? Where, exactly, does one draw the line between being sex-ually aggressive and being "into" domination? To some, these behaviors may sound like an exhilarating Friday night. For others, the behaviors may seem extreme or even dangerous.

The line between extreme sexual thrill and real danger depends largely on the concept of consent, and the agreement between those engaged in a "scene." To consent to a behavior means that one agrees to engage in it. Without consent, *any* sexual behavior could be considered assault or abuse. While dominants and submissives engage in a form of power exchange, being submissive doesn't mean that a person is ok with, or consents to, everything a dominant partner wants. Boundaries are discussed and negotiated beforehand and, in some cases (like the relationship between the fictitious Grey and Steele), a contract may even be drawn up explicitly stating what a person would or wouldn't be ok with happening sexually during the scene. "Safe-words," or signals, which indicate a person wants to turn down the intensity or stop, are agreed upon if required. Once these boundaries are established, behaviors that may appear to an onlooker to be abusive are actually expressions of a carefully crafted and consensual sexual arrangement.

Because of the taboo nature of BDSM, those who enjoy the behaviors have sought friendship and more from others who consider themselves "kinky." These individuals, couples, and groups form what is known as the "BDSM community" (sometimes referred to as the "kink community"). This network, active online and in real life, plays a large role in educating those new to "kink" and providing support and a sense of togetherness for those who want it. Community members and organizations promote and encourage community-developed guiding principles such as "safe, sane, and consensual" (SSC) or "risk aware consensual kink" (RACK), which serve to remind each other to acknowledge risk and "play" safe. Like any other community, members of the BDSM community look out for each other in many ways. Aside from making friends, the network provides access to potential partners who have similar sexual or relationship interests. People may gain reputations as being particularly skilled at certain behaviors, or particularly caring when negotiating boundaries or following up with partners. Likewise, people may also earn bad reputations if they become known for ignoring preestablished boundaries and safewords, or crossing other lines. This word-of-mouth policing has been seen as a way to keep people safe and keep the community healthy.

But despite attempts to keep BDSM play completely safe, there are risks involved. For those aroused by physical pain and/or bondage there is the ever-present risk that serious injury, or worse, might occur. While community norms dictate that BDSM play should be safe, sane, and consensual, not everyone follows these dictates. Sexual assault, by force or by ignoring pre-established boundaries, is a growing concern among community members. The taboo nature of BDSM may make it difficult for someone who has been assaulted to come forward, even within the community. As the popularity and awareness of BDSM increase, community members fear that those who are interested but inexperienced or uneducated may both intentionally and unintentionally cause harm.

The immense popularity of the *50 Shades of Grey* novel has catapulted kink and BDSM into mainstream American culture. Some members of the kink community have complained about the books, arguing that the boundary-crossing actions of Christian Grey do not represent the overarching values of safe, sane, and consensual, which are respected and practiced by most. Others see it as a way to bring BDSM out of the shadows and into the conversation about mainstream sexuality.

The increase in awareness comes at a time in which the community is experiencing a dynamic shift. The Internet has taken the concept of community to a much larger scale, allowing for conversations to happen outside of local clubs and creating nationally recognized community leaders. While the reputations of "good" or "bad" members were discussed in local scenes, online message boards have allowed these conversations to be undertaken in a much more public manner.

In the YES selection, sexuality educator Wayne V. Pawlowski explains BDSM and describes it as a normal, healthy form of sexual expression that exists on a long continuum of possible behaviors. While some are more common than others, he reveals, all must be consenting to truly be part of the BDSM community. Rachel White, a journalist who covers issues of sexuality and gender, highlights the recent increase in BDSM's popularity among college students. She also details recent controversies within the BDSM community involving alleged sexual assaults and the divisive responses by community members and leaders.

YES ↵

Wayne V. Pawlowski

BDSM: The Ultimate Expression of Healthy Sexuality

What is BDSM? We will get to definitions in a moment, but let's start off by saying that it (BDSM) is perhaps one of the most misunderstood forms of sexual expression today. It is not only misunderstood, it is feared; prosecuted as abuse/assault; depicted as something engaged in by mentally disturbed, sexual predators who torture, rape, kill, and dismember their victims; and the behaviors associated with it are classified as mental disorders in the psychiatric diagnostic criteria of the *Diagnostic and Statistical Manual of Mental Disorders* (commonly known as the DSM) and the *International Classification of Diseases* (ICD). Given all of this, individuals who engage in BDSM behaviors rarely talk about their interests with people outside of the "BDSM Community." The end result is that BDSM and BDSM behaviors remain "in the closet" and misunderstood.

It is known that BDSM behaviors occur among all genders, sexual orientations, races, ages, sexual identity groups, social groups, and economic groups. And, they have occurred throughout recorded history and across cultures. Beyond these general statements, however, there is very little solid and reliable research as to the number of individuals who engage in and/or who fantasize about BDSM behaviors. And, in part because of its secrecy, there is almost no research data describing the population of individuals who are regular or periodic BDSM "players" and/or who are members of the "BDSM Community." As a result, the misunderstanding and myths about BDSM continue to pervade the culture and the psychiatric view of BDSM behaviors.

Much has been written and discussed about:

- The weaknesses of the psychiatric diagnostic criteria for BDSM behaviors,
- The lack of research and data to back up the diagnostic criteria,
- The inaccurate and inconsistent application of diagnoses of BDSM behaviors,
- The gender bias in the diagnostic descriptions (overwhelmingly male),
- The discrepancies between the descriptions of BDSM behaviors in the *Diagnostic and Statistical Manual* and the *International Classification of Diseases*, and,
- The lack of a clear and consistently applied distinction between individuals who engage in BDSM behaviors *consensually and safely* versus those who force, rape, torture, and/or otherwise engage in non-consensual, violent behaviors.

The bottom line is that the *Diagnostic and Statistical Manual* is not a useful place to go to try to understand BDSM, or the people who engage in BDSM behaviors. In addition, as with other previously "pathologized" behaviors that the *Diagnostic and Statistical Manual* eventually "de-pathologized" (masturbation and same-sex sexual behavior, to name two), BDSM behaviors as they are engaged in by those who identify with the "BDSM Community" bear little to no resemblance to the behaviors described in the psychiatric diagnostic criteria. The subtleties and distinctions among BDSM behaviors as practiced and understood by those who engage in those behaviors (hereafter, for brevity sake, referred to as "practitioners") are lost on the majority of the psychiatric community (those who write the psychiatric diagnostic criteria), the legal community (police, courts, lawyers), and the culture as a whole.

So, in order to understand how BDSM and engaging in BDSM behaviors can be the ultimate, healthy expression of self and of sexuality we must first step away from the psychiatric diagnostic criteria and from the legal and cultural misperceptions and interpretations. Next we must clarify what BDSM is and isn't, then we must examine BDSM behaviors in the context of "normal," "conventional" behaviors, and lastly, we must try to let go of our preconceived biases and see the incredibly healthy aspects of how BDSM play is conducted and experienced.

What BDSM Is and Isn't

BDSM is an acronym for a wide range of behaviors, both sexual and non-sexual. It is actually a complex interplay of three separate and distinct "worlds" of behavior, none of which are inherently overtly sexual but most of which can and often do play out in powerfully erotic ways. BDSM includes the world of *BD*, the world of *Ds* and the world of *SM*. While these three worlds can and frequently do overlap (hence the acronym "BDSM"), they can and frequently do travel totally and completely separately from each other.

Recognizing that the language used to describe BDSM is in flux and that different regions of the US and the world will use different terms to describe the same behaviors, let us attempt to clarify the three "worlds" mentioned above.

BD is the world of "bondage and dominance," "bondage and domination," or "bondage and discipline" (remember, language varies from place to place and person to person so all three descriptions are simply different words used to define *BD*). *BD* always involves some sort of restraint—bondage—and is frequently, but not always, paired with some sort of domination and/or punishment/discipline.

Ds is the world of "Dominance and submission" or "Domination and submission." (Remember the note above about variations in language.) And, yes, the uppercase "D" and lowercase "s" are intentional. *Ds* involves some sort of "superiority" and "inferiority"; the domination of one individual over another and/or the submission of one individual to another.

SM is the world of "sadism and masochism" or "sadomasochism." *SM* involves some sort of playing with and/or giving (sadism) and receiving (masochism) of pain and/or other sensations.

So, BDSM encompasses a wide range of behaviors and activities. Common elements that are "played with" in most BDSM behaviors are power (exchanging it, taking it, and/or giving it up), the mind (psychology), and sensation (using or depriving use of the senses and working with the chemicals released by the body when pain and/or intense sensations are experienced).

BDSM play often occurs as much psychologically as it does physically so "using" the mind, the brain, and the imagination is a powerful and well-exercised skill among BDSM practitioners. It is the psychological aspect of BDSM that gives BDSM play its meaning and context. Sometimes, BDSM play is *primarily* psychology rather than physical. When it is, things like domination and submission may not look at all like what people expect. In fact, predominantly psychological BDSM "behaviors" may not be at all "visible" or evident to an observer even when they are occurring in a very public arena. More will be said about the psychological aspects of BDSM later in this article.

As with every other aspect of their lives, practitioners of BDSM make on-going decisions about what role BDSM behaviors will play in their general lives and in their sexual lives. Their BDSM behaviors may be "real" or role play, one-time-only, 24/7, on-going, short-term, long-term, periodic, primarily erotically sexual, primarily non-sexual, a part of one relationship only, or a part of every relationship. There is no single way that BDSM behaviors are integrated into practitioners' lives, sexual lives, and/or love making in the same way that there is no single way that other more "conventional" behaviors are integrated into the lives, sexual lives, and/or love making of people in general.

Normal/Conventional or Abnormal/Unconventional

For most non-practitioners, BDSM is viewed as "unconventional" and/or "exotic" behavior at best or abnormal and dangerous at worst. In fact, BDSM play is nothing more or less than an extension of the "normal," "conven-

tional" behaviors that most "traditional" couples engage in with great frequency. Most behaviors in life are engaged in along a continuum from mild/gentle to moderate to extreme/intense. (See Figure 1.) BDSM is simply the more extreme/intense end of the continuum of normal, conventional behavioral expression.

Figure 1

Continuum of Expression of Conventional Behaviors

◄---►

Mild	Moderate	Extreme

BD Behaviors

During love making it is not uncommon for one partner to "hold" the other partner "in place" at a particular moment (e.g., holding a partner's head in place during oral sex), or to tie a partner's hands with underwear or a scarf. Many couples view these behaviors as nothing more than playful and exciting ways to enhance their intimacy. Most would not view them as BDSM. They are, however, all forms of "restraint" and "restraint" in BDSM parlance is "bondage." These playful and exciting behaviors are simply the mild or gentle end of a continuum of behaviors that may, at the extreme end, involve having someone completely immobilized, caged, or chained to a wall. (See Figure 2.) The only difference between holding a person's head in place and having someone completely immobilized is the level of intensity and drama of the behaviors, the psychological meaning of the behaviors, the way the behaviors "look," and how the behaviors are experienced by the participants. The behaviors themselves are the same; one partner is restraining another. And, again, restraint is another word for bondage and bondage is a part of the world of *BD*.

Figure 2

Continuum of BD Behaviors

Partner's hands tied with scarf.	Partner handcuffed to bed.	Partner immobilized/caged.

◄---►

Mild	Moderate	Extreme

Ds Behaviors

A partner may playfully and lightheartedly say, "You get no sex from me unless you bring me a glass of wine and light some candles first!" This is a conventional, light-hearted occurrence among many "traditional" couples; sex is playfully "withheld" and later "granted" upon the completion of a task. As we saw with *BD*, this playful behavior is nothing less than the gentle end of *Ds*. It is servitude, "requiring" one partner to "serve" the other with sex as the "reward." The more intense end of this behavior might be a full-time live in "slave" who is "allowed" to have sex with the Dominant partner as a result of satisfactorily completing his/her chores. (See Figure 3.) Again, both of these behaviors are essentially the same as they both involve servitude. What is different about them is the intensity and drama of the behaviors, their psychological meaning, how they "look," and how they are experienced by the participants.

Figure 3

Continuum of Ds Behaviors

No sex without a glass of wine.   Full-time live-in slave.

◄ - ►

Mild   Moderate   Extreme

SM Behaviors

A light slap on the buttocks or gently pinching a partner as orgasm nears is common "conventional" behavior among "traditional" couples. But, as with the *BD* and *Ds* examples, this light slap and gentle pinch are nothing less than the mild or gentle end of the *SM* continuum . . . playing with sensations. The moderate place on this continuum might be lightly spanking a partner. The extreme end of the continuum might be severely whipping or flogging a partner. (See Figure 4.) Again, all of these behaviors are the same in that they involve administering some sort of sensation to a partner in order to heighten erotic feeling. What is different about them is the intensity of the behaviors, their psychological meaning, how they "look," and how they are experienced by the participants.

Figure 4

Continuum of SM Behaviors

Light slap on buttocks   Light spanking   Severe whipping

◄ - ►

Mild   Moderate   Extreme

Some readers might be horrified to think of or to interpret their "normal," "conventional," "vanilla," "ordinary" behaviors as BDSM behaviors . . . but in fact, they are just that. Perhaps they are the mild or gentle end of BDSM; but they are BDSM nonetheless. Or, to put it the other way, BDSM behaviors are nothing more than the extreme end of "normal," "ordinary," "conventional" behaviors.

The importance of the "psychological meaning" of behavior was mentioned earlier and it cannot be emphasized enough how important psychological meaning is to BDSM practitioners. The experience of any behavior and how the behavior "feels," comes directly from the meaning that has been given to the behavior by the people involved in it. It also comes from the context in which the behavior occurs. If a behavior is labeled and/or identified as a BDSM behavior for a particular couple, it will be EXPERIENCED as a BDSM behavior by that couple. If the exact same behavior is not given that label or identified in that way, it will be experienced completely differently; likely it will be experienced as ordinary, conventional behavior.

It was mentioned earlier that predominantly psychological BDSM behavior may not be visible even if it is occurring in a very public arena. An example of this is someone sitting alone on a park bench. That individual may well be doing nothing more or less than sitting alone on a park bench. However, if that individual is a submissive that has been ordered to sit there until his/her Dom returns, that submissive will be engaging in an intense and powerful BDSM experience. The behavior alone looks very conventional—sitting on a park bench—but the psychological meaning of that sitting is profoundly influenced by the meaning assigned to it by the individuals involved.

Healthy Sexuality and Healthy Relationships

Because the meaning of behavior comes from knowing and understanding its context, for BDSM behaviors to "work" they must be discussed, analyzed, clearly understood, and agreed upon. This means individuals must share with their partners their wants, needs, desires, fantasies, limits, fears, etc. It means they must *communicate and negotiate* in great detail and clarity about what they want, what they like, what they are willing to do, what they are not willing to do, what the relationship means to them right now, and what it might mean tomorrow; and, after-the-fact, they must communicate again about what the experience was like for them.

All of this requires the development of self-awareness, communication skills, listening skills, high self-esteem, awareness of boundaries (one's own and others'), awareness of personal likes and dislikes, negotiation skills, etc.

What could be healthier than for individuals to be encouraged to develop and practice all of these things? And then, what could be better for couples than to engage in this level of communication, negotiation, and feedback as they enter into and develop relationships?

As part of their belief in and need for communication, openness, and full consent, BDSM practitioners have developed a number of guiding principles which are taught and followed by the "community" and by those who seriously engage in BDSM activities. These principles include *SSC* (Safe, Sane, Consensual) and/or *RACK* (Risk Aware Consensual Kink), *Hurt Not Harm, Negotiation, Relationship of Equals, Safe Words, After Care, Self-Affirming Not Self-Destructive,* and *Never Under the Influence.*

This paper does not allow for a full explanation of each of these principles, but the list itself conveys the BDSM Community's interest in and desire to talk openly and honestly about safety, limits, can-do's, can't-dos, how to monitor and take care of each other while in the midst of play, how to take care of each other when play is done, etc. All of this illustrates the fact that BDSM practitioners are not the disturbed, compulsive, driven, dangerous individuals who engage in pathological behaviors as described in the *Diagnostic and Statistical Manual* and as seen on TV. Instead, in reality, they are serious, cautious, thoughtful, caring individuals who negotiate with equal partners to engage in behaviors that are mutually satisfying, mutually desired, and enacted as safely as possible. They believe that two people can only enter into a BDSM relationship if they both fully understand each other, they both fully understand what they are going to do together, and, they both fully and completely consent to what will happen before, during, and after the behavior. These beliefs, qualities, interactions, and behaviors epitomize healthy sexuality and sexually healthy relationships.

WAYNE V. PAWLOWSKI is an independent consultant, trainer, and clinical social worker based in the Washington, DC, area. He has more than 20 years of experience in sexuality education, reproductive health, and family planning.

Rachel White

The Story of 'No': S&M Clubs Sprout Up On Ivy Campuses, and Coercion Becomes an Issue

Sometimes my friends and I stop each other mid-sentence and say, 'Oh my god, you guys. We go to Harvard. This is so weird,'" Maria, a junior, said recently over Skype chat.

Harvard had been Maria's dream school for years. (She requested a pseudonym, but not because she's not proud of her alma mater.) A valedictorian of her New England public high school, she got in on the basis of a 4.0 GPA and started working toward an English major. Last year, she began looking around for some extracurricular activities to enrich her college experience. There were more than 400 student groups to choose from. Maria chose a group called Munch. Her goal was to meet new people, to explore something new, maybe to release some of the pressure that comes with trying to compete in an intimidating hothouse of rampant overachievement.

Maria is petite, with honey-blonde hair and brown eyes. They widened as she ticked off a few of the areas she hoped to explore in her free time: "Bondage, handcuffs, ice play, ..."

Maria is, she said, less a masochist than a submissive. "So a lot of taking orders and stuff like that," she explained. "I'm really into the whole exhibitionist thing, semi-public places, mirrors . . . ." In addition to educational meetings on campus, Munch members have occasionally gotten together in private to "play." Since joining, Maria's had a chance to explore some of her fantasies. "I've been hit with a riding crop, a belt, a paddle, canes, a flogger . . . floggers are my favorite."

The popularity of *50 Shades of Grey* has accelerated a mainstreaming of the BDSM subculture already underway—the initials stand for bondage, discipline, sadism and masochism—and the trend has been especially pronounced in our more elite institutions of higher learning. Columbia has a BDSM group. So do Tufts, MIT, Yale and the University of Chicago. Brown, UPenn and Cornell have hosted BDSM educators for on-campus seminars entitled "The Freedom of Kink" and "Kink for All." It looks like conservatives who have long viewed the Ivy League a bastion of depravity may have a point after all.

But some young members of such groups are finding the subculture is offering them more of an education than they expected, confronting them with serious issues involving consent, disclosure, anonymity, sexual violence, guilt and innocence, crime and punishment.

While the scene's mantra—"safe, sane and consensual"—is heard so often it might as well be translated into needlepoint, violations of these maxims are common. In the last year, hundreds of people have come forward to describe the abuse they've suffered within the scene. The victims are mostly women, and like *50 Shades'* fictional 22-year-old Anastasia Steele, many are also young, submissive and uncertain about their boundaries.

In December, Victoria (not her real name), a 20-year-old English major at an Ivy League school, had decided to skip reading period, apply more makeup than usual and venture on her own to a kinky meet-up she had read about on FetLife, a social networking service for fetishists. Victoria didn't have any experience with submissive sex, but she had been drawn to it for years; she sometimes had fantasies about dungeons or about being restrained or embarrassed, and she recalled family trips to Medieval Times having given her an unusual erotic charge.

The meeting was fun. Victoria had interesting conversations about neurobiology and religion and, of course, about kinky sex. It was near the end of the evening when a man walked in whom she recognized; he had tried to form an S&M club on her campus a few years before. Eric had a doughy, impish face and slicked-back hair, and he wore his cell phone in a carrier on his hip.

A week later the two went to a "play-party." After some reluctance, Victoria agreed to negotiate some tentative participation, defining safe words and off-limits actions. But once the two were alone in a corner, she said, Eric put a knife to her throat and began groping her. Victoria was shaken, but she couldn't help doubting herself. Maybe this was how it was supposed to be, she figured.

The next day, when Eric asked her to send him an email stating what had happened and describing it as consensual, she complied. "At the time, I felt like this must be normal," she said. "Now it seems obvious he was just building up a defense."

The BDSM scene can be violent by nature. Physical and psychological power, and the lack thereof, are at the heart of the erotic experience. As a result, sexual assault can be harder to define and harder to prove. But that's not to say it doesn't happen. Indeed, awareness of the problem seems to be growing, and controversies around the issue have been roiling the tight-knit fetish community all year.

Kitty Stryker and Maggie Mayhem were up late one night, chatting online. Both are known as sex-positive activists and celebrities within the sadomasochism world. That night, they began to swap sexual-assault stories and realized the experience was more common than either had known. The pair began collecting similar tales online, and it wasn't long before they had amassed more than 300 anecdotes. The stories ranged from more benign assaults (unwanted groping) to tales of being drugged and raped. Many of the victims described abusers who were well-known members of the community, people who hosted parties or helped to organize the scene.

"What we found is that the abuse was systematic," said Ms. Stryker, who regularly goes by a pseudonym. "People had these stories, but when they went to report them to community leaders, they were dismissed as drama. Not only that, but people were ostracized for reporting. It becomes clear how easy it is for an abuser to swoop in on a newbie." Meanwhile, Andy, a 24-year-old law student who lives in New York City, also began collecting abuse stories, publishing them directly on FetLife. Andy is something of a New York scene fixture, known for throwing massive BDSM galas that include such attractions as "glitter bathtubs" and fake-blood tableaux modeled on the TV series *Dexter*. A transgendered male, he quickly collected hundreds of anecdotes, many from fellow New Yorkers, some of which called out abusers by FetLife username. "I knew the people they were naming," Andy said. "There were party organizers and influential people that users were saying had done horrible things to them," he said. Publishing these accounts on the social network had a galvanizing effect. Every time someone "loved" a post it showed up on their feed. Soon, everyone on the site knew who was being accused of what—though they didn't always know the identities of the accusers.

When FetLife employees caught wind of the posts, they began removing usernames. Employees warned that lodging criminal accusations against users violated the site's terms of service. CEO John Baku then got involved, stating that he was sorry for everyone who'd experienced abuse and suggesting that victims go to the police. (Mr. Baku declined to comment for this article.) The CEO's involvement spurred hundreds of comments from users, many siding with the site's administrators and warning of an epidemic of false accusations. Others backed Andy, arguing that the community should police itself and support victims. BDSM is illegal in some states, and many practitioners do not feel comfortable going to the police.

"The types of abuse that happen when you are new and vulnerable are happening to us now," Andy said. It was a fall afternoon, and he was sitting in an East Village cafe, wearing a fedora, white suspenders and a black Janelle Monae shirt. "There are people in the New York scene that everyone knows are bad news, and people tell you but no one does anything about it. Since FetLife has emerged, we've had this giant influx of young people coming into the scene who haven't been around long enough to hear the whispers."

As word spread about the multiple accounts of consent violation, the National Coalition for Sexual Freedom (NCSF) launched a survey. "We haven't closed it yet, but so far we have 5,000 responses, and over 30 percent of them had have their previously negotiated limit violated, which I think is horrific," said spokesperson Susan Wright. "There is still confusion between consensual BDSM and assault."

As the debate around naming abusers wore on, FetLife stuck to its policy.

Things got more complicated when Mr. Baku himself was accused. The story came to light on the personal blog of a woman named called SinShine Love. "Let it be clear," she wrote, "the reason John sees no problem with any of this rape apologist bullshit is because he has a foggy ass notion of consent and acceptable behavior himself. And because he personally benefits from people like me staying silent."

Mr. Baku issued an apology for his behavior on FetLife, stating that he was drunk the night in question, though he didn't specifically admit to abuse.

"We enforce the idea that you can say no to anything," said Holli, a leader of Columbia University's BDSM group, Conversio Virium. "There are a lot of young, inexperienced people that come to us for guidance and an introduction to the scene. A lot of them become easy targets for people to prey on at play parties. Sometimes young people like to say 'Yes, yes, yes' to everyone they encounter at a fetish party or event, but if you say 'yes' when you mean 'I'm not so sure about this,' the lines about whether actual consent was given start to blur."

Samantha Berstler, a student at Harvard who had studied the scene, supports Conversio Virium but questions the group's willingness to admit non-students. "Why not just put a big neon sign on the door that says, 'Vulnerable young nubile college students, many without strong support networks in the city yet, please come take advantage of them?'" she wondered.

Every time she logs into FetLife she sees the same story, Ms. Berstler added. "Someone else I know is writing that a relationship was completely abusive, and of course she was young and a college student and pretty and new."

Consent is paramount at Harvard's BDSM group, Munch, said the group's leader, who asked to be identified as Michael. Right now, the university is considering giving the group its official backing, provided it adopts specific policies to educate members on how to deal with abuse. "We are working on developing standardized policies," he said. "Right now that mostly exists with the function of an email list—anyone who joins the list gets a spiel."

Victoria could have used the support of a good student group. After she and Eric broke up, she told her friends about the darker elements of their relationship—how he would repeatedly threaten to rape her and how maybe sometimes what he did actually seemed like rape, and how he once casually suggested he might be a serial killer. She said she had sometimes felt forced into sex acts, including electrocution and "fire play."

Everyone agreed that this was abuse, but when she talked about reporting it, they waffled.

The NCSF has been working on new community guidelines about what constitutes consent and what doesn't. Ms. Wright says she's also been developing an app with FetLife that will direct members who have been abused to the authorities, as well as a new program that helps victims report to the police in general.

Meanwhile, despite FetLife's best efforts, alleged abusers are still being publicly identified. A tech-savvy member of the BDSM community named MayMay recently developed an app that puts a yellow square around the profile photo of anyone who has been accused of abuse, along with a description of their alleged misdeeds. The yellow square can only be seen within the app, a free download.

After her breakup with Eric, Victoria sought out the help of a therapist and was diagnosed with PTSD. Eventually, she decided to press charges.

"I met a lawyer and we just picked the three most obvious instances of rape," she recalled. "He said it wouldn't make sense to file a report of 20 instances. I was worried that if I made the report, Eric would come attack me or kill me, and I didn't want to put my life in danger unless I was certain something would come of it." Victoria's lawyer went to a friend who was a DA and asked what he would do with such a case.

Victoria was sitting in the school library weeks later when she received the email from her lawyer. The DA said he would throw the case out. BDSM scenarios are just too complicated to prosecute, he said.

One afternoon, Michael again met with school administrators about Munch gaining official recognition as a student group. Michael and two other group leaders sat and waited for their turn to be seen. Other student group leaders had arrived late and were wearing shorts. Michael and the other Munch members had worn suits. They were nervous.

The meeting was tense, but Michael felt it went well. "One of the big concerns that they had were issues of consent, and I'm proud to say we did a good job of representing ourselves as a group that takes consent very seriously," he said. He hopes that Munch can become a leader in larger discussions about sexual abuse on campus, taking its consent-is-paramount model to the "vanilla" world. Harvard will make a determination about the group's official status at the end of November.

Rachel White is a journalist who covers issues of sexuality and gender. Her work has appeared in *The Atlantic, The New York Observer, Cosmopolitan,* and *Time Out New York.*

EXPLORING THE ISSUE

Is BDSM a Healthy Form of Sexual Expression?

Critical Thinking and Reflection

1. What types of behaviors are included on the BD continuum? The DS continuum? The SM continuum?
2. What is sexual consent? What are ways in which consent can be negotiated?
3. What are skills any couple, according to Pawlowski, could learn from those who engage in BDSM?
4. Do communication and negotiation of boundaries ensure that a "scene" will be risk-free?
5. Should BDSM clubs be sanctioned on college campuses? Why or why not?

Is There Common Ground?

The line between pleasure and pain has been the subject of erotic writings for centuries, and artwork from around the world depicts sadistic and masochistic sexual acts. Is this proof that BDSM is a natural, healthy expression of our sexuality? Or simply a proof that sexual exploitation is not a modern phenomenon?

During recent tours, pop stars Britney Spears and Rihanna have incorporated steamy, bondage-inspired costumes and dance routines into their stage show. When allegations of domestic violence arose between Rihanna and her partner, many online commentators pointed to her BDSM-style outfits as "evidence" of "risky" lifestyle choices. This victim-blaming attitude often accompanies incidents of sexual violence that become public and, in this particular case, speaks to the taboo nature of BDSM.

The alleged assaults detailed by Rachel White are but one of the potential risks faced by BDSM practitioners. In April 2009, a Tennessee man died of suffocation after his wife left him alone, bound and gagged, for over 20 hours. While this event received a great deal of media attention, it is important to remember that many people explore this or other BDSM-related fantasies every day, and that sexual assault can happen to anyone—not just those into BDSM.

Pawlowski attempts to place BDSM behaviors along a continuum in order to cast them as merely less conventional expressions of common sexual activities. Do you agree with his analysis? Why or why not? He continues by attempting to counter the "pathology" label given by the DSM and "as seen on TV" depictions of BDSM. Do you feel any BDSM activities are unhealthy or pathological? Some? None? All? How did you decide?

White highlights the risks involved for practitioners of BDSM, as well as the changes and challenges being faced by the community itself. What is the value of community when it comes to stigmatized or taboo expressions of sexuality? What, if anything, can one do to reduce the risks involved in BDSM play? Is BDSM sexual activity inherently riskier or less healthy than "vanilla" sexual encounters?

Create Central

www.mhhe.com/createcentral

Additional Resources

Alison, L., Santtila, P., Sandnabba, N.K., and Nordling, N. (2001). Sadomasochistically oriented behavior: Diversity in practice and meaning. *Archives of Sexual Behavior, 30*(1), 1–12.

Anderson-Minshall, D. We were kinky long before *50 Shades of Gray," The Advocate,* May 8, 2013.

Moore, A. (2009). Rethinking gendered perversion and degeneration in visions of sadism and masochism, 1886–1930. *Journal of the History of Sexuality, 18*(1). doi: 10.1353/sex.0.0034.

Newmahr, S. (2011). *Playing on the edge: Sadomasochism, risk, and intimacy.* Bloomington: Indiana University Press.

Kleinplatz, P.J., Moser, C. *Sadomasochism: powerful pleasures.* (2006). Kleinplatz, P.J., Moser, C., editors. New York, NY: Harrington Park Press.

Sagarin, B.J., Cutler, B., Cutler, N., Lawler-Sagarin, K.A., and Matuszewich, L. (2008). Hormonal changes and couple bonding in consensual sadomasochistic activity. *Archives of Sexual Behavior, 38,* 186–200. doi: 10.1007/s10508-9374-5.

Internet References . . .

Community-Academic Consortium for Research on Alternative Sexualities

This organization researches and disseminates information about and in support of individuals who participate in alternative sexual communities, including kink communities.

https://carasresearch.org/index.php

Consent Alone Is Not Enough

A discussion of the definition of consent within the BDSM community and sexual experience. This article is published through the Woodhull Alliance, an organization dedicated to sexual freedom as a basic human right.

www.woodhullalliance.org/2013/sex-and-politics/ consent-alone-is-not-enough/

The Trouble with Bondage

This article, by William Saletan, highlights the risks associated with extreme kink and argues that BDSM play is far from mainstream sexual behavior.

www.slate.com/articles/health_and_science/ human_nature/2013/03/bondage_dominance_ submission_and_sadomasochism_why_s_m_will_ never_go_mainstream.2.html

The National Coalition for Sexual Freedom (NCSF)

The NCSF advocates, through education and advocacy, for the rights of "consenting adults who engage in alternative sexual and relationship expressions." They also provide a list of "Kink-Aware Professionals," including counselors, therapists, and doctors who are trained in the unique and diverse needs of members of the kink community.

www.ncsfreedom.org

Selected, Edited, and with Issue Framing Material by:
Ryan W. McKee, *Widener University*
and
William J. Taverner, *Center for Family Life Education*

ISSUE

Can Sex Be Addictive?

YES: Patrick J. Carnes, from "Sex Addiction: Frequently Asked Questions" (2013), www.sexhelp.com/sex-education/what-is-sex-addiction-faqs

NO: Lawrence A. Siegel and Richard M. Siegel, from "Sex Addiction: Semantics or Science," Original essay written for this volume (2011)

Learning Outcomes

After reading this issue, you should be able to:

- Describe several sexual behaviors/scenarios that could be classified as problematic ("compulsive" or "addictive").
- Compare the addiction model for behaviors like drinking or gambling and contrast it with the addiction model for sexual behaviors.
- Describe the importance of medical and academic sources like the DSM on the legitimacy of the "sex addiction" model.
- Describe the influence popular media sources have on the cultural acceptance of the "sex addiction" model.
- Explain the influence personal values have in determining whether sexual behaviors/scenarios are seen as problematic.

ISSUE SUMMARY

YES: Patrick J. Carnes, considered by many to be an expert on sexual addiction, answers some common questions about this phenomenon, as featured on the website www.sexhelp.com. Carnes discusses the nature of sexual addiction, ways in which it might be manifested, and offers suggestions for treatment.

NO: Sex therapist Lawrence A. Siegel and sex therapist/educator Richard M. Siegel counter that sexual addiction is grounded in "moralistic ideology masquerading as science." They argue that while some sexual behaviors may be dysfunctional, the term "sexual addiction" pathologizes many common forms of sexual expression that are not problematic.

The name Tiger Woods once conjured an image of competition, championships, and multi-million-dollar endorsements. The champion golfer was on pace to win more major tournaments than anyone in history. But after his multiple extra-marital affairs were revealed, his name became synonymous with one term—"sex addict." Woods sought to keep much about his situation private, but apologized to family and fans at a press conference. Questions and diagnoses were tossed about from television studios to dining rooms worldwide. "Why would he risk his family and fortune?" "He MUST be addicted to sex!" "Sex wasn't his problem, hubris was!"

While Woods' behavior was blamed on addiction by many in the general public, the concept of sex addiction is a controversial subject among experts in the fields of sexology and sex therapy. At the heart of the controversy is a seemingly simple question that has no easy answer: *How much sex is too much?*

Consider this exchange from the classic Woody Allen movie, *Annie Hall.* Two characters, Alvy and Annie, have just been asked by their therapists if they have sex "often."

> *Alvie*: Hardly ever. Maybe three times a week.
> *Annie*: Constantly. I'd say three times a week.

Whether or not one can (or is) having too much sex might be a matter of perspective, as it seems to be for Alvie (wanting more) and Annie (wanting less). On the other hand, some members of the sexological community will clearly tell you that there is a point at which sex can become too much.

Another important consideration is how a person defines sex. Does it include masturbation? Does it include oral or anal intercourse, in addition to vaginal intercourse? Are nongenital touching behaviors, like kissing or massage, sexual in nature? And how about the viewing of online pornography, or the reading of an erotic novel like *Fifty Shades of Grey*? Is sex outside of a committed relationship or marriage necessarily a sign of addiction? Answers will depend on whom you ask.

Much of modern understanding of sexual addiction comes from the work of Patrick J. Carnes, who authored *Don't Call It Love: Recovery from Sexual Addiction.* Carnes co-founded the Society for the Advancement of Sexual Health in 1987, an organization dedicated to "helping those who suffer from out of control sexual behavior." Today, Carnes is considered a leading authority on sexual addiction, in a field that includes prevention services, treatment services (including a 12-step recovery model), professional conferences, an academic journal *(Sexual Addiction and Compulsivity)*, and more.

The website for Sex Addicts Anonymous (saa-recovery.org), which points visitors to links for resources and meeting information, details the frustration of sex addicts who feel they are "powerless over our sexual thoughts and behaviors and that our preoccupation with sex was causing progressively severe adverse consequences for us, our families, and our friends. Despite many failed promises to ourselves and attempts to change, we discovered that we were unable to stop acting out sexually by ourselves."

The framing of sex as a compulsive and addictive behavior is nothing new. The idea that masturbation and frequent intercourse could send a person into a downward spiral of unhealthiness was presented in advice columns, "health" journals, and other periodicals during the Victorian era and the early 1900s. Consider the following excerpt about masturbation from John Harvey Kellogg's *Plain Facts for Old and Young*, written in 1891:

> As a sin against nature, it has no parallel except in sodomy. It is known by the terms self-pollution, self-abuse, masturbation, onanism, voluntary pollution, and solitary or secret vice. The habit is by no means confined to boys; girls also indulge in it, though it is to be hoped, to a less fearful extent than boys, at least in this country. Of all the vices to which human beings are addicted, no other so rapidly undermines the constitution, and so

certainly makes a complete wreck of an individual as this, especially when the habit is begun at an early age. It wastes the most precious part of the blood, uses up the vital forces, and finally leaves the poor victim a most utterly ruined and loathsome object.

Nineteenth-century preacher Sylvester Graham also described a litany of ailments that would affect the masturbator, or anyone who had "frequent" intercourse before age 30. If the names Kellogg and Graham ring a bell, it may be because the food products they created, cornflakes and graham crackers, were made because they would supposedly help suppress the sexual urges of some of the earliest "sex addicts" (which could have been just about anyone)!

More recently, attempts at measuring sexual addiction have taken on more a more scientific tone, though critics of this term pose that it is simply the same old Victorian idea, repackaged for a new century. Many modern-day sexologists call the idea of sexual addiction nonsense, stating that the very term "sexual addiction" invites comparison to other addictions in which the object of dependence (heroin, nicotine, alcohol, gambling, etc.) is inherently harmful. They explain that sex, as a normal biological drive, should not be placed in the same category. Efforts to create an addiction out of sex do nothing more than feed a hungry new addiction treatment industry that is erotophobic, at its core.

Recently, this subject has been at the forefront of the mental health community's debate over revisions to the fifth edition of the *Diagnostic and Statistical Manual of Mental Disorders (DSM5)*, published by the American Psychiatric Association. The workgroups charged with updating what is considered by many to be the "holy scripture" of psychology poured over research on sex addiction and letters from advocates and organizations on all sides of the debate. They considered the scientific evidence for and against the phenomenon, the impact and validity of terms like "out-of-control," "compulsion," and diagnoses such as "sex addiction" and "hypersexual disorder." Ultimately, both sex addiction and hypersexual disorder were omitted from the *DSM5*.

In the YES and NO selections, Patrick J. Carnes explains the nature of sexual addiction, signs of possible sexual addiction, codependency, and different types of treatment. Sex therapists Lawrence A. Siegel and Richard M. Siegel reject the notion of "sexual addiction" as unscientific and moralistic.

YES ↵

Patrick J. Carnes

Sex Addiction: Frequently Asked Questions

What Is Sexual Addiction?

Sexual addiction is defined as any sexually related, compulsive behavior that interferes with normal living and causes severe stress on family, friends, loved ones, and one's work environment.

Sexual addiction has also been called hypersexuality, sexual dependency, and sexual compulsivity. By any name, it is a compulsive behavior that completely dominates the addict's life. Sexual addicts make sex a priority over family, friends, and work. Sex becomes the governing principle of an addict's life. They are willing to sacrifice what they cherish most in order to preserve and continue their unhealthy behavior.

No single behavior pattern defines sexual addiction. These behaviors can take control of addicts' lives and become unmanageable. Common behaviors include, but are not limited to compulsive masturbation, compulsive heterosexual and homosexual relationships, pornography, prostitution, exhibitionism, voyeurism, indecent phone calls, and anonymous sexual encounters. Even the healthiest forms of human sexual expression can turn into self-defeating behaviors.

What Behavior Patterns Indicate that Sex Addiction May Be Present?

While an actual diagnosis for sexual addiction should be carried out by a mental health professional, the behavior patterns below can indicate the presence of sexual addiction. Individuals who see any of these patterns in their own life, or in the life of someone they care about, should seek help from a certified professional.

- *Acting out: a pattern of out-of-control sexual behavior.*

  Examples may include:

  - Compulsive masturbation
  - Indulging in excessive pornography
  - Having chronic affairs
  - Exhibitionism
  - Dangerous sexual practices
  - Prostitution
  - Anonymous sex
  - Compulsive sexual episodes
  - Voyeurism
- *Experiencing severe consequences due to sexual behavior, and an inability to stop despite these adverse consequences.*

- *Persistent pursuit of self-destructive sexual behavior.*
- *Ongoing desire or effort to limit sexual behavior.*
- *Sexual obsession and fantasy as a primary coping strategy.*
- *Behaviors increase in intensity or risk.*
- *Severe mood changes related to sexual activity.*
- *Inordinate amounts of time spent obtaining sex, being sexual, and recovering from sexual experiences.*
- *Neglect of important social, occupational, or recreational activities due to sexual behavior.*

What Is Sexual Anorexia?

Sexual anorexia is an obsessive state in which the physical, mental, and emotional task of avoiding sex dominates one's life. Like self-starvation with food or compulsive dieting or hoarding with money, deprivation of sex can make one feel powerful and defended against all hurts. As with any other altered state of consciousness, such as those brought on by chemical use, compulsive gambling or eating, or any other addiction, the preoccupation of avoiding sex can also be devastating. In this case, sex becomes a furtive enemy to be continually kept at bay, even at the price of annihilating a part of oneself.

Specialists in sexual medicine have long noted the close parallels between food disorders and sexual disorders. Many professionals have observed how food anorexia and sexual anorexia share common characteristics. In both cases, the sufferers starve themselves in the midst of plenty. Both types of anorexia feature the essential loss of self, the same distortions of thought, and the agonizing struggle for control over the self and others. Both share the same extreme self-hatred and sense of profound alienation. But while the food anorexic is obsessed with the self-denial of physical nourishment, the sexual anorexic focuses his or her anxiety on sex. As a result, the sexual anorexic will typically experience the following:

- A dread of sexual pleasure
- A morbid and persistent fear of sexual contact
- Obsession and hyper vigilance around sexual matters
- Avoidance of anything connected with sex
- Preoccupation with others being sexual
- Distortions of body appearance
- Extreme loathing of body functions
- Obsessive self-doubt about sexual adequacy
- Rigid, judgmental attitudes about sex
- Excessive fear and preoccupation with sexual diseases

- Obsessive concern or worry about the sexual activity of others
- Shame and self-loathing over sexual experiences
- Depression about sexual adequacy and functioning
- Self-destructive behavior to limit, stop, or avoid sex

Both men and women can suffer from sexual anorexia. Their personal histories often include sexual exploitation, some form of severely traumatic sexual rejection or both. It is also possible that a person can be both sexually addicted and sexually anorexic, acting out sexually in meaningless relationships, and paralyzed sexually with intimate relationships.

Sexual Dependency and Other Addictions

Sexual addiction can be understood by comparing it to other types of addictions. Individuals addicted to alcohol or other drugs, for example, develop a relationship with their "chemical(s) of choice"—a relationship that takes precedence over any and all other aspects of their lives. Addicts find they need drugs just to feel normal.

With a sexual addiction, there is a parallel situation occurring. Sex—like food or drugs in other addictions—provides the "high" and addicts become dependent on this sexual high to feel normal. They substitute unhealthy relationships for healthy ones. They opt for temporary pleasure rather than the deeper qualities of "normal," intimate relationships.

Sexual addiction follows the same progressive nature of other addictions. Sexual addicts struggle to control their behaviors, and experience despair over their constant failure to do so. Their loss of self-esteem grows, fueling the need to escape even further into their addictive behaviors. A sense of powerlessness pervades the life of an addict.

How Many People Are Affected by Sexual Addiction?

Estimates range from three to six percent of the population.

What Are Multiple Addictions?

It is not uncommon for people to be addicted to one or more processes or substances. As a matter of fact, research has shown that the more trauma an individual has experienced in the past, the higher the probability there is more than one addiction present.

Dual addictions directly related to sexual addiction include:

- Chemical dependency (42%)
- Eating disorder (38%)
- Compulsive working (28%)
- Compulsive spending (26%)
- Compulsive gambling (5%)

Sexual Addiction and Abuse

Research has shown that a very high correlation exists between childhood abuse and sexual addiction in adulthood.

A poll of female and male sex addicts revealed that:

- 97% suffered from emotional abuse
- 83% suffered from sexual abuse
- 71% suffered from physical abuse

There is a growing body of evidence that suggests early child abuse, especially sexual, is a primary factor in the onset of sex addiction. Apparent biological shifts occur in the brain, which heighten the brain's arousal mechanisms and limit one's ability to filter behaviors.

Are More Sex Addicts Male or Female?

It remains unclear whether one gender has a higher incidence of sexual addiction over the other. Research [Dr. Carne's] shows that approximately 20–25% of all patients who seek help for sexual dependency are women. (This same male–female ratio is found among those recovering from alcohol addiction, drug addiction and pathological gambling.) The great irony is that sex addiction in women appears to be increasing. In recent, very large studies of online behavior, 40% of those struggling with sexually compulsive behavior are women.

Why Don't Sexual Addicts "Just Stop" Their Destructive Behavior?

The key to understanding the loss of control present in addicts is to understand the concept of the "hijacked brain." Addicts essentially have rewired their brains so that they perform certain behaviors (drinking, drug use, eating, gambling, sex, etc.) even when they are intending to do something quite different. Triggers to these maladaptive responses are usually stress, emotional pain, or specific childhood scenarios of sexual abuse or sexual trauma. Breakthrough scientific discoveries about brain function are helping us to understand the biology of this disease.

How Is Sexual Addiction Diagnosed?

To help professionals determine whether a sexual addiction is present, the Sexual Addiction Screening Test (SAST), an assessment tool specially designed for this purpose, has been developed [(www.sexhelp.com/am-i-a-sex-addict/sex-addiction-test)].

What Is the Role of Cybersex?

Today, over 70% of sex addicts report having problematic online sexual behavior. Two-thirds of those engaged have such despair over their internet activities that they experience suicidal thoughts. Sexual acting out online has been shown to manifest in similar off-line behavior. People who already were sex addicts find the Internet accelerates their problem. Those who develop an addiction in the online space quickly start to act out in new ways off-line. One of the pioneering researchers of this problem, the late Dr. Al Cooper, described online sexual behavior as the "crack-cocaine" of sexual compulsivity.

Where Can I Find Help with a Sexual Addiction or Sexual Anorexia?

1. Take our online Sexual Addiction Screening Test, the SAST.
2. Contact a Certified Sex Addiction Therapist (CSAT®) for help. Find a therapist in your area using our Therapist Locator or by calling 800-708-1796 in the U.S. or 480-488-0150 outside the U.S.
3. Start a twelve-step program.
4. Visit GentlePath.com to find books, DVDs, audios and other resources for recovery.

Getting Help: The First Step

The first step in seeking help is to admit that a problem exists. Though marital, professional, and societal consequences may follow, admission of the problems must come, no matter the cost. Unfortunately, fear of these consequences keeps many sexual addicts from seeking help, and the consequences can be dire.

Many resources are available to provide information, support, and assistance for sexual addicts trying to regain control of their lives. These include inpatient and outpatient treatment, professional associations, self-help groups, and aftercare support groups.

Are Sexual Addicts Ever Cured?

Like other types of addicts, some sexual addicts may never be "cured." Sexual addicts achieve a state of recovery, but maintaining that recovery can be a lifelong, day-by-day process. The twelve-step treatment approach teaches addicts to take their recovery "one day at a time," concentrating on the present, not the future.

Is There Any Help Available for the Partners of Sex Addicts?

Partners of sexual addicts, like partners of alcoholics, can also benefit from counseling and support groups. Discovering your loved one is a sex addict can be a very traumatic experience for family members. Inpatient and outpatient programs, counseling, and support groups are all available to help them regain control of their lives and support the recovery of their partner. There are also books and resources for partners of sex addicts

---

PATRICK J. CARNES is a nationally known speaker on the topic of sex addiction. He is the author of numerous books, including *Facing the Shadow: Starting Sexual and Relationship Recovery* and *In the Shadows of the Net: Breaking Free of Compulsive Online Sexual Behavior.*

Lawrence A. Siegel and
Richard M. Siegel

→ **NO**

Sex Addiction: Semantics or Science?

With the dizzying blur of events that was 2010—from unprecedented economic turmoil and panic to our military continuing to be mired in Iraq and Afghanistan, and even the emergence of a new "Tea Party" movement and the most vitriolic bipartisanship in decades—it seems the year will most likely be remembered as the Year of the Tiger. And though it was, in fact, that very year in the Chinese calendar, we are of course talking about the golfer, Tiger Woods. And now, as we roll into 2011, Mr. Woods is slowly, slowly beginning to be thought of as a golfer again, rather than the latest and most notorious "poster boy" for the sex addiction industry—which, it should be noted, is enjoying a windfall of popularity and exponentially growing profit, as well as the predictable explosion of "experts" and "sex addiction therapists" swarming markets all over the country, offering vague promises of "recovery" from any one of a hundred forms of so-called "sex addiction."

Nevermind (as the public, the media, and the industry itself do) that there is no such medically or psychologically recognized diagnosis, and that an outrageously expensive and completely unproven "treatment" thrives without the slightest oversight or accountability. And despite the industry's assertions that the medical and psychological establishment has simply not caught up with what they just know to be true, there has still not been any scientific research conducted to either confirm such a diagnosis or show effectiveness of any kind of "sex addiction treatment."

The whole idea of "sex addiction" is a metaphor gone amuck, and is borne out of a moralistic ideology masquerading as science. It is a concept that seems to serve no other purpose than to relegate sexual expression to the level of shameful acts, except within the extremely narrow and myopic scope of a monogamous, heterosexual marriage. Sexual diversity? Interests in unusual forms or frequency of sexual expression? Choosing not to be monogamous? Advocates of "sex addiction" would likely see these as the uncontrollable acts of a sexually pathological individual; one who needs curing.

To be clear, we do not deny the fact that, for some people, sexual behavior can become problematic, even dysfunctional or unmanageable. Our objection is with the use of the term "sexual addiction" to describe a virtually unlimited array of—in fact, practically ANY—aspect of sexual expression that falls outside of the typically Christian view of marriage. We believe that the term contributes to a generally sex-negative, pleasure-phobic tone in American society, and it also tends to "pathologize" most forms of sexual expression that fall outside of a narrow view of what "normal" sex is supposed to look like. This is a point made clear by sex addiction advocates' own rhetoric. Three of the guiding principles of Sexaholics Anonymous include the notion that (1) sex is most healthy in the context of a monogamous, heterosexual relationship; (2) sexual expression has "obvious" limits; and (3) it is unhealthy to engage in any sexual activity for the sole purpose of feeling better, either emotionally or to escape one's problems. These principles do not represent either science or most people's experience. They, in fact, represent a restrictive and repressive view of sex and sexuality and reflect an arrogance that sex addiction proponents are the keepers of the scepter of morality and normalcy. Moreover, the concept of "sex addiction" comes out of a shame-based, arbitrarily judgmental addiction model and does not speak to the wide range of sexual diversity, both in and outside the context of a committed relationship.

A primary objection to the use of the term "sex addiction," an objection shared with regard to other supposed behavioral "addictions," is that the term *addiction* has long ago been discredited. Back in 1964, the World Health Organization (WHO) declared the term "addiction" to be clinically invalid and recommended in favor of dependence, which can exist in varying degrees of severity, as opposed to an all-or-nothing disease entity (as it is still commonly perceived) (1). This is when we began to see the terms *chemical dependency* and *substance abuse*, terms considered to be much more appropriate and clinically useful. This, however, did not sit well with the addiction industry. Another objection to the concept of "sex addiction" is that it is a misnomer whose very foundation as a clinically significant diagnosis is built on flawed and faulty premises. For example, a common assertion put forth by proponents of sex addiction states that the chemical actions in the brain during sexual activity are the same as the chemical activity involved in alcohol and drug use. They, therefore, claim that both sexual activity and substance abuse share reward and reinforcement mechanisms that produce the "craving" and "addictive" behaviors. This assertion is flawed on several levels, not the least of which is that it is based on drawing conclusions from brain scan imaging that are devoid of any real interpretive foundation, a "leap of faith," so to speak. Furthermore, it is somewhat of a stretch to equate the neurophysiological mechanisms which underlie chemical dependency, tolerance, and withdrawal with the underlying mechanisms of what is most often compulsive or anxiety-reducing behaviors like gambling, shopping, sex, and other so-called "process addictions."

Another example often cited by sex addiction proponents is the assertion that, like alcohol and drugs, the "sex addict" is completely incapable of controlling his or her self-destructive behavior. Of course, this begs the question of how, then, can one change behavior they are incapable of controlling? More importantly, however, is the unique excuse this "disease" model provides for abdicating personal responsibility. "It's not my fault, I have a disease." More often than not, it seems that "I can't stop" is the ultimate excuse for "I don't want to stop." Finally, a major assertion put out by sex addiction advocates is that anyone who is hypersexual in any way (e.g., frequent masturbation, anonymous "hook ups," infidelity, and cybersex) must have been abused as children or adolescents. Again, the flaws here are obvious and serve to continue to relegate any type of frequent sexual engagement to the pathological and unseemly—Tiger Woods was merely one of a long list of celebrity indiscretions made public. But what made Mr. Woods' case unique was that he seemed to have been diagnosed by the media, based on assumptions made from rumors and leaked reports, along with a paparazzi's photograph of him outside a sex addiction treatment center in Mississippi. Confirmation of his admission, then, was proof enough of his "disease."

Of course, the seemingly never-ending parade of politician sex scandals, each with the requisite and routine news conference of "mea culpas" and high-profile treatment stays (some even the fodder for "reality television" shows like "Celebrity Sex Rehab") that have become *de rigueur* for any famous person caught having an affair.

This becomes even more troubling in light of the fact that many professionals in this industry rely on patients' self diagnosis, often giving legitimacy to the notion that if one feels they are an addict, then they are one. One would be hard pressed to find any other area of clinical management that is based on patients diagnosing themselves.

Every clinician knows that "addiction" is not a word that appears anywhere in the *Diagnostic and Statistical Manual,* or "DSM," the diagnostic guidebook used by psychiatrists and psychologists to make any psychopathological diagnosis. Nor does it appear in any of the International Classification of Diseases (ICD-10), codes used for classifying medical diagnoses. "Abuse" and "dependence" do appear in the DSM, relevant only to substance use patterns, but "addiction" does not. Similarly, there is an ICD-10 code for "substance dependence," but not addiction. Why? Perhaps because the word means different things to different people, especially when used in so many different contexts. Even without acknowledging the many trivial uses of the addiction concept, such as bumper stickers that proclaim,

"addicted to sports, not drugs," cookies that claim to be *"deliciously addicting,"* Garfield coffee mugs that warn *"don't talk to me until after my first cup,"* or T-shirts that say *"chocoholic,"* there aren't even consistent *clinical* definitions for the concept of addiction. A 1993 study, published in the *American Journal of Drug and Alcohol Abuse,* compared the diagnostic criteria for substance abuse and dependence between the DSM and ICD-10. The results showed very little agreement between the two (2).

Pharmacologists, researchers who study the effects of drugs, define addiction primarily based on the presence of tolerance and withdrawal. Both of these phenomena are based on pharmacological and toxicological concepts of "cellular adaptation," wherein the body, at the very cellular level, becomes accustomed to the constant presence of a substance, and readjusts for "normal" function; in other words, whatever the "normal" response was before regular use of the substance began returns. This adaptation first accounts for tolerance, wherein an increasing dose of the substance to which the system has adapted is needed to maintain the same level of "normal." Then it results in withdrawal, wherein any discontinuation of the substance disrupts the "new" equilibrium the system has achieved and symptoms of "withdrawal sickness" ensue. This is probably most often attributed to addiction to opiates, such as heroin, because of its comparison to "having a monkey on one's back," with a constantly growing appetite, and its notorious "cold turkey" withdrawal. But perhaps it is most commonly observed with the chronic use of drugs with less sinister reputations, such as caffeine, nicotine, or alcohol.

Traditional psychotherapists may typically define addiction as a faulty coping mechanism, or more accurately, the *result* of using a faulty coping mechanism to deal with some underlying issue. Another way to consider this is to see addiction as the symptom, rather than the disease, which is why the traditional therapist, of any theoretical orientation, is likely to want to find the causative issue or issues, and either teach the patient more effective coping mechanisms or resolve the unresolved issue(s) altogether. This is backed up by a number of studies which show that the vast majority of so-called "sex addicts" display an extremely high co-morbidity rate with mood, anxiety, and personality disorders. Keep in mind that psychotherapists are legally and ethically bound to adhere to established and accepted standards of diagnosis and treatment, regardless of whatever cultural fads may be enjoying popularity.

Another definition of addiction has emerged, and seems to have taken center-stage, since the development of a pseudo-medical specialty known as "addictionology" within the last twenty or so years. Made up primarily of physicians, but including a variety of "addiction professionals," this field has helped to forge a treatment industry based on the disease model of addiction that is at the core of 12-Step "fellowships," such as Alcoholics Anonymous and Narcotics Anonymous. Ironically, despite the resistance to medical or psychiatric treatment historically expressed in AA or NA, their philosophy has become the mainstay of the addictionological paradigm. This becomes especially ironic considering these programs also eschew any attempt to empirically validate their rhetorical effectiveness, seeking validation only on the basis of recommending the program to others.

If the concept of chemical addictions, which have a neurophysiological basis that can be measured and observed, yields no clinical consensus, how, then, can we legitimize the much vaguer notion that individuals can be "addicted" to behavior, people, emotions, or even one's own brain chemistry? Other than to undermine responsibility and self-determination, we really can't. It does a tremendous disservice to our clients and patients to brand them with a label so full of judgment, arbitrary opinion, and fatuous science. It robs individuals of the ability to find their own levels of comfort and, ultimately, be the determining force in directing their own lives. There is a significant and qualitative difference between the person who acts because he or she can't (not a choice, but a position of default) and the person who is empowered to choose not to. As clinicians, we should loathe sending our clients and patients down such a fearful, shameful road.

In 1989, Patrick Carnes, founder of the sex addiction movement, wrote a book entitled *Contrary to Love*. The book is rife with rhetoric and personal ideology that reveals a lack of training, knowledge, and understanding of sexuality and sexual expression, not surprising for someone whose background is solely in the disease model of alcoholism. To illustrate the importance of understanding that perspective, we will simply paraphrase the oft-quoted Abraham Maslow: If the only tool in your toolbox is a hammer, then everything begins to look like a nail. This, while seemingly a harsh judgment, is clearly reflected in the Sex Addiction Screening Test (SAST). Even a cursory glance at the items on the SAST shows a deep-seated bias against most forms of sexual expression. Unlike other legitimate screening and assessment tools, there is no scientific foundation that would show this tool to be credible (i.e., tests of reliability and validity). Instead, Carnes developed this "test" by simply culling his own ideas from his book. Annie Sprinkle, America's first adult-film-star-turned-PhD-Sexologist, has written a very good web article on the myth of sex addiction. In it, she also describes some of the shortcomings of the SAST. While not describing the complete test here, a listing of some of the assessment questions are listed below, along with commentary (3).

1. *Have you subscribed to sexually explicit magazines like* Playboy *or* Penthouse? This question is based in the assumption that it is unhealthy to view images of naked bodies. Does that mean that the millions of people who subscribe to or buy adult magazines are sex addicts? Are adolescent boys who look at the *Sports Illustrated Swimsuit* edition budding sex addicts? By extension, if looking at *Playboy* or *Penthouse* is unhealthy and pathological, then those millions of people who look at hardcore magazines or Internet porn should be hospitalized!

2. *Do you often find yourself preoccupied with sexual thoughts?* This is totally nebulous. What does "preoccupied" mean? How often does one have to think about sex in order to constitute preoccupation? Research has shown that men, on average, think about sex every eight seconds; does that mean that men are inherently sex addicts?

3. *Do you feel that your sexual behavior is not normal?* What is normal? What do they use as a comparison? As sexologists, we can state unequivocally that the majority of people's sexual concerns relate, in one way or another, to the question "Am I normal?" This is incredibly vague, nebulous, and laughably unscientific.

4. *Are any of your sexual activities against the law?* This question is also steeped in a bias that there is only a narrowly acceptable realm of sexual expression. It assumes that any sexual behavior that is against the law is bad. Is being or engaging a prostitute a sign of pathology? What about the fact that oral sex, anal sex, and woman-on-top sex are illegal in several states?

5. *Have you ever felt degraded by your sexual behavior?* Again, there is a serious lack of quantification here. Does regretting a sexual encounter constitute feeling degraded? Does performing oral sex for your partner, even though you think it's degrading, constitute a pathology or compromise? What if one's partner does something during sex play that is unexpected and perceived as degrading (like ejaculating on someone's face or body)? What if someone enjoys feeling degraded? This question pathologizes at least half of the S/M and B/D communities. Moreover, anyone who has had a long and active sexual life may likely, at one point, to have felt degraded by something they've done. It is important to note that this question does not ask if one consistently puts oneself in a position of being degraded and later experiences intense guilt and shame but, rather, have you ever felt degraded. We suspect that most people can lay claim to that, to some degree or another.

6. *Has sex been a way for you to escape your problems?* Is there a better way to escape one's problems temporarily? This is a common bias used against both sex and alcohol use: using sex or alcohol to provide relief from anxieties or problems is inherently problematic. It also begs the question: why are things like sex and alcohol not appropriate to change how one is feeling but Zoloft, Paxil, Xanax, and Klonopin are? The truth of the matter is that sex is often an excellent and healthy way to occasionally experience relief from life's stressors and problems, more often working better than any medication.

7. *When you have sex, do you feel depressed afterwards?* Sex is often a great way to get in touch with one's feelings. Oftentimes, people do feel depressed after a sexual experience, for any number of reasons. Furthermore, this doesn't mean that sex was the depressing part! Perhaps people feel depressed because they had dashed expectations of the person they were involved with. Unfulfilled expectations, lack of communication, and inattentiveness to one's needs and desires often result in post-coital feelings of sadness and disappointment. In addition, asking someone if they "feel depressed" is arbitrary, subjective, and clinically invalid.

8. *Do you feel controlled by your sexual desire?* Again, we are being asked to make an arbitrary, subjective, and clinically invalid assessment. There is an undercurrent here that seems to imply that a strong sexual desire is somehow not normal. Human beings are biologically programmed to strongly desire sex. Our clients and patients might be better served if we addressed not their desires, but how and when they *act* upon them.

It is worth further noting that the concept of "sex addiction" is one with very little clinical relevance or usefulness, despite its popularity. Healthy sexual expression encompasses a wide array of forms, functions, and frequency, as well as myriad emotional dynamics and personal experiences. Healthy behavior, in general, and sexual behavior, in particular, exists on a continuum rather than as a quantifiable point. Using the addiction model to describe sexual behavior simply adds to the shame and stigma that is already too often attached to various forms of sexual expression. Can sexual behaviors become problematic? Most certainly. However, we must be careful to not overpathologize even problematic sexual behaviors because, most often, they are symptomatic expressions rather than primary problems.

For many years, sexologists have described compulsive sexual behavior, where sexual obsessions and compulsions are recurrent, distressing, and interfere with daily functioning. The actual number of people suffering from this type of sexual problem is relatively small. Compulsive sexual behaviors are generally divided into two broad categories: *paraphilic* and *non-paraphilic* (4). Paraphilias are defined as recurrent, intensely arousing fantasies, sexual urges, or behaviors involving non-human objects, pain and humiliation, or children (5). Paraphilic behaviors are usually non-conventional forms of sexual expression that, in the extreme, can be harmful to relationships and individuals. Some examples of paraphilias listed in the DSM are pedophilia (sexual attraction to children), exhibitionism (exposing one's genitals in public), voyeurism (sexual excitement from watching an unsuspecting person), sexual sadism (sexual excitement from dominating or inflicting pain), sexual masochism (sexual excitement from being dominated or receiving pain), transvestic fetishism (sexual excitement from wearing clothes of the other

sex), and frotteurism (sexual excitement from rubbing up against or fondling an unsuspecting person). All of these behaviors exist on a continuum of healthy fantasy play to dangerous, abusive, and illegal acts. A sexologist is able to view these behaviors in varying degrees, knowing the difference between teacher-student fantasy role play and cruising a playground for victims; between provocative exhibitionist displays (including public displays of affection) and illegal, abusive public exposure. For those with a "sex addiction" perspective, simply having paraphilic thoughts or desires of any kind is reason to brand the individual a "sex addict."

The other category of compulsive sexual behavior is non-paraphilic or "normaphilic," and generally involves more conventional sexual behaviors which, when taken to the extreme, cause marked distress and interference with daily functioning. This category includes a fixation on an unattainable partner, compulsive masturbation, compulsive love relationships, and compulsive sexuality in a relationship. The most vocal criticism of the idea of compulsive sexual behavior as a clinical disorder appears to center on the overpathologizing of these behaviors. Unless specifically trained in sexuality, most clinicians are either uncomfortable or unfamiliar with the wide range of "normal" sexual behavior and fail to distinguish between individuals who experience conflict between their values and sexual behavior, and those with obsessive sexual behavior (6). When diagnosing compulsive sexual behavior overall, there is little consensus even among sexologists. However, it still provides a more useful clinical framework for the professional trained in sexuality and sexual health.

To recognize that sexual behavior can be problematic is not the same as labeling the behaviors as "sexually compulsive" or "sexual addiction." The reality is that sexual problems are quite common and are usually due to non-pathological factors. Quite simply, people make mistakes (some more than others). People also act impulsively, not always making good sexual choices. When people do make mistakes, act impulsively, and make bad decisions, it often negatively impacts their relationships; sometimes even their lives. Moreover, people do often use sex as a coping mechanism or, to borrow from addiction language, a "medicating behavior" that can become problematic. While this can be a useful metaphor, it has been taken literally by proponents of the "sex addiction" approach. Thus, an entire field has as its foundation a metaphor run amuck.

However, this is qualitatively different from the concept that problematic sexual behavior means the individual is a "sexual addict" with uncontrollable urges and potentially dangerous intent. Most problematic sexual behavior can be effectively redirected (and cured) through psychosexual education, counseling, and sex therapy. According to proponents of "sex addiction," problematic sexual behavior cannot be cured. Rather, the "sex addict" is destined for a life of maintaining a constant vigil to prevent the behavior from reoccurring, often to the point of obsession, and will be engaged in a lifelong process of a fear-based "recovery."

Unfortunately, as with its chemical counterparts, it is just not the reality for most people. More unfortunately, this view causes people to live in fear of that ever-present "demon" lurking around every corner: themselves.

References

1. Center for Substance Abuse Treatment (CSAT) and Substance Abuse and Mental Health Services Administration (SAMHSA). Substance use disorders: A guide to the use of language. 2004.
2. Rappaport M, Tipp J, Schuckit M. A comparison of ICD-10 and DSM-III criteria for substance abuse and dependence. American Journal of Drug and Alcohol Abuse. June, 1993.
3. Sprinkle, A. Sex addiction. Online article. Accessed 11/5/06 from www.anniesprinkle.org.
4. Coleman E. What sexual scientists know about compulsive sexual behavior. Electronic series of the Society for the Scientific Study of Sexuality (SSSS). Vol 2(1). 1996. Accessed 11/5/06 from www.sexscience.org.
5. American Psychiatric Association. Diagnostic and Statistical Manual of Mental Disorders. 4th edition, TR. Washington: American Psychiatric Publishing. June, 2000.
6. Coleman E. What sexual scientists know about compulsive sexual behavior. Electronic series of the Society for the Scientific Study of Sexuality (SSSS). Vol 2(1). 1996. Accessed 11/5/06 from www.sexscience.org.

LAWRENCE A. SIEGEL is a clinical sexologist and president of the Sage Institute for Family Development in Boynton Beach, Florida.

RICHARD M. SIEGEL is a licensed mental health counselor and certified sex therapist. He is the education director of the Sage Institute for Family Development in Boynton Beach, Florida.

EXPLORING THE ISSUE

Can Sex Be Addictive?

Critical Thinking and Reflection

1. What is the difference between addiction and compulsion?
2. At what point would a person's sexual behaviors, or frequency of sexual activity, lead you to become concerned for their health?
3. What role does the media play in the widespread acceptance of sex addiction as a legitimate mental health issue?
4. What are the reasons for sex addiction, or hypersexual disorder, being omitted from the DSM-5? What impact does its omission have on how we see the issue?

Is There Common Ground?

Thanks in part to celebrity sex scandals, sex addiction is presented as a very real and problematic issue in the popular media. Among sexologists, however, the legitimacy of the sex addiction model is far from settled. At the heart of this debate is the true meaning of a word many have trouble defining—addiction.

Think of the many things that might be considered addictive—alcohol, caffeine, tobacco, other drugs—and assess whether or not they are part of your life, or the lives of your family or friends. What makes something addictive? Is it how often a person indulges in it? Is it the degree to which it seems recreational or compulsive? Is it how much control a person has in deciding whether or not to engage in it? Or, is addiction more about what might be considered a social vice?

How about nonchemical behaviors that some might consider compulsive? Are people who surf the Internet for hours "addicted"? How about a political "junkie" who constantly scours newspapers and blogs for new information? The person who never misses an episode of their favorite TV crime fighting drama? Teens (and adults) who play video games for hours at a time? What about the person who spends every Sunday glued to the TV watching football, or the one who builds their life around their favorite reality TV shows? The person who constantly checks and updates their social media accounts? Can a person be addicted to their artistic or musical pursuits? Fitness and exercise? Are these harmless habits ways to relax and blow off steam? Which behaviors escape the realm of "addiction" because they are more socially functional (or accepted)?

Does something become addictive only when it is undesired or otherwise interferes with one's life? Does this apply to spending more time with one's hobbies than a significant other, family, or job might like? Does skipping class to play video games or engage in online gambling put one at the cusp of addiction? Considering sexual behaviors, is it possible to be addicted to masturbation or other sexual behaviors, as Carnes asserts? Is looking at online porn for hours different than playing an online game for hours? Is skipping class to have intercourse with a partner a sign of addiction? Is there a line between healthy sexual expression and compulsion or addiction? And if so, where is that line drawn?

Did you agree with Carnes' examples of behaviors that may indicate sexual addiction? Do you agree or disagree with Siegel and Siegel's critiques of Carnes' assessment criteria? Is sex addiction a serious problem, as Carnes asserts? Or is the assigning of an "addiction" status to otherwise healthy and consensual activities simply adding to the modern trend of the medicalization of sexuality, while recalling an era when sexuality was simply demonized?

Create Central

www.mhhe.com/createcentral

Additional Resources

Carnes, P. (2001). *Out of the Shadows: Understanding Sexual Addiction*, 3rd ed. Center City, MN: Hazelden.

Kafka, M.P. (2010). Hypersexual disorder: A proposed diagnosis for DSM-V. *Archives of Sexual Behavior, 39*(2), 377–400.

Klein, M. (2012). *America's War on Sex: The Continuing Attack on Law, Lust, and Liberty*. Westport, CT: Praeger.

Ley, D. (2012). *The Myth of Sex Addiction*. Lanham, MD: Rowman & Littlefield Publishers.

Moser, C. (2011). Hypersexual disorder: Just more muddled thinking. *Archives of Sexual Behavior, 40*(2), 227–229.

Internet References . . .

Sex Addiction: Rejected Yet Again by APA

This article, by David Ley, defends the APA's decision to exclude classifications of both "sex addiction" and "hypersexual behavior disorder" from the DSM-5.

www.psychologytoday.com/blog/women-who-stray/201212/sex-addiction-rejected-yet-again-apa

Sex Addiction Beyond the DSM-V

In this article, by Alexandra Katehakis, the therapeutic impact of the APA's decision to exclude "hypersexual behavior disorder" from the DSM-5 is discussed.

www.psychologytoday.com/blog/sex-lies-trauma/201212/sex-addiction-beyond-the-dsm-v

The International Institute for Trauma and Addiction Professionals

This organization was founded by Patrick Carnes and aims to "set the standard for professional certification materials used in education and recovery." Here you can take the Sexual Addiction Screening Test (SAST) described in this issue.

www.sexhelp.com

Sex Addicts Anonymous

This is the webpage for the 12-step program dedicated to helping men and women find relief and support from their addictive sexual behaviors.

www.saa-recovery.org

Why "Sexual Addiction" Is Not a Useful Diagnosis—And Why It Matters

This essay, by Marty Klein, outlines the professional and political implications of the acceptance of the sex addiction model. He argues that the concept does little to help people, while fueling an "addictionologist" agenda and industry.

www.saa-recovery.org

The American Association of Sexuality Educators, Counselors, and Therapists (AASECT)

AASECT is an interdisciplinary professional organization for educators, counselors, therapists, and others whose work is relevant to the promotion of healthy sexuality. Here you can find AASECT-certified therapists in your area, books by members, and learn about training opportunities the field of sexology.

www.aasect.org